DUO!

DUO!

THE BEST SCENES

FOR TWO FOR THE 21ST CENTURY

EDITED BY
JOYCE E. HENRY
REBECCA DUNN JAROFF
BOB SHUMAN

APPLAUSE THEATRE & CINEMA BOOKS
An Imprint of Hal Leonard Corporation
New York

Published in 2009 by Applause Theatre & Cinema Books
An Imprint of Hal Leonard Corporation
7777 West Bluemound Road
Milwaukee, WI 53213

Trade Book Division Editorial Offices
19 West 21st Street, New York, NY 10010

Printed in the United States of America

Book design by UB Communications

Library of Congress Cataloging-in-Publication Data

Duo! : the best scenes for two for the 21st century / edited by Joyce E. Henry, Rebecca
Dunn Jaroff, and Bob Shuman.
     p. cm.
   Summary: The scenes contained in this volume are presented exactly as written by the
playwrights, with no internal deletions. The introductions to each follow the headings
"Characters," "Scene," and "Time"; the playwrights' stage directions are contained in
parentheses. If any two-character scene is interrupted by a third character, some external
business, or an event which would be difficult to reproduce in a classroom or audition
situation, we have enclosed the section in brackets as a suggested cut.
   ISBN 978-1-55783-702-8
  1. Acting. 2. Dialogues, English. 3. English drama–21st century. 4. American drama–
21st century. I. Henry, Joyce E. II. Jaroff, Rebecca Dunn. III. Shuman, Bob.
   PN2080.D86 2009
    792.02'8–dc22
                              2009019163

www.applausepub.com

CONTENTS

SCENES FOR TWO MEN

SCENES FOR TWO WOMEN

SCENES FOR TWO MEN

ONE-ACTS FOR TWO

EDITORS' NOTE

The scenes contained in this volume are presented exactly as written by the playwrights, with no internal deletions. Our introductions to each follow the headings "Characters," "Scene," and "Time"; the playwrights' stage directions are contained in parentheses. If any two-character scene is interrupted by a third character, some external business, or an event which would be difficult to reproduce in a classroom or audition situation, we have enclosed the section in brackets as a suggested cut.

Some scenes may be longer than are called for in your situation. Although the material may provide important clues to your motivation and background, you may need to cut some in the interest of time. As appropriate, mention to the audience that the scene is abridged.

FOREWORD
BY VIVIAN MATALON

As a director and teacher, I know how valuable a book of scenes from plays can be. In my opinion a scene book is an essential tool for any performer or student of acting. It provides a wealth of choices to challenge your technical skills and emotional range, and it may spark your interest in a contemporary playwright or two. The scenes in *DUO!* were drawn from plays written since the year 2000, and they are varied in content and approach. Some are comic, some dramatic. They offer characters of different ages and ethnicities. Some make statements about current issues; some develop complex characters and conflicts; and some suggest the fabric of the future American theatre. You will find scenes written by well-known playwrights, and others by playwrights who are unknown and unsung—yet. But none is so hackneyed that the listener/teacher/director will be thinking, "Oh God, not that scene again!" Above all, make every effort humanly possible to read the entire play before committing yourself to a scene. Buy the script, borrow it, read it quietly in a corner of the Drama Book Shop or Barnes & Noble, but read the whole script! Only then can you make informed choices about your character and the scene in which he or she appears. Select your scene carefully. If you are a beginning acting student, it may be hard for you to know what characters are "right" for you. Do not give yourself too difficult a challenge each time you approach a scene. Of course you want to stretch yourself and try to face a few acting problems, but give yourself the possibility of solving them. A six-foot-two male should not attempt to play Toulouse Lautrec (Toulouse Lautrec is not included in this volume, although Vincent van Gogh is).

I once angered a student by saying that a 300-pound female would not be cast as Blanche Dubois and should probably not try the role. She argued that a director should look beyond stereotypes. And she was right, to an extent. A 300-pound Blanche would bring an unusual dimension to the role. (Blanche Dubois is not included in this volume, but Vivien Leigh is.) The student would have done much better to focus her talent on the wonderful character role of Eunice. So be realistic: choose a character that offers challenges, not obstacles.

Scene work can be so much more rewarding than struggling with an acting exercise. In a scene you have a partner; you have to consider the choices he or she makes and react to them. "Learn to work off the other fellow," was one of Sanford Meisner's sage pieces of advice. I deplore the current emphasis on acting exercises, notably Meisner's "Repetition exercise" in which partners repeat the same phrase over and over to each other. It is, one must remember, an actor's ability to interpret a text that brings audiences to plays and not his or her skill at repeating such inanities as, "Your eyes are blue," or recalling the day the family dog died. And incidentally, Meisner, whom I was fortunate enough to know well, and with whom I studied for seven years, devised the Repetition exercise very late in his career, and many of his most eminent former students were never exposed to it. He intended that it be used for beginning students only and, even then, for no more than six weeks before going to work on a text.

The play's the thing! So choose a scene that excites you, that you feel passionate about, that stimulates your imagination, that takes you beyond yourself and the "Your eyes are blue" syndrome. And have fun with it. As Meisner once said, "Don't bring that dreary thing you call your life on the stage."

VIVIAN MATALON

A graduate of the Neighborhood Playhouse School of the Theatre, Vivian Matalon has earned a distinguished reputation as a director on Broadway, in London's West End, and in regional theatres throughout America, Great Britain, and Canada. His Broadway productions include the Tony Award–winning *Morning's at Seven* with Teresa Wright and Maureen O'Sullivan; *After the Rain*; *Noël Coward in Two Key*, with Hume Cronyn and Jessica Tandy; *Brigadoon*; *The Tap Dance Kid*, for which he received a Tony nomination; and Stephen Temperley's *Souvenir*.

SCENES FOR A MAN
AND A WOMAN

THE ALTRUISTS

BY NICKY SILVER

CHARACTERS
RONALD *(34), a flamboyant dumpling;* SYDNEY *(29), his sister, a shallow and utterly self-absorbed soap-opera actress*

SCENE
A New York City apartment

TIME
One Sunday

SYDNEY *believes that* SHE *has killed her radical lover, Ethan.* SHE *is seeking help from her older brother,* RONALD.

SYDNEY: I hate my life. My life is over.

RONALD: Don't say that.

SYDNEY: Why not? It's true. What am I? I'm a 29-year-old soap-opera actress. Even if I get off, if I claim temporary insanity—

RONALD: Temporary?

SYDNEY: Screw you. Even if I claim self-defense, or a chemical imbalance, the latter of which I think is highly likely. You know I'm on Atkins—

RONALD: What?

SYDNEY: Atkins. The Atkins Diet, the all-the-protein-and-fat-you-can-shove-down-your-greasy-throat diet. That could make a person crazy, couldn't it?

RONALD: Something has.

SYDNEY: There was that woman, that matronly woman, she shot her diet doctor and she got off!

RONALD: No she didn't

SYDNEY: I detest you. Couldn't you let me be falsely optimistic for even a moment? So, all right, all right, I claim self-defense. Then what? The show'll drop me like a bad habit. They're just looking for some reason to get rid of me. I can tell. They think I'm fat and old. My God, they dress me in nun's outfits! At 29, I'm too old for TV and too young for prison. I can't go to prison, they'd eat me alive.

RONALD: You won't go to prison.

SYDNEY: It's all lesbians. You know that, don't you? All lesbians! They'll go insane. When, I ask you, when, do you think they've ever seen a waistline like mine! I'm scared! I don't like lesbians. I'm afraid of them.

RONALD: You like Cybil and Audrey

SYDNEY: Not really.

RONALD: I've always known you were shallow, but I never thought you were homophobic.

SYDNEY: I'm not! I'm just scared of lesbians.

RONALD: What do you think the word means?

SYDNEY: Don't criticize me! Can't you see I'm in trouble! I have nowhere else to turn. You're my brother, you're supposed to love me! LOVE ME, GOODDAMN YOU! HELP ME!

RONALD: Okay, Okay... stop crying. (**HE** *hugs her.*)

SYDNEY: Thank you.

RONALD: I'll help you.

SYDNEY: You will?

RONALD: Of course.

SYDNEY: I do love you.

RONALD: I know.

SYDNEY: You're my brother.

RONALD: Are you hungry?

SYDNEY: No, no, I'm in ketosis.

RONALD: What?

SYDNEY: Deprived of carbohydrates, my body's burning fat cells for fuel.

RONALD: Oh. Well, calm down.

SYDNEY: I knew, Ronald, I knew despite all of our differences, that you'd come through for me. Maybe we could make it look like a suicide? Ethan drank too much and he got depressed a lot. I could forge a note, you could wipe off the gun—

RONALD: Sydney?

SYDNEY: What?

RONALD: Three times. You shot him three times.

SYDNEY: Oh yes. Right. Probably hard to make that look like suicide.

RONALD: Why don't you go wash your face.

SYDNEY: That's good. That's a good idea. I'll feel better after I wash my face. (**SHE** *walks toward the bathroom and looks in.*) When did you last launder these towels?

RONALD: (*Thinking.*) Uuuuuhhhhh—

AUGUST: OSAGE COUNTY

CHARACTERS
BILL FORDHAM *(49), a college professor, recently separated because of an affair with a student;* **BARBARA FORDHAM** *(46), the injured wife, overly dependable and stoic*

SCENE
A large country house outside Pawhuska, Oklahoma, sixty miles northwest of Tulsa

TIME
August 2007

BARBARA copes with the collapse of her marriage, her mother's drug addiction, and her father's recent disappearance. BILL has accompanied his estranged wife and their teenage daughter to his mother-in-law's home during the family emergency.

BILL: Look what I found. Isn't that great?

BARBARA: We have copies.

BILL: I don't think I remember a hardback edition. I forgot there was ever a time they published poetry in hardback. Hell, I forgot there was ever a time they published poetry at all.

BARBARA: I'm not going to be able to sleep in this heat.

BILL: I wonder if this is worth something.

BARBARA: I'm sure it's not.

BILL: You never know. First edition, hardback, mint condition? Academy Fellowship, uh . . . Wallace Stevens Award? That's right, isn't it?

BARBARA: Mm-hm.

BILL: This book was a big deal.

BARBARA: It wasn't that big a deal.

BILL: In those circles, it was.

Barbara: Those are small circles.

Bill: (*Reads from the book.*) "Dedicated to my Violet." That's nice. Christ…I can't imagine the kind of pressure he must've felt after this came out. Probably every word he wrote after this, he had to be thinking, "What are they going to say about this? Are they going to compare it to *Meadowlark*?"

Barbara: Did Jean go to bed?

Bill: She just turned out the light. You would think, though, at some point, you just say, "To hell with this," and you write something anyway and who cares what they say about it. I mean I don't know, myself—

Barbara: Will you please shut up about that fucking book?!

Bill: What's the matter?

Barbara: You are just dripping with envy over these…thirty poems my father wrote back in the fucking sixties, for God's sake. Don't you hear yourself?

Bill: You're mistaken. I have great admiration for these poems, not envy—

Barbara: Reciting his list of awards—

Bill: I was merely talking about the value—

Barbara: My father didn't write anymore for a lot of reasons, but critical opinion was not one of them, hard as that may be for you to believe. I know how important that stuff is to you.

Bill: What are you attacking me for? I haven't done anything.

Barbara: I'm sure that's what you tell *Sissy*, too, so she can comfort you, reassure you: "No, Billy, you haven't done anything."

Bill: What does that have to do—why are you bringing that up?

Barbara: They're all symptoms of your male menopause, whether it's you struggling with the "creative question," or screwing a girl who still wears a retainer.

Bill: All right, look. I'm here for you. Because I want to be with you, in a difficult time. But I'm not going to be held hostage in this room so you can attack me—

Barbara: I'm sorry, I didn't mean to hold you hostage. You really should go then.

Bill: I'm not going anywhere. I flew to Oklahoma to be here with you and now you're stuck with me. And her name is Cindy.

Barbara: I know her stupid name. At least do me the courtesy of recognizing me when I'm demeaning you.

BILL: Violet really has a way of putting you in attack mode, you know it?

BARBARA: She doesn't have anything to do with it.

BILL: Don't you believe it. You feel such rage for her that you can't help dishing it in my direction—

BARBARA: I swear to God, you psychoanalyze me right now, I skin you.

BILL: You may not agree with my methods, but you know I'm right.

BARBARA: Your "methods." Thank you, Doctor, but I actually don't need any help from my mother to feel rage.

BILL: You want to argue? Is that what you need to do? Well, pick a subject, all right, and let me know what it is, so I can have a fighting chance—

BARBARA: The subject is me! I am the subject, you narcissistic motherfucker! I am in pain! I need help!

THE AUTOMATA PIETA
BY CONSTANCE CONGDON

CHARACTERS

ELVIS YAZZI *(20s) is a Navajo man who's just been working construction;* BAMBI *(teens) is a famous fashion doll, made of plastic (yes, she's a Barbie doll).*

SCENE

Northern Arizona, near the Navajo reservation

TIME

The present

From Part 1, THE ARK OF THE DARK: BAMBI *belongs to two young girls, sisters.* SHE *was separated from them when their mother threw the doll out because the girls kept fighting over her. Then* SHE *was drenched in toxic waste when, instead of going to a proper site, a truck dumped its contents on her in the desert. This caused* BAMBI *to became life-size, alive, and naked—*SHE *can only walk on her tippy toes.* BAMBI *found some garbage bags and fashioned a dress for herself when* ELVIS *encountered her, wandering.* HE *took her to the Many Farms Mall on the rez and bought her some real clothes. Now* HE *has taken her to his girlfriend's trailer to clean her up. When frightened,* BAMBI *wants to go back to the box* SHE *came in.*

(*Lights up on a space that contains a vanity and mirror.* ELVIS *enters.*)

ELVIS: Molly? Moll? Yo, baby?

> (BAMBI *enters, dressed in cheap mall clothes, on her tippy toes, carrying the mall shoes.*)

> She's not here.

> (BAMBI *sees herself in a mirror, has a minor breakdown, and starts jumping up and down in distress.*)

ELVIS: Bambi! Bambi! What is it?

BAMBI: Back in the box! Back in the box! Back in the box!!!!

> (ELVIS *grabs her and holds her in a tight grip.* SHE *calms down.*)

> That's nice.

ELVIS: What's wrong?

BAMBI: I want back in the box I came in.

ELVIS: I don't remember any box.

BAMBI: Lucky you. Once you've had a perfectly good box with a big plastic window to see out of and lots of twist ties to hold you in just the right places, you never forget it. I expect my box is lost somewhere. Recycled. Who knows. It's sad. Don't let go.

ELVIS: I won't. Most girls don't like this. Molly didn't like it, anyway.

BAMBI: That was me in the mirror.

ELVIS: Uh-huh.

BAMBI: I don't like it.

ELVIS: You look good.

BAMBI: I look very large.

ELVIS: You look alive.

BAMBI: My hair looks very, very terrible, Elvis.

ELVIS: We can get that fixed.

BAMBI: How? Where? WHEN?

ELVIS: I don't know. (**BAMBI** *looks frozen in panic.*) Now. Sit.

(**BAMBI** *tries to sit at the vanity table—they both work on bending her legs so* **SHE** *fits on the chair.* **ELVIS** *finds a brush and stuff and begins to try to handle* **BAMBI'S** *huge mass of hair.* **HE** *tries combing it—some of it comes out and* **HE** *is horrified and hides the loose strands somewhere.* **HE** *tries to put on a barrette—doesn't work—starts going through the drawers of the vanity, then exits to look elsewhere in the apartment.*)

BAMBI: Don't leave me with this scary-looking girl. Oh, that's right—it's me.

(*Hyperventilation—***SHE** *tries to calm down. Sounds of* **ELVIS** *rummaging through stuff.*)

BAMBI: What are you looking for?

ELVIS: (*Offstage.*) Staple gun.

(**BAMBI** *tries to do something with her hair, but her doll arm position won't allow it.*)

BAMBI: God made me so I can never fix my own hair. She is stupid. What a stupid, stupid god!!

(**Elvis** *re-enters with a big rubber band.*)

Elvis: I took this off of a bunch of carrots in the frig. Okay. (**Elvis** *grabs her hair and wrangles it into a ponytail.*) There. That didn't hurt, did it?

Bambi: I look good.

Elvis: Bambi. Just don't ever tell anybody I did this. Okay? Okay?

Bambi: But you did such a good job.

Elvis: Just don't tell anybody.

Bambi: Okay. I don't know anybody to tell.

Elvis: When you do—don't.

Bambi: Okay. I look good.

Elvis: Okay. Let's get out of here before Molly comes back. She wouldn't understand any of this.

Bambi: Is this hair spray?

Elvis: You can't take that.

Bambi: Help me with these knee positions so I can stand.

Elvis: Okay.

(**He** *does.*)

This makes me just a little queasy. We have to find a way to make your arms work and these feet and—

Bambi: Maybe things will be better in the morning.

Elvis: Oh Jeez. Man. I have to take you home. You've got no place to stay.

Bambi: Do you have a speed boat? Fun house? Closet?

Elvis: I've got a closet.

Bambi: That will be fine.

Elvis: My life—has been so completely changed. By you.

Bambi: Is that a happy thing? Are you happy, Elvis?

Elvis: No. Come on.

(**They** *exit.*)

"BENCH SEAT" from AUTOBAHN
BY NEIL LaBUTE

CHARACTERS
GUY *(20s), a graduate student in a university town;* GIRL *(20s), not formally educated and working at the local Walmart*

SCENE
The bench seat of an automobile overlooking a scenic view where lovers come to either make out or break up

TIME
The present

GUY *is trying to get out of his present relationship, but* GIRL *has been down this road before, literally.*

GUY: No, look, not at all! I was just trying to say that.... See, I'd like to talk about the future, that's all...what our future might be.

GIRL: Oh.

GUY: Like, if you see us having one of those. A future together, I mean.

GIRL: Well, yeah, duh. Sure. (*Beat.*) Sure I do.

GUY: Okay. Right. And would that be...what? Here, or...?

GIRL: Wherever. They have Wal-Marts all over, so I can transfer anywhere.

GUY: Right. Of course.

GIRL: I know engineers work in all parts of the world, so I'm willing to do whatever. You tell me.

GUY: 'Kay. It's just that...you know...I think it's gonna be...well...

GIRL: My parents'd be fine with it, too, so no problem there. I mean, they'd probably wonder why you couldn't just get a job around here, what with the Boeing plant nearby and all, but hey...they're not the end of the world.

GUY: Sure. (*Beat.*) You mean "it." It's not the end of the world.

GIRL: I don't really like it when you do that. Correct me.

GUY: Sorry, I wasn't . . . I was only . . .

GIRL: Just so you know. (HE *nods and stops, trying to regroup.* SHE *slides slowly over to him, cuddles again.*) Whatever you want, that's what I'd like. However you wanna work things out is cool. (*Laughs.*) I was just so sure you were gonna let me have it, you know, tell me to take a hike or something, that I was really shaking. I was almost kinda mad on the way up, I don't know if you noticed or not, . . .

GUY: Ummm, a little, I guess, but . . .

GIRL: Yeah, I was sorta steaming. I mean, you have to understand . . . this guy before you—I showed you his photo that one time, remember?—he really hurt me and I think I'm so hypersensitive to another incident like that one that I'm still jumpy, I am. Like, two years later. (*Beat.*) Afterward, and I don't mean just when I was walking back home, but for months after, I wanted to hurt him, I really did. I would follow him to class and send 'im shit, all this shit through the mail, little dead field mice and crap. . . . I was so out of it! Yeah. I'd find out when he was going on dates and stuff—his roommate was this one wrestler who marginally liked me—and I'd show up at the restaurant or down over at the Cineplex and go to the same show . . . whatever. One time, this once, I waited in some bathroom stall at an Applebee's for, like, an hour. I screamed at this chick he took to his softball game. I mean, like, in her face! (*Yells.*) AAAAAAAHHHHHH!!! If you could've seen her . . . man, it was priceless. (*Remembering now.*) See, he ended up having to take some summer classes to finish up, so I really let him have it. Totally spooked him. He even called the cops once, but I was, like, so what? Fuck him. I just kept it up, but was very sly about it, too. Made it seem all totally random, from these different mail stations in other towns and stuff. . . . They couldn't really do a thing about it. The police. (*Beat.*) I got his new e-mail address about five months ago—through one of those "Find Your Classmate!" deals out on the Internet—and I've sent him a few nasty ones. These, like . . . all these pictures of horses shitting in a woman's mouth and various acts of that nature . . . because, you know, that's basically what he did to me. Just outright . . . took a shit right on me and then probably laughed about it, too. All the way home. (*Thinks.*) How do you say it in the past, anyway? You know, like, past tense? When you've already shit on someone. . . .

GUY: Ummm . . . shat, I think.

GIRL: Really?

Guy: Yeah. It's . . . I mean, I'm not so sure if it's the same for *horses*, but with people, yes. It's shat.

Girl: Well . . . that's what he did. This Mr. Grad Student with a Trust Fund. He shat on me and sent me packing, and that is wrong. That is a bad, bad thing to do to someone, a someone who loves you, so I said to myself, I said, "Hey, little man, no! Uh-uh! I'm not through with you yet. Nope. And maybe not for a long time, either." (*Beat.*) So, see, that's what I was thinking about on the way up here. Sorry if I was being all weird.

Guy: No, that's . . . no. Didn't notice.

Girl: Good. 'Kay, that's great. (**She** *settles into the crook of his arm.* **He** *is frozen, like a deer on the interstate.*) You wanna make out some more, or should we go drive . . . ?

Guy: Umm . . . huh. Why don't we, maybe, sit for a bit? All right?

Girl: Sure. Fine.

Guy: We could just sit here . . . and relax.

Girl: That's nice.

Guy: Yeah. Let's stay . . . and relax.

(*The* **Girl's** *eyes start to flutter and* **She** *closes them.* **He** *is wide awake.*)

Girl: Tell me again.

Guy: What?

Girl: How much . . .

Guy: Huh?

Girl: . . . You know . . . how much more it was. More than good . . .

Guy: Oh. (*Indicates.*) This much. It was this much more . . . this, this much.

(*The* **Girl** *drifts off. The* **Guy** *sits with his hands held wide, his eyes open, staring off into the night.*)

BLACK THANG
BY ATO ESSANDOH

CHARACTERS
SAM *(30s), attractive, intelligent Black man;* MATTIE *(30s), attractive, intelligent Black woman*

SCENE
New York City

TIME
The present

When MATTIE *and* SAM *began dating three months before,* SHE *said* SHE *did not want to become emotionally involved with anyone and persuaded* SAM *to sign a contract stating that they mutually agreed not to become emotionally attached. If the contract were broken, all ties would be nullified. But neither can hold to the contract.*

(SAM'S *apartment.* SAM *and* MATTIE *languish in bed.*)

SAM: So what do you want to do now?

MATTIE: I don't know.

SAM: Do you want me to call you a cab?

MATTIE: What?

SAM: A cab.

MATTIE: Do you want me to leave?

SAM: Well I—

MATTIE: Because if you want me to leave I will.

SAM: No I thought you wanted to leave.

MATTIE: What would give you that impression?

SAM: It's what always happens. I just assumed that—

MATTIE: You assumed?

SAM: Well yeah—

MATTIE: Sam. If I wanted to leave, I would just leave. I would just say, "Sam, I'm leaving." And then I would leave. Thus relieving you of the burden of assumption.

SAM: Whatever Mattie. I was just being polite. As in, if you, Mattie want to leave, I will graciously call you a cab Mattie.

MATTIE: What's gracious about calling me a cab Sam? I'm not a retard Sam. I know how to use a phone Sam. I've called a cab or two in my life Sam. In fact I would say I'm pretty darn good at cab-calling Sam. Thank you very much Sam.

SAM: Okay—

MATTIE: Okay so no need for the shroud of chivalry Sam! If you want me to leave, just say leave—

SAM: I never said I wanted you to leave!

MATTIE: So why are you trying to call me a cab?

SAM: Can we just drop the cab!

MATTIE: You brought it up!

SAM: Okay! All right! I'm sorry about the cab Mattie!

MATTIE: I don't want an apology Sam.

SAM: Then what do you want Mattie?

MATTIE: Clarity.

SAM: Clarity?

MATTIE: Clarity.

SAM: Clarity about what?

MATTIE: Clarity on whether or not you want me to leave. Do you?

SAM: No! Do you?

MATTIE: No!

SAM: Fine!

MATTIE: Fine!

(*Pause.*)

SAM: Are you PMS-ing or something?

MATTIE: Oh my God! That is so fucking typical. Of course you would say that—

SAM: I'm just asking—

MATTIE: (*Mimicking* **SAM**.) "Are you PMS-ing or something? Are you PMS-ing or something?" Could you at least be a little more creative in your stupidity?

SAM: What's wrong with you?

MATTIE: Nothing. Nothing's wrong with me, that's the point! But no! Dr. Sam over here, recent graduate of the University of Assumption specializing in Assumptionology automatically assumes that I am having my period.

(*Slight pause.*)

SAM: You know what maybe you should leave.

MATTIE: Oh now he wants me to leave. Fine I'm leaving—

SAM: Oh Jesus Christ Mattie what is this about—

MATTIE: Why do you want to know? I'm leaving remember—

SAM: Mattie!

MATTIE: Yes?

SAM: Can you at least tell me what is wrong with you?

MATTIE: Well to do that would mean I have to stay and since you don't want me to stay I—

SAM: Mattie. Stop it.... What's wrong?

MATTIE: Nothing. Oh my God. Am I not being clear? No. No I'm not. I realize that I'm not being clear.... Okay look. I've gotta go. Okay? I promise not to let the door hit my ass on the way out. Heh heh heh. Okay? See ya—I mean bye. Bye. Bye Sam.

DEAD MAN'S CELL PHONE
BY SARAH RUHL

CHARACTERS

JEAN *(late 20s) was the last person to see Gordon alive and has his cell phone.*
DWIGHT *(late 20s) is Gordon's brother.* THEY *are in a love haze in the back of his store. (Hermia is Gordon's widow.)*

SCENE

Dwight's stationery store

TIME

The present

JEAN has been trying to contact and visit Gordon's friends and relatives.

DWIGHT: I was dreaming about you. And a letter press. I dreamed you were the letter Z.

JEAN: Why Z?

DWIGHT: Two lines—us—connected by a diagonal. Z.

JEAN: Oh, Dwight.

DWIGHT : If we are ever parted, and can't recognize each other, because of death, or some other calamity—just say the letter Z—to me—it will be our password.

JEAN: Z.

DWIGHT: Let's never be parted. I don't need more than twelve hours to know you, Jean. Do you? Tell me you don't. We exchanged little bits of our souls— I have a little of yours and you have a little of mine—like a torn jacket—you gave me one of your buttons. I—I love you Jean.

(The phone rings.)

DWIGHT: Don't get that.

JEAN: It'll just take a second. (*To the phone.*) Hello? Are you sitting down? This might come as a very great shock to you. But Gordon has passed away.

DWIGHT: (*Overlapping.*) Jean? Who's on the phone?

JEAN: I'm sorry, who is this? (*To* **DWIGHT**.) A business colleague. (*To the phone.*) The funeral was yesterday. Yes, it was a very nice service. It was Catholic so it wasn't very personal—I'm sorry—are you Catholic? Oh, good—I mean—

DWIGHT: (*Whispering.*) Jean—come here. . . .

(*A pause while the broker offers* **JEAN** *his condolences.*)

JEAN: (*To* **DWIGHT**.) I'm on the phone! (*To the phone.*) Yes, incoming. Thank you, but if you want to offer condolences, the best thing would probably be to write to Hermia and Harriet Gottlieb. Their address is 111 Shank Avenue.

DWIGHT: (*No longer whispering.*) Jean!

JEAN: (*To* **DWIGHT**.) I'm on the phone! (*To the phone.*) I don't know anything about a living will—no—I'm sorry. I have to go. I hope you have a pleasant day in spite of the bad news. Good-bye.

(**SHE** *hangs up.*)

DWIGHT: Who was that?

JEAN: A business colleague.

DWIGHT: I don't think you want to get mixed up in that.

JEAN: Oh, Dwight, I'll be all right.

DWIGHT: I forbid you to talk to Gordon's colleagues.

JEAN: You *forbid* me?

DWIGHT: Get rid of the phone. Give it up. It's bad luck.

JEAN: It brought me to you, didn't it?

DWIGHT: It's not good for you. Life is for the living. Me. You. Living. Life, life, life!

(*The phone rings.*)

If you answer that phone, Jean, if you answer that phone—

JEAN: What?

DWIGHT: I will!—it will make me sad.

JEAN: I have to answer it, Dwight. Sometimes it seems like you didn't even love your own brother.

(**SHE** *answers it.* **DWIGHT** *crumples.*)

JEAN: (*To the phone.*) Hello? Jean speaking. (*To* **DWIGHT**.) It's Hermia. She needs a ride home.

DEVELOPING IN A DARK ROOM

BY JOSEPH CATALFANO

CHARACTERS

MEREDITH *(mid-30s), a soon-to-be-divorced woman in a relationship with a rising political candidate;* MARK *(late 30s), her ex-husband, suddenly seeking custody of their mysteriously mute son*

SCENE

An affluent suburban home

TIME

The week before elections

(MEREDITH *opens the door to* MARK.)

MEREDITH: (*Surprised.*) How did you find me?

MARK: You're dating a pretty high-profile political candidate. Everyone knows about the great David Glass around here. You weren't that tough to find.

MEREDITH: Why are you here?

MARK: I have some news you might want to hear in person.

MEREDITH: I thought we were speaking through our lawyers from now on.

MARK: I think you'll want to hear me out.

MEREDITH: I don't think I—

MARK: Five minutes.

(SHE *hesitates, then walks into the living room.* MARK *takes a few steps in after her.*)

MEREDITH: I'm not talking without my lawyer.

MARK: Did he advise you not to talk to me after my last visit? He seemed pretty anxious to prevent a scene.

MEREDITH: You have three minutes.

MARK: A reporter called me this morning, wanting to talk about you.

MEREDITH: What did you say?

MARK: He left a message asking me to call him back but I think we both know why he's calling. We could be on the front page of tomorrow's paper if I pick up the phone, but I doubt your new boyfriend wants us to hang our dirty laundry out in the town square a week before the election.

MEREDITH: So you're here to blackmail me?

MARK: It doesn't have to be this difficult.

MEREDITH: After thirteen years of marriage and having a child together it's come to this?

MARK: I came home that night and you two were just gone. Vanished. Thirteen years with a person and you think you know her.

MEREDITH: What about a husband who stops coming home to you at night? When did I stop being enough for you?

MARK: We've been growing apart for years. We were different then.

MEREDITH: And when did this happen?

MARK: You want me to get out a calendar? We could never see eye-to-eye on anything.

MEREDITH: Including how to deal with our son.

MARK: We need to move forward and stop looking back at what we can't fix.

MEREDITH: We never really tried to fix anything. We stopped speaking to each other after Jesse stopped talking.

MARK: People change and sometimes there's no reason or logic to it. You start to want different things out of life. You just move on.

MEREDITH: What about Jesse? Why do you suddenly want custody?

MARK: He's my son and I can provide a stable life for him.

MEREDITH: And I can't? You just gave up on us—walked out and stopped coming home.

MARK: I always provided for you both.

MEREDITH: You gave up on your son.

MARK: (*Irritated.*) How dare you. We took him to two psychologists.

MEREDITH: You can't just hand your child off to someone and hope they take care of the problem. You can't put him on medication and walk away.

MARK: That's not what we were doing.

MEREDITH: I didn't see you give up your job. Instead, you gave up on me and found someone else.

MARK: I don't have to listen to this: I have a right as a father—

MEREDITH: You should have exercised that right when he was waiting for you at the door and you never came home.

MARK: Oh, c'mon.

MEREDITH: Is she worth it?

MARK: What?

MEREDITH: Just tell me: When you didn't come home, was it her?

MARK: Look—all you want to do is blame someone, and I'm not—

MEREDITH: I'm still your wife—

MARK: On paper. Stop this constant badgering, blaming, accusing, everything. It doesn't get us anywhere and it doesn't help Jesse either.

MEREDITH: I want to know why his father wants to walk back into his life after being gone for so long. What happened? Do you suddenly feel guilty for all the times you weren't there for him? Has it just occurred to you that maybe Jesse stopped talking when you stopped caring?

MARK: He understands the pressure I was under.

MEREDITH: He's 12 years old, Mark. How do you know he understands when he doesn't talk to you, or me, or anyone?

MARK: I'm all for responsibility but when is it my turn to make myself happy?

MEREDITH: It's all about you, isn't it? (**MARK** *doesn't answer.*) Then let it go. Both of us. We're starting over here.

MARK: Is he getting professional help?

MEREDITH: When he stopped talking we put too much pressure on him. We were all over him. I'm trying something new.

MARK: You mean that camera hanging around his neck?

MEREDITH: He takes it everywhere with him.

MARK: That's the crazy artist talking, not a professional doctor.

MEREDITH: You never try to understand.

MARK: And you think that's healthy? You think that's the answer? Some cheap old camera?

MEREDITH: If he starts developing pictures he could start communicating again. It's better than medication or doctors who want to hook him up to machines or get into his head.

MARK: You're obviously not thinking clearly anymore. I have to return a phone call.

MEREDITH: Before you pick up the phone, think of your son. For once—try to think about someone besides yourself. I think you're here because of her. Or to relieve yourself of some guilt.

MARK: I'm done here.

MEREDITH: Do you really want to expose him to this kind of attention if this gets into the papers? That would be pretty careless for the loving father.

MARK: You should have thought about that before you moved in with a politician. This could drag out for months, maybe years. Or we could end this within a few days. It's your call.

MEREDITH: Get out.

(**MARK** *opens the door and leaves.* **MEREDITH** *slams the door after him.* **SHE** *holds back tears.*)

ECSTATIC STATES
BY JULIANA FRANCIS KELLY

CHARACTERS

MATTIE JOYCE *(30s to early 60s), a Spiritualist medium;* **THE GHOST OF COLONEL JAMES HARVEY BLOOD** *(30s to mid-50s), a nineteenth-century Civil War hero who, after the war, abandoned his respectable job and family to live with Mrs. Victoria C. Woodhull, a Spiritualist medium who ran for President of the United States in 1872*

SCENE

MATTIE'S *home office in Lily Dale, a declining Spiritualist community in upstate New York*

TIME

The present

All morning, **MATTIE,** *running low on money, has been trying to straighten out her finances. Her attempts, however, have been thwarted by a series of visits from increasingly disruptive ghosts, all of whom have had some connection to the great nineteenth-century trance medium Victoria C. Woodhull.*

MATTIE: *(On phone.)* Account summary. Account...no...Go back. Account summary. *(Beat.)* Oh, hi there—I actually didn't want to talk to a person today, I just wanted the machine voice to tell me my balance.

(Sound of spectral gunfire; **MATTIE** *looks distracted.)*

Ooh, that um, credit protector program sounds really great but—

(The ghost of radical reformer and Civil War hero **COLONEL JAMES HARVEY BLOOD** *crashes on, wounded, disoriented, in the heat of battle.* **HE** *sings as* **HE** *fires five shots from his rifle.)*

BLOOD: The stars above in Heaven now are looking...kindly...down.

(BANG!)

MATTIE: *(On the phone.)* Gotta go!

*(**SHE** hangs up the phone.)*

BLOOD: Old John Brown's body is a-mouldering all around. *(BANG!)* Old John

Brown's (*BANG! BANG!*) rifles red with blood-spots turned to—(*BANG!*) The soul goes marching on!

Mattie: Hello?

Blood: (*Without seeing* **Mattie**.) Hello.

Mattie: Hello?

(**Blood** *sees* **Mattie** *and mistakes her for the love of his life, nineteenth-century radical reformer and presidential candidate Victoria Woodhull.*)

Blood: Victoria!

Mattie: I'm sorry, what?

Blood: Mrs. Woodhull!

Mattie: Wait a minute—do you *mean*—

(**Blood** *embraces* **Mattie**.)

Blood: I still love you, Mrs. Woodhull! I love you in the present, I love you in the past, I love you in the future! I love you even now while I am assailed with horrors. I see you, stepping through the smoke: *La Liberté guidant le peuple,* and I am filled with a love that outlasts any nightmare, that busts up the old, grinding ideas of time and space, and which flows freely into all your open doors and windows

Mattie: I'm sorry, but you are really mixed up!

Blood: I'm mixed up?

Mattie: Yes, you are because—

Blood: Let's have an argument!

Mattie: What?

Blood: Throw something at me!

Mattie: Is this a poltergeist?

(**Mattie** *grabs her phone and dials.*)

Blood: Go on—fling the inkwell at my head!

(**Blood** *snatches a bobble-headed angel off* **Mattie's** *computer monitor and throws it at himself.*)

Blood: Oh, you voluptuous scamp, you brave vibration, you free lover…

MATTIE: (*Excitedly.*) Barbara, are you there? Pick up if you're there! I've got the wildest manifestation over here, it's really something, you should—

(*Barbara's machine cuts her off.*)

Oh, stupid machine—

(**BLOOD** *staggers and leans against* **MATTIE**.)

MATTIE: Whoa—hello.

BLOOD: (*Softly.*) I really do love you, Victoria, I've been walking over half the country to find you and tell you—

(**BLOOD**'s *knees give out from under him.*)

BLOOD: Kiss me.

MATTIE: No.

(**BLOOD** *kisses* **MATTIE**, *then takes out a knife.*)

Uh . . .

(**BLOOD** *holds up his hand to silence her.* **HE** *cuts away a bandage on his leg revealing a gory wound.*)

Oh God—

BLOOD: Kiss me again

(**BLOOD** *kisses* **MATTIE** *again, reties his bandage as a tourniquet, takes out a flask, douses his wound with alcohol, and plunges his knife into his leg.*)

BLOOD: (*A horrifying wail. Lights strobe in pain as* **BLOOD** *digs out two bullets.* **HE** *stands up and looks at* **MATTIE** *sadly.*) You're not Victoria.

MATTIE: No, but there seems to be some kind of . . . Victoria storm kicking up around here.

(**BLOOD** *bows.*)

BLOOD: Madam

(**HE** *limps slowly away. Quietly to himself—from the poet Mirabai.*)

In a sudden, the sight. . . . Your look of light, stills all . . . all call a halt . . . you've lost your path. . . .

ELEPHANT
BY MARGIE STOKLEY

CHARACTERS
ELLEN *(early 20s), an artist;* JAY *(mid-20s) a U.S. Marine*

SCENE
ELLEN'S *studio*

TIME
May 1997

A flashback. ELLEN *is in her studio.* SHE *is screaming to* JAY *as if* HE'S *in another room. Both have been drinking, but* JAY *is not as obviously drunk.*

ELLEN: Jay! Jay! Come on. I'm ready! Jay. God dammit . . . why do shirts have buttons? I HATE BUTTONS! Where are you? I told you I have something to show you . . . come here.

JAY: I'm here . . . it's blank? I thought you wanted to show me your work?

ELLEN: Who cares. . . . (SHE *reveals herself to him and strikes a pose; most of her shirt is off.*) . . . ME! I wanted to show you me! (SHE *throws her shirt to the ground.*) What do you think?

JAY: (*Amused.*) Oh, boy.

ELLEN: (*Looking at her canvas.*) You're right. Its white. Weird. Why white? White why? White why, why white why . . .

(JAY *gets down on one knee, then both knees, and then* HE *puts one up.* ELLEN *is baffled by how* HE *is positioning himself.* HE *takes her hands.* SHE *goes to join him on her knees.*)

JAY: No. Don't come down here . . . wait.

ELLEN: But . . . (SHE *almost falls as* SHE *tries to stand.*)

JAY: You stand. Okay, I am going to kneel.

ELLEN: You are kneeling, okay. I'll stand. Here we go.

JAY: I love you. You make me . . .

ELLEN: Ohhhhh, monkey!

JAY: Wait. You are really going to want to listen. (*A pause.*) I love you. You make me a better person, more alive, more thoughtful but most of all more interested... in everything! I laugh more, I feel more, and I definitely talk more. Hell, I write thank-you cards now because of being with you. I want to thank you for all the time you've shared with me and ask you to share every day that follows with me as well. Ellen, you are charming, strong, beautiful, and now half-naked.... I need you in my life. Will you marry me?

ELLEN: Jay... you love me?

JAY: I love you. Will you marry me?

ELLEN: You've only known me for two weeks.

JAY: I know but... I feel.... How do you feel?

ELLEN: (*In shock.*) I love you. I do. Oh my god! Holy shit!

(**ELLEN** *begins to jump up and down and spin in ecstasy. After a moment,* **JAY** *begins jumping with her.*)

JAY: Marry me?

ELLEN: (*Ecstatic.*) You've got to be kidding me.... I can't believe it.... I am in love! I didn't even realize it... and you... you just knew. Amazing! (**SHE** *pulls him close and kisses him.*) I love you. I love you. I love you.

JAY: Will you marry me?

ELLEN: I don't know... don't kill this moment. I am so excited that I feel it. Come here, my love. (**SHE** *caresses his face.*) My love, I like that.

ELLIOT, A SOLDIER'S FUGUE
BY QUIARA ALEGRÍA HUDES

CHARACTERS
ELLIOT *(early 20s) is a soldier fighting in Iraq;* GINNY *(50s), his mother, recounts his experiences through his letters back home.*

SCENE
The stage. Two wallets are on the ground.

TIME
The present

GINNY *reads from a letter as* ELLIOT *acts out its contents.*

GINNY:
> In my dreams, he said.
> Everything is in green.
> Green from the night-vision goggles.
> Green Iraq.
> Verdant Falluja.
> Emerald Tikrit.

(ELLIOT *enters.* HE *puts on night-vision goggles.*)

ELLIOT: (*To imaginary night-patrol partner.*) Waikiki man, whatchu gonna eat first thing when you get home? I don't know. Probably start me off with some French toast from Denny's. Don't even get me near the cereal aisle. I'll go crazy. I yearn for some cereal. If you had to choose between Cocoa Puffs and Count Chocula, what would you choose? Wheaties or Life? Fruity Pebbles or Crunchberry? You know my mom don't even buy Cap'n Crunch. She buys King Vitamin. Cereal so cheap, it don't even come in a box. It comes in a bag like them cheap Jewish noodles.

GINNY:
> Nightmares every night, he said.
> A dream about the first guy he actually saw that he killed.
> A dream that doesn't let you forget a face.

ELLIOT: The ultimate Denny's challenge. Would you go for the Grand Slam or the French Toast Combo? Wait. Or Western Eggs with Hash Browns? Yo, hash browns with ketchup. Condiments. Mustard, tartar sauce. I need me some condiments.

GINNY:
>Green moon.
>Green star.
>Green blink of the eye.
>Green teeth.
>The same thing plays over and over.

(**ELLIOT'S** *attention is suddenly distracted.*)

ELLIOT: Yo, you see that?

GINNY:
>The green profile of a machine in the distance.

ELLIOT: Waikiki, look straight ahead. Straight, at that busted wall. Shit. You see that guy? What's in his hand? He's got an AK. What do you mean, "I don't know." Do you see him? (**ELLIOT** *looks out.*) We got some hostiles. Permission to shoot. (*Pause.*) Permission to open fire. (*Pause.*) Is this your first? Shit, this is my first, too. All right. You ready?

GINNY:
>In the dream, aiming in.
>In the dream, knowing his aim is exact.
>In the dream, closing his eyes.

(**ELLIOT** *closes his eyes.*)

ELLIOT: Bang. (**ELLIOT** *opens his eyes.*)

GINNY:
>Opening his eyes.
>The man is on the ground.

ELLIOT: Hostile down. Uh, target down. (**ELLIOT** *gets up, disoriented from adrenaline.*)

GINNY:
>In the dream, a sudden movement.

ELLIOT: Bang bang. Oh shit. That fucked moved. Did you see that? He moved, right? Mother f. Target down. Yes, I'm sure. Target down.

GINNY:
>Nightmares every night, he said.
>A dream about the first guy he actually saw that he killed.

[(**POP** *enters, sits on the ground.* **HE'S** *trying to stay awake.* **HE** *looks through binoculars.*)

GRANDPOP: In my dreams, he said.]

GINNY:
Walking toward the guy.

(**ELLIOT** *walks to the wallet.*)

[**GRANDPOP:** Everything is a whisper.]

GINNY:
Standing over the guy.

(**ELLIOT** *looks down at the wallet.*)

[**GRANDPOP:** Breathing is delicate.]

GINNY:
A green face.

[**GRANDPOP:** Whisper of water in the river.]

GINNY:
A green forehead.

[**GRANDPOP:** Buzz of mosquito.]

GINNY:
A green upper lip.

[**GRANDPOP:** Quiet Dong-Ha.]

GINNY:
A green river of blood.

(**ELLIOT** *kneels down, reaches to the wallet on the ground before him. It represents the dead man.* **HE** *puts his hand on the wallet and remains in that position.*)

ERRATICA
BY REINA HARDY

CHARACTERS
HOOPER *(40s), a librarian who also holds several advanced research degrees;*
STAFFORD *(40s), a successful academic who has not endeared herself to* HOOPER,
but now has an interest in cultivating a relationship

SCENE
Various floors of research library

TIME
Now

STAFFORD: Hooper? Are you in here? Hooper?

(SHE *enters, virtually blind in the dim light. Her hands grope at shelves.* HOOPER *contrives to stand quietly behind her as* SHE *fumbles.*)

Hooper?

HOOPER: Hi.

(STAFFORD *starts, realizes* SHE *has been stroking* DR. HOOPER'S *chest, starts again, and composes herself.* SHE *respects* HOOPER, *against her will.*)

STAFFORD: Evening, Dr. Hooper.

HOOPER: Professor. Good to see you. What brings you up to stack eleven?

STAFFORD: The same thing that brought me to stacks one through ten—I have a favor to ask you. Why aren't you in your office?

HOOPER: This. (*Holds up the book.*) *Depositions of the Clay Island Fraud Trials.* Wild-haired little history grad was frantic for it. Convinced her professor would turn her out in the alleys if she didn't find it for him. I wouldn't be surprised if he was the one misplaced the damn thing—back in his student days. God knows no one else has ever read it.

STAFFORD: (*Taking the book from him and examining it.*) You found it here? Three floors and sixty-seven call numbers away from its rightful place?

HOOPER: Yeah. (HE *shakes his head.*)

STAFFORD: How?

HOOPER: I had a feeling. Look, it was only a few floors off. Not, for example, buried under a tree, or in the guts of a broken jukebox in the basement under Commons. I consider it an easy find when I don't have to leave the building. On to better things. You had a favor to ask me?

STAFFORD: Yes.

HOOPER: *You?* Spectacular. I just won half a dozen bets. Well, go on. Shoot.

STAFFORD: I want a look at the diary.

HOOPER: Which diary?

STAFFORD: You know which diary. The diary.

HOOPER: You mean Quinberry? Sorry. I wasn't sure. I remember you not being impressed with my Quinberry.

STAFFORD: Circumstances have changed. I...can see the potentially revolutionary nature of the find.

HOOPER: Now, that's a little rich from you, Professor, but I'll allow it.

STAFFORD: Go on, smirk. You've got your way.

HOOPER: (*As HE speaks,* STAFFORD *follows him round about the stage and audience in a way that suggests traversing the floors of the library.*) Forgive me for looking so satisfied, but for a man like me—Quinberry was my lodestar, understand. My Ultima Thule, my one true love. I looked for her for years, in five countries. Common opinion held her to be apocryphal, but I had a feeling. She was out there. And no matter what I was doing, no matter where I was, she was never far from my thoughts.

STAFFORD: Could you possibly slow down a little bit? You've got this place set up like an obstacle course.

HOOPER: Places to go, things to find. You know, if you want to keep up, you shouldn't wear such devastatingly sexy shoes. Do you need help over that?

STAFFORD: No.

HOOPER: Of course not.

STAFFORD: You were saying, about the Quinberry?

HOOPER: Hardest find of my life. But lively, dangerous, funny as hell, incredibly useful as an indicator of the sociopolitical roles of middle-class women in Elizabethan times—well, from the little I've been able to piece together so far. Something that good is worth the sweat. You know, I crossed an ocean for her. Three times. Ah, there.

(HE *pops the* Depositions *back into its rightful place.*)

You can see why the disregard of someone like yourself might grate on me. These past few weeks have been a season of glory for me. I can't think of any librarian more . . . adored, frankly. But you just sat in your office, didn't come to the talks or the presentations. "Quinberry," you said. "She's not so great." You, who I'm not ashamed to say, I respect.

STAFFORD: I had no idea.

HOOPER: Hmmph.

(HE *turns, and starts for his office door—another suggestive journey over the stage away.* SHE *follows.*)

STAFFORD: But now I've come around. I want to see the book.

HOOPER: Yeah, and I should be happy—but you know? I've got a feeling.

STAFFORD: No.

HOOPER: I think your motives are ulterior.

STAFFORD: Nonsense.

HOOPER: You're a bad liar, professor. You're too devoted to your own notion of truth. You'd call a bride ugly at her wedding. No, Quinberry goes first to the translator.

STAFFORD: He won't get here for weeks.

HOOPER: You couldn't properly understand the shorthand anyway.

STAFFORD: I've been studying up. I want a crack.

HOOPER: You're pleading like an undergrad. That's exciting. I like it. Keep on, it's working.

STAFFORD: I could get a vague idea, I could figure out what and who we were dealing with. Please. I know I can be a little hard to deal with.

HOOPER: Ha.

(HE *reaches his door and begins to fiddle with the lock.*)

STAFFORD: But I've never said that you don't do decent work.

HOOPER: Hm.

STAFFORD: You do . . . good work, Dr. Hooper.

HOOPER: (*Stops. Long, slow smile.*) All right, professor. Your foot's in the door.

STAFFORD: Good. When I can have the text?

HOOPER: Ease up, I hadn't said you won. I said you had a chance. First, I want to know why you've really changed your mind, and just what you want with my baby. Second, I want more abject flattery. We'll have dinner, talk it all out. I'll pick you up at your office at half past six tomorrow.

STAFFORD: Doctor, really, you will not—

HOOPER: Friday then. It's a date.

EXPECTING ISABEL
BY LISA LOOMER

CHARACTERS
NICK *(40), Italian-American artist and believer;* MIRANDA *(30s), a wonderer, not a cynic, a woman who questions everything*

SCENE
The playground

TIME
The present

NICK *and* MIRANDA *are fifty thousand dollars in debt from their various desperate efforts to conceive a child.* NICK'S *unwillingness to proceed further has resulted in an estrangement in their marriage and both have returned to their mothers.* NICK *haunts the neighborhood playground, hoping* MIRANDA *will appear.*

NICK: I knew she'd show up at the playground eventually. Lila lives just a couple of blocks away. (*Looks at watch.*) And martini time is five. (MIRANDA *enters the playground and sees him.*)

MIRANDA: (*Tentative; bit cool.*) Hi.

NICK: (*Turns; "surprised."*) Oh hey—hi. (*Pause.*) How you doin'?

MIRANDA: (*Defensive.*) I'm fine. Well, my hair's falling out, but they say that's just the hormones leaving my system.

NICK: Looks good. Gives you . . . more face.

MIRANDA: (*Smiles despite herself.*) Yeah? How are you?

NICK: Me? Great—

MIRANDA: (*Bit hurt.*) Yeah?

NICK: Well, not great. . . . I'm good. . . . I'm . . . lousy.

MIRANDA: So, uh, what are you doing down here?

NICK: I had a job interview nearby.

MIRANDA: (*Surprised.*) Really? How'd it go?

NICK: Well... I got it.

MIRANDA: (*Excited for him.*) You did? Nick, that's wonderful!

NICK: Hey, sit down a minute—

MIRANDA: No, that's okay— (**SHE** *keeps her distance.* **HE** *forges on.*)

NICK: I'm painting a mural for a kid's room. Folks live in the Dakota.

MIRANDA: What are you painting?

NICK: Well, the parents are in international law. They want *Guernica. Guernica* with Disney characters. But they want it in browns and beiges to work with the apartment. (*To audience.*) I knew that would get her—

MIRANDA: Oh Nick. Well, at least you got a job!

NICK: And their neighbor wants me to paint her kid's room, too. She wants bunnies on the walls. Bunnies with open arms. Seems her and her husband adopted a child from this orphanage in Romania where the kids spend their first couple of years strapped to a bed. (*Beat.*) And I got to thinking...

MIRANDA: Yeah?

NICK: All those kids out there... (*Pause.*) And we're knocking ourselves out to bring another one into the world.

MIRANDA: Who's knocking themselves out? I went to a sperm bank—

NICK: And you know, I gotta admit I'm just a little surprised you'd do something like that with a stranger. (*To audience.*) This is a woman that's squeamish about taking a lick from someone else's ice cream!

MIRANDA: Nick, I was just looking into—

NICK: What? Like window shopping? You know, I don't even know if I want to be with a woman who's been with another man's—

MIRANDA: I went to a sperm bank! I didn't make a withdrawal—!

NICK: You didn't? (**SHE** *shakes her head no.*) No. (*Relieved and moved.*) Well, good. That's... really good. 'Cause you know, I've been thinking.... (*Pause; emotional.*) See, I always thought we'd have a kid with your brains... and my hands. And if it was a girl, she'd have yellow hair... but maybe know her way around the kitchen.

MIRANDA: (*Fighting tears.*) Nick, I—I can't think about that child. I can't talk about that child. I can't. (*In the present.*) Please. Give me a minute.

NICK: Okay. (**SHE** *turns away from the audience. Continuing, to audience.*) But last night I'm watching the game with my family and I'm thinkin'— (*Pause.*) What if the kid had my brother's brains and her mother's . . . (**HE** *mimes drinking.*) I mean, it's not like ordering Chinese— (**MIRANDA** *turns.*)

MIRANDA: (*Softly.*) We would have had a wonderful child. (**SHE** *sits on a park bench.*)

NICK: Yes, we would. (*To audience.*) Maybe. (*Sits; to her.*) See, you . . . and my mother—and Einstein—you want to believe there's some order out there. That if you eat the right lunch—or say the novena—or find the right formula—then things'll work out. Because God doesn't play dice with the universe, right? But what if He does? What if He's got a serious gambling problem? Then what difference does it make if the kid comes from our bodies, or a test tube . . . or . . . or if we just adopt? (*Pause.*)

MIRANDA: You want to . . . adopt?

NICK: (*Looks out at playground/audience.*) Look at those kids. Do you think you could love one of them?

MIRANDA: (**SHE** *looks out. Trying.*) I guess. . . . I mean—love is love. Right? (*Beat, turns to him.*) You really think you can just love someone for the rest of your life that wasn't related to you at all?

NICK: (*The proof.*) Well, I love you—

MIRANDA: (*Throws her arms around him.*) Oh, Nick, I love you too. I miss you! And I hate living with my mother!

NICK: (*Kissing her.*) Oh, baby, I hate living with my mother too. (*To audience.*) So I moved into Lila's because she had a three-bedroom apartment. And now that we weren't trying to make a baby, we started to make love again.

[(*Lila enters—in her apartment.* **SHE** *sees them kissing and exits fast.*)]

And we started to talk about adoption.

FORCE CONTINUUM
BY KIA CORTHRON

CHARACTERS
MRAI *(30s), a black woman;* DRAY *(teens, 20s), a black man*

SCENE
DRAY's *living room*

TIME
The present

(MRAI *is a teacher in the public school;* SHE *has taken in her artist, unemployed, high-school-dropout brother, who is not very helpful.* DRAY *is on a couch, his back against big pillows, relaxed, watching TV, painting on paper with watercolors, and talking on the cordless telephone. Offstage a baby screams. Meanwhile:*

(1) – MRAI *enters, charging through, exits to the kitchen;*
(2) – MRAI *returns with baby bottle, exits back from where* SHE'D *originally entered;*
(3) – MRAI *enters, searching frantically;*
(4) – MRAI *finds baby powder and exits from where* SHE'D *entered;*
(5) – MRAI *enters, searching more frantically;*
(6) – MRAI *finds pacifier and exits from where* SHE'D *entered;*
(7) – *Baby stops crying.*)

DRAY: I don't like movies like that. (*Pause.*) I dunno, (*1*) like I hate movies that leave you hangin' up in the air at the end, I figure I done invested *my* time, (*2*) the least they own me— (*Pause.*) No! That was a *great* movie! I see that again, wanna go? (*Pause.*) Every time we out you say Dutch treat, Dutch treat dag, Cinda, you my girlfriend, can't you pay for me once in a while? (*Pause.*) (*3*) Yes! You ever get their Everything Pizza? And the garlic's like this thick juice you can pour— Yeah! (*4*) Why ontchu come over, we pop in a video? (*Pause.*) Well how 'bout this? We both go to the video store, (*5*) you pick out whatchu want, I pick out mine, we double feature? (*Pause.*) That ain't fair, I might not like whatchu pick out but I'm willin' to watch it, I don't complain. (*Pause.*) I don't complain! What was that dumb movie (*6*) you had me watch with that guy. (*Pause.*) That *guy*, with the black hair, he was in the other movie too. (*Pause.*) Yeah, (7) you had me watch that I didn't say nothin'— No I just— Well I have my opinion—

MRAI: (*Enters, turns off the TV.*) Off the phone.

DRAY: Excuse me, Cinda. (*To* **MRAI**.) Huh?

MRAI: Hang up, Dray!

DRAY: How come?

MRAI: Lazy! Spoiled! You see me tryin' to quiet the baby?

DRAY: Your baby. (**MRAI** *seething.*) *What?* How many people it take to quiet her? (*Into receiver.*) Call ya later. (*Hangs up.*)

MRAI: You do the dishes?

DRAY: (*Back to painting.*) Yeah. Sweep the kitchen? Yeah. Read a story to Nina? Yeah. Take out the trash? Yeah. (**DRAY** *remote-controls the TV back on,* **MRAI** *snaps it off.*)

MRAI: I gotta work! (**MRAI** *picks up papers off the desk. They are stories written by fourth-graders:* **MRAI**'s *a teacher. Sits to grade them. Eventually mutters.*) Every black man I know talk like cops public enemy number one, pull 'em over no reason and same black men first to turn on the cop shows. (**DRAY** *chuckles. Quiet awhile,* **DRAY** *painting,* **MRAI** *grading.*) Readin' to Nina wasn't on your chore list. Thank you.

DRAY: (*Not looking up.*) You're welcome.

MRAI: She likes her uncle readin' to her.

DRAY: First grade. Pretty soon she be doin' it herself.

MRAI: I'm not sorry I took you. (**DRAY** *looks at her.*) In case you were wonderin'.

DRAY: I wasn't.

MRAI: I think . . . I dunno, after you dropped out. Just lyin' around the house—

DRAY: I got a job.

MRAI: Sellin' watercolors a Times Square and the downtown skyline to tourists is a bit too freelance for Mom to count. (**DRAY** *goes back to his painting.*) To me it counts. I get on you a lot but you doin' good. (*Ring.*) If that's Cinda I'm throwin' the phone out!

DRAY: Hello? (*Glances at* MRAI.) Lemme call you back. (DRAY *hangs up. Back to painting. Not looking up.*) I wa'n't too much for Mom to handle. She and I had a disagreement over whether ten grades was enough education for me. By winnin' the argument I forfeited my room. And she, martyr, my son Dray he too much. Could my good offspring please take in her shiftless little brother? (MRAI *gazes at him. His painting uninterrupted.*) No chore readin' to Nina nohow. You know I like kids' books.

MRAI: I'm takin' another job. (HE *looks at her.*) Not just you. I was thinkin' about it before. School ain't cuttin' it.

DRAY: When? Midnight to three?

MRAI: Close. Midnight to seven. Proofreading.

DRAY: Maybe you oughta consider askin' their father to contribute.

MRAI: He didn't do a damn thing for 'em while he was here, you think—?

(MRAI *suddenly inhales harshly.* DRAY *looks at her. Happens again.*)

DRAY: Mrai? (*It gets worse:* MRAI *can't breathe. Slamming open desk drawers, searching.*) Mrai! (DRAY *jumps to* MRAI, *snatches an inhaler out of drawer, gives to her.* SHE *sucks. Eventually relaxes.*)

MRAI: If my family don't kill me the asthma will.

DRAY: I'll get a job!

MRAI: Toldja I'd planned on moonlighting before you showed up. (*Beat.*)

Talk about it later. (DRAY *resumes his relaxed painting position.* MRAI *resumes her work. Now looks through her papers: something lost. Scours the desk drawers, surrounding books, etc.*)

DRAY: What? (MRAI *continues her search.*) Sharisa Warner? (MRAI *looks at him.* HE *picks up a fourth-grader paper, reads.*) "My father gave me five shiny nickels and went away."

MRAI: (*Snatching paper.*) Why'd you take that?

DRAY: It's a good story—best one. Give her a A.

MRAI: Why you snoopin' through my work? Drawin' on my students' papers?

DRAY: Sketches. Ideas.

MRAI: Dray— (DRAY *shows his illustrations, beautifully rendered, with captions. One painting per line.*)

Dray:

My father gave me five shiny nickels and went away.
After school, I buy a gumball.
Tuesday I get red, cinnamon not cherry.
Wednesday black. I hate licorice. Garbage.
Thursday grape, my sister's favorite. She say, "Thank you."
Friday yellow. Banana. Yay!
Saturday white. Boring and no more nickels.
"Hi Sharisa!"
Zero nickels left and I feel all rich.

(*The last picture is of a little girl on her daddy's lap or being embraced by him.*)

I'ma remember her name. Collaborator. The children's book business.

(**Mrai**, *torn between anger and pride, gazes at the pictures.*)

FREEDOM HIGH
BY ADAM KRAAR

CHARACTERS
HENRY *(26), African American, works with the Freedom Riders during the Civil Rights movement.* JESSICA *(21) is a white college student from an upper-class background.*

SCENE
The woods near a college campus in Ohio

TIME
1964

HENRY *has been training mostly white student volunteers to travel to Mississippi and help register African Americans to vote, but wrestles with doubts about the project.* JESSICA *is concerned about the increased tensions between* HENRY *and the volunteers.*

(HENRY *enters, walking quickly, carrying a small branch he's torn off of a tree.* JESSICA *comes up behind him, out of breath.*)

JESSICA: Henry... wait.

HENRY: ... You followin' me?

JESSICA: I just wanna ask—

HENRY: You don't wanna talk to me right now. Dig?

JESSICA: We weren't laughing at you. We're laughing at the documentary. That pink lady, rambling on about how Negroes don't want to vote?

HENRY: Go talk to Roz.

JESSICA: (*Blocking his way.*) You're the one keeps saying we're gonna get killed. Is that what you really think?

HENRY: ... Yeah.

JESSICA: So—what?—we should disband the whole Project?

HENRY: Just... leave me be.

JESSICA: Henry, the whole future of the Movement—

HENRY: You're not part of the Movement, okay?

JESSICA: Oh, yeah?

HENRY: Yeah. You're just a . . .

JESSICA: What? Rich white kid?

HENRY: I got nothin' against you bein' white, but once you're in Mississippi, it's . . . it's not a game—

JESSICA: I know.

HENRY: You don't! You don't know. And that's why this Project is. . . . 'Cause not only you gonna get killed, you gonna get all of us killed.

JESSICA: So why, why did you come here?

(**HENRY** *waves this off and starts to walk away.*)

JESSICA: You at least owe me—

HENRY: I don't owe you nothin'.

JESSICA: (*A new tack.*) No one was paying attention. Now they are.

HENRY: Summer's gonna end. All a you gonna go back north. And so are the cameras.

JESSICA: I won't leave at the end of the summer. I'll stay—

HENRY: You won't last a month.

JESSICA: You don't know me. I may be a klutz, I may say too much, but there's more to me. . . . You're being just as bigoted . . . as they are.

HENRY: Who?

JESSICA: Those people in Mississippi—

HENRY: (*Appalled.*) What?!

JESSICA: It's the same damn thing. You create all these tests— Of course we're not gonna live up to what you can do. That doesn't mean we're incapable— I know, I know I haven't seen the kind of violence you have. But when I heard about those girls, torn to pieces in their Sunday school? I cried, I had nightmares—

HENRY: Not the same as a bomb going off in your kitchen.

JESSICA: I'm sure; you need to tell us about that. But I know—I know!—what it's like to be invisible. I'm invisible to my own family!

HENRY: 'Scuse me.

JESSICA: (*Turning to face him.*) No! This is my country too, dig? I have every right to be part of this. You hear me?

HENRY: I hear you, but—

JESSICA: I also have great capabilities—great, vast capabilities!—that I have not been given the chance to.... You think just 'cause I went to Radcliffe, I haven't known discrimination?

HENRY: ... You better off joining the Peace Corps—

JESSICA: No! If we don't go to Mississippi, what's going to happen? Where's it gonna end?... Talk to me!

HENRY: I don't know where it's gonna end.

JESSICA: More killing? A race war? That what you want?

HENRY: It's not about what I want, what you want. Jesus! The dogs are outta the pound. They smell blood. (**HE** *stops himself.*)

JESSICA: What are you talking about? You got something to say? Say it! I don't know the way it is? Tell me!

HENRY: ... Things I been seein' 'round the country.

JESSICA: (*Curious, receptive.*) Yeah? Like what?

HENRY: Like, I was up in New York City, spent time with some Negro teenagers. They livin' in buildings a lot more disgusting than a Mississippi sharecropper. They go a mile downtown and see white folks with money fallin' outta their coats, then go uptown and the police tells 'em they can't play on the street. Man, when it gets hot up there, and they get chased off the streets ... somethin's gonna blow.

JESSICA: Is that why you changed?

(*We hear a dog barking, getting closer.*)

HENRY: We gotta run— Come on!

JESSICA: Hey— Look, it's just someone's pet. See?

[(*Man's voice calling offstage to a dog.*) Come on, boy.]

(*The barking stops. Pause.*)

JESSICA: We're not in Mississippi yet. . . . Hey, you know, I have a car here. What do you say we get off this campus, go into town, and get some lemonade? I bet you haven't even been in town yet. Come on, we won't even talk about the damn Project.

HENRY: . . . Promise?

JESSICA: Cross my heart. . . . Come on.

(**THEY** *exit.*)

GAP
BY CAROL S. LASHOF

CHARACTERS
FRAN PETERSON *(30s–40s) is an English teacher at Urban Public, a large, diverse high school in an avowedly liberal American city.* **WILL** *(16), African American, is a very bright young man who is failing in school, primarily because of poor attendance.*

SCENE
A high school classroom

TIME
The present

FRAN PETERSON *is sitting at her desk reading papers.* **WILL** *enters the room.* **FRAN** *is absorbed in her work, and does not immediately look up.* **WILL** *clears his throat.*

WILL: Uh. Hi, Ms. Peterson.

FRAN: Oh, hi. Uh...

WILL: You wanted to see me.

FRAN: Yes, yes, of course, I was...

(**SHE** *gestures vaguely at the stack of papers in front of her.*)

WILL: I could come back. Tomorrow. Or whatever.

FRAN: No, no. Please. Sit down. I wanted to talk to you about your paper. (*Pause.*) Have a seat.

(**WILL** *sits. Pause.*)

FRAN: Your paper on *All Quiet on the Western Front.*

WILL: Yeah. That's the only paper we've written so far this fall.

FRAN: Yes. Right. So. Did you like the book?

WILL: Yeah. It was good.

FRAN: What makes it good?

WILL: Don't you think it's good?

FRAN: Yes, of course I do. But I wanted to know what you thought about it.

WILL: I kind of already put what I thought in my paper. Did you like the paper?

FRAN: Yes, it was good.

WILL: What makes it good?

(FRAN *suddenly realizes that* WILL *is making fun of her.* SHE *shoots him a quick glance but we can see her stifle any further reaction.* SHE *turns her attention to the stack of papers on her desk, shuffles through them, and extracts* WILL'S *essay.*)

FRAN: The title is "Trauma and Disassociation ... "

WILL: "... on the Western Front." Yeah.

FRAN: Interesting title.

WILL: (*Shrugs.*) I thought it fit.

FRAN: You thought it fit because ... ?

WILL: Because it's about trauma and disassociation?

FRAN: I haven't ever heard you use those words in class. Or anybody.

WILL: Well, nobody would use those words in class.

FRAN: In fact, you've missed rather a lot of classes.

(WILL *shrugs. Pause.*)

WILL: You said you wanted to talk to me about the paper.

(FRAN *studies the paper for a moment, glances quickly at* WILL, *sighs, and adopts a peppy tone.*)

FRAN: Let's go through some of this together, shall we? Could you read ... ?

(FRAN *hands the paper to* WILL *and points to the opening sentence.* WILL *reads.*)

WILL: "Shells fall around you, they scream through every fragment of your soul. The only reason you can even move is because you're fighting for your life in the dirt."

(WILL *stops and looks up quizzically.*)

FRAN: That's good. Keep going.

WILL: You circled *you* in red. And *your.*

FRAN: Oh. Because in the guidelines for the essay, I said not to use the second person. The second person is when you—

WILL: Yes, I know, it's when you use *you*. But how else could I say it without using *you*?

FRAN: Well. You could say *Paul*: "The only reason *Paul* can even move is because *he* is fighting. . . ."

WILL: But I don't just mean Paul. I mean anybody. I want it to be like you're there.

FRAN: Oh. Well, you could say . . . uh, no. Well . . . I suppose maybe that's the exception, I guess, that proves the rule. (*Pause.*) Let's go on. . . . Here, this paragraph . . .

(**FRAN** *points to a line on the paper and* **WILL** *reads.*)

WILL: "War consumes Paul to the point where he is disassociated from his past, present, and future. He lives in utter isolation, with only the Front as a constant."

FRAN: "War consumes Paul to the point where he is disassociated from his past, present, and future"?

WILL: Yeah.

FRAN: Could you explain how you arrived at that analysis?

WILL: How I arrived at it?

FRAN: The ideas. Where did they come from?

WILL: From reading the book?

FRAN: And anywhere else?

WILL: From thinking about it?

FRAN: (*Pause.*) How about these particular words: *consumes . . . disassociated. . . .*

WILL: I was going to say, "War eats Paul up," but I thought *consumes* sounded better.

FRAN: (*Pause.*) Well, yes, it does. That's true. And *disassociated*?

WILL: My dad uses that word a lot. He works with Vietnam vets.

FRAN: Oh, I see! Did he help you with this paper?

WILL: A little. He read it and circled my mistakes. Like he usually does. But then he makes me correct them on my own.

(*Pause.* **FRAN** *looks at* **WILL**, *then down at the paper.*)

FRAN: To be honest—

WILL: You don't think I wrote the paper.

FRAN: I didn't say that. Maybe you had some inappropriate help or...

WILL: I wrote the paper by myself. Yeah, my dad proofread it. But it's my ideas. My words.

FRAN: I'm not accusing...I'm just trying to understand. There's an inconsistency between the way you talk in class and the way you write....

WILL: Yeah, I know that. I don't talk the way I write. Does anybody?

FRAN: It's not only that. I looked up your STAR reports from last year, and your writing score—

WILL: I hate those tests! Before you even get to the test part, they ask you for your race and your parents' income and how many years they've gone to school and your student ID number and what language you speak at home and, I dunno, what kind of breakfast cereal you ate this morning, and by the time I get to the real questions, my brain is boiling, and I just stare at the words and read them again and again. .

(*Silence.* **FRAN** *looks at* **WILL** *directly and openly for the first time in their conversation.*)

FRAN: Will, I'm sorry, I—

(**WILL** *stands up.*)

WILL: I enjoyed reading *All Quiet on the Western Front,* and I even enjoyed writing the paper. And I don't care what grade I got on it. I don't cheat. And I could speak the way I write, if I chose to do so, but I prefer to talk the way everybody else does. So, thank you, Ms. Peterson, for the informative conversation. And have a nice day.

(**WILL** *bows to her and walks away.* **FRAN** *stands up hurriedly to follow him.*)

FRAN: Will, wait, please. I apologize.... Can we talk...?

(**WILL** *leaves the room, closing the door firmly behind him, but not slamming it.* **FRAN** *wilts.*)

FRAN: Shit.

GEORGE & MARTHA
BY KAREN FINLEY

CHARACTERS
MARTHA STEWART *(older), the domestic doyenne, and* GEORGE W. BUSH *(younger), the president*

SCENE
*A hotel room, the presidential suite—*MARTHA *calls it a dump. There is a bed, a TV, some type of bar for refreshments, liquor, a nightstand, and a telephone. Interpret the suite as lavishly or as minimally as desired.*

The characters can be nude and body-painted. MARTHA *is in black-and-white convict stripes, pearl necklace, and gold knee-high boots. Red and white vertical stripes are painted on* GEORGE'S *chest with white stars on blue arms. His legs have scattered stars with the lone star of Texas on his back. HE wears a blue double-breasted, gold-buttoned jacket and has a belt that reads "Boy Toy." HE wears cowboy boots. Both wear wigs.*

TIME
During the GEORGE W. BUSH *administration, specifically the 2004 Republican convention in New York City*

GEORGE *and* MARTHA *are sitting up in bed having a conversation. They play with each other's hands and bodies in a very unconscious style common with lovers.*

MARTHA: George, I need to redesign the world.

GEORGE: Honey, can't we keep your work out of our love life? I just want to get a little high and watch *The Sopranos.*

MARTHA: I can go big on this, George, with your help. It is more than infrastructure, George. We can redesign America with a Middle East craze. After Pearl Harbor Hawaii overtook home decorating in the fifties. Everyone was wearing a muumuu and throwing tiki parties. With Kmart, everyone in the US will be living in a tent and building their own mosque with the help of Home Depot.

GEORGE: Sweetheart, I know we both are involved with domestic issues but Kmart is not Iraq.

MARTHA: Kmart isn't Iraq but that doesn't mean Iraq can't be Kmart.

GEORGE: Honey, I hate to disappoint you but Cheney isn't making money in shower curtains.

MARTHA: You need to rethink Bed, Bath and Beyond, George. (*Passionate, holding* **GEORGE** *by the shoulders.*) Everyone has a kitchen, George. I want to redo Iraq's lifestyle. This is more than religion, George. Once I introduce a culture to shabby chic and Extra Virgin Olive Oil, they are paying lifetime dues to be in Martha's club. We are talking utensils. Utensils, George. UTENSILS. Everyone has a utensil. An herb garden.

GEORGE: Not an herb garden, Martha. Too peacey. We want them to buy things, Martha, not grow them. (*Pause.*) Cheney thinks it is all in fast food.

MARTHA: Cheney? You are listening to that bald-headed, uncouth fart machine on his sense of style for America? George, you are going to need me. America needs to transform those hooded prisoners into the perfect black dress. I have the perfect solution, George.

GEORGE: Easy, Martha.

MARTHA: Yes, that is why I want to start McMohammed Kabob. It's a good thing.

(**GEORGE** *looks at her perplexed, listening.* **HE** *turns off the television.*)

MARTHA: Look, George. Sony in Japan was started by American money— McMohammed Kabob. And if we are lucky, play our cards right, Micky McJesus will be coming in a six-pack on the Gaza Strip.

GEORGE: (*Coming to his senses.*) You're right, Martha. These people need to liquor up so they can find OUR GOD OUR WAY. It's time these people learned to take the edge off with alcohol. That's the way I found Jesus. Alcohol. Drank myself to oblivion until I found the Lord.

MARTHA: George, we don't want them to be shitting red, white, and blue. Only wiping their ass on the good old U.S.A. greenback.

GEORGE: We could bring in McDonalds, Disney, and throw in a theme park and call it Mickey McMohammed. Make a movie, a cartoon on the Passion of Mohammed. Make Mohammed a mouse. The Moslems need a mouse. Make it a Moslem mouse. A Mouslem. Make Mohammed a Mouseketeer. Then we get the kids' meals and toy franchise and everyone is happy. And another thing.

MARTHA: Make it a good thing.

GEORGE: (*Exasperated, concerned, hesitant.*) I don't know, Martha. It might not look good.

MARTHA: MIGHT NOT LOOK GOOD? This is new, George. Since when have you been concerned about appearances?

GEORGE: I want to save the theme park for when I leave the White House.

MARTHA: Oh, don't start now with priorities, George. You can never be spontaneous. Oh, go read a book with Laura and turn on the night light.

GEORGE: Martha, I can never process anything with you.

MARTHA: Okay, I am listening.

GEORGE: I plan—

MARTHA: (*Sarcastically.*) Oh, George has a plan.

GEORGE: I plan to make a theme park based on all the presidents.

MARTHA: (*Sarcastically.*) *All the presidents??* Really, George? That is quite an undertaking.

GEORGE: (*Sounding presidential.*) It will be a theme park based on all the presidents.

MARTHA: You just said that, dear. All the presidents. Don't need to repeat yourself.

GEORGE: It will be a theme park based on each and every presidency. And considering—

MARTHA: Considering . . . sounds very NPR. Sounds liberal, considering??

GEORGE: And considering—

MARTHA: Are you really going to consider everything, George? Are you? Are you considerate, George? Really, George, you have never considered anything except the easy way out of anything.

GEORGE: Since there is always a new president—

MARTHA: Never knew that, George. Thought we were in a dictatorship or monarchy under King George. Thanks for telling the subjects!!

GEORGE: (*Getting mad.*) Since there is always a new president, the theme park will continue to grow and grow. And I will make appearances. And my library will be there, too.

MARTHA: Since you don't read, there will have to be plenty of open space for Frisbees—

THE GRAND DESIGN
BY SUSAN MILLER

CHARACTERS

JOSH *(late 30s) is a recently divorced scientist who is somewhat angst-ridden, but guided by his curiosity and governed by his sense of humor;* FRANCES *(late 50s–early 60s), his mother, who shares her son's qualities, is on a journey of discovery.*

SCENE
The stage

TIME
The present

(JOSH *and* FRANCES *occupy opposite sides of a stage to indicate the geographical distance between them. They are addressing the audience as the scene begins.*)

FRANCES: My son is kind of a poet scientist. He's got this grant to come up with a message for alien civilizations. To let them know who we are. He's hit a wall. And I've left town. On foot.

JOSH: My mother is walking. She's walking with no clear purpose all across the United States. It's her response to the—situation. To turning a certain age. To my breakup. It's her memorial to the nature of our times. (*Beat.*) She calls me from the road.

FRANCES: I'm on the Eleanor Roosevelt Trail.

(*A succession of calls.*)

I'm standing outside a church on top of a hill in Ohio where the Underground Railroad connected. (*Beat.*) I don't know where I am. But I see cows.

I'm covering ground. I'm walking past the things I know.

I met this person who picks the places to stop along the way. You know when you get directions—on your computer. What's that called—map something? Well, they actually send people out to find interesting things to do along the routes. I just never thought of that. There are all kinds of jobs I never thought about.

JOSH: Look, I'm sorry. I'm sorry things didn't work out and I didn't give you grandchildren and—

FRANCES: (*To audience.*) He thinks I'm out here because he failed in his marriage. I'm out here because I failed. To know what to do next. I was sad. And I started walking. I was walking in circles all around the house. Finally, I just took it outside. And I'm not the only one out here. There are mothers walking all over the place. (*Beat.*) I'm worried he won't find love.

(*The phone rings in Josh's house. Although they begin talking to each other, as if on the phone, this is dropped shortly and they just address each other directly.*)

FRANCES: Hi, Sweetie!

JOSH: Mom? Where are you?

FRANCES: If I wanted to be located, I would stay home.

JOSH: Are you just walking aimlessly or do you have some kind of plan?

FRANCES: I do have a plan. To walk aimlessly. All right, the story so far. I just had pie. They use shortening and whole eggs and I don't care. Because while I eat my pie and have my coffee, I'm not drowning in the facts. There is no true history of the United States. I am not guilty. I am not wanting. I am not disappointed. So, how are you coming with your memo to alien civilizations?

JOSH: See, when you say it like that—

FRANCES: Like what?

JOSH: Like how you said it.

FRANCES: Like how I said memo or how's it coming?

JOSH: How you said it like you had no opinion or no opinion you'd be ready to reveal, even though we can be pretty sure that you are always in possession of an opinion. Anyhow, I'm now writing a memo. It's more like an equation. You know? Which lays out the thing to be discovered or proven. It's not necessarily what we are—it's what we could be.

FRANCES: (*Struck.*) That's lovely.

JOSH: For a lie, you mean.

FRANCES: Maybe it's a lie we need.

JOSH: Well, I do, I guess. I need it. (*Beat.*) See, the big discoveries—gravity, particle theory, chaos, DNA—they place us. They put us in the physical world. But they're just descriptions. Of our physical properties. Our propensities. What we're capable of—what's possible, what we've already accomplished, I mean how do you—first...I thought, well, fucking, of course. Sexual congress. For them to see how we do it and how much we like to do it. But, fucking causes so much confusion and anxiety. And what if they interpret two figures expressing their ardor as some kind of cruel rite? And the truth is, fucking doesn't last. And, then, what about madness, disorders of the mind, bodies that aren't whole? (*Beat.*) I should just tell them that to be human is to impose yourself on the world. This is how I see it, so this is how it is.

FRANCES: (*A beat.*) Or—you could take this grant money and give it away to actual people. So they could eat, go to school, and maybe collectively expand and redefine the concept of what it is to be human.

JOSH: Okay, sister, listen, didn't I give up my beautiful SUV when you were on your moral imperative not to drive big, gas-guzzling automobiles, thus entrenching us in a relationship with oil-producing nations and consequently undermining what we tout to be our own unique position of being free in the world?

FRANCES: I was quoting. I didn't come up with that myself, which is disturbing, because I don't always see how things fit and I'm always completely thrown to learn there's a relationship between a simple thing like buying a car or a carton of milk and the decline of civilization.

JOSH: Well, just put your two cents in about this, would you, and help me out here. I mean, is it sentimental to think there's something—anything—we have in common with everyone else on earth?

FRANCES: What everyone wants to know is who am I going to be? And then, who am I going to be with who'll make it not so terrible to *be* me? And if you have children, well, who are they going to be and who are they going to be with and will I like who they are and who they're with and how do I keep them safe? (*Beat.*) Maybe you're reaching, Josh. Maybe the story of one person is all they need to know about us.

JOSH: Where the hell are you?

FRANCES: In my tent.

JOSH: You are not in any kind of a tent.

FRANCES: In my tent outside of my room at the motel. You don't think I'd really pee in the open, do you? You should go outside. It is an alarmingly beautiful night.

JOSH: I can't go outside. I can't think outside.

FRANCES: Did you open my letter yet?

JOSH: (*Avoiding.*) I haven't had the chance—actually.

FRANCES: I know you're carrying it around in your pocket and it's getting smushed and I need you to read it.

JOSH: I know you want me to read it, Frances. So it must be important. And that, of course, brings up my morbid fear of important letters.

FRANCES: Josh.

JOSH: And I don't really have the time right now.

FRANCES: (*Retreating.*) Okay.

JOSH: I'm in over my head with this thing.

FRANCES: Look, if the aliens have a sense of humor, they'll see the irony. Or they'll receive it like the French do when you try to speak their language. (*A beat.*) Tell me . . . just show me what you've got so far.

JOSH: Just—you know, I'm still working on it.

GROUNDWORK OF THE
METAPHYSIC OF MORALS
BY YOUNG JEAN LEE

CHARACTERS
SHEILA *and* TERRENCE *are in their mid-to-late twenties, both WASP-y white.*

SCENE
Fu Manchu's testing room with a mechanical tester (a big, loud machine) and trap door

TIME
1932, afternoon

Groundwork of the Metaphysic of Morals *is based on the 1932 adventure movie* Mask of Fu Manchu. SHEILA *and* TERRENCE *offer to trade Genghis Khan's mask and shield for the return of* SHEILA's *father, an archaeologist who has been kidnapped by Fu Manchu. Captured by the evil genius themselves,* SHEILA *and* TERRENCE *escape to Fu Manchu's testing room.*

SHEILA *and* TERRENCE *enter.* TERRENCE *stares into the trap-door opening in the floor while* SHEILA *stands behind him.*

SHEILA: We should probably go soon.

(TERRENCE *continues to stare down into the opening.*)

Come on, Terrence. Let's get out of here.

TERRENCE: What were they thinking, anyway? Everyone knows that white people are just going to do whatever they want and there's nothing you can do to stop them.

SHEILA: Come on, Terrence.

TERRENCE: Why were they so unhappy?

SHEILA: I don't know.

TERRENCE: Maybe we did something to them. Maybe it was our fault.

SHEILA: Why would it be our fault?

TERRENCE: What if the whole world is a structure that is built up around white people and men controlling everything and being superior? What if everything, including the way we breathe, is structured by this?

SHEILA: There's no such thing as a master structure. It's all just individuals working toward their goals.

TERRENCE: How do you know?

SHEILA: I don't like to think in terms of race. I like to see people as human individuals.

TERRENCE: Huh.

SHEILA: I don't even think there's any such thing as race.

TERRENCE: Huh, interesting.

SHEILA: It's based on facts, on historical evidence.

TERRENCE: What about racism?

SHEILA: Slavery was racism, and when you drag a black man behind your truck for mile upon mile.

TERRENCE: Maybe you shouldn't say that.

SHEILA: No! I'm going to fight, because this kind of reverse racism makes me mad! People think I won't stand up for myself, but I will!

TERRENCE: You seem very mad.

SHEILA: I'm going to show everyone that I can make it, that I can succeed without these complaints of racism bringing me down, making me feel bad about myself! I want everything to be fair and nondiscriminatory and based on logic, and fuck you! Everything I think is based on logic! (*Pause.*) Maybe we should get out of here.

TERRENCE: I would like to stay a minute.

(SHEILA *exits. Pause.*)

Orientals, I miss you! Though I know it is probably horrible and racist for me to say this, there was something about your culture that I valued so much. There was your incredible hospitality, and your wonderful food and religion and oh, everything! And I don't understand. I don't understand why we have to shoot and kill each other like this, but I promise I will try to understand better from now on. I accept the theory about everything being an evil structure that makes every breath we take, that makes the very idea of breathing, serve the white man. And I am aware that right at this moment, *right at this moment* I am being evil and disgusting. But I will try and try and try and try, and every day I will try harder to be responsible. I will be responsible.

(*Beat.* **TERRENCE** *exits.*)

HENRY
BY CLAUDIA BARNETT

CHARACTERS
HIM *(20s) has returned to be with his former lover;* HER *(20s) remains ambivalent about that.*

SCENE
A room (his). A bed with two blankets, one spread over the bed and the other folded into a square. They are having a picnic.

TIME
The present

HIM: I owe you an apology.

HER: For what?

HIM: For leaving you.

HER: For leaving me? When?

HIM: I've been gone six months.

HER: Six months? But we just put a deposit on the banquet hall. It seems like yesterday.

HIM: I left you.

HER: (SHE *walks away from the picnic.*) That's right. You did. Ran off with another woman. How could you do that? You've caused me so much pain. My heart. My lungs. My toes.

HIM: You burned my stuff.

HER: All of it. Huge bonfire. Roasted marshmallows. But I couldn't eat them. I felt ill.

HIM: We were going to get married. I gave you a ring.

HER: Do you want your ring back? Is that why you invited me here?

HIM: Didn't you burn it? I just assumed.

HER: Diamonds don't burn. I tried. I guess you want it back. Well, you can't have it.

Hɪᴍ: No, you keep it.

Hᴇʀ: If you don't want it, neither do I. Here. It's yours.

(**Sʜᴇ** *removes the ring from her finger and hands it to him.* **Hᴇ** *takes it and inspects it.*)

Hɪᴍ: It's smaller than I remembered.

Hᴇʀ: It is small.

Hɪᴍ: But it's pretty.

Hᴇʀ: It's okay.

Hɪᴍ: Now you're hurt?

Hᴇʀ: Now? It's been two years. Two years of hurt. You ran away. Didn't even leave a note. And suddenly here you are with smoked turkey and brie. I don't eat that anymore, you know. I'm a vegetarian. And lactose intolerant. You don't know a thing.

(**Hᴇ** *wraps the blanket around the picnic and ties it up. The picnic somehow disappears.*)

Hɪᴍ: I think you should keep the ring.

Hᴇʀ: No, thanks. We broke up. Dear Abby says to give the ring back. So does my mother. And besides, it reminds me of you.

Hɪᴍ: Is that so bad?

Hᴇʀ: The pain is in my heart. My lungs. My hands. How could you leave me?

Hɪᴍ: For another woman.

Hᴇʀ: For another woman. And you didn't even leave a note.

Hɪᴍ: I didn't want to hurt you.

Hᴇʀ: And so you didn't leave a note?

Hɪᴍ: I left you because she was pregnant. And I wanted to do the right thing.

Hᴇʀ: The right thing

Hɪᴍ: You always talked about children, and I always said no. But here I was having one. So I thought it best not to tell you.

Hᴇʀ: You didn't want me to be jealous.

Him: So I went to Minneapolis.

Her: I've never been to Minneapolis.

Him: I couldn't help myself.

Her: You couldn't.

Him: She was like a siren singing for a sailor, but I wasn't smart enough to plug my ears. So I followed her. Fell for her. Impregnated her.

Her: Against your will.

Him: I had no will. She raped me, shackled me, kept me prisoner. Forced me to have her baby.

Her: But you're a man.

Him: Such things can happen.

Her: So I've heard, but I can't imagine.

Him: She has magical powers. And the tongue of a cat.

Her: I don't want to hear about her tongue.

Him: Then I left her.

Her: What about the baby?

Him: She didn't want it. She laid it out with the trash one morning at daybreak. That broke the spell, and together we escaped.

Her: We?

Him: Me and Henry.

Her: Henry?

Him: My son.

(*A doll appears.* **He** *takes it and holds it like a baby. A brief baby's cry.*)

Her: I knew I heard a baby. He's beautiful.

Him: He has six toes.

Her: On each foot?

Him: Yes.

Her: How romantic.

Him: But only one nose.

Her: That's for the best.

Him: So will you marry me and be his mother?

Her: Of course not. I'm already someone's mother. I have a baby of my own.

Him: You do?

(*A second doll appears, accompanied by the sound of a brief baby's cry.* **She** *takes the doll and holds it as if it were a baby.*)

Her: Oh, yes. She's lovely, too. And she also has six toes.

Him: On each foot.

Her: And one nose.

Him: How old is she?

Her: She's the same age as Henry.

Him: Well, then she must be mine.

Her: She might not.

Him: But we were together...

Her: But Henry's not mine. So there your logic falls apart.

Him: I think they like each other.

Her: I think they have gas.

Him: I love you, you know.

Her: Yes, I know. But I'm not magical, so I can't keep you.

Him: But I love you.

Her: You're not very strong.

Him: I can lift the bed.

Her: Please don't. That's not what I meant.

Him: We could live happily ever after: you, me, Henry, and...

Her: Henrietta.

Him: Henrietta?

Her: Yes.

Him: Yes, you'll marry me?

Her: Yes, her name is Henrietta.

(*The dolls disappear.* **He** *kneels and offers her the ring.*)

Him: Please will you marry me?

Her: I always knew you'd come crawling back. But I can't take you back. Not after the way you've hurt me. I feel the pain in my heart. My lungs. My toes. All six of them.

Him: But we have the ring, the china pattern, the banquet hall.

Her: We had those things, but now they're gone.

Him: We still have the ring.

Her: That's not the same ring. I got it in a gumball machine. It's made of peppermint candy.

(**He** *puts the ring in his mouth and swallows.*)

Him: Delicious.

(*The sound of a baby crying, once, briefly.*)

Her: Now everything is gone.

(*The sound of the baby crying begins again and rapidly intensifies. His doll reappears. The noise seems to be coming from the doll.* **He** *does not know what to do.* **He** *holds the doll up high, gently shakes it, and tries to hand it to her.* **She** *watches him calmly but does not move.*)

THE IMPOSSIBILITY OF
MOST THINGS
BY ALBERT INNAURATO

CHARACTERS

MICHAEL CRENSHAW *(18) meets* GOLDA PEARLSTEIN *(18) for the first time.*
(In the play they are older actors playing 18.)

SCENE

Outside a large hall at Harvard. A freshman orientation party is going on.
There's a banner on the wall: WELCOME CLASS OF '78.

TIME

Fall 1974

Students in preppy attire with mild hippie touches dance by behind a dull
window. MICHAEL CRENSHAW *comes out of the party and lights a cigarette.* HE
is a nice-looking, rather boyish 18-year-old.

A livelier dance starts up inside. An 18-year-old, GOLDA, *pushes out of the*
hall—looking for MICHAEL, *though* SHE *hides that.* SHE'S *wearing a long, too-*
loose dress. Her hair is down. SHE *is more unflatteringly dressed than anything*
else, but it makes her seem less attractive and a little chubby. SHE *stops, aware of*
MICHAEL. SHE *sneaks a look at him.* SHE *looks away.* HE *sneaks a look at her,*
then looks away. SHE *settles down on a piece of wall across from him.* HE *sneaks*
another look at her. SHE *looks up and catches him.* THEY *both look away.*
Finally, MICHAEL *edges across the stage until* HE *is sitting beside* GOLDA. THEY
smile shyly at one another.

MICHAEL: What's your name?

GOLDA: Death and Torment.

MICHAEL: I thought you looked familiar. I'm Michael, Outcast of Groton.

GOLDA: Why?

MICHAEL: Opera.

GOLDA: Yes. That's non-U.

MICHAEL: I found Callas when I was thirteen. She got me through Groton. I
have come to believe that obsession is salvation. I feel that way about opera,

reading, and sex. And about acting. I want to act, you see, Death and Torment.

GOLDA: I'm really Golda. Golda Pearlstein. (*Beat.*) You didn't laugh.

MICHAEL: You carry it well. I am very uncomfortable, yet there's nothing wrong with my name. It's Crenshaw. Of the Grosse Pointe Crenshaws. Do you like opera?

GOLDA: Does *Cabaret* count as an opera?

MICHAEL: I shouldn't have brought it up.

GOLDA: You can hide loving opera. It's something you can do in the dark. You look fine.

MICHAEL: I do?

GOLDA: Oh, yes. In fact, I feel a crush coming on.

MICHAEL: By crush, you don't mean an Italian ice?

GOLDA: If only I did. Perhaps we should part now before I make a total fool of myself.

MICHAEL: Well, I realize it's not a contest, but I can make a fool of myself faster than any other human in history.

GOLDA: Wanna bet?

MICHAEL: You're on.

GOLDA: You see, I saw you earlier. I've been seeing you all week. It's orientation week so I've been getting oriented to you. You look a little like Prince Valiant in a movie I saw in grade school. My older sister, Jennifer—and I'm Golda, right?—made out noisily right behind me with her first boyfriend, a blond jock named, as it happens, Jock. Somehow the combination of Prince Valiant—dark-haired, blue-eyed, strong, yet a poet; hell in a duel—yet clearly in need of thick motherly paps to cry on—Jennifer tonguing Jock, the overheated movie theater, and my hands sticky from Juicy Fruits—has eroticized your type of soft hard Wasp for me forever. And Michael, Outcast of Groton, unlike the celluloid Prince Valiant, you are the real thing, not some male starlet decked out in tin.

MICHAEL: (*Beat.*) You win.

GOLDA: Told you.

MICHAEL: You're funny and, I can tell, sweet. I notice also a latent but pronounced sexual allure.

GOLDA: Please!

MICHAEL: The baby fat will melt away. You have pretty hands and feet. (**HE** *pulls the fabric of her dress tight.*) Meaty breasts. (**HE** *walks behind her and makes the dress snug.*) And a robust fin de siècle derrière many a real man will want to knead. I'm homosexual.

GOLDA: So was Prince Valiant.

MICHAEL: (*Beat.*) What movie is this?

GOLDA: Who's talking movies?

MICHAEL: I see.

GOLDA: Don't worry, I've grown up bathing in the impossibility of most things. I mean, things you want. There's a law, like gravity, "You want it? You can't have it!"

(*Beat.* **THEY** *listen to the music.*)

MICHAEL: Strange the power of cheap music.

GOLDA: Is that Cole Porter or Noël Coward?

MICHAEL: Is there a difference? I was almost in *Private Lives* once.

GOLDA: At Groton?

MICHAEL: Not exactly. You see, Golda, my slightly younger sibling, Cynthia, was at Andover. The Drama Teacher, Mr. Shingles, was doing *Private Lives*. Thirty-six women auditioned. No genital males did. I determined to try out. True actors are hungry. We were between plays at Groton. And Groton, you see, ill-fated Groton, is a bastion of the higher stand-up comedy type writing of, say, Neil (not Noël) Simon. So I hitchhiked to Andover. You know:

(*Singing about freedom à la Janis Joplin from "Me and Bobby McGee."* **GOLDA** *is utterly lost.*)

Janis Joplin is just like Callas, only hoarser. At Andover, I auditioned for Mr. Shingles, fat and hysterical, not entirely my style. Later he was fired and sent to jail for binding the hockey team in Saran Wrap. Don't ask. Of course, I got the part. In fact, I got both male parts. Cynthia was cast in both female parts. It would be an early postmodern *Private Lives* with intimations of incest. But one of her classmates, a jealous girl named Wisteria Wicket.

(**GOLDA** *laughs.*)

I'm serious, why do you laugh? Do you think perhaps I'm Ivy Compton-Burnett in preppy drag? (*Back to the story.*) Wisteria Wicket turned me in. I claimed asylum as a political refugee from Groton. I was returned there for disciplinary action. I was barred from all Neil Simon plays for the foreseeable future. Later, as we were watching my father and younger brother play tennis while my beloved sister watched and wept—Dada wouldn't play with girls— my mother said to me: "You are a disgrace, Michael Crenshaw, a noisy, unpopular scamp. And since Dada plans to disinherit you, you may well need Neil Simon or equivalent to live as an actor." "You know, Mama," I replied, "though I realize Neil Simon is the only commercial playwright we have in the foreseeable future of these early seventies, I feel confident that TV-type writing will lose its power, that a society in which most people have gone to college and fought for civil rights and objected to pointless slaughter and illegal bombings in a far-off place called Vietnam will transcend that type of entertainment and start to value the arts." Her eyes teared, she squeezed her face shut. She sneezed. Hay fever. Tell me, Miss Pearlstein, Golda if I may, can I be wrong about that?

GOLDA: (*Beat.*) Is Neil Simon all that bad? I mean, I like *Barefoot in the Park* and *The Odd Couple* is great. You have to grant he's very skillful. *Plaza Suite* is ingenious. (*Beat.*) Isn't it?

MICHAEL: (*Beat.*) I have a bottle of Mateus in my room.

GOLDA: Really? I have some pot.

MICHAEL: Really? I have four 'ludes.

GOLDA: Really? I've got a soupçon of horse.

MICHAEL: Inject?

GOLDA: Smoke.

MICHAEL: We're downer doers, delicious. Let's go.

GOLDA: Roommates?

MICHAEL: I have a single. Emotional problems.

GOLDA: I should have tried that. What did you claim?

MICHAEL: An obsession with male genitals.

GOLDA: Oh, a man thing.

MICHAEL: What are you going to do here this semester?

GOLDA: I was thinking of auditioning at Lowell House. They are casting for their spring play. I'd like to be an actress.

MICHAEL: You won't be an actress, really, you're not cheap enough. I know. I am. Tell me about your writing.

GOLDA: (*Surprised, ill at ease.*) My writing?

MICHAEL: Uh-huh.

GOLDA: (*Uncomfortable.*) I can't spell. Jennifer, my older sister, corrects my spelling. She's an aspiring andrologist studying animal sperm at the University of Guelph.

MICHAEL: The University of Guelph?

GOLDA: In Ontario. She's won many awards, starting with harvesting our—well, actually my—hamsters' ejaculate when she was fourteen.

MICHAEL: Mazeltov. Is that the word?

GOLDA: I don't know. We're assimilated.

MICHAEL: (*Raising an eyebrow.*) But they named you Golda?

GOLDA: I think I was their offering to the Dybbuk. He never came, so they were stuck with me and I was stuck with Golda. Anyhoo, Jennifer is no longer generally available.

MICHAEL: I didn't inquire about your spelling. (*Beat.*) Come, come, I told you two of my guilty secrets: loving opera and Janis Joplin—my being queer is too obvious to be a secret. So tell one of yours.

GOLDA: (*Hesitant.*) Novels. But for now I write plays—preparation. When I write prose, I feel so lonely. And I don't understand anything. Novels require more insight and less stupidity. Maybe I can learn.... (*Beat.*) I'm so sorry. Listen to me! Sophomoric yet only a freshman. How dare I say I want to write? As though anyone would care. As though just by saying it, I am.

MICHAEL: Golda— (**He** *shudders.*) Pardon me, your name hurts my mouth—I am a little sissy who will die young. We butterflies know talent. Don't ask me how. We know it. Gol...Whatsaname, I'm sincere when I tell you, I can sense it in you. You won't be happy, no, I think not. And I don't know if you'll be successful. You will be what you already are.

(**He's** *meant it and* **She** *understands that in some bizarre way,* **He's** *right.* **She** *doesn't know what to say.*)

Golda: I'm . . . (*Beat.*) Michael, Outcast of Groton, I'm afraid.

Michael: I'm afraid too.

Golda: Of what?

Michael: Of . . . of what. That's it. Of what.

(**She** *looks at him, concerned.*)

Michael: (**He** *smiles.*) I'm sure there will be a part for you at Lowell House.

Golda: How do you know?

Michael: I've curried favor. I serviced several seniors.

Golda: Already.

Michael: The early bird gets the worm.

Golda: So to speak. (*Beat.*) What's the play? They're awfully secretive.

Michael: *Madame Butterfly.*

Golda: That's a play?

Michael: Was a play first. By John Luther Long. Tell you what, come to my room. Perhaps I can convert you to opera.

Golda: I don't want to imply I'm tin-eared. I can hear the tunes in *A Funny Thing* . . . but not in anything else.

(**They** *start to walk off arm in arm.*)

Michael: I see. Maria—Madame Callas—may be quite a lot for you to start. But there's always Anna Moffo. Nice. Safe. Comfy. American. Bland. And by the way all the Moffo fans I know are arty New Yorkers, hence have excellent connections for Quaaludes. . . . (**They** *are almost offstage.*)

Golda: Yum! (**They're** *offstage.*)

THE LAST FREAK SHOW
BY PHILIP ZWERLING

CHARACTERS

AL ZIPPERSTEIN *(mid-30s), born and bred in the Bronx, runs a ramshackle traveling freak show in Texas, slightly out of his element;* IRENE FORTUNATA *(20s), elegant and seductive with an edge, arrives to discuss a business proposition.*

SCENE
Texas Panhandle

TIME
July 1933

AL ZIPPERSTEIN *sits behind the desk with his feet up and an unlighted cigar in his mouth. HE wears a stained wife-beater T-shirt and a worn fedora. HE is juggling three balls in the air and each time tosses them higher. At some point one of the balls, above the audience's sight line, fails to come down. AL looks for it as HE catches the other two balls. HE can't see it anywhere. The phone on his desk rings and HE grabs for it.*

AL: (*A quick, well-practiced spiel.*) Zipperstein Family Circus and Freak Show: geeks, freaks, and oddities for the whole family. We entertain, educate, elucidate, and electrify audiences from Moscow to Minneapolis and Paris to Philadelphia with pinheads and snake women. . . . Oh, hi, howya' doin', Robbie? Beatin' them rich Dallas broads off with a stick? Doin' a little après-horizontal rhumba shopping at Nieman-Marcus? Yeah. . . . Yeah. . . . What? (*Suddenly agitated.*) But you said the big D was a go. . . . You said. . . . They can't do that. I'll drag their heinies into court if they cancel. . . . Yeah. . . . Yeah. . . . Yeah. . . . But. . . . But Robbie, you gotta . . . but. . . . Robbie it's two hundred degrees in the shade out here in Lubbock and there ain't no shade. Electric Girl is shortin' out. Monkey Boy's off his bananas, Helga's tattoos are running down her legs and puddlin' ink in her shoes, and the Siamese twins are slipping apart. Help me out here, Robbie . . . Robbie. . . . Robbie?

(AL *slams down the phone when HE realizes it has gone dead. The lost ball now falls from above and lands on his head. HE puts his head down on the desk and sighs. There is a knock as on wood and a young, attractive woman, stylishly dressed, enters.*)

IRENE: I tried to knock. . . . (*Seeing AL with his head down.*) I'm sorry, are you okay?

AL: (*Raises his head, sees* **IRENE**, *and shakes off his gloom, rises while speaking, shrugs into the garish jacket hung on his chair, and approaches* **IRENE**.) Okay? Why never better in my life. How could I not be okay when a beautiful woman, like yourself, exactly like yourself, enters my humble office unannounced and shines her pulchritudinous glow upon my straw-covered hovel. My countenance is lifted by your mere presence, Miss . . . ?

IRENE: (*Offering her hand in response.*) Fortunata . . . Irene Fortunata.

AL: Fortunata? From the Italian *forunato* . . . fortunate . . . one upon whom the gods and nature have smiled and made her fortune. . . .

(**HE** *ushers her into the only other chair, dusting some hay or paper off of it and watches attentively as* **SHE** *slowly sits and crosses her legs.*)

But it is we, Miss Fortunata, it is we who are fortunate, we who are the happy recipients of your beauty, charm, and . . . (*Addressing her legs.*) peerless form. (**HE** *sits atop his desk facing her.*) And I feel myself especially fortunate today that you should perambulate your pulchritude into my presence at this very hour of this very day at this very moment of my own good fortune.

IRENE: Really? I perhaps thought I had come at a bad time for you. You seemed . . . sad.

AL: Sad? Sad, you say? Al Zipperstein doesn't know the meaning of that particular word. Al Zipperstein does not wallow in the valleys of despond. He moves from peak to peak and success to success as his entertainment establishment progresses across this fair land, enthralling audiences from coast to coast.

IRENE: Well, I'm glad to hear that . . . Mr. Zipperstein. I . . .

AL: Al, Al, please call me Al. Let's begin our relationship on a note of unfettered informality upon which our incessantly increasing intimacy may grow and deepen, expand. . . .

IRENE: (*Cutting him off.*) As you please. Al, then

(**SHE** *takes out a gold cigarette case and elegantly places a cigarette between her lips.* **SHE** *waits until* **HE** *finally gets the idea and searches for a match to light it for her. When* **HE** *fails to find a match in any of his pockets,* **SHE** *offers him her lighter and* **HE** *lights the cigarette.* **SHE** *inhales deeply and blows smoke in his direction.*)

Al, I am here on business.

AL: Business? Business is what I am all about. Al Zipperstein is all business all the time. Just a moment ago I was telephonically communicating with my show business agent in Dallas, the capital of this vast state, to arrange our future performances before the very economic and cultural elite of this land not so long ago seized by force of arms from menacing Mexicans and...

IRENE: Austin...(**HE** *looks puzzled.* **SHE** *explains.*) Actually Austin is the capital of Texas.

AL: Smart and beautiful. Yes, Miss Fortunata, it is Miss, I hope?

(**IRENE** *nods in the affirmative.*)

Yes indeed, smart and beautiful and unattached. But what do I know, Miss Fortunata, a poor boy born in the Bronx ghetto of immigrant yids and cruelly thrust into this Gentile world to claw his way up from the gutter to at last walk proudly among the crowned heads of Europe and to traverse each of our own forty-eight states many times over. I forget capitals, sometimes, they pass so quickly, even the state I'm in....

IRENE: Business, Mr. Zipperstein...

(**HE** *shakes his head "no."*)

Al. Business, Al. I am here, on behalf of myself and my...associates to offer you four hundred dollars for one of your...(*Searches for the word.*)... exhibits.

AL: Ah, Miss Fortunata, lovely as you are, so lovely, so ethereal, but not wise in the alternate world of carnival life. You speak like a "Gilly," the hoi poloi...the uninformed from out there. (**HE** *waves his hand around to indicate the circus world outside.*) We do not have "exhibits" at Zipperstein's. No, not at all. Nothing is dead here. There are no lifeless abnormal forms stuffed into formaldehyde vats. No "gaffed" shows here, my dear. No "made" freaks decked out in costumes and makeup to deceive the rubes. Everything at Zipperstein's is alive and real, as real as they were born and made by a benevolent god, a god whose sense of humor...strayed perhaps...in forming human beings not unlike ourselves but with a bit more hair here, a pointed head there, or the body of an alligator down here. Their piteous existence simply makes the lives of the rest of us so much richer and develops our more tender sympathies for those less fortunate.

IRENE: Five hundred dollars, Al. Five hundred dollars for the Monkey Boy. Cash...(**SHE** *lifts her purse.*)...now.

AL: You embarrass me, Miss Fortunata. You embarrass yourself. Let me show you something that will astound you....

(HE *rummages behind the desk, disappears there, and reappears with a glass bottle perhaps two feet tall. Inside is what appears to be a large human fetus but with two heads.* IRENE *jumps to her feet in horror.*)

IRENE: Good God. What an abomination.

AL: Not exactly. (HE *turns the bottle so that we can see that the fetus has a tail.*) See the tail. It was displayed at a freak show in Edinburg in front of a large mural heralding it as "The Devil's Spawn." The gulls paid a dime to see it close up inside the tent. (HE *shakes the bottle so that the fetus bounces up and down.*) It's a bouncer, you see. God had nothing to do with it—just a man and bottles of India rubber.

IRENE: (*Moving closer for a better look.*) You mean it's fake.

AL: Gaffed, as we say. A made freak is a fake freak, which is easy to do with your dead "exhibits." I bought it when that show folded to remind myself of the difference. On my lot it's all real. That's why we're nearly the last freak show still in business. Your lack of knowledge shows me you're a "gilly," someone unfamiliar with our ways. (*Beat.*) Now Monkey Boy, or Macalaca, as I refer to him in our face-to-face close personal relations, grows in popularity week by week... by the day even. People flock to see what many eminent scientists think may be the Missing Link within Charles Darwin's controversial Theory of Evolution. He's the real thing. His contributions to Science may be unlimited. And yet I am so often touched by his kindly disposition, hidden like a jewel behind untold yards of thick and matted hair encrusted with the vermin of the Malay jungle where he was discovered just eight months ago....

IRENE: Six hundred dollars.

AL: (*Switching tactics.*) I can make more than that off him in two months, lady. One month if the damn heat breaks. Where do you get off...

(HE *stands again and wags his finger at her.* SHE *stands and* HE *backs up to give her room, finds his finger pointing unbecomingly at her bosom, and embarrassed, puts it down.*)

IRENE: That was my final offer... Mr. Zipperstein. Your miserable menagerie of traveling geeks is an affront to the sensibilities of educated Americans. The current national economic difficulties put your kind of so-called entertainment at peril of extinction ... Al. Think about it, sell Monkey Boy now, and you may last another year. Perhaps Roosevelt's New Deal will rescue you by then. You know, one Jew from New York helping another and all. Your sort sticks together, I'm told. (**SHE** *turns to leave, walks a few steps, and faces him again.*) Six hundred dollars, Al, it's not an insignificant sum.

AL: (**HE** *stands also.*) Not even close, tootsie.

IRENE: I won't ask you again. But I will warn you, my friends and I are used to getting what we want.

AL: (**HE** *regards her attractive body one more time.*) I don't doubt that you do. But in this case, it will be over my dead body, sister.

IRENE: That would be a pity, Al, a pity. But, in the end, unfortunately, quite acceptable to my colleagues. (**SHE** *offers her hand.* **AL** *does not take it.*) We'll meet again, I'm sure.

AL: Oh, yes, come again, Miss Fortunata. Accept this ducat, a free admission to our show. (*Proffering a ticket to her.*) It'll be as close as you ever get to Monkey Boy.

(**IRENE** *sashays out as* **AL** *follows her exit greedily with his eyes.*)

CHARACTERS
SAM *(late 20s), a determined returner of junk mail;* POSY *(late 20s),* SAM's *long-distance accomplice*

SCENE
A campground in the West and a small cluttered apartment on the other side of America

TIME
The present

SAM *and* POSY *have plotted together to return all junk mail in their postage-paid envelopes, filled with objects to increase the weight so that the companies would have to pay postage due.* SAM *works on the East Coast,* POSY *on the West.*

SAM: Posy.

POSY: What?

SAM: I'm just saying your name. It's nice.

POSY: Thanks. (*Silence. Snoring.* POSY *looks toward the tent.*)

SAM: You should always come here.

POSY: Where?

SAM: To where I am.

POSY: You won't tell me where you live. (SAM *doesn't respond.*) How am I supposed to get there if you refuse to tell me where you live?

SAM: We could meet halfway.

POSY: I'm not going to meet someone halfway I can't trust because he won't tell me where he's from.

SAM: It's got a stupid name.

POSY: Sprott.

SAM: How'd you know?

Posy: I did a reverse directory lookup. Back after the first time we ever talked. You live in Sprott. Perry County, Alabama. Now what's so bad about that?

Sam: You don't know Sprott. It's Podunk. You've got to be from it to understand it. Okay? Let's go someplace else. I take my motorcycle and get on the 65 and you take your SUV and . . . how do you get out of town?

Posy: The 10.

Sam: Yeah. You take your SUV up the 10 and . . . I don't know. Put your finger on a map. Cleveland, maybe. Minneapolis. Saint Paul. Chicago. We could start a life together.

Posy: Oh. I don't know.

Sam: I might have flash. I could be a revolutionary.

(**Posy** *doesn't respond.*)

All right then. You could be revolutionary. Come on, Posy. What are you doing up there sitting on some mountaintop with an SUV and a husband you don't love and a life so boring you've got to entertain yourself by going through your neighbors' mail?

Posy: That's not why I do it.

Sam: I know you. You want more. Come on, Posy, you don't have a job. I say we start our own business. I say we quit talking and start that group we're always going on about. Millions of people all over America, headed by us.

Posy: Oh, I don't know.

Sam: Sure you do. I hear there's people out there with money, and if they like what you're doing they'll give it to you for free.

Posy: No.

Sam: That's what I hear. We could at least check it out. We could have a website. You could be president. We could write a whole handbook of stuff. Stone, you know, how to weigh down envelopes so they cost more from me, and you could talk about how to collect large quantities of envelopes to send back in the first place. Come on, Posy. This time it's our turn. What are we doing talking for hours on the phone when if we got together we could rule the world, we could change the order of things, we could—

Posy: Sam?

Sam: We could lead the resistance like nobody's business.

Posy: Sam. I can't come.

Sam: Why? Because you're married to a fat dude who pays too much taxes and doesn't believe resistance is possible? He's over. The future is ours. You say I don't know you, but I know more about you than he ever will.

Posy: I think he's waking up. I think I have to go now.

Sam: Are you chickenshit?

Posy: What?

Sam: He's not waking up. If you hang up the phone it's not because of that.

(**Posy** *toys with the idea of hanging up, but* **She** *doesn't. Sounds of night and quiet.*)

Posy, did you hang up, or is it the reception?

(**Posy** *doesn't answer.*)

Maybe I just thought I knew you. Viva La Revoluciòn, you know. So here I am thinking I'm talking to some brave-ass revolutionary chick and really I'm talking to some middle-aged housewife.

Posy: I'm not middle-aged.

Sam: I knew you were still there.

LET IT GO
BY CRYSTAL FIELD

CHARACTERS
MERRILEE *(19), a young girl whose brother, Joe, was killed in Iraq;* PATRICK *(19),* MERRILEE'S *boyfriend*

SCENE
Next to Joe's freshly dug grave, in the cemetery of a small town called Kinderhook, in upstate New York

TIME
Immediately after the burial of MERRILEE'S *brother, during the Iraq War*

Family and friends have dispersed. MERRILEE *is alone.* SHE *stands there, thinking.* PATRICK *re-enters.*

PATRICK: (*Taps her shoulder.*) One . . . two . . . three . . . you're it!

(SHE *doesn't speak.*)

Merri, you goin' home for lunch?

MERRILEE: No . . .

PATRICK: It's a late lunch. They'll wait for you.

MERRILEE: I'm not goin'

PATRICK: Where you goin' then?

MERRILEE: I'm goin' to New York City.

PATRICK: New York City!!! Why you goin' there?

MERRILEE: Because.

PATRICK: Why because?

MERRILEE: Because my brother said someday we'd go.

PATRICK: I'll go with you.

MERRILEE: No, you won't go with me.

PATRICK: Why not?

MERRILEE: 'Cause this is something I gotta do alone

PATRICK: (*Puts his arm around her shoulder.*) You lost your feelin' for me?

MERRILEE: No, I haven't lost my feelin' for you.

PATRICK: (*Gets close.*) Your dress is so pretty.

MERRILEE: I gotta go— If I don't go this minute, I'll never go—

(**PATRICK** *slides his finger down her dress, from neckline to below her belly button.*)

PATRICK: I know somethin' deep is bothering you. I just can't put my finger on it.

MERRILEE: Patrick . . . (**SHE** *feels for him . . . can't help it.*)

PATRICK: You're shakin'. You're tremblin'. (*Pause*) We could go up Mount Tremper. It'll be dark soon—the moon'll come out—that yellow moon— round like your golden belly. . . . (**HE** *kisses her.*) But if we go . . . you're gonna go anyway. . . . Here you are, a tremblin' and a shakin', and you're gonna go anyway.

MERRILEE: I gotta find something—I gotta find some sign—some witches' brew—some amulet. Something—something that'll let me have some peace.

PATRICK: Remember that night two weeks ago? That golden moon right after the Liberty Dance— Your dress was 'a flutterin' and 'a shimmerin' in the moonlight. . . .

MERRILEE: My brother's still hangin' here. . . . I can feel him. . . . Wrote me so many times. . . .

PATRICK: Joey was brave—he was brave. He was independent—he was really brave. He had a real rep in his unit.

MERRILEE: He wrote me— "It's my third tour. I'm doomed. This time, I'm gonna get it. There's a bullet with my number on it—"

PATRICK: Let's just go up Mount Tremper. You'll feel good—you'll feel better.

MERRILEE: I can't, Patrick. . . . I want to, but I can't!

(*Pause.* **THEY** *stare at each other.*)

PATRICK: You think you can keep a secret?

MERRILEE: A secret?

PATRICK: Yeah—a deep, dark and no talkin' secret.

MERRILEE: Yes, I can keep a secret. (*Pause.*)

PATRICK: I'm not goin' to any late lunch, either. I'm goin' to a meetin'.

MERRILEE: A meetin'—

PATRICK: Over at the university. I'm goin' to an antiwar meetin'.

MERRILEE: You goin' over there?!—with the Reds!—With the Anarchist Commies?!

PATRICK: I'm goin' over there. I'm gonna listen to them.

MERRILEE: How you know where to meet?

PATRICK: Merrilee—one a Dan's friends called me up. A friend from the Army...told me all about Dan and him. He told me the SUV they was drivin' didn't have armor plate. They was just sittin' ducks.

MERRILEE: He told you that!

PATRICK: I'm goin' over—I'm goin' over there and listen....They's called Vets Against the War—all veterans. All of 'em. Some really hurt bad—organizing a protest.

MERRILEE: Organizing—

PATRICK: Merri-Merri-Merrilee...beautiful Merri. Come on—go with me. He said Joe knew it was comin'. He said if he don't get back, to come get me— I'd know what to do.

MERRILEE: He told you all that?

PATRICK: He did—he did...he told me.

MERRILEE: How you know he wasn't lyin'? Just to convince you—proselytysin'. Like the Seventh-Day Adventists do around here.

PATRICK: Merri, can you keep this thing all to yourself—

MERRILEE: I can.

PATRICK: He give me this— (*Shows her Joe's dog tags.*) Joe gave 'em to him at the hospital...just before he went.

MERRILEE: Is it a sign?

PATRICK: It's the sign you was lookin' for. Come on—we'll go to the meetin' and then we'll go up Mount Tremper, and then, if you still wanta go to New York City, you can go—

Merrilee: I'm gonna take you up on that, Patrick. I'm gonna try.

Patrick: Come on, Merri-Merri-Merrilee. Let's go find the car.

MAGGIE MAY
BY TOM O'BRIEN

CHARACTERS
DONNY *(late 20s), a hopeless romantic;* MAGGIE *(late 20s), a down-to-earth kind of girl*

SCENE
A hotel room in the Bahamas

TIME
The present

DONNY *has duped* MAGGIE *into going to the Bahamas with him, telling her* HE *has won a sweepstakes. In reality* HE *wants to have a relationship with her.*

(DONNY *and* MAGGIE *come running in, soaked and laughing.*)

MAGGIE: Oh, my God. I can't believe it.

DONNY: It's fucking pouring.

MAGGIE: I think it's a sign.

DONNY: It's just a passing storm.

MAGGIE: No, it's probably a hurricane.

DONNY: Oh, that's the attitude.

MAGGIE: No wonder they gave you a free trip. It's hurricane season.

DONNY: Okay, Miss Negative. (*Goes to the window.*) Oh, yeah, I think it's letting up.

(*Another crash of thunder and lightning.*)

This sucks.

MAGGIE: C'mon, let's make the best of it. What's in the ol' minibar? (*Goes to the minibar and opens it.*)

DONNY: I didn't even know we had a minibar.

MAGGIE: Let's see, what do we have here?

DONNY: (*Hops on the bed and picks up the remote control.*) Oh, dude, we have pay per view.

MAGGIE: And we have rum!

DONNY: We have rum in the minibar? That's fantastic.

MAGGIE: This is the Bahamas. They have rum everywhere. I'm gonna make rum punch.

DONNY: Yes, we'll get drunk and watch... *Tuck Everlasting.*

(**DONNY** *watches TV as* **MAGGIE** *looks around the room.*)

MAGGIE: Hey, is there sugar anywhere?

DONNY: Where?

MAGGIE: I don't know. Have you seen any?

DONNY: Have I seen any sugar in the room? I don't know. Where would that be?

MAGGIE: I don't know.

DONNY: (*Beat.*) Are you dating anyone right now?

MAGGIE: What?

DONNY: I don't know. I just thought... I don't know. Are you?

MAGGIE: Umm... I don't know, sort of.

DONNY: Sort of? I'm glad I'm not that guy.

MAGGIE: No, its nothing serious.

DONNY: Yeah, from your end, but that poor bastard. What's his name?

MAGGIE: Why?

DONNY: Just wondering. I'm sorry. I didn't mean to...

MAGGIE: No, I just... what made you think of that?

DONNY: Do you like him?

MAGGIE: No, I hate him.

DONNY: I mean, do you like him as much as you liked me?

MAGGIE: Will you stop?

DONNY: What? We're just a couple of friends talking.

MAGGIE: What about you?

DONNY: No, I just sit at home looking at a picture of you.

MAGGIE: Shut up. Who are you dating?

DONNY: Never mind that. What's his name?

MAGGIE: It's not. . . . I'm not telling you.

DONNY: It's Bob, isn't it?

MAGGIE: No.

DONNY: Greg?

MAGGIE: What's your girlfriend's name?

DONNY: Maggie.

MAGGIE: Shut up. What's her name?

DONNY: None of your business.

MAGGIE: Good, I'm not telling you what my boyfriend's name is.

DONNY: Oh, my God. What are you, six?

MAGGIE: You started it.

DONNY: Do you think if I had a girlfriend you'd be here right now?

MAGGIE: Well, I don't know. Maybe you'll meet someone down here.

DONNY: That's true. We should work out a system. Like sock on the door means don't come in.

MAGGIE: What is this, a frat house?

DONNY: Well, you might meet someone too.

MAGGIE: I'm not gonna take them back to the room.

DONNY: Okay, Miss Prude.

MAGGIE: I'm not a prude.

DONNY: That's true. You're not.

MAGGIE: Hey.

DONNY: What? I'm just agreeing with you.

MAGGIE: Just behave.

DONNY: Jeez, I can't win.

(**MAGGIE** *starts to go.*)

Where are you going?

MAGGIE: I need juice for this punch.

DONNY: It's pouring out.

MAGGIE: I'm just going down to the lobby.

DONNY: Want me to come?

MAGGIE: I think I'll be fine.

DONNY: Okay.

MARE'S NEST
BY JOSEPH GOODRICH

CHARACTERS

DONNELLY *(40–60) is a high-strung, well-to-do older man;* ROSE *(early 20s) is a young domestic servant.* SHE'S *determined to break through her employer's fears and suspicions and befriend him. This hasn't been an easy task, but* ROSE *has applied herself and* DONNELLY'S *beginning to melt. Sadie is* DONELLY'S *sister; she runs the household for him.*

SCENE

DONNELLY'S *New York City townhouse*

TIME

Winter of 1943

DONNELLY *is typing a letter at the desk.* ROSE *stands in front of it.* DONNELLY *finishes typing, removes the letter from the typewriter carriage, signs it, folds it, places it in an envelope, licks a stamp, and places it on the envelope, then sets the envelope on the desk.*

DONNELLY: Give this to Sadie, if you'd be so kind. Tell her to have it registered and bring back the receipt.

ROSE: I'd be happy to, Mr. Donnelly, but I can't.

DONNELLY: And why is that? A sudden paralysis of the lower extremities?

ROSE: Sadie's not here to give it to.

DONNELLY: Where is she?

ROSE: Out shopping. Said she'd be back for dinner.

DONNELLY: Oh—it's Thursday, isn't it?

ROSE: Yes, sir.

DONNELLY: A very good day for Macy's, Wanamaker's, Bergdorf Goodman, and the Russian Tea Room; a very bad day for the U.S. Post Office and my bank account.... Well, it'll just have to wait till tomorrow, I suppose. (*Pause.*)

ROSE: Is it a very important letter?

DONNELLY: It is to me. And perhaps to its recipient.

Rose: I'll take it to the post office.

Donnelly: That's very kind of you, but... it's not necessary

Rose: I'm going to the cleaners with the suits. I could just as easily stop by the post office, too.

Donnelly: No, I couldn't impose on you like that.

Rose: You wouldn't be imposing.

Donnelly: It can wait till tomorrow.

Rose: I'd be happy to do it. I'd *like* to. (*Pause.*)

Donnelly: Sadie's always done it in the past. I don't know how she'd.... I wouldn't want to upset her. I wouldn't want to make her feel somehow less... essential.

Rose: I won't tell her if you won't. (*Pause.*) She'll never know, Mr. Donnelly. I'd run right to the post office and then run right back. (*Pause.*) She could take the suits, instead. Tomorrow. Tell her you *want* her to do it. That no one else can take suits to the dry cleaners like she can.

Donnelly: But she'll just give them to you.

Rose: But she'll feel special because you asked her to—you see? That way, no one's feelings are hurt, and your letter gets mailed today. (*Pause.*)

Donnelly: ... You couldn't just drop it in the box, you understand. You'd have to go to one of the clerks to have it registered. —And you'd have to get a receipt for it. I need the receipt, Rose. That's very important.

Rose: I'll bring you ten receipts. (*Pause.*)

Donnelly: I'm tempted, Rose. I'm very tempted. (*Pause.*) No, I don't think so. I can't risk it. Thank you, though, for thinking of it.

(**He** *rolls a new sheet of paper into the typewriter's carriage, begins typing.*)

Rose: Mr. Donnelly? (**Donnelly** *stops typing.*) I was just wondering... did you get a chance to look through that magazine?

Donnelly: Magazine? —Oh. Oh, yes. Yes, I have. Yes. A very interesting article, if somewhat... salacious in tone.

Rose: Salacious?

Donnelly: ... Racy.

ROSE: Oh, sure. That's *Radio Mirror* all over. If Oscar Levant really romanced all those gals like they say he'd never have time to be on the radio at all. Am I right?

DONNELLY: I . . . I assume so.

ROSE: Anyway, I think he's married. I *think*. . . . You gotta take it all with a grain a salt. I myself don't believe a word of it. But you know, I like the pictures. I like to see what they look like. I mean, sometimes you're surprised. Olan Soule, for instance. The way he sounds you'd think he'd be Don Ameche or something. But no—he's just a little shrimp of a guy. Like a train conductor or something.

DONNELLY: I wasn't aware of that. That's very—disappointing.

ROSE: Well, that's the kind of stuff you learn if you read that magazine.

DONNELLY: I'll be certain to get it back to you.

ROSE: Oh, Mr. Donnelly, keep it.

DONNELLY: I couldn't.

ROSE: Why not? I'm through with it.

DONNELLY: But you'll want it back eventually, won't you?

ROSE: I read it from front to back already. You're welcome to it. I'd just throw it away, anyway. In fact, I'll tell you what. Every issue I get, when I'm done with it, you can have it. How 'bout that?

DONNELLY: I don't know if—if I . . .

ROSE: They have a lot of articles about *Information, Please.*

DONNELLY: . . . Do they?

ROSE: I see 'em all the time. Practically every other issue.

DONNELLY: Well . . . if that's the case—and you really wouldn't mind parting with them when you've perused them to your satisfaction—then. . . . Yes, I'd be happy to uh, uhmm . . . take them off your hands.

ROSE: Meanwhile— (**SHE** *holds up the letter.*) I'll take *this* off of *yours*. (*Pause.*) Let me, Mr. Donnelly. It would make me so happy to do something for you. (*Pause.*)

DONNELLY: Registered, remember. And bring me the receipt. That's very important.

ROSE: I will.

DONNELLY: Don't forget.

ROSE: I won't.

DONNELLY: I know you won't. I asked Sadie how you were doing. She said you're doing very well. "Very reliable" is how she described you.

ROSE: . . . She did?

DONNELLY: Oh, yes. That's high praise, coming from her.

ROSE: Oh.

DONNELLY: So I have every reason to believe you'll be back with my receipt in— (HE *checks his wristwatch.*) —approximately twenty minutes. Normally, I'd say it shouldn't take more than fifteen minutes, but the recent snowfall has to be considered. And I have. I've considered it and rejected it as a significant impediment. Granted, I'm assuming that sufficient time has elapsed for shoveling and foot traffic to have "done their stuff," as they say. And I don't believe that's an unreasonable assumption. . . . However, one never knows, things being as they are, and I've added an additional five minutes to the standard fifteen. So I won't begin actively speculating on the reasons for your tardiness until— (HE *checks his wristwatch.*) —eleven forty-seven AM, Eastern War Time. Unless, of course, you're not tardy at all.

ROSE: Twenty minutes, just to the post office?

DONNELLY: And back.

ROSE: That's a piece of cake, Mr. Donnelly.

DONNELLY: Is it now?

ROSE: I can do it in a lot less than that.

DONNELLY: If you go bucketing down the streets like a madwoman—yes.

ROSE: I bet I could do it in ten.

DONNELLY: I won't have you dashing about on my account.

ROSE: I wouldn't dash.

DONNELLY: You could break a leg on those streets!

ROSE: Then you'd just have to shoot me.

DONNELLY: You could slip and fall. You'd crack open your skull like an overripe muskmelon.

ROSE: No, I wouldn't.

DONNELLY: It can't be done, Rose. Not in ten minutes.

(ROSE *reaches into a pocket, takes out a coin.*)

ROSE: I got a nickel here says it can.

DONNELLY: Rose—it's impossible.

ROSE: You want to bet on that, Mr. Donnelly? (*Pause.*)

DONNELLY: Well . . . yes. All right. Yes. Yes—why not? I'll take your bet, Rose. And I'll double it. . . . I think I've got a dime here somewhere. . . .

ROSE: Oh no, Mr. Donnelly. You hold on to your money.

DONNELLY: I've got to put something up if we're going to have a bet.

ROSE: I think we could make it a little more interesting. If you're willing. (*Pause.*)

DONNELLY: What do you propose?

ROSE: Here's what I'm thinking. If I make it to the post office and back—

DONNELLY: In ten minutes.

ROSE: In ten minutes . . .

DONNELLY: With a receipt, mind you.

ROSE: In ten minutes, with a receipt . . . *then* . . . Monday night, you let me listen to your show with you.

DONNELLY: . . . My show?

ROSE: *Information, Please.* If I win, I get to listen to the show with you.

DONNELLY: . . . In *here*?

ROSE: Yeah.

DONNELLY: . . . With *me*?

ROSE: Yeah. (*Pause.*)

DONNELLY: *Why?*

ROSE: I figure between you and the show, I could learn something. So what do you say, Mr. Donnelly? Is it a bet?

DONNELLY: ...Mmmm...

ROSE: Be a sport. Come on. (*Pause.*)

DONNELLY: ...Ten minutes?

ROSE: From the time I go through that door to the time I come back in.

DONNELLY: And all you want—if you win—is to listen to *Information, Please?*

ROSE: With you.

DONNELLY: That's a terribly strange.... (*Silence.*)

ROSE: What have you got to lose, Mr. Donnelly? You'd listen to it, anyway. And besides, you're positive I can't do it, so—

DONNELLY: You can't.

ROSE: Then why not take the bet? (*Pause.*)

DONNELLY: Ten minutes. (**HE** *looks at his wristwatch.*) Starting...now.

ROSE: Thank you, Mr. Donnelly. (**SHE** *hurries out of the room. Pause.*)

(**DONNELLY** *begins typing.* **HE** *stops.* **HE** *touches his chin, his nose, the top of his head—then his right ear, then his left ear—then the top of his head, his nose, his chin—then places the hand flat on the desk....*)

DONNELLY: She can't win. She won't win. She can't win.

(**HE** *begins to type.* **HE** *stops.*)

She won't. (*Pause.*) She won't.

THE MERCY SEAT
BY NEIL LaBUTE

CHARACTERS
BEN *(30s), a confused man, is caught between the love for his wife and young daughters and his passion for* **ABBY** *(40s), a co-worker.*

SCENE
New York City

TIME
Not long ago

ABBY *believes that* **BEN** *was about to leave his wife for her, but then the 9/11 explosions seemed a good opportunity for* **BEN** *to fake his death and run away with* **ABBY**, *who just wants him to follow through with the phone call* **SHE** *thought was meant for his wife. A slash (/) indicates overlapping dialogue.*

BEN: What?

ABBY: The call you were going to make. Yesterday, before all this.

BEN: Huh?

ABBY: I cannot do this. This "ride the rails" thing with you. (*Beat.*) If we're going to make it, you and me, I mean...then you need to call your wife and kids and let them know what's going on. Tell them the truth.

BEN: Oh. So...this was all a...what, trick? Some kind of...

ABBY: No, not a *trick*. I just can't...

BEN: Get me to go out on a limb for you and then push me off the fucking branch?!

ABBY: I'm just saying I can't do what you're asking me!

BEN: Fine...fuck, fine, we'll just...

ABBY: I don't wanna carry all that shit around, I'm not willing to do that!!

BEN: Shit, SHIT! Shit on you for doing this.

ABBY: I'm not "doing" anything, Ben, I'm asking you to.

BEN: You know I can't! I cannot do that!! / No, no, NO!!

ABBY: Why?! / WHY NOT?!!

BEN: Because it ruins it. It ruins the ending.

(**ABBY** *takes this in, processing.* **BEN** *fiddles with the door.*)

ABBY: This is not a movie, Ben.

BEN: I'm not saying that.

ABBY: You can't dictate how life is supposed to—

BEN: Yeah, I could. . . . In this *one* instance, I could've! (*Beat.*) We had no chance here. . . . A day ago, we were just another two people fucking each other and pretending that we had something special. Now we've got a chance to actually make it that. Special . . .

ABBY: It wasn't special?

BEN: It was an *affair*, Abby, fuck, can't we just be . . . ?

ABBY: It was special to me.

BEN: Of course it was "special," that's the wrong word. I just mean that it was common, regular. It happens. But this thing . . . this disaster . . . makes what we're doing . . . possible.

ABBY: I see. . . . Now I see.

BEN: All we have to do is walk away, Abby! Not run . . . just walk. Walk off into the sunset.

ABBY: All right. Okay. Duly noted. (*Beat.*) But after you make the call.

BEN: Shit . . . Abby . . . / Don't ask me to—

ABBY: I *need* you to do that for me. / Will you? Ben?

BEN: I can't . . . / . . . oh God—

ABBY: Please . . . / Ben, please . . . for me . . . *Please.*

BEN: Yes. (*Beat.*) Okay.

ABBY: Thank you.

BEN: I will. (*Beat.*) You, umm, you want me to . . . what, make the call that I was gonna make yesterday, right? The call I said I was going to make before this . . . all this . . . happened.

Abby: That's what I want. Yes.

Ben: All right, Abby, I'll do that.

(**Ben** *crosses back to the couch and sits, rubbing his eyes. Pulls his cell phone out of his pocket and switches it on.* **Abby** *starts across the room.*)

Abby: I'll give you your privacy.

Ben: No, you don't have to.

Abby: It's okay, you should have time to... / It's fine.

Ben: I want you to hear this, Abby. / ABBY! (**Abby** *stops and looks at him.*) You need to hear this.... Go ahead, take a seat.

(**Abby** *crosses back toward the kitchen and sits on the edge of a stool near the counter.* **Ben** *takes a deep breath, then dials a number and waits. After a moment,* **Abby's** *phone begins to ring.* **She** *looks up, startled, and mimes to* **Ben:** *"What should I do?"* **She** *starts to panic, but* **Ben** *motions for her to take the call.*)

Abby: Hello?

Ben: Hi.

Abby: Ben? Why're you...?

Ben: Just listen. Okay? Just... listen to me. (*Beat.*) So... this was the call I was going to make yesterday.

Abby: No, no, I don't want you to *pretend* with me, I want you to call them and—

Ben: Abby, shut the fuck up and listen! I was going to call *you* yesterday, not them. I was gonna make this call on my way to work, and then I thought, What the hell, it's only a few blocks over, I'll stop in and talk to her. Tell her face-to-face. Be brave, like she's always asking me to be... she deserves that. (*Beat.*) I wasn't gonna phone home, Abby, I can't do that. You can call my wife, spill your guts if you want to, but I'll never be able to... can't do that. (*Beat.*) That's why all... *this*... suddenly seemed so logical, like the only thing possible. And I wanted it. God, I did! But now.... Look, I think you're great, and we've had, umm, the most amazing...

Abby: Ben... don't.

Ben: No, I promised you I'd make a call, and this is it. I'm calling to tell you I can't do this anymore, I'm tired of dodging and hiding and all the, just, bad shit I've done so effortlessly since we met. If you'd taken this...meal ticket...of ours, then great. I'd've worked in a fucking *lumberyard* the rest of my days to be with you, but if you wanna make me come clean about what I've done, purge all my sins for some un-fucking-fathomable reason...I mean, if I'm publicly forced to choose between those little girls' hearts and your *thighs*, well then, there's just not much question. (*Beat.*) Sorry, Abby, I'm really very...I don't know. Just sorry. G'bye.

(**BEN** *clicks off the call. After a moment, his cell phone begins ringing and continues while they sit staring at each other.* **ABBY** *slowly hangs up.* **BEN** *finally snaps his phone shut.*)

MR. LUCKY'S
BY STEPHEN FIFE

CHARACTERS
ALISON *(20s), single;* TOM *(20s), single*

SCENE
A fairly upscale bar

TIME
Now

Both ALISON *and* TOM *have come to Mr. Lucky's Bar hoping to meet someone. After one glance, each is very impressed with the other.*

(TOM *and* ALISON *are seated on bar stools.*)

TOM: (*To audience.*) I've been sitting here a few moments, just taking in all the ambience: the burnished wood and low lighting, the posters of showgirls from the Ziegfield Follies—girls who are dead now, it's true, but my God, what legs. . . . I look around, and I have a really good feeling about this place. A better feeling than I've had about any place in a while. . . . I'm pretty sure I've never been here.

ALISON: (*To audience.*) I come to this bar all the time. All the time. No one interesting ever comes here.

TOM: I passed by this place lots of times, I'm sure of that much. Lots of times before tonight. I really don't know why I never came in.

ALISON: It's like there's a sign on the door. "Interesting guys stay away. Pathetic morons are welcome."

TOM: Maybe it was the name. Yeah, I guess that was it. "Mr. Lucky's."

ALISON: Once or twice I saw someone. Some guy. He'd sit down and nod at the bartender, then order a draft in a confident voice. My interest was piqued, I glanced over, flashed him my best cryptic smile. . . . Then he'd look back, he'd turn the full force of his gaze on me, and I'd see the words printed right there on his forehead: "More of the Same."

TOM: I was a little put off at first, ya know, that's a lot of pressure to put on a guy. But now I think I can deal with it. I think I've gone through enough bad times that I'm ready for something good. Yeah. "Mr. Lucky's."

ALISON: "Mr. Lucky's." Yeah, right. I guess that's why I came here in the first place. Walked in off the dark street one night, the street filled with muggers and stalkers and guys shaking little jars filled with their vital fluids, and plopped my rear down on this overstuffed barstool. Just to prove a point, to prove that that name was all crap. (*Pause.*) I think I've more than succeeded. (**SHE** *drains her drink, stands.*)

(**ALISON** *and* **TOM** *glance at each other. Their eyes meet. Pause.* **BOTH** *look away.* **ALISON** *sits.*)

ALISON: Wow.

TOM: Wow.

ALISON: Wow.

TOM: Wow.

ALISON: What planet did he beam down from?

TOM: Wow.

ALISON: I'm afraid to look over again, I'm afraid he's gonna be like one of those premium channels you're not supposed to be getting. . . .

TOM: Wow. I mean—wow. She is exactly. . .

ALISON: I'm afraid he's gonna suddenly fade out or else his face will be all scrambled up, with black lines across it. . . .

TOM: I mean, exactly. Exactly.

ALISON: You're crazy, Alison, really crazy. Your reception doesn't pick up this station. This isn't part of your package.

TOM: It's like she walked right out of my brain and sat down on that barstool and ordered a drink. It's like a chunk of my brain is enjoying a drink there.

(*Pause.* **TOM** *glances over at* **ALISON**. **SHE** *glances at him.* **THEY** *can't avoid catching each other's eye.*)

TOM: Hi.

ALISON: Hi.

TOM: How's it goin'?

ALISON: Good.

TOM: Good.

ALISON: How's it goin' with you?

TOM: Good.

ALISON: Good.

(*Pause.*)

TOM: Good. (*Pause.* **HE** *looks away. To the audience.*) Oh God.

ALISON: (*To audience.*) God.

TOM: Good. Good. What is that?

ALISON: Good, Alison. Good. That was real good.

TOM: Beer nuts are good. Cheeseburgers are good. Joe Cocker Live at the Hollywood Bowl is good. But this is not good.

ALISON: See, this is the thing: I've talked with so many morons, I can't even remember what real people say anymore. People who actually eat with a knife and a fork.

TOM: (*To* **ALISON.**) Can I get you another drink?

ALISON: What?

TOM: Can I buy you a drink?

ALISON: No.

TOM: Okay.

ALISON: No, I'm just fine.

TOM: Okay.

ALISON: Thank you but no. (*Pause.*) No, thank you. (*Pause.*)

TOM: Me too.

ALISON: What?

TOM: I'm fine too. With my drink I mean.

ALISON: Oh.

TOM: Yeah . . .

ALISON: Good.

TOM: Good.

ALISON: Good.

(*Desperate pause.*)

TOM: (*To audience.*) Ah.

ALISON: (*To audience.*) Ooo.

TOM: (*To audience.*) Come on, think of something. . . .

ALISON: (*To audience.*) This is like a nightmare. . . .

TOM: (*To audience.*) I can't be this stupid. . . .

ALISON: (*To audience.*) I can't be this stupid. . . .

(*Pause.*)

TOM: I didn't mean to insult you.

ALISON: What?

TOM: I mean, I hope I didn't insult you. Before. When I asked . . .

ALISON: Who says I felt insulted?

TOM: Well, the tone of your voice . . . I thought maybe—

ALISON: Believe me, I don't feel insulted.

TOM: Well, good. I'm glad. It's just the way you said No. There was just so much . . . no in it.

ALISON: Oh, you would know if I felt insulted, believe me.

TOM: Yeah?

ALISON: Yeah. There would be absolutely no question about it.

TOM: Huh. Well, I guess I was wrong then.

ALISON: I guess you were.

TOM: So you have a real temper, huh? I think that's good. I mean, healthy. You live longer that way.

ALISON: See, this is what I would've done if I felt insulted.

(**SHE** *tosses the contents of her drink in his face. Pause. The liquid drips from his face.*)

ORSON'S SHADOW
BY AUSTIN PENDLETON

CHARACTERS

LARRY *(Sir Laurence Olivier) (53), world-famous actor, trying to raise money to produce a film of the "Scottish play," is estranged from his wife, actress* **VIVIEN LEIGH** *(47), who is subject to recurrent manic episodes.*

SCENE

The stage of the Royal Court Theatre

TIME

1960

VIVIEN *is leaving the next day for New York and would like* **LARRY** *to come for supper with her at Notley, their home.* **LARRY** *has just told Kenneth Tynan and Joan Plowright, his current love, that* **HE** *will call* **VIVIEN** *to "break it off."*

VIVIEN: Hello? (**VIVIEN** *has entered, ringing phone in hand, at Notley. There is no set for Notley; there are lights, though.*)

LARRY: Hello, darling.

VIVIEN: Larry.

LARRY: You don't sound out of breath. I was afraid you'd be in the garden and have to dash in.

VIVIEN: I was in the garden.

LARRY: Oh. Good, then. I am shutting my eyes and imagining how lovely it is.

VIVIEN: I'm going to miss it.

LARRY: Of course. But then New York will be over, and it will go well for you, and you can have the summer there, which is my favorite time of the year at Notley, and we can bask in it, and— (**HE** *stops. Pause.*)

VIVIEN: Why did you pause?

LARRY: I—I'm just—so excited for you. New York, on your own. Are you excited, darling?

VIVIEN: More frightened, actually—

LARRY: There is nothing to be frightened—

VIVIEN: Can you hurry up here?

LARRY: Darling—

VIVIEN: I'll have them put out a light supper, and some wine—

LARRY: You are marvelous in that play, Vivien.

VIVIEN: I'm not frightened about the play.

LARRY: But there is nothing else to be frightened of, my—

VIVIEN: Do you remember the last time I was in New York?

LARRY: Well, when we took the Cleopatra plays there after London—

VIVIEN: That was ten years ago.

LARRY: And what a ten years it has been, hasn't it, and you have come so far. Well, we both have. And I know this will be your first time on the New York stage without me, without being half of the Oliviers, which must be bloody boring—

VIVIEN: The last time I was in New York was with you, just last year.

LARRY: I don't—

VIVIEN: When you took *The Entertainer* there.

LARRY: Of course! Of course! You came for the opening, such madness—

VIVIEN: And you had a run-through and every actor in New York was asked, and you were inspired and we all rushed round to tell you and you would not hear of it. You said, "Tonight means nothing to me. Because I did not know what I was doing." But I've been wondering. Since I'm going to New York, why don't I try to do what you did that one night, except why don't I try to do it every night, just not know what I'm doing—

LARRY: Oh, darling—

VIVIEN: What?

LARRY: You musn't.

VIVIEN: Why not?

LARRY: Because you know, darling, how much it means to you, the regularity of it—

Vivien: Larry—

Larry: The reassuring rhythm in the theatre of knowing exactly what it is that you must do each night—

Vivien: But that's because I'm crazy, Larry.

Larry: Put it however you wish to put it—

Vivien: There is no wish involved here—

Larry: Darling, I'm telling you this for your own good—

Vivien: I know you are!

Larry: And, really, that's why you're so exquisite on the stage, because everything is held in place so carefully—

Vivien: Marlon Brando changes it every time.

Larry: Well, then.

Vivien: He never knows what he's going to do.

Larry: I think perhaps he gives off that illusion.

Vivien: When we were filming *Streetcar* he never did the same thing twice. Kazan adored it, that's the kind of director he is.

Larry: You've told me this.

Vivien: And what I never told you is that I'd amuse myself, thinking, "Larry would go mad." When you directed it here, in London, in fucking London, you used to tell us what to do precisely, at every moment, and not to change, never to change—

Larry: I did this for you, of course—

Vivien: I'd add one gesture, you'd say, "Well, a little baroque this evening, aren't we?"

Larry: I think you're remembering inaccurately—

Vivien: I remember everything you've ever done!

Larry: Well, then perhaps you'll remember that everything I've done for many years has been to protect you, because I know better than anyone—

Vivien: I'm going to try it, Larry.

Larry: (*Flares.*) Well, good, then! Have a bash at it, I say!

(*Pause.*)

VIVIEN: What—what—

LARRY: What is it, darling.

VIVIEN: What wine would you like tonight?

LARRY: Darling, I have this bloody meeting here in town. As I've told you.

VIVIEN: Where is this meeting?

LARRY: What?

VIVIEN: The meeting.

LARRY: Oh! Oh, its—

VIVIEN: Oh, really, I'm not coming there, I'm not going to track you down.

LARRY: Of course! I didn't—

VIVIEN: I just want to know where you are.

LARRY: I'm in an office somewhere. I'm not even sure—

VIVIEN: Larry—

LARRY: I mean, I was brought here. I'm afraid I was abducted, actually!—

VIVIEN: You've never been abducted in your life—

LARRY: I'm sorry if I got a little cross just now. It's just, your telling me about that run-through in New York does make me think of when you came to see the play in London, the first night I ever played it in front of any audience, when you came round and told me I'd disgraced myself—

VIVIEN: I never said you had disgraced yourself.

LARRY: You said, "What the fuck do you think you're doing with that blues song?" And—

VIVIEN: Larry—

LARRY: What?

VIVIEN: What were you doing with that blues song?

LARRY: Tony told me to do it! And I did! And I'm afraid that's what happens every time I just do something, I'm afraid that you all say, "Oh, Larry, musn't do that, no," no, all the rest of you can do that, but, no, Larry is the captain, isn't he?—

Vivien: That is not what I meant!

Larry: And so I was never able to do it again, I acceded to your wishes, darling, as I try to do, and once again I was severely compromised—

Vivien: You bastard!

Larry: And I'm afraid that many people were quite disappointed, Tony, the other members of the cast—

Vivien: I was trying to protect the other members of the cast!

Larry: Are you saying they need to be protected from me?

Vivien: There were people who were acting from their hearts that night! That— Brenda—your wife, that marvelous Joan Plowright, and you just had to wipe them out, you had to hurl yourself against a wall and pretend that you were Bessie Smith! Bessie Smith! Do you know the first thing about poor Bessie Smith?

Larry: (*Alarmed.*) Vivien—

Vivien: She bled to death! You bastard! She bled to death because they would not treat her at a Southern hospital! Do you know what that feels like! Do you know what it feels like to be left to die, to be put into a strait jacket?—

Larry: I'm coming out there.

Vivien: No!

Larry: I'll be there in no time.

Vivien: Larry—

Larry: Of course there may be traffic.

Vivien: You have your meeting.

Larry: You don't want me to come out, then.

Vivien: It's just that—

Larry: You're afraid of me.

Vivien: Larry, it's just that I'm afraid I feel the mania a bit, and I know that frightens you.

Larry: You mean you're afraid I'm going to hit you.

Vivien: Larry, listen to me. That was my fault. I was crazy. You don't understand just how it is—

LARRY: How what is?

VIVIEN: An attack of mania. It is impossible to sleep, and terrifying if anybody else can sleep—

LARRY: Are you saying, then, that I don't understand?—

VIVIEN: I think you just can't understand sometimes that I am crazy, that's—

LARRY: That's quite a thing to say, after all that—

VIVIEN: And if you could, I think you'd be much happier, because you would not take me quite so seriously. You wouldn't feel this guilt, which makes you such a bore. What have I done to you, I sometimes wonder. My life has a moral, it really has a moral. If you're manic-depressive, never marry the minister's son. Even if he is the sexiest man in the world.

LARRY: Sexier than Brando?

VIVIEN: Do stop.

LARRY: Did you and Brando—

VIVIEN: Oh, well, I'm fairly sure I would remember that.

LARRY: Because I know you and Kazan—

VIVIEN: That what? We what?

LARRY: Darling, in New York one night I went to Sardi's and Kazan was at a table with the actors from whatever naturalistic thing he was directing then, and I heard him say to them, "You see that man? I fucked his wife."

VIVIEN: He said that?

LARRY: And I moved on, not having heard, you know, and I thought, it happened on the film of *Streetcar*, and you would never have been in that film if I had not directed you in it on the stage, that marvelous play about, I have to say, a nymphomaniac—

VIVIEN: She is not a nymphomaniac!

LARRY: Which I took on after I'd been asked to join a club with Winston Churchill! I had everything to lose!

VIVIEN: Oh, now you're saying I kept you from Winston Churchill!

LARRY: And then to hear it said in public that he fucked you? He fucked you, darling!

VIVIEN: Well, it's a dirty job but somebody's got to do it.

LARRY: Oh, darling—

VIVIEN: Darling, how do you know he even meant it? He likes to excite his actors, as I told you.

LARRY: I am an animal onstage, and cannot be an animal everywhere—

VIVIEN: What are you wearing?

LARRY: What?

VIVIEN: Right now. What are you wearing?

LARRY: What am I wearing?

VIVIEN: Please. Tell me.

LARRY: Well, the—well, the velvet jacket—

VIVIEN: Lovely.

[**JOAN:** We really must go.

LARRY: (*Hissing.*) No!]

VIVIEN: Who's that?

LARRY: One of the people I'm meeting with.

VIVIEN: He sounds tough.

LARRY: He is.

VIVIEN: Are they listening to this?

LARRY: Someone just popped in to see how long I'd—it's all right—

VIVIEN: What is this meeting about?

LARRY: Oh—you know.

VIVIEN: No, I don't know.

LARRY: Well, since you must know I'm trying to get the money for our film—

VIVIEN: What?

LARRY: And I didn't want to mention it because I know how you can get your hopes up.

VIVIEN: Oh, Larry, who is going to put money in that film?

LARRY: Darling, I can get the money.

VIVIEN: Let me go to New York! Let me get on with my stage work! Let me be something other than an aging film star!—

LARRY: I can get the money! You forget that you're a legendary film actress.

VIVIEN: Mary Pickford is a legendary film actress, but I don't see anybody putting up the money to star her in a movie of *Macbeth*!—

LARRY: VIVIEN! Vivien, why did you say that?

VIVIEN: What did I say—

LARRY: The name of that character, the title of that play!

VIVIEN: Are you out of your mind?

LARRY: I am not out of my mind, you know how dangerous—

VIVIEN: Darling, you are actually upset about this!—

LARRY: Don't you know me at all?

VIVIEN: Larry, all right, I'm sorry I said it, but what does it matter?

LARRY: What does it matter?

VIVIEN: It only matters if you're in a theatre when you say it, and I'm not in a theatre right now—

LARRY: But I am! (*Pause.*) I mean— (*Long pause.*)

VIVIEN: Where are you?

LARRY: At the Royal Court.

VIVIEN: Yes.

LARRY: I'll come out.

VIVIEN: Are you going to do another play there?

LARRY: Yes.

VIVIEN: What?

LARRY: *Rhinoceros.*

VIVIEN: That one we saw in Paris?

LARRY: Yes.

VIVIEN: You hated that play.

LARRY: Well, you know, though, it was something new, wasn't it.

VIVIEN: You hated *Rhinoceros*. We laughed about it.

LARRY: Darling, I'm playing the one who stands alone at the end, who refuses to turn into a rhino like the rest of them, which is marvelous when one begins to delve because until that point, if you'll remember, he keeps saying, "I'm afraid of life," so—

VIVIEN: "I'm afraid of life"?

LARRY: Well, it's a challenge for me, isn't it. And, as I say, you know me—

VIVIEN: A challenge?!

LARRY: Yes, and—

VIVIEN: You have no idea what that is, to be afraid of life.

LARRY: How dare you say that to me.

VIVIEN: Larry?

LARRY: What?

VIVIEN: The girl is going to have to be so charming. In the play.

LARRY: I—yes. Yes. That's very smart, you're very smart about—

VIVIEN: I love you.

LARRY: And I—the same—

VIVIEN: Has someone popped his head back in again?

LARRY: Yes.

VIVIEN: Shall I let you go, then?

LARRY: I am so very proud of you.

VIVIEN: I'll be back in the summer. We can have a summer here together. And we needn't have people out on weekends, I know how that exhausts you, and you're going to be exhausted, oh my poor darling, if you've just been playing someone who's afraid of life. (*Silence.*) Larry?

LARRY: I—I—

VIVIEN: *Au revoir.*

OUR LADY OF 121ST STREET
BY STEPHEN ADLY GUIRGIS

CHARACTERS
EDWIN *(late 30s) is an irreverent and street-wise Latino man who is basically a good guy;* **MARCIA** *(mid-30s) is a bit uptight, but knows it. Both are attending the funeral of her aunt, a much beloved nun and teacher.*

SCENE
In and around the Ortiz Funeral Home, Harlem

TIME
The present

EDWIN: Hello, sorry for that. I'm, uh, Edwin Velasquez.

MARCIA: Marcia Cook, could you open up that window, please?!

EDWIN: It's closed 'cuz of the A.C.

MARCIA: So smoke outside!! I'm sorry, but I'm an asthmatic!

EDWIN: Ass-what?

MARCIA: Asthma? Hello! I have asthma. I mean the sign says: *"Prohibido Fumar,"* right? But, of course, *I'm the bitch,* just because other people don't give a hoot about anyone else except themselves, so they have no goddamned—

EDWIN: Hey, look—

MARCIA: I mean, I could die! Okay?! I could literally have an asthma attack and drop dead right here! So I'd appreciate it if you would stop gawking at me and open the damn window before I start to really get upset!

EDWIN: It's open, it's open!

MARCIA: I'm really sorry—

EDWIN: Apology accepted.

MARCIA: Apology? See, that's the whole problem right there. I shouldn't have to go off on people and get labeled some kind of overreacting person just to get them to obey a damn law which they're supposed to just obey because it's the goddamn law! I shouldn't have to even ask!

Edwin: You're very right—

Marcia: I mean, *I* didn't put up that "No Smoking" sign.

Edwin: No, you didn't.

Marcia: 'Cuz if there was a sign here that said "Smoking: *Mucho Gusto*!!" I would've just not said a word and suffered silently and possibly died; or I would've just found another place to sit, like outside in the stifling humidity or something, okay, because— Don't look at me like that!

Edwin: Like what?

Marcia: Like I'm some kind of lunatic, or bitch, or rabble rouser!

Edwin: What's a rabble rouser?

(**Marcia** *collapses.*)

Marcia: Oh, my God!

Edwin: What's wrong?

Marcia: Palpitations!

Edwin: Palpi-who?

Marcia: Danger! Danger!

Edwin: What should I do?

Marcia: My inhaler...please...my bag!

Edwin: What? This?

Marcia: Oh, God....Yes....Thank...

(**Marcia** *inhales deeply several times.*)

Edwin: Should I call 911?

Marcia: No! Oh, God! Danger! I'm—count ten, Marcia—ten, nine, five—

Edwin: Eight!

Marcia: Eight?

Edwin: (*Helping her.*) Seven...

Marcia: Six?

Edwin: Dass right—

MARCIA and **EDWIN**: Five . . . four . . . three . . . two . . . one.

(*Pause.*)

MARCIA: Oh, my God.

EDWIN: That was scary.

MARCIA: Oh, my God.

EDWIN: It's okay.

MARCIA: Hold me?

EDWIN: Yeah . . . yeah, sure.

(**EDWIN** *cradles* **MARCIA**. *A beat.*)

MARCIA: You saved my life.

EDWIN: Actually, I was one of the smokers that caused your conniption.

MARCIA: Look, I rarely feel grateful for anything, so could you just shut up and let me be grateful for a second?

(*Pause.*)

EDWIN: You're a very strange lady.

MARCIA: Ssh.

PARADISE
GLYN O'MALLEY

CHARACTERS
BASSAM *(late 20s), a Palestinian engaged in the Intifada against the Israelis;*
FATIMA *(17), a Palestinian girl*

SCENE
Warehouse Headquarters

TIME
Winter 2002

FATIMA *has dreamed of becoming a writer. Now her brother has been killed by the Israelis, and she is desperate to find the means to get her parents out of the Middle East.*

(**BASSAM** *takes off his scarf, and uses it to demonstrate how and where the vest will be placed.* **SHE** *allows him to touch her; there is great intimacy in this.*)

BASSAM: I will place it . . . here. And . . .

FATIMA: Go on.

BASSAM: There will be no pain. It will explode into your heart. You will be gone the moment it detonates.

(**FATIMA** *winces.*)

Are you *certain*?

FATIMA: (*Beat.*) How many soldiers can I kill?

BASSAM: There will be nails, shrapnel, bullets outside in the belt. The wider you open your arms, the more of them will find a target. Once the . . . detonator...is unlocked . . . you have only to touch one wire to it, open your arms and . . .

FATIMA: Can I do it *now*?

BASSAM: You must prepare yourself.

FATIMA: I am.

BASSAM: You cannot be too emotional, Fatima.

FATIMA: I don't feel anything anymore.

BASSAM: (*Thinking on his feet.*) Tomorrow, then...just before sundown. Perfect! The marketplace outside the settlement near the road to the camp. There are usually soldiers, and there will be a rush of shopping for their Shabbat.

FATIMA: I don't want to hurt any of our people!

BASSAM: You will do it inside the market. They won't be there.

FATIMA: The money for my parents.

BASSAM: I will bring it to them myself.

FATIMA: SWEAR IT!

BASSAM: (**HE** *raises a hand.*) Before God, the Just, the Merciful, I swear to you that your parents will receive from this hand twenty-five thousand American dollars for your sacrifice.

FATIMA: (**SHE** *relaxes a little.*) Thank you. Thank you. It is the first time I have felt...relief since Ahmed.

BASSAM: Tomorrow, he will greet you.

FATIMA: Tell my dad, my mom...

BASSAM: You can yourself. Write what is in your heart, and I will bring it to them with the...rest.

FATIMA: I don't want them to mourn.

BASSAM: They will. It's only natural. But they are proud patriots. It will be sweet sorrow. They'll know you will be safe now forever, and your gift will change their lives.

FATIMA: YES! Yes! Watch over them, Bassam. Promise me.

BASSAM: They will be under our protection. I promise.

FATIMA: (*Laughs mildly.*) It's funny—I'm hungry.

BASSAM: Then we'll make a feast. Anything you want.

FATIMA: No. It's better that I leave all this with hunger, and leave the wasps nothing to feed on.

BASSAM: As you wish.

FATIMA: (*Awkward.*) Now...what?

Bassam: It would help so many if you would speak.

Fatima: Speak?

Bassam: On a video. We can make one. It will memorialize your action, your gift to the Palestinian people. Will you do that?

Fatima: And my parents will have it along with my letter to remember me?

Bassam: Yes.

Fatima: Then...?

Bassam: You go home and sleep.

Fatima: Will I...

Bassam: What?

Fatima: Will I be...alone?

Bassam: I'll be with you every step of the way.

(*Hands her a cell phone.*)

My number is the only one in this. Tonight, if you...lose...heart...press this bottom. I will be there for you. I will listen. I will help.

Fatima: I won't lose heart.

Bassam: At noon tomorrow, go to Al Asqa. Fortify yourself. Clear your mind of everything else but this great gift you're about to make. I will meet you there. I will guide you, and map out the plan of how to get you to the market without passing through checkpoints. You will have the cell phone at all times. If you change your mind at any point, you just press the button. One ring and I know it is all off. Now, place the key back around your neck.

(**Fatima** *does so.*)

God has now seen you accept the will He has placed in your soul.

(**He** *wraps her head in a Kaffiyeh.*)

I envy you this glorious honor. Your name will be sung among the nations. Your picture will look down on the cowards who call themselves our allies. The most important word you have ever written will be heard by all the world! Welcome, Fatima! Welcome to the Martyr's Brigade!

PARADISE PARK
BY CHARLES MEE

CHARACTERS
BENNY *(20s), Black;* ELLA *(20s), white*

SCENE
An amusement park—like Coney Island or one of the Disney parks

TIME
Today

BENNY *has been thinking about* ELLA, *a young woman* HE'S *met earlier by pure chance.* SHE'S *been nice to him—though not making a pass by any means—but her niceness gets his attention. In the midst of one of the amusement park's attractions, both are lost in the woods.*

THE WOODS

ELLA:
Whose woods are these?

BENNY:
I don't know.
So.
I guess we're lost in the woods together.

ELLA:
I've never been lost in the woods.

BENNY:
Neither have I.

ELLA:
I'm glad I'm not alone.

BENNY:
So am I.
I like nature,
but I'm a little bit afraid of it.

ELLA:
Well, sure.

BENNY:

    Of the dark parts especially.
    I'd like nature better if it were better lit.
    I think everyone is, you know,
    basically afraid of the dark.
    Even amoebas.
    I mean, every life form,
    you take them out of the light
    and they begin to feel some anxiety.
    I do.

ELLA:

    I do.

BENNY:

    Light, basically, is how you orient yourself
    and a person without a sense of orientation
    I mean, if you don't know where you are
    and where you're going
    and about where you are on the line of the place where you are
    and the destination where you're going
    a person begins to freak out.
    I think that's why
    in jazz
    they always play the melody at the top
    and then
    once you know the tune
    you think: right, let them riff
    because I know where I am
    and I know that, in the end,
    they're going to come back to the melody
    You know what I mean?

ELLA:

    Well.
    Sure.

BENNY:

    It's like
    a love story
    you can just get lost in a love story because
    we know

whatever happens along the way
we might get confused or we might get lost
or it's on again off again
and it goes down some blind alley
but that's how real life is
that's how it really is to be in love
sometimes you never know
sometimes it seems like it is just drifting
or it becomes hopeless
but it doesn't matter
because in the end
with a love story
you know
either they are going to get together
or they're not.

ELLA:
Right.

(*Silence.*)

Do you think
you could ever live in the woods?

BENNY:
You mean, forever?

ELLA:
Well, for a long time.
Say, like five years.

(*Silence.*)

BENNY:
Five years.

(*Silence.*)

With you?

(*Silence.*)

ELLA:
Oh.
Oh.

Okay.
With me.

(*Silence.*)

BENNY:

Yes.

(*Silence.*)

ELLA:

Oh.

BENNY:

I've thought about it before
living in the country
because that would be beautiful
and I've always found it frightening
cut off from the world
as it seems to me
all alone
and
with nothing to do
but wait to get to be eighty years old
or ninety
and die.
You know, you might have thought you were going to be a doctor
or go to the moon
or just have a nice civil-service job
a career and all the ordinary stuff of life
not throw it away on a great sort of romantic gamble
like you think
oh
I'd like to go to the country for the weekend
but to just fling myself out into the universe
and drift among the stars
and have this be my destiny
take the gamble that this would be a meaningful life
and one you would really like forever
the only life you have.
I mean, not that I'm a morbid person
but, you know, it seems to me,

if you're out there alone
maybe with a farm and fields and trees
and the night sky, the stars
you start to think pretty quickly
how you're all alone
and you just have your life on earth
and then it's over
and it hasn't been much more than a wink
in the life of the stars
and you haven't done anything
that you think is worth an entire life on earth
so I've always felt a lot safer living in the city
where you can't see the stars at night.

ELLA:

Unh-hunh.

BENNY:

There you have your friends and things to do
you get all caught up
and it's fun
I'm not against having fun
what I mean is
going to movies, having dinner, hanging out
you can forget entirely that you're a mortal person
it seems: this could go on forever
until, I suppose, you meet someone, and you think:

(*Silence.*)

I could live with you forever in the woods.
And that would be a life.

(*Silence.* **SHE** *starts to back away from him.*)

Or not, you know. Or not.
I didn't mean to come on so strong.
I just start talking, and I don't know when to stop.

ELLA:

Stop.

BENNY:

Right.

ELLA:
Good.
Maybe we could just take a walk in the woods.

BENNY:
Right. Good.
Good idea.
Let's do that.

ELLA:
Shh.

BENNY:
Right.
Quiet
like deer.

(**THEY** *turn and walk into the woods.*)

PERSEPHONE UNDERGROUND
BY CAROL S. LASHOF

CHARACTERS
PERSEPHONE *(16–20), daughter of Demeter, the goddess of the harvest;* HADES'
SON *(20s), the son of the god of Hell, determined to take* PERSEPHONE *back
"home" with him*

SCENE
A meadow near Athens

TIME
The mythic past; evening

PERSEPHONE *has run off from her mother's wedding to investigate the enticing
music* SHE *heard earlier coming from a cave, unwittingly falling prey to* HADES'
SON, *who is determined to take her back with him to the underworld.*

(*The meadow.* HADES' SON *emerges from the cave. As far as possible, his appearance
should suggest both his divinity and his other- [or more precisely under-] worldliness.
Utterly quiet,* HE *sits on the ground as* PERSEPHONE *enters running. Breathless,*
SHE *pauses before approaching the entrance of the cave.* SHE *is about to enter when*
SHE *sees* HADES' SON.)

HADES' SON: Hello.

PERSEPHONE: Hello.

HADES' SON: Where were you running to?

PERSEPHONE: I don't know.

HADES' SON: Are you running away?

(PERSEPHONE *shrugs uncertainly.*)

PERSEPHONE: Everyone seemed to think it was such a beautiful wedding.

HADES' SON: Whose wedding was it?

PERSEPHONE: Don't you know?

(HE *shakes his head.*)

Where did you come from?

(**He** *gestures towards the cave.*)

You live there? In that cave?

HADES' SON: No. Underground.

PERSEPHONE: No one lives underground. Except the shadows of the dead. (*Pause.*) And Hades. Their king. But you are too young to be him.

HADES' SON: I am not a shadow.

(**He** *stretches his hand towards her.* **SHE** *draws back.*)

My father says I am never to come above ground, but it's so beautiful—the surface of the earth, all silver and shadow. And the breeze is so soft.

PERSEPHONE: If you could see it in the daylight, the colors would dazzle you.

HADES' SON: They would blind me. The sunlight would blind me.

(**SHE** *utters a wordless cry of pity and reaches toward him.*)

PERSEPHONE: It must be awful to live underground.

HADES' SON: Oh, no! There's a glorious world there. There are waterfalls a thousand feet high and vast caverns where the softest whisper echoes forever. There's a cliff formed of pure obsidian and a river of molten lead—

PERSEPHONE: If it's so wonderful down there, then why are you sitting here in the dark, sighing for a whiff of fresh air?

HADES' SON: Because the air is sweet.

(**He** *reaches for the blossoms that are tucked into her sash.* **SHE** *undoes her sash and lets the blossoms fall.* **He** *gathers them up.*)

PERSEPHONE: They're Narcissus. Named for the boy who died of love for his own reflection.

HADES' SON: Yes, I know the story. He saw his own face reflected in a pool of water. And fell in love. And died of longing.

PERSEPHONE: And Echo pined away for love of him because she could not tell her love. She hid silently in the shadows until she became a shadow herself with no body, a shadow of a voice with no words of her own.

HADES' SON: If she had come out of the shadows, if she had spoken to him . . .

PERSEPHONE: If he had looked up and seen her there . . .

HADES' SON: Would she have run away?

PERSEPHONE: Would he have been afraid of the love in her eyes?

HADES' SON: Why wouldn't he be flooded with gladness?

PERSEPHONE: Why shouldn't she fly to his arms?

[(*The voices of the Athenian girls are heard offstage, calling for* **PERSEPHONE**.)]

I have to go.

HADES' SON: Why?

PERSEPHONE: My friends are looking for me. If they find me here with you ...

HADES' SON: What would they do?

PERSEPHONE: Shhh.

[(*The voices seem for a moment to be coming closer; then they begin to recede into the distance.*)]

When I was here earlier, I heard the strangest music. It seemed to be coming from under the earth.

HADES' SON: Come with me?

PERSEPHONE: To the Underworld?

HADES' SON: It's a world of endless adventure ....

(**HE** *holds out his hand to her.* **SHE** *holds back.*)

PERSEPHONE: I've heard that no one comes back from the Underworld.

HADES' SON: That's not true. You can come and go as you please—so long as you don't eat anything grown from the earth while you're there. Every bite of fruit, anything with roots in the ground, binds your soul more tightly to Hades.

(**PERSEPHONE** *shudders.*)

Of course, the truth is that we don't have much in the way of fresh fruits and vegetables down below anyway. Naturally, we live mostly on ambrosia, my father and I.

PERSEPHONE: Who is your father?

HADES' SON: The king of the Underworld.

PERSEPHONE: (*Horrified.*) Hades? You are the son of Hades?

HADES' SON: Yes.

PERSEPHONE: I heard he had a son, but I thought...

(SHE *trails off, stops, embarrassed.*)

HADES' SON: Yes? What?

PERSEPHONE: Oh, you know. People say things.

HADES' SON: What do they say?

(*Pause.* HE *waits for her to continue speaking.*)

PERSEPHONE: They say that... that your mother was a shade, that you were brewed in a caldron and nursed on the roots of trees....

HADES' SON: That's true.

PERSEPHONE: And they say that your father is ashamed of you and keeps your existence a secret. That he has given you no name so that no one will trouble to know you.

HADES' SON: That's also true. (*Pause.*) Do they say anything else?

PERSEPHONE: Only that... that you are deformed and ugly. (*Pause. Hastily.*) But that's not true.

[(*The voices of* PERSEPHONE'S *friends are heard coming closer again, more urgent and anxious now.*)]

You'd better go.

HADES' SON: Come with me! (*Pause.*) You'll be back before dawn.

PERSEPHONE: I can't....

HADES' SON: Why not? (*Pause.*) You're a goddess. What do you have to fear in the land of the dead?

(HE *holds out his hand.* SHE *hesitates.*)

Come with me?

(HE *stands still and quiet, waiting for her. Finally,* SHE *takes his hand and* THEY *exit together into the cave.*)

PROPHECY

CHARACTERS
ALAN GOLDEN *(60s), a Jewish-American father;* MARIAM JABAR *(24), his estranged daughter, whose mother is Palestinian-Lebanese.*

SCENE
ALAN GOLDEN'S *office at the Refugee Relief Committee, a prominent not-for-profit organization in Manhattan*

TIME
2006

MARIAM *arrived in New York last night. Her mother, Hala Jabar, was once* ALAN'S *colleague; they had an affair and* HE *promised to marry her if she got pregnant.* HE *did not, however, as* HE *was unable to leave his infertile wife, Sarah. Hala then returned to the Middle East where she works for the United Nations.* MARIAM *was raised by her mother in Lebanon and the Occupied Palestinian Territories.* SHE *clutches a large leather lady's handbag to her chest.*

MARIAM: Hello, Alan. Thank you for making some more time.

ALAN: I've cleared the whole afternoon. We barely got started last night. Come in.

(HE *moves to hug her, but* SHE *steps away.*)

There is so much more about you I'm dying to know. (*Silence.*) Sit down, please, Mariam.

(HE *points out two chairs around a low table, and* HE *holds one out for her, and then sits.* SHE *keeps holding on to her bag.*)

Mariam. How very lovely you are. Like Hala. People must tell you that. How long will you stay in New York?

MARIAM: Long enough. But I want to know about you.

ALAN: You do? Sure. That's so nice. Well, what's to know? I'm still executive director here. Your mother worked...she had the office right next door. Does Hala ever speak about those years? (*Silence.*) Well, I'm rather overwhelmed at the moment. We're trying to figure out how to get some aid into Tyre, then, of course, there's Gaza. There's always Gaza, as we say around here. Not to mention Iraq.

MARIAM: It's an overwhelming moment, yes.

ALAN: You look so much like Hala.

MARIAM: I have your nose. (**THEY** *laugh, nervously.*)

ALAN: Sorry. That was a mistake.

MARIAM: Don't be sorry about that.

ALAN: Good. (*Pause.*) All right, Mariam. Look, I'll tell you. I never intended to leave your mother. It was Sarah. By the time I had sorted things, and Sarah was, well, resigned to the way things were, your mother didn't want me anymore. How is she? How is Hala?

MARIAM: Hala was traveling the road north from Tyre with a convoy of women and children when the road was hit. The first ambulance, clearly marked, it could be seen from the sky, was destroyed. Deliberately targeted, Hala says.

ALAN: (**HE** *reacts to this angrily.*) We heard. (*Pause.*) Hala would be in the thick of it all.

MARIAM: Everyone, now, is in the thick of it, I think.

ALAN: True. Does she know you're here? That you've come?

MARIAM: It was a beautiful summer in Lebanon, Alan. Our house on the Corniche overlooks the sea. In the morning there were birds, at night music. So many friends had come home. We were laughing all the time. Hala made me leave, to go to London, she thought. I never left Heathrow. I got on a plane for New York.

ALAN: I'm very glad.

MARIAM: I am glad, too.

ALAN: I'm happy about that.

MARIAM: Happy?

ALAN: Thrilled, I'd say, yes. We have missed so many years. I will work hard, Mariam, to become a real father to you.

MARIAM: There's no need. I'm grown.

ALAN: Even for a grown-up, a father is.... I miss my own father quite a bit. It went so fast, your growing up. I thought about you every birthday, what you'd be wearing, where I would take you. I always wanted you to ride the merry-go-round in Central Park. I never knew the actual date.

MARIAM: June twenty-seventh.

ALAN: Close! I always thought the first of July. Somehow, I think, I was not surprised to see you as you are now, in the hijab, too. A father knows his daughter, somehow, even if...

MARIAM: I never felt I knew you.

ALAN: We can be father and daughter, now. I'll show you the city. What would you like to see? Do you like opera, museums, food, we have the best restaurants, shopping, do you like to shop? Read? Hip-hop? There are mosques. We have quite a few Arab neighborhoods. There are so many people I'd like you to meet. You'll stay for a while, I hope. You could think of studying here, at Columbia.

MARIAM: I'll stay as long as it takes.

ALAN: Months? Weeks?

MARIAM: It won't be that long.

ALAN: No?

MARIAM: I don't think you know why I've come.

ALAN: I had hoped to see me.

MARIAM: That's true.

ALAN: To get to know me a bit.

MARIAM: Yes, to see you at work. I wanted to be here in this building with you and all these good people, all these innocent civilians, at this particular time, when so many innocent civilians in my part of the world.... You do good work, all of you. You send aid to people like me. You send protein bars and bottles of cooking oil, not olive oil, of course, vegetable oil, but still, we can cook up the dried chick peas, and rice, if we have clean water, that is. If the water purification plants have not been bombed, if crude oil has not been dumped in the sea, killing the fish. Never mind. You send ready meals, if you have to, dump them on us from the sky. And you send little pieces of paper telling us to leave our houses before they are bombed. That is very kind. The good people in the United States continue to think they are good because of the work you do here helping refugees. The more refugees your country makes, the more people like you try to help.

ALAN: That is one way of looking at it, I suppose.

MARIAM: Do you look at it another way?

ALAN: I try. There is always evil in the world, and there is always good.

MARIAM: True.

ALAN: I do what I can to tip the balance our way.

MARIAM: That is admirable, Alan.

ALAN: Thank you. Your mother, too, Hala feels the same way. Felt. I'm certain, still does.

MARIAM: Oh, yes. My mother thinks exactly like you. But let me ask you, Alan, one thing. I have come here just to ask you. Why, when you tip the balance, as you say, why is it always Muslims who must die? Why does the balance never tip the other way? There is a bomb ticking right now inside my bag. Please answer soon.

ALAN: Don't talk like that. Not even inside my office. It's fine to be outraged, of course. I am also outraged. But someone might overhear you, even here. That would put you at risk.

MARIAM: I understand.

ALAN: Fine, then, okay. We all know what's going on. What do you think I do day in and day out? But I want to tell you something else: My father, your grandfather, he lived in times worse than these, and he never gave up. He wasted not one instant on revenge. He got people out. Snatched from the Nazis. He saved lives. Often, of course, it does feel useless. I feel hopeless . . . but I learned from him, from what he did, individuals can make a difference to other individuals. That may be all we can do. But we must do that much.

MARIAM: That is true.

ALAN: In times like these, it does feel overwhelming. That's why family is so important. My father left a legacy to me. I intend to pass his legacy to you. I have letters to you, Mariam, a drawer full, returned by your mother, unopened. I wanted to know you. I tried to imagine what you needed to hear at every time, every age. You can read them. Tell me if I got anything right.

MARIAM: That would be nice.

ALAN: I sent money, too.

MARIAM: Naturally. Of course.

ALAN: I wanted you to have the best. Be the best. Your mother and I spoke about a new race. It was foolish, romantic talk, of course. But we believed it in those days, and we still do, Hala, too, I am certain of that, in peace, somehow, in justice, in living together, side by side, that someday clearer heads will prevail. We believed in you, too, Mariam. We believed that in making you from our flesh we were going to give something beautiful not just to ourselves but to the world. I am so sorry I wasn't there to see you grow up.

MARIAM: In Lebanon for the Civil War? In East Jerusalem? Where?

ALAN: I am sorry, Mariam. I have a great deal to be sorry for. But please know how thrilled, how blessed I feel, truly, I don't use that word lightly, that you came to find me. We can be father and daughter, at last. It's a gift. Amazing at this time in my life to have one more chance. I am so happy that you've come.

MARIAM: One more chance?

ALAN: I might live to know my grandchildren, a wonderful thought. I am a fortunate man, Mariam, because you've come.

MARIAM: (**SHE** *stands, clutching the bag to her chest.*) I see. I thought it would be nice if you knew me, if you understood everything in your last minutes, if your whole life flashed before you, and you got to know at the very last moment that this child who was supposed to bring in the new world, only you never got to watch her grow up, unfortunate, that, but there was always a war on, after all, and how could you leave your important job to go there, anyway. It was always so unsafe. But I wanted you to know, now, at last, about the new world you made with your big dreams, your empty words, and the murderous actions they cover up, the peace plans, the road maps running every which way, they have to bulldoze so many houses to get there, and put up such a big wall, build a fence around Gaza, such a nice prison they built, to keep the fishermen from being able to fish, and there is nowhere to run, you get blown up if you go to the beach, if you leave, you can't get back in, and, then, why not send Lebanon back to the Stone Age, the people, after all, are so primitive, but none of that matters, now, at all, because most of all I wanted to see your face at the moment you understand it is your own flesh who is going to blow you up.

(*At this,* ALAN *makes a lunge for her, and* HE *grabs her bag.*)

I wouldn't open the clasp.

(HE *stands frozen, holding the bag away from him, not knowing what to do.* MARIAM *laughs.*)

We are all terrorists, after all.

(SHE *takes the bag away from him.*)

ALAN: Forget about me. I'm an old man. Don't ruin your life.

MARIAM: Don't you know, we love death more than life? We love martyrdom. Get ready, Alan. I'm going to give you a treat. Parents are always already dead. They don't get to hear this:

(MARIAM *begins to recite the Kaddish.*)

Yeetgadal v'yeetkadash sh'mey rabbah
B'almach dee v'rah kheer'utey
V'yanleekh malkhutei, b'chahyeykhohn, uv' yohmeykhohn
Uv'chahyei d'chohl beyt yisrael

(ALAN *freezes.* MARIAM *opens the bag and dumps its contents onto the floor: lipsticks, pens, her passport, a diary, a wallet, keys, the usual stuff, a book.* ALAN *feels like a fool, but* HE *relaxes.* MARIAM *picks up the book.*)

See Under Love by David Grossman. A great Israeli novelist. A great Holocaust book. And do you know that David Grossman had a son, Uri? He was a tank commander in the ground invasion. His father had just signed a petition with other Jewish intellectuals calling for an end to the fighting. This war could have ended before Uri Grossman got killed by a Hezbollah rocket. He was 20 years old. And you think we are the only ones who love to make martyrs? Do you think we are the only ones who love death? (SHE *trembles.*) Like an ocean, like two seas crashing together between the rocks, and that is my bloodstream, that churning is always my heart. You cannot imagine the power with which my heart beats. How does my heart not jump from my chest? How does my blood not rush out? You wanted something else. I believe you wished for a son. In your mind I would be a great man. I would have had a bar mitzvah. I would have done good. I would have figured out how. Like your father, like you.

ALAN: No. Mariam. It was you I wanted. All the time, I wanted you.

(**ALAN** *goes to her and* **HE** *holds her and comforts her.*)

MARIAM: It's too hard.

ALAN: I know that, believe me, my dear one, my daughter, my child, I do understand.

REBEL MOON
BY BRIAN GRANGER

CHARACTERS
BERTO *(20), an Hispanic man dating Mara;* **LISETTE** *(18), also Hispanic, Mara's younger sister*

SCENE
Outside **LISETTE**'s *apartment building in an inner-city neighborhood*

TIME
The present

BERTO *and Mara have been fighting and* **LISETTE** *has been eavesdropping. As* **BERTO** *comes back to try and make up with Mara,* **LISETTE** *seizes her opportunity.*

BERTO: Mara!

(*The door to the fire escape opens and* **LISETTE** *steps out onto the fire escape balcony.*)

LISETTE: Stop yelling. You're so loud you don't even realize.

BERTO: What? Were you listening in to our fight?

LISETTE: Hell, yes. This shit is way better than what's on TV right now.

BERTO: Where is Mara?

LISETTE: Not coming. She said to take those tickets and—

BERTO: Ah, crap. I should have known. She's been like this for the past couple of weeks. You're the smart sister. What's her problem?

LISETTE: I don't know. She and I don't really chat it up like homegirls.

BERTO: I treat her nice, don't I?

LISETTE: Like a queen. A lot of girls would love to have you as their man.

BERTO: Yeah, right.

LISETTE: No, it's true. I hear girls talk about you all the time at school. How hot you are. They fantasize things about you all the time.

Berto: What kind of things?

Lisette: How you are in bed. Your size. Lots of stuff I would be embarrassed to say.

Berto: You don't seem embarrassed so far, and you're saying a lot.

Lisette: That's cause I ain't easily shocked like my sister. And fantasies are interesting.

Berto: Well. Girls can say what they want. None of it's worth a damn. Especially all that flowery poetry bullshit. Nothing a girl has to say is worth listening to, far as I'm concerned.

Lisette: I agree. Girls do way too much talking.

(*Pause.*)

Berto: You're strange.

Lisette: Is that bad?

Berto: I didn't say it was bad. Just different. I never figured you and your sister would be so different, but you are.

Lisette: Good. I don't want to be like her. She's annoying. And she's fat.

Berto: Listen to you.

Lisette: It's true. You weren't lying to her. She just didn't want to hear it. And not just from you—I try to tell her she's gaining weight and she gets all crazy with me, too. (**Lisette** *unties and reties her hair over the next few lines, arching her back as* **She** *does this.*) You see, it's all because our mother was fat, rest her soul. We loved Mama, but as kids Mara and I used to promise each other that we would never get fat. I'm keeping my promise. Mara... Mara's pissed off at herself and at the world. I don't need to hear her mouth any more than you do.

Berto: She used to have your body, you know. When we first met.

Lisette: She was hot, wasn't she? I used to think she was so pretty.

(**Lisette** *begins stretching, dancer-like, using the bars of the fire escape.* **She's** *very flexible.* **Berto** *is awestruck.*)

Lisette: She's still pretty. But it's like, she's let herself go, you know? It's like she doesn't care about pleasing you anymore.

Berto: Yeah.

LISETTE: I think a woman needs to please her man. All the time. Anywhere and everywhere and every way he wants it. She needs to keep her body firm and beautiful for her man. Because that is the way every man truly wants his woman's body to be. He might feel emotions for her, feel responsible for her. Committed. But he wants the tight body, always.

BERTO: What are you doing?

LISETTE: I'm stretching, silly. You know I take dance classes.

BERTO: No. You know what I mean, chica. What are you doing?

(*A pause as* **LISETTE** *looks back into the apartment toward* **MARA**, *somewhere offstage.* **SHE** *turns back to* **BERTO**.)

LISETTE: Like I said. I'm stretching.

(*Pause.*)

BERTO: I wish I didn't have to waste these tickets.

LISETTE: You don't have to. I'll be down in a minute. Gonna grab my jacket.

(**LISETTE** *exits.*)

(*As the lights fade out, Berto looks at* **MARA'S** *window with the tickets in hand.* **HE** *turns and holds up the tickets in the moonlight, like a trophy.*)

RED LIGHT WINTER
BY ADAM RAPP

CHARACTERS
MATT *(30), an aspiring playwright currently trying to write a play and/or commit suicide;* CHRISTINA *(25), a prostitute hired to cheer him up*

SCENE
A rundown hotel room in Amsterdam

TIME
The present

CHRISTINA *pretends to be a waiflike French girl, but is actually an American woman working in Amsterdam's red light district.* SHE *is supposed to help* MATT *overcome his recent impotence, but is already smitten with* MATT'S *roommate, who recently procured her services.*

MATT: So let me get this straight. You guys quote-unquote *made love* three times.

CHRISTINA: I wanted four but he wouldn't stop talking about you.

MATT: What did he say?

CHRISTINA: How important you are to him. And how he felt strange making love because he wanted to introduce me to you. He cares about you very much.

MATT: Oh, no doubt. . . . So are you like all smitten with him or something?

CHRISTINA: What is smitten?

MATT: Love. Are you in love with him?

CHRISTINA: I don't know. Just now when he was leaving I suddenly felt like I would never see him again and it made me feel very sad.

MATT: Well you probably won't . . . see him again, I mean.

(CHRISTINA *turns away, smokes for a moment.* MATT *crosses back to the desk.*)

Christina, as a human being or whatever, I feel I should say something. And this isn't intended to burst your bubble, or like cockblock him because he really is like a brother to me, but Davis's mother is alive and well. She actually teaches comparative literature at Brandeis.

And regarding his melancholy, the only angstrom of quote-unquote *sadness* that I've ever been privy to was the time when he cried because he wasn't named a Rhodes scholar.

(**CHRISTINA** *puts her cigarette out and reaches into her bag and removes a small snow globe of the New York City skyline.* **SHE** *shakes it and watches it snow for a moment.*)

What's that?

(**SHE** *hands it to him.*)

Did Davis give you this?

CHRISTINA: It's beautiful.

MATT: Yeah, he bought this at a gift shop near the train station in Paris.

CHRISTINA: I was very moved to receive it.

MATT: I'm sure.

CHRISTINA: I wish to someday go to New York.

MATT: Well, you should come visit.

(**HE** *hands the snow globe back to her.* **SHE** *stares at it for a moment, then puts it in her bag.*)

So regarding this whole thing, we don't have to like, um, *do* anything if you don't want to. I mean you seemed pretty upset there and I wouldn't want to feel like obligat—

CHRISTINA: It's okay. I would like to be with you.

MATT: Really? I mean, I can't guarantee you like orgasming in triplicate.

CHRISTINA: That's not important.

MATT: More water?

CHRISTINA: No, thank you.

MATT: Another cigarette?

(**SHE** *nods.* **HE** *gives her another cigarette, lights her, then sits on the other bed.*)

So before we continue, I have to say something. And I might be totally off base here.

CHRISTINA: What.

MATT: You're not French, are you? I mean you might be, right? But I'm almost totally sure you're like this very talented imposter. So you can like stop the routine. I won't tell anybody. I mean your accent is spot-on perfect, and the slight lack of knowledge of English vocabulary is very subtle and authentic, i.e., your purported ignorance of words like *smitten* and *demarcate* and um *scribe*, but you sort of blew it when you sang. I mean, you have this totally like mellifluous voice or whatever, and your song really is affecting—it's just that there was a moment or two there where you suddenly sounded really Midwestern. I'm from Illinois so I have these like Des Plaines River Valley superpowers.... I mean, if you want to continue in like character or whatever it's fine with me.

(*Suddenly a cell phone starts ringing.* CHRISTINA *goes into her bag, removes it, stands and faces the corner for privacy, answers.*)

CHRISTINA: Hello? Oui...Oui...Oui...No...No...(*She hangs up.*)

MATT: Who was that?

(SHE *turns to face him.*)

CHRISTINA: (*Dropping the accent, American English now.*) Albert.

MATT: Your boyfriend?

CHRISTINA: My husband.

MATT: You're married?

CHRISTINA: It was arranged. He's gay, lives in Paris.

SCENES FROM AN UNFINISHED LIFE
BY LEIGH KENNICOTT

CHARCTERS
MARK *(early 30s), a dark, athletic, young man;* FLORRIE *(28), moderately attractive*

SCENE
A coffee shop in San Francisco

TIME
The present

MARK *is in the doghouse, and he knows it.* HE *and* FLORRIE *were an item until* SHE *got pregnant. Now, in the aftermath,* HE *wants her back, but* SHE *is insulted. Still, part of her wants to hang on to the relationship.*

MARK: Hey.

FLORRIE: Hey.

(HE *looks at the menu. Sets it down.*)

MARK: Did you get my message?

FLORRIE: Which one?

MARK: From Effie and Edgar?

FLORRIE: No. Stop that. What message?

MARK: When I had to go out of town.

FLORRIE: For the month, right?

MARK: Well, not—

FLORRIE: I know. You were hiding. And it wasn't a month. It was six weeks.

MARK: Well, you know. It's ski season.

FLORRIE: *That's* where you went?

MARK: After the month.

FLORRIE: And did you know what *I* was doing?

MARK: (*Ineffectually.*) There was nothing I could do to help.

FLORRIE: Except hold my hand!

MARK: I took some emergency time off. I had to think.

FLORRIE: How fitting.

(**THEY** *both look at the menu.*)

Well?

MARK: Well, I'm—glad you agreed to see me.

FLORRIE: (*Menacingly.*) I meant the food.

MARK: Oh. I don't— I'm not hungry. But you eat.

FLORRIE: Whyyy?

MARK: I'll pay.

FLORRIE: You keep doing that. I meant, why did you suddenly want to see me?

MARK: Be—because I thought . . . and I suddenly realized how much I love you.

FLORRIE: Hmmm. Why don't I believe you?

MARK: I know. I panicked.

FLORRIE: Edgar said it was because you were broke.

MARK: I was. I am. (*Forlorn.*) I just couldn't handle it.

FLORRIE: Oh. (*Beat.*) And I could.

MARK: (**HE'S** *silent. Then.*) I missed you.

FLORRIE: So now, you just want to get back together, no questions asked?

MARK: Effie and Edgar—

FLORRIE: Are spies.

MARK: No. They begged me to call you.

FLORRIE: That's what they said.

MARK: I just wasn't ready—for that.

FLORRIE: Oh, icing on the cake!

MARK: I know it doesn't look good.

FLORRIE: Good!? You know, right now, you're not in the best position to ask me to have anything more to do with you.

MARK: (*Bristling. This is not going his way.*) Why did you agree to meet me then?

FLORRIE: To see what you would say. And so far, you haven't offered much.

MARK: But Effie said—

FLORRIE: The problem's over. It's gone from my body.

MARK: (*Uncharacteristically gentle.*) I'm sorry. What happened? How did you—

FLORRIE: No. It would be a privilege to know.

MARK: But it was my—

FLORRIE: Oh, don't trot that out. Don't even—

MARK: (*Reaches for her hand.*) Florrie . . .

FLORRIE: (*Recoils.* **SHE** *jumps up with her purse.*) Don't! Ever! Tempt me! Again!

(**SHE** *turns and hurries out of the coffee shop.*)

SCRIPTED
BY MARK HARVEY LEVINE

CHARACTERS
SIMON *(25–40) is married to* ELAINE *(25–40). Their morning gets off to an interesting start when* SIMON *finds a script on their nightstand.*

SCENE
A bedroom

TIME
The morning

(SIMON *and* ELAINE *lie in bed, asleep. The alarm goes off.*)

ELAINE: Oh, God, don't make me get up...

(SIMON *reaches over to turn off the alarm. His hand rests on a very thick stack of pages, held together with two brads—a script.* HE *picks it up.*)

ELAINE: What time is it?

(SIMON *is engrossed in the script.*)

ELAINE: Simon? What time is it?

SIMON: (*Reading from the script.*) "It's...7:20..."

ELAINE: You didn't even look at the clock...

(SIMON *looks at the clock.*)

SIMON: It *is* 7:20...

    (SIMON *looks back at the script. Reading.*)

    "It *is* 7:20..."

ELAINE: Whatcha got?

SIMON: This isn't yours?

ELAINE: No.

SIMON: I found it...on the nightstand...

ELAINE: What is it?

SIMON: It's ... a ... script ...

ELAINE: You mean like for a movie?

SIMON: No ... for us. It's us. It's— This is what's happening right now.

ELAINE: What? What are you talking about ...?

SIMON: Say something. Say anything.

ELAINE AND SIMON: (*Simultaneously.*) The cows are barking at midnight! How did you do that? Stop that! *Stop it!!*

ELAINE: Simon, my God, how are you doing this?

SIMON: I don't know! I don't know! I just found the script. Our script. This is— I know everything you're about to say.

ELAINE: What do you mean?! What do you mean?!

SIMON: Look! Read it!

ELAINE: Oh my God ... it knows what I'm going to say ... what I'm saying ... right now.... Aaugh!

(**SHE** *drops the script.* **HE** *picks it up.*)

SIMON: And we can't seem to help ... (*Turns page.*) ... saying what we're supposed to say.

ELAINE: Well ... *just don't.* Say something different. Look at your next line, and say something else. Anything else ...

SIMON: (*Struggling.*) I ... can't ...

(**ELAINE** *grabs the script.*)

ELAINE: (*Reading.*) "I can't." (*Panicking.*) Okay. Okay. Okay.

SIMON: All right, let's not panic.

ELAINE: I'm not panicking ...

SIMON: Yes you are—it says so, in parentheses ... "Elaine ... panicking ... "

ELAINE: Don't look at it! Just don't look! Put it down! Put it down!

(**SHE** *throws the script to the floor. They cross as far away from it as they can, clutching each other.*)

SIMON: All right ... let's stay calm ... let's try to think here ...

ELAINE: How can we stay calm?! Simon, we've got our lives…our own words written down and plonked on our nightstand!

SIMON: It wasn't there last night…

ELAINE: So who put it here? Who wrote this? Someone came in while we were asleep? Into our apartment?

SIMON: I don't think it was a person…How could anyone know what we're going to say? Elaine, I think…someone…is trying to tell us something…

ELAINE: Someone?

SIMON: Y'know…God…

ELAINE: No! No No No! Stop that! I don't want God to tell me things! I hate signs and symbols!! The God I believe in does NOT drop scripts off in the middle of the night!

SIMON: Maybe it's a warning! Maybe something horrible happens today…and we have a chance to prevent it…

ELAINE: You think?

SIMON: We have to see.

ELAINE: Okay, but don't let go of me.

(*Together, they shuffle over to the script.* **SIMON** *gingerly picks it up. Pause. Dramatically,* **HE** *opens it.*)

ELAINE: AAAAAUGH!

(**SIMON** *drops it.*)

ELAINE: Sorry. Sorry. I'm just scared. Go ahead, I'm not even gonna look.

(**HE** *picks the script up again.* **ELAINE** *looks away.* **HE** *starts to read.*)

SIMON: Okay…okay. Let's see. Well, I'm going to be late for work. Probably 'cause I'm standing here reading this thing. (*Flips ahead more.*) You sing show tunes while you grade papers?

ELAINE: Only when I'm upset. You don't find this horribly frightening?

SIMON: No…I mean, yes, but…I think it's kinda neat… (*Reads further.*) Your mom's gonna call.

ELAINE: Oh, great.

(**SHE** *looks at the script.*)

ELAINE: My God...our whole conversation is in here. Oh, this is so embarrassing. Look—it takes us three pages to get off the phone. (*Reading both parts.*) "All right...," "Okay...," "I'll talk to you later...," "All right...," "So everything's okay?" "Everything's okay." "All right..." "Okay..." God! We sound so stupid all written down like this.

SIMON: Look at me...I never finish a sentence, I mean...all my lines end in "dot, dot, dot..."

ELAINE: Simon...I'm scared.

SIMON: I know, sweetie...

ELAINE: No, I mean, what if...what if one of us...dies...in this? What if that's why this is here?

SIMON: Well, then...we'll just avoid whatever it was. I mean, y'know, if it's a car wreck or something, then we'll just stay inside...

ELAINE: That never works. You've watched "The Twilight Zone." Y'know, the car crashes through the house anyway.

SIMON: Well, then, lemme look at the end. Let's see how this thing ends.

ELAINE: Oh God. Okay.

SIMON: I mean, we have to know...

ELAINE: Okay.

(*Terrified,* **HE** *turns to the last page. They both exhale in relief.*)

SIMON: We're alive!

ELAINE: We just say good NIGHT AND GO TO BED. THAT'S NICE.

SIMON: It looks like our whole day is here...

ELAINE: Okay, then. Let's read it from the beginning. I want to know what happens.

SIMON: Are you sure?

ELAINE: Yeah...Yes.

SIMON: Okay...here we go...

SHYNESS IS NICE
BY MARC SPITZ

CHARACTERS
FITZGERALD *(30s), a brand new junkie;* BLIXA *(30s), an Australian pimp*

SCENE
A spare New York City Apartment

TIME
The present

FITZGERALD *plans to introduce his two 30-year-old virgin friends to the joys of sex.* HE *will provide* BLIXA *with twenty bags of heroin, and* SHE, *in turn, will provide him with a prostitute.*

(BLIXA, *tough in leather jacket enters, quickly.*)

FITZGERALD: You know you're early.

BLIXA: I'm only ten minutes early.

FITZGERALD: I figured you'd have a hard time finding this place.

BLIXA: I've got an excellent sense of direction.

FITZGERALD: What are you? One of those aboriginals?

BLIXA: Do I look Aborigine?

FITZGERALD: You wanna beer?

BLIXA: All right. Do you have any Foster's?

FITZGERALD: I've got Bud and Bud Lite. That's American for beer. Have a seat. I'll get you a brew. Nice and cold.

BLIXA: (*Looks around. Nowhere to sit.* SHE *finally sits on the floor.*) Nice place.

FITZGERALD: Yeah. . . . You like it?

(FITZGERALD *exits. Returns with two beers. Hands her one.*)

It's a twist-off.

BLIXA: (*Opens beer. Gulps it.*) American beer tastes like piss. Where's the thing we talked about? Do you have it?

FITZGERALD: You know what I always wanted to ask you people? What's up with the fucking platypuses?

BLIXA: How should I know?

FITZGERALD: They're mammals, but they lay eggs. I mean, how can they get away with that shit?

BLIXA: Where is it?

FITZGERALD: I got it. Don't worry. So how long have you been pimpin'?

BLIXA: A few months.

FITZGERALD: Wait, so you're not a pimp back home?

BLIXA: No. I work in a pub.

FITZGERALD: You're a waitress?

BLIXA: Not anymore.

FITZGERALD: Fucking incredible. So you thought you'd come to America and pimp. That's cool.

BLIXA: I couldn't get a legitimate work visa.

FITZGERALD: And this Kylie, she was down with the plan?

BLIXA: We both need the money. America is very expensive.

FITZGERALD: No shit. And this Kylie . . . she a waitress too?

BLIXA: She was. Now she's my bitch.

FITZGERALD: Right. And she doesn't mind all the random fucking.

BLIXA: Kylie's a smart girl . . . she knows herself. Very useful asset.

FITZGERALD: Sure. Sure.

BLIXA: Kylie gets blind drunk and fucks boys at random anyway. So I simply suggested we organize ourselves.

FITZGERALD: So how come she's the bitch and you're the pimp? Why not vice versa?

BLIXA: Men like Kylie better.

FITZGERALD: Why's that?

BLIXA: They tend to think I'm hard.

FITZGERALD: Aw... you're not hard. You're all right.

BLIXA: Let me ask you something....

FITZGERALD: Shoot....

BLIXA: Your two mates, are they really virgins?

FITZGERALD: Swear to fuck.

BLIXA: Amazing. Why? Fear of AIDS?

FITZGERALD: Nah. Fear of disappointing Morrisey. (*Beat.*) Say, what the fuck is Vegemite anyway?

BLIXA: It's a spread.

FITZGERALD: Cool.

BLIXA: Why is it any of your business whether or not they have sex? It's a personal issue.

FITZGERALD: How old are you?

BLIXA: I just turned thirty.

FITZGERALD: Me too. And you know what that shit's like. It's a transition. I mean, look, you packed up and moved to America to start a new life as a pimp right? That's the kind of shit you do when you're thirty. You pimp. You experiment with drugs. Normal shit.

BLIXA: And your mates, they're not experimental enough for you.

FITZGERALD: No. They don't experiment with dick. And it's become painful to hang out with them. Boring! They're my last two friends. I mean, you need friends, right? You, you've got your bitch. These are our friends. Who has the patience to make new ones? I'd rather keep 'em than be alone but they gotta loosen up.

BLIXA: Why do they have to experiment with sex and hard drugs in order to loosen up?

FITZGERALD: 'Cause... this is America.

BLIXA: (*Pulls a gun. Places it on the floor.*) Do you mind? It's weighing down my coat.

FITZGERALD: (*Cools significantly. Stares at it.*) No, I can hang that up for you if you want. (*Pulls out inhaler. Takes a hit.*)

BLIXA: Are you asthmatic?

FITZGERALD: No. (*Stares at the gun again. Swallows some pills.*) You want some crackers or something?

BLIXA: That's all right. I didn't plan to stay long. I assumed I'd just get my payment and go.

FITZGERALD: Right... so I suppose you'll be wanting that... now.

BLIXA: Yes. Now would be fine.

FITZGERALD: So this chick... she's good-looking, huh? (*Picks up the gun, holds it, sucks on the inhaler some more.*)

BLIXA: Careful with that. It's loaded.

(FITZGERALD *puts the gun down, swallows more pills.*)

BLIXA: What's that?

FITZGERALD: Vitamins.

BLIXA: Vitamins?

FITZGERALD: And minerals. Keeps you from getting cancer.

BLIXA: (*Grabs the bottle.*) Xanax. (*Long, painful beat.*) That's a palindrome.

FITZGERALD: It's an antianxiety medication, all right?

BLIXA: Do I make you anxious?

FITZGERALD: Nah, I just never had a gun all up in my place before.

BLIXA: (*Takes the gun back.*) She's very attractive. Your mates won't be disappointed. Will I be disappointed?

FITZGERALD: Huh? (*Nervous.*) Nah. This is great shit. Great shit. Here. I'll prove it.

(FITZGERALD *removes the single bag from his pants pocket. Opens it. Lays out a line on the floor. Pulls out a dollar bill. Hands it to* BLIXA.)

FITZGERALD: Test it out, babe. On me.

BLIXA: (*Takes the dollar.*) You know when I met you at the bar, I thought you were cute.

FITZGERALD: I am cute.

BLIXA: I don't usually make these kind of arrangements. It's not really orthodox.

FITZGERALD: Yeah? Your Pimpin' for Dummies handbook frowns on it, huh? Chapter one . . . cash only. Chapter two, get yourself a big-ass gun to enforce cash-only policy. You even know how to use that thing?

BLIXA: (*Holds up gun. Points it at* FITZGERALD). I know how to use it.

FITZGERALD: Yeah? Cool.

BLIXA: You're very arrogant.

FITZGERALD: Thanks.

BLIXA: So are all your business transactions made with heroin?

FITZGERALD: I invested in a lot of it.

BLIXA: You don't have any cash?

FITZGERALD: I got thirty bucks . . . somewhere.

BLIXA: (*Takes a snort.*) It's strong.

FITZGERALD: It is.

BLIXA: It's good.

FITZGERALD: It is.

BLIXA: I'm high.

FITZGERALD: You are.

BLIXA: So where do you get it?

FITZGERALD: Oh, it's everywhere in America.

BLIXA: Wow. I'm really high.

FITZGERALD: You really are. You want another beer?

BLIXA: Sure.

FITZGERALD: You wanna mess around?

BLIXA: Maybe.

FITZGERALD: Oh yeah? Really?

(**BLIXA** *does another line.*)

I'm a little high. A little fucked up, too. Maybe we could just kiss a little. That'd be good.

(**BLIXA** *leans in and kisses him. Bites his lip.*)

Ow. That's my lip, babe.

BLIXA: I know.

(*They begin to make out, roll around on the floor.*)

You have twenty bags?

FITZGERALD: Yeah. That's the deal, right?

BLIXA: You're not gonna fuck me.

FITZGERALD: Well . . . I'm kinda too high. Maybe you could just gimme head.

BLIXA: No. You're not gonna fuck me.

FITZGERALD: Nah, nah. I'm all about maintaining good diplomatic relations.

BLIXA: Don't think you can burn me 'cause I'm foreign. I know how to use this. If I'm fucked here, I'll find you and you'll pay.

FITZGERALD: I got it. Now put away that boomerang and hunt my crock.

SOME GIRL(s)
BY NEIL LaBUTE

CHARACTERS
GUY *(33), engaged and looking for answers;* SAM *(30s), his ex-girlfriend from high school*

SCENE
A standard hotel room

TIME
The present

GUY *confronts his past relationships as* HE *finally prepares to make a commitment, hoping to figure out what went wrong before* HE *gets married.* SAM *is the first of four ex-girlfriends with whom* GUY *meets.*

SAM: You're very careful with your things.

GUY: Yeah, I picked that up somewhere. . . .

SAM: You must've, because you sure were never like that when I knew you. Back then . . .

GUY: Well, we were just kids, right?

SAM: Eighteen. When you dumped me, I mean. That's an adult.

GUY: True, but that's what it seemed like. To me. *Kids.*

SAM: Whatever. Whatever *you* say . . .

GUY: You are angry.

SAM: Maybe just a touch. Yep.

GUY: Huh. All right . . . Sam, I'm gonna be open with you here. Totally up front. Honest.

SAM: That's promising a lot. . . .

GUY: I know, I know it is, but I'm gonna be, and, well, I just am. (*Beat.*) I think the reason we broke up back then—

SAM: Not we. You. *You* ended it.

GUY: Yes, but...

SAM: It wasn't a "we" thing. "We" was when we were a couple, *we* decided to start dating, *we* would choose what movie to go to on Friday night, but the finishing-it-off part? That was *you*. . . .

GUY: I know that. I do. I do know it. . . . So, yeah, I stopped calling, coming over, but it wasn't any one thing that prompted it, it wasn't . . . and for some reason, I always had the idea that you thought you'd done something . . . some . . .

SAM: No . . . (*Beat.*) I . . . no.

GUY: Oh. 'Cause my mom said that the two of you had talked, and—not, like, recently, I mean, but back in the day, back whenever—and she . . .

SAM: . . . I never said that. . . .

GUY: No, but implied it, *insinuated* that I'd led you to believe that you'd done something, and—

SAM: I don't think that was the case. . . .

GUY: . . . and I just wanted you to know, as in better late than never, that it wasn't anything of the sort.

SAM: I know. I *know* that. . . . I mean, why would I think that? I wouldn't.

GUY: Right, so I'm just reiterating for you, then—albeit a bit late in the game— you did nothing wrong.

SAM: Thanks.

GUY: It was me. All me. I needed to, ahh . . .

SAM: What? What did you "need"?

GUY: Or "wanted" to, I dunno. I felt, like, at the time . . . I wanted to have my freedom, do the college thing somewhere other than over at Community or maybe just pursue my writing stuff. Whatever. And *you* were a girl that I could sort of look at, you know, take a glance at and maybe . . . see her whole future.

SAM: Really?

GUY: A bit. Yeah. And that's not bad or anything, it's not, but you're just that type of woman. And I think, if I can say this . . .

SAM: . . . Go on, you're on a roll. . . .

Guy: ... History has proved me right. It has. You ended up almost exactly like I figured you would.

Sam: Oh, have I, now? (*Beat.*) Huh...

Guy: ... Well, kinda. (*Beat.*) I mean, still here, with kids and your husband doing what I pretty much would've guessed he'd be doing... and back then, when I'm just this scared teenager staring eternity in the face, I could see *myself* with that produce manager's vest on and I suppose I got nervous and backed out of the situation the best way I knew how.... (*Beat.*) So.

Sam: ... He's not the produce manager. He runs the store. The whole thing.

Guy: Oh. Okay.

Sam: He's the *store* manager. There is a difference.

Guy: Granted. Sorry...

Sam: Forget it.

Guy: ... I am sorry. You're not mad, are you?

Sam: No, I'm fine.

Guy: Because I didn't want to...

Sam: I said I'm fine. Just believe me, okay? I believe you, so why don't you go ahead and believe me....

Guy: ... All right. I'll... yeah. Fine.

Sam: ... And that's really it? That's the *whole* reason why we suddenly just ended like that? Because you had a *vision* of working at some Safeway for the rest of your life?

Guy: Basically, yeah... I mean...

Sam: Not some other girl?

Guy: Umm, no, not that I... I don't, you know. I don't *recall* anybody else.

Sam: No? You don't?

Guy: Uh-uh.

Sam: 'Cause I always had this vague, you know... this *worry* about that. Back in "the day." Back whenever...

Guy: No... we were going out for, like...

SAM: Two years. A little over.... We were "promised" to each other for two years. (*Beat.*) And you never went to the prom with somebody else? Right?

GUY: ... No. You know that. No, I even ... I worked that night. *On* prom night. (*Beat.*) It was our senior spring, and after we broke up I was—

SAM: *You*, okay? *You* broke it off. Just say it.... (*Beat.*) Look, I don't even wanna think about this, not at all, I don't. I'm a *mother* now ... a wife and a mother and this is like some ancient Greek history! Why did you have to call me about this? Do this to me ...? Huh?

GUY: I wanted to ... I don't know. To just make sure that we were ... okay.

SAM: Yeah, fine, yes ... we're okay. A-OK. Is that what you needed? Is that gonna be enough to get you back to your something special life in ... where is it, again?

GUY: New York. I have a place in Brooklyn now, but I teach up near ... doesn't matter. It's all ... New York. City.

(*Silence for a moment as this all gets processed.*)

SAM: Wow. Geez, it's amazing how ... it's all still pretty fresh. You know? I mean, you think it's gone, put in some box under your bed, but God ... somebody mentions a dance or a boy you knew and it's, like, just *right* there. Instantly it's ... there.

GUY: Yep. That's true.

SAM: Yeah. (*Beat.*) Guess it's partly due to the whole "virginity" thing....

GUY: ... Right. I feel the same way.

SAM: Well, that's great. *Terrific.* At least we have that....

GUY: I am sorry about stirring up all the— (*Checks his watch.*) It's almost quarter of.

SAM: 'Kay. Thanks.... (*Beat.*) I know that you're looking at my face. I feel you doing that—it's a skin thing. Sometimes after a baby your pigment can get all ... doesn't matter. Anyway, take care. Good to see you, I guess....

GUY: Hey, Sam ... you, too. Seriously. I hope I didn't ...

SOME GIRL(s)
BY NEIL LaBUTE

CHARACTERS
GUY *(33), engaged and looking for answers;* LINDSAY *(30s–40s), his former co-worker*

SCENE
A standard hotel room

TIME
The present

GUY *invites* LINDSAY, *a married woman with whom* HE *had sex years ago, to a hotel room in an effort to fix his mistakes before* HE *gets married.* LINDSAY *is the third of four ex-girlfriends that* GUY *contacts.*

LINDSAY: . . . And, so, how do we go about it? Making that happen?

GUY: I'm not sure. . . .

LINDSAY: How do you help me, you know . . . get back some of the dignity I lost? A small bit of that back . . . ?

GUY: Well . . . I could . . . I mean, I suppose I *could* go out there, you know, to the car, and talk to him. If that's what you really, *really* want . . .

LINDSAY: Hmmm . . .

GUY: . . . something like that. I don't see what we gain by it, but . . .

LINDSAY: No, you're right. It doesn't really even out . . . not after all the time that's passed. Uh-uh.

GUY: . . . Or I could . . . ahhh . . .

LINDSAY: . . . You wanna know what he thinks? My husband, I mean . . . what he thinks you should do?

GUY: Ummmmm . . . no, what?

LINDSAY: This woman you're marrying . . . you haven't said much about her. . . .

GUY: Not that much to tell, really. . . .

LINDSAY: . . . She'd probably be surprised to hear that.

GUY: I mean, not *so* much. Studying to be a nurse, and, ahhh . . . you know. Some girl is all. This girl that I'm . . .

LINDSAY: Yes?

GUY: I mean, she's *terrific*, of course, she's definitely that. But . . .

LINDSAY: . . . What? She's what?

GUY: Nothing. I just . . . I'm not really so keen to drag her into this.

LINDSAY: I see. Fine. (*Smiles.*) She's younger than me, right?

GUY: Hmmm?

LINDSAY: Younger than me.

GUY: Ahh, yeah. Yes. She's 23. Well, in April . . .

LINDSAY: Nice. How nice. *Youth.* (*Beat.*) Back then, when it was over, I was sure that was one of the reasons, the *main* reason, that you didn't stay. That you left me. My age.

GUY: . . . No, not just that . . . I mean, no.

LINDSAY: Well, that's what I imagined. Told myself, anyway. That it wasn't for a real reason, not some reason that would actually *matter* . . . but because I was older than you.

GUY: I liked your age. I did. . . .

LINDSAY: And the fact that your bride-to-be is younger sort of nails it for me. I mean, kind of.

GUY: Lindsay, no, it really wasn't . . .

LINDSAY: So tell me something—what's the, tell me what you think would be the most hurtful thing you could do to her? This fiancée of yours . . .

GUY: Listen . . . I don't even want to . . .

LINDSAY: . . . It's speculation. That's all. We are just *imagining*. So . . . what would it be?

GUY: I dunno.

LINDSAY: So, what if . . . you cheated on her? Even though you're not married yet.

GUY: ... She'd hate it. I mean, what do you think?

LINDSAY: I believe she would, because she trusts you. She's put her trust *into* you.

GUY: Yes.

LINDSAY: See, that's what my husband thinks, too. He said that very thing. That the worst thing wouldn't be what we could do to you ... but to her. For you to hurt her in some way...

GUY: Oh.

LINDSAY: ... And I agree. I agree with that. Because it's the other person who feels the pain.

GUY: Right. Maybe we should, ummmm ...

LINDSAY: So, I mean, since you've *promised* to make things all better... that's what we'd like you to do.

GUY: I'm not following you ...

LINDSAY: We would like you to sleep with me. Again. *Now.*

GUY: What ...? Why?

LINDSAY: Because you don't want to. And she wouldn't want you to, either.

GUY: But, I don't see where that ...

LINDSAY: It's not really for you to see. It really is for somebody else. These someone *elses* that you hurt a while ago and didn't have the guts to say "I'm sorry" to. (*Beat.*) Do you want the drapes open or closed?

GUY: Wait, no.... Look, I realize that you're mad, Lindsay, I get that now.

LINDSAY: Good, I'm glad that's coming across for you....

GUY: I do understand that. Totally. But I cannot ... no. I can't.

LINDSAY: Yes, you can.

GUY: No ...

LINDSAY: Yes ...

GUY: ... Noooo ...

LINDSAY: I said yes.

GUY: Ahh, and I said no, okay? I mean, I can do this all day long, if you'd like, but...(*Beat.*) I *want* to do something here, I do, but I can't do...that.

LINDSAY: You said you *would*. You said you would make it up to me.

GUY: I know, I know that, but...I *can't*.

LINDSAY: Can and will. You *will* do this! Do it while my husband sits down there in our Outback and waits for me....

(*The man takes this in. The woman goes for another sip of water but realizes the bottle is empty.*)

GUY: Why would I do that? I mean...and you, why would *you* want to? It's...

LINDSAY: Does she know?

GUY: What? Does who know...?

LINDSAY: About your little trip here. All these stops you're making...

GUY: You mean...?

LINDSAY: You know *exactly* what I mean. Does your girlfriend know about this?

GUY: ...No. God, no.

(*The woman moves to her coat, takes a piece of paper out.*)

LINDSAY: Shall we call her? It's Alex, right? My husband tracked her down.

SOUND
BY ROBERT PATRICK

CHARACTERS
DOROTHY PARKER *(30-ish) is a pert, pretty New Yorker;* NOËL COWARD *(30-ish) is smooth, groomed, British.*

SCENE
A party at Gloria Swanson's mansion in a room decorated like a South Seas saloon

TIME
1920s

As Gloria Swanson pursues the hot new actor, Rudolph Valentino—with whom she wants to co-star in a self-produced film version of Camille, *directed by Erich Von Stroheim and backed by Mary Pickford—*DOROTHY *sits on a stool, drinking;* NOËL *appears at the door.*

DOROTHY: Aloha.

NOËL: This is the seventeenth bar I've found in this historical exhibit. How many bars does it take to make a prison?

DOROTHY: One, if you work it right.

NOËL: May I come in and gather some local color? I'm writing a book called *Around the World by Tramp Steamer.*

DOROTHY: Come right in, Mister Steamer. May I call you Tramp?

NOËL: (*Saunters in and takes a stool.*) All the best people do. Well, the Austrian director is meditating in the Florentine ballroom. The Man of the West is demonstrating rope tricks to America's Sweetheart in a Japanese pavilion. The Merry Widow is having a nervous breakdown in the French gardens. And the god and goddess of love are romping in a Pompeian swimming pool. What's playing in the Honolulu Room?

DOROTHY: (*Pours him a drink.*) Hamlet contemplates suicide.

NOËL: You're very quiet.

DOROTHY: I'm not speaking to myself. (*Toasts him.*) Hamlet toasts the ghost and downs the hatch.

Noël: You're all talk. How can they turn a book of yours into a film?

Dorothy: How does one turn anything into a film? By spreading it very, very thin.

Noël: They do seem to squeak by without us, don't they?

Dorothy: In Hollywood, to coin a phrase, the word is out. They get paid for not talking—like blackmailers.

Noël: I know I should resent that, but I can't help thinking—

Dorothy: That doesn't pay any better than writing.

Noël: —that there is a certain poetry in their shadow-shows. There are, after all, very few things that people actually do. We stand, sit, and lie, walk, run, and crawl—

Dorothy: And drink more than is good for us, if we know what's good for us.

Noël: —and the silent cinema reduces all the complexities of life to those few rudimentary reflexes: kiss, kill, coddle—

Dorothy: Rape, pillage and foreclose.

Noël: —and yet, even as we writers sink here in the West, I find I pity a generation brought up purely on pantomime. Those few things people do are so repetitious, so boring—

Dorothy: Rape and pillage never pall.

Noël: —and it is only the style of the great poets, Shakespeare, Homer, Milton, Moses—

Dorothy: Irving Berlin. God, I love that man!

Noël: —that give poor little life any meaning at all. I weep not only for us as they bar us from Paradise, but for them in a world of gestures, without any meaning at all.

Dorothy: Not that I don't relish our growing closeness, but why aren't they filming you in Britain?

Noël: Only Americans can make movies. The British cannot distinguish between a film and a fog.

Dorothy: Speaking of fogs, I told my producer that Hamlet had an Oedipus Complex. He said, "A boy is always smart to get into real estate."

Noël: I told mine he should do a film about Socrates, and he asked me, "What are Socrates?"

DOROTHY: So do you think the Princess from Pittsburgh will succeed in making Rudolph Vaselino?

NOËL: There's no forecasting Americans in love. You celebrate Saint Valentine's Day with a massacre.

DOROTHY: Love should be so simple. A loves B. B loves A. They roll around on each other and spell AB, BA, ABBA, BABA. But there are all those other letters waiting in line and the thing turns into alphabet soup. I envy the Babylonians. They didn't have any vowels.

NOËL: How you do go on.

DOROTHY: Well, if you can be Peter Pan, I can be Wendy.

NOËL: What are we doing in this illiterate Eden?

DOROTHY: I'm trying to present a moving target to the little boy with the arrows. No, on the train coming out here I wrote a hateful movie about Broadway. On the train back, I'll write a hateful play about Hollywood. It's a living. Your turn.

NOËL: I'm running from bigger boys with bigger arrows. No, I wish to understand this curious beast, America, and Hollywood seems to be its heart.

DOROTHY: Or some part bloody and beating.

NOËL: If I could comprehend the film industry, I think I should have a grip on the U.S.A.

DOROTHY: Fate has sent me to you. It's simple. The film industry consists of Jewish producers in California trying to convince Catholic bankers in New York that they know which fantasies will sell to Protestant farmers in Nebraska.

NOËL: The only great religion omitted is the Muslims.

DOROTHY: They have something better.

NOËL: And what is that?

DOROTHY: Hashish.

NOËL: Gesundheit.

(**THEY** *toast one another and toss down another drink.*)

SOUVENIR
BY STEPHEN TEMPERLY

CHARACTERS

FLORENCE FOSTER JENKINS *(middle-aged), a wealthy woman without musical talent who labors under the misguided belief that* SHE *is a major vocal artist;* COSIMO MCMOON *(29), a not-so-successful song composer, and* FLORENCE'S *rather unenthusiastic accompanist*

SCENE
An elegant music room at the Ritz-Carlton

TIME
The 1930s

MCMOON *has just finished playing "Crazy Rhythm" on the piano as* FLORENCE FOSTER JENKINS *enters.*

FLORENCE FOSTER JENKINS: Is that what they call jazz? Is it? Goodness, Cosme! (*Caresses the piano.*) You've quite shocked the Bechstein.

COSIMO MCMOON: Music is music.

FLORENCE FOSTER JENKINS: And people sing that song and they dance? Is that what happens? Your friends, for example. When you and Kurt—such a personable young man!—when you and he are entertaining young ladies. You bad boys.

COSIMO MCMOON: (*Embarrassed.*) Shouldn't we get to work

FLORENCE FOSTER JENKINS: (*Crossing away from him, oblivious.*) I could almost picture myself singing it. I imagine it would create quite a sensation.

COSIMO MCMOON: Here at the Ritz? . . . I don't know. Your audience expects something different.

FLORENCE FOSTER JENKINS: Ah! But what if we were to find ourselves with a different kind of audience?

COSIMO MCMOON: Different?

FLORENCE FOSTER JENKINS: Different.

COSIMO MCMOON: In what way?

Florence Foster Jenkins: Suppose we suddenly found ourselves with more seats to sell?

Cosimo McMoon: More...seats?

Florence Foster Jenkins: Many more.

Cosimo McMoon: But you've...Madame J, you've been sold out for weeks!

Florence Foster Jenkins: True.

Cosimo McMoon: Why would you need more seats?

Florence Foster Jenkins: So that many more music lovers could pay their two-forty to attend.

Cosimo McMoon: You've already got five hundred coming. Isn't that enough?

Florence Foster Jenkins: Think of my charities, Cosme! Think what such a box-office boost could mean.

Cosimo McMoon: Boost?

Florence Foster Jenkins: Boost. You see, it's been proposed.... Quite out of the blue. That we move our recital. To a larger...venue. Which is rather exciting. Don't you think?

Cosimo McMoon: But... (**He** *rises and crosses to her.*) I thought you were happy here at the Ritz.

Florence Foster Jenkins: Up to a point.

Cosimo McMoon: I thought you liked the intimacy of the ballroom.

Florence Foster Jenkins: Yes and no.

Cosimo McMoon: Exactly what are we talking? How much larger?

Florence Foster Jenkins: Believe me, we will make quite a splash. There is considerable anticipation among those in the know.

Cosimo McMoon: And you just...?! I mean, its arranged?! Just like that?!

Florence Foster Jenkins: It's come as a shock. I quite understand.

Cosimo McMoon: I should say so.

Florence Foster Jenkins: I was telephoned, Cosme. And this was *proposed*.

Cosimo McMoon: Proposed? (*Crosses away, returning to the piano bench.*) What was proposed? Move us where? The Hippodrome?

FLORENCE FOSTER JENKINS: Not. Quite.

COSIMO McMOON: Where? (*Terrified,* **HE** *jumps to his feet and rushes back to her.*) Dear God—tell me where!

FLORENCE FOSTER JENKINS: (*Reverently.*) Town Hall.

COSIMO McMOON: (*Appalled.*) Town Hall?

FLORENCE FOSTER JENKINS: It's been proposed that we move our recital there, Cosme. Where they have guaranteed there will not be a single empty seat. Not one!

COSIMO McMOON: But...!

FLORENCE FOSTER JENKINS: Of course I knew I had a following. I'm not blind after all. But I must say, I had no idea I was quite so... popular! (**SHE** *sits in the chair.*)

COSIMO McMOON: I can't believe what you're telling me.

FLORENCE FOSTER JENKINS: I could hardly believe it myself.

COSIMO McMOON: (*His hysteria growing.*) I mean, what have I been doing all this time? All this rehearsing! This isn't easy for me. I'm trying to... what's right for you. (*He snaps, lashing out at her.*) I could just let you *sing!* You know? But I don't. Because I worry. And because I do the decent thing everyone assumes I'll just go along...! With whatever... crazy...! (*Becoming speechless.*)

FLORENCE FOSTER JENKINS: (*To calm him.*) Shh! Cosme, dear Cosme, think what's at stake. In these perilous times. With so many in need. How can I refuse? We must all try to do some good in the world.

COSIMO McMOON: (*His vehemence born of desperation.*) But at what *price?*

FLORENCE FOSTER JENKINS: (*Startled.*) I beg your pardon?

COSIMO McMOON: At what *price?*

FLORENCE FOSTER JENKINS: I don't understand.

COSIMO McMOON: Your artistic standards. What of them?

FLORENCE FOSTER JENKINS: (**SHE** *moves to him, alarmed.*) *Como dice?*

(*Now that* **HE** *has her attention,* **HE** *pursues his advantage, improvising frantically.*)

COSIMO McMOON: Your voice in a barn like Town Hall?

FLORENCE FOSTER JENKINS: Barn?

COSIMO MCMOON: They didn't tell you? About the acoustics? I mean it's famous. For how you can't hear.

FLORENCE FOSTER JENKINS: You can't?

COSIMO MCMOON: You think you've gone deaf.

FLORENCE FOSTER JENKINS: Deaf?

COSIMO MCMOON: (*Advances on her, backing her into the chair.*) To go from our little room to that great monster...! It's something that should be approached gradually, very gradually. If at all.

FLORENCE FOSTER JENKINS: Surely we can rehearse. Prepare.

COSIMO MCMOON: And what if *strain* should be induced? What then?

FLORENCE FOSTER JENKINS: (*Unnerved.*) Strain? (*With one hand* **SHE** *caresses her throat.*)

COSIMO MCMOON: It could undermine all we've worked for. I can't allow that. Won't. I don't care what they say.

FLORENCE FOSTER JENKINS: (*Her other hand goes to her throat.*) Strain?

COSIMO MCMOON: Strain. (*Seeing that* **HE** *has won,* **HE** *crosses back to the piano.*) Mrs. Jenkins, listen, if your concern is extra revenue—wouldn't the same result be achieved by adding an additional recital here at the Ritz? At least that way there won't be any...

FLORENCE FOSTER JENKINS: Strain. (*Humbly.*) What can I say? You saved me from myself.

COSIMO MCMOON: (*Modestly.*) Well.

FLORENCE FOSTER JENKINS: *Mille grazie, signor buon fortuna.*

COSIMO MCMOON: (*Sits.*) *Prego.* I guess.

FLORENCE FOSTER JENKINS: To abuse my voice is unthinkable. After all, one is not a trombone.

COSIMO MCMOON: Exactly!

FLORENCE FOSTER JENKINS: We shall add two more recitals to our present schedule.

COSIMO MCMOON: Two...!

FLORENCE FOSTER JENKINS: (*To indulge him.*) Very well—three. But no more! How right you are, Cosme. And how very wise. There is no good reason to move. There is every reason to stay. I shall explain to Town Hall. Let them find someone else to sing in their barn! Some mezzo or other. (*Gathering her possessions from the table.*) Forgive me for not consulting you first. It shall not happen again. Strain!

SOUVENIR
BY STEPHEN TEMPERLY

CHARACTERS
FLORENCE FOSTER JENKINS *(middle-aged), a wealthy woman without musical talent who labors under the misguided belief that* **SHE** *is a major vocal artist;* **COSIMO McMOON** *(40s), a not-so-successful song composer who has become her devoted accompanist*

SCENE
A backstage dressing room at Carnegie Hall

TIME
1944

FLORENCE FOSTER JENKINS *has just completed a Carnegie Hall concert, and realized that the audience has found her not a great concert artist as* **SHE** *had believed, but a hilarious joke.*

FLORENCE FOSTER JENKINS: Why didn't you tell me?

COSIMO McMOON: (*Unable to answer directly.*) They gave me a piano. (*A pause.*) So I could warm up.

(**SHE** *crosses in silence to the piano.* **COSME** *observes her, uncertain how best to proceed in the face of such a disaster.*)

FLORENCE FOSTER JENKINS: (*Simply.*) You didn't tell me. Why didn't you tell me?

COSIMO McMOON: (*After a pause.*) Toscanini dresses here. (*A pause.*) Right in this room.

FLORENCE FOSTER JENKINS: When I begged you.

COSIMO McMOON: Think of that.

FLORENCE FOSTER JENKINS: Cosme, why didn't you tell me?

COSIMO McMOON: What? What is it, Madame Flo?

FLORENCE FOSTER JENKINS: Have I been so... (**SHE** *can hardly bring herself to say the word.*) foolish?

COSIMO McMOON: (*Not to be deflected from his course.*) I thought it went... very well.

FLORENCE FOSTER JENKINS: Have I?

COSIMO MCMOON: Really. Very well.

FLORENCE FOSTER JENKINS: How could you let me make such a fool of myself?

COSIMO MCMOON: I don't... you just had a huge success. Out there. Huge.

FLORENCE FOSTER JENKINS: (*Turns away from him.*) Don't!

COSIMO MCMOON: Didn't you hear them at the end?

FLORENCE FOSTER JENKINS: At the end. They... (**SHE** *sits on the chaise.*) Cosme, I heard them...!

COSIMO MCMOON: They were just... loving you. Didn't you hear? It was... quite huge. Didn't you hear that?

FLORENCE FOSTER JENKINS: I thought...

(**SHE** *turns from him.* **HE** *rises.*)

COSIMO MCMOON: What? What did you think?

FLORENCE FOSTER JENKINS: I didn't know what to think!

COSIMO MCMOON: Let me tell you... I don't mind admitting I was quite nervous. Before we began. I didn't know how they were going to take you. But, boy! They really loved you.

FLORENCE FOSTER JENKINS: Did they?

COSIMO MCMOON: Loved. You. A whole big concert hall full of strangers and they loved you.

FLORENCE FOSTER JENKINS: Did they really?

COSIMO MCMOON: Really.

FLORENCE FOSTER JENKINS: Cosme, would you tell me?

COSIMO MCMOON: (*Crosses toward her.*) On my way in I was talking to a soldier—just a kid—he was tickled pink he was going to get to hear you. He didn't know where he'd end up. But wherever he goes he's going to have some happy memories after tonight. He'll be one happy G.I.

FLORENCE FOSTER JENKINS: Happy?

COSIMO MCMOON: Oh, yes! Very happy! You could hear them. They were just eating it up. You could hear them. Didn't you hear them? Didn't you hear how happy they were?

FLORENCE FOSTER JENKINS: I heard, I thought...

COSIMO McMOON: What did you hear?

FLORENCE FOSTER JENKINS: I thought they were laughing, Cosme. Were they? Were they laughing? You expect that in "The Laughing Song." That's to be expected. But the "Ave"? My beloved "Ave"? Why would they laugh? I don't understand.

COSIMO McMOON: (*Comes closer, choosing his words with care. Very gently.*) You've heard of nervous laughter? You know how when an audience sees something just overwhelming and they can't deal with their emotion...the only way they can release it sometimes is to laugh. You must know that. That's so well known. I'm surprised you don't know that. You could ask anyone and they'll tell you. How many singers today can provoke that kind of reaction? I'll tell you—very few. There are very, very few.

FLORENCE FOSTER JENKINS: I saw them with handkerchiefs....I'd seen that before but I thought...I imagined something quite...

COSIMO McMOON: Well, of course. You wouldn't want them sobbing, would you? Just bawling their eyes out.

FLORENCE FOSTER JENKINS: I didn't know what was wrong. I thought I was in voice.

COSIMO McMOON: You were. You were in *fine* voice.

FLORENCE FOSTER JENKINS: Some things I always sing well, but one or two I thought I'd never sung better. The Mozart, for example...

(**HE** *sits beside her.*)

COSIMO McMOON: Unforgettable!

FLORENCE FOSTER JENKINS: Dear Cosme...! (**SHE** *brings her handkerchief up to cover her eyes and sobs as if her heart is breaking.*)

COSIMO McMOON: (*Tenderly.*) I don't know why you're upset. I thought you'd be happy. Why aren't you happy? Look what you did. You had a triumph. (*Emphatically.*) You gave those people something they'll never forget.

FLORENCE FOSTER JENKINS: (*Speaking with difficulty, through her tears.*) You wouldn't...ever tell me things...that weren't true...would you, Cosme? For whatever reason. You wouldn't ever...lie to me?

COSIMO McMOON: I would never do that. Never.

Florence Foster Jenkins: You promise me? You swear?

Cosimo McMoon: (*Holds up one hand.*) I swear on all that's holy I would never lie to you. Never. Do you believe me?

Florence Foster Jenkins: I'm . . .

Cosimo McMoon: Do you? (*Mock rough.*) You better believe me!

(**He** *pretends to box with her as with a child.* **She** *laughs abruptly.* **They** *laugh together.* **She** *dries her tears.*)

Florence Foster Jenkins: I was so afraid . . .

Cosimo McMoon: I don't know what you think went on out there.

Florence Foster Jenkins: I didn't know what to think.

Cosimo McMoon: You're overtired. From all the excitement.

Florence Foster Jenkins: I felt . . . I felt I was lost. I didn't like that.

Cosimo McMoon: No one likes that.

Florence Foster Jenkins: I felt . . . (*With a burst of energy, rising.*) I *do* feel quite tired!

Cosimo McMoon: You're bound to be tired. Look what you did!

(**She** *makes her way to the piano, touches it gently.*)

Florence Foster Jenkins: Toscanini really dresses here? If only he could have heard me tonight! I imagine he would have much to say. (*Shyly.*) Cosme, if Mr. Mozart had been here, do you think he'd have been pleased?

Cosimo McMoon: I think he'd have been very pleased. Very.

Florence Foster Jenkins: I do hope he'd have been pleased. And Mr. Verdi. Mr. Gounod. All of them. (**She** *sits on the bench, allowing her fingertips to caress the keys. Almost mournful.*) Since I was a girl, you know, I've dreamed of such a night. And now it's gone. It was ahead of me. It was there to be hoped for. But now it's over. It's in the past. A memory. If only we could live in the music forever, Cosme. If only it could go on and on. But of course it can't. Of course it has to end. (*With an abrupt change of tone.*) I must get changed! (**She** *rises to face him as* **He** *sits on the chaise.*) You will come to the party, won't you? You won't desert me.

Cosimo McMoon: (*Solemnly, He rises to face her.*) As if I could.

FLORENCE FOSTER JENKINS: (*Almost shyly.*) I should so like to leave with you. Perhaps you would escort me to our reception? Unless...

COSIMO McMOON: (*With a formal tenderness.*) I should be honored. (**HE** *offers his hands.*) Truly.

FLORENCE FOSTER JENKINS: (*Taking his hands.*) Thank you. Dear Cosme. Thank you. For telling me the truth. In my heart of hearts I never really doubted that you would.

(*Exit, FFJ.* **HE** *watches her go.*)

COSIMO McMOON: Within a month she was dead.

STUFF HAPPENS
BY DAVID HARE

CHARACTERS
COLIN POWELL *(50s), U.S. Secretary of State, who is becoming more and more* persona non grata *as an opponent of the administration's plan to go to war with Iraq;* CONDOLEEZZA RICE *(40s), the tough-minded head of the National Security Agency, with close personal ties to President George W. Bush*

SCENE
Condi's office

TIME
Post-9/11, pre-Iraq invasion

(RICE *is in her office at night.* POWELL *appears.*)

POWELL: Condi...you busy?

RICE: I'm busy. Busy enough. Come in.

(THEY *both smile.*)

How you getting on? You close?

POWELL: Still that word.

RICE: The President's very firm about this. Lose the little things, you start losing the big ones.

POWELL: (HE *nods slightly.*) Condi, the French aren't stupid. They know we'll go to war if we have to.

RICE: So?

POWELL: I'm trying to avoid war.

RICE: We're all trying to avoid war.

POWELL: Yeah. (POWELL *looks at her, not believing her.*) Look, they're offering a formula. It's words. Words set out in a certain order. It satisfies their honour and it satisfies us. They're going to say we need a second resolution, we're going to say we don't. You can read it either way.

RICE: That good, eh?

(**THEY** *both smile.*)

POWELL: All we want is a headline: 'US Achieves Iraq Resolution'. I can get fourteen votes. . . .

RICE: Fourteen?

POWELL: Maybe fifteen. Even Syria. Who knows? But I have to give in to the French. On this one thing. It's a way of saying, 'Look, we're not going to give you nothing.'

(**RICE** *stares, undecided.*)

We were going to do this in two weeks, remember? Do we want it to take longer? Do we want it to fail? I don't think so.

RICE: Do you like this guy?

POWELL: He's a self-defined intellectual who writes biographies of Napoleon. He destroyed my daughter's wedding to discuss 'and' and 'or'.

RICE: You like him.

(**POWELL** *looks her in the eye.*)

POWELL: Condi, I'm telling you: He gave me his word.

RICE: Okay.

POWELL: That means something.

(**THEY** *stare at one another a moment.*)

Do you think . . . do you think you could speak to the President?

RICE: Why don't you speak to him?

(**THEY** *both know the answer, so neither speaks.*)

POWELL: No point in being a trusted adviser unless she gives some trusted advice.

(**RICE** *smiles in assent.*)

Thank you.

(**POWELL** *goes.* **RICE** *sits alone.*)

THEY'RE JUST LIKE US
BY BOO KILLEBREW

CHARACTERS
RICHARD *(late 20s, early 30s) has found a life "softer" than the fast-paced New York scene as a high-school drama teacher;* BETH *(late 20s, early 30s) yearns to be a famous Oscar-winning actress, but cannot forget the love they had together.*

SCENE
RICHARD'S *house*

TIME
The present

(RICHARD *walks into his house.* BETH *is in there, pacing.* HE *is surprised to see her.*)

RICHARD: How did you get into my house?

BETH: I broke your window.

RICHARD: You broke the window?

BETH: I am a passionate person.

RICHARD: What are you doing here?

BETH: I wanted to see you.

RICHARD: So you just show up and break my window?

BETH: I am an impulsive and passionate woman. Don't worry, the paparazzi don't know I'm here.

RICHARD: Okay.

(SHE *goes to kiss him and* HE *pushes her away. It is awkward.*)

BETH: It's really good to see you.

RICHARD: Yeah?

BETH: You know I really missed you.

RICHARD: Yeah?

BETH: Of course. It's nice to see your face.

RICHARD: Thank you.

BETH: How are you?

RICHARD: Peaceful and quiet and easy and good.

BETH: Good, are you—

RICHARD: Not a lot of buzz, buzz, buzzing going on around here, it's not loud here. I can slow down and sit still.

BETH: Yeah, I've been trying to go a little slower myself these days. I'm walking slower, leaving my cell phone at home, sitting in the park, petting dogs, calling my mom. I really have slowed down and it feels really good.

RICHARD: Yeah?

BETH: Yeah.

RICHARD: Really?

BETH: You don't believe me?

RICHARD: No, I believe you. I'm glad you're doing whatever you need to do to make yourself happy.

BETH: Thanks.

(*Pause.*)

RICHARD: How's the career?

BETH: Fine, I'm not really worried about it these days, like I said, I'm just trying to take it one day at a time.

RICHARD: Right.

BETH: I did get a new agent.

RICHARD: Yeah?

BETH: He really believes that I am a character actress, which is what I've known for years, so it's good that we are on the same page.

RICHARD: Great.

BETH: Oh, I did an eight-episode arc on that show "Divine Justice."

RICHARD: Great show.

BETH: Yeah, I was the head of an Internet pedophile sex-slave ring while that actor—the one who is sort of cross-eyed—talked about evidence and all that.

RICHARD: Great.

(*Pause.*)

BETH: I'm thinking about taking a break.

RICHARD: Really?

BETH: Yeah—just taking off and going somewhere quiet and resting and swimming and driving and all that.

RICHARD: You think you'd like that?

BETH: You know I would like that.

RICHARD: Where would you go?

BETH: Oh, I don't know. (*Gives him a little smile.*) Somewhere with space and roads and soft people.

RICHARD: Where would that be?

BETH: Why are you being such an asshole?

RICHARD: What?

BETH: You know exactly how you're behaving and don't act like you don't.

RICHARD: I don't know what—

BETH: I came all the way down here! I flew down here to see you. To tell you I'm sorry! That I will stop living my life the way I was living it if that will make you happy. I want to be with you. You know that's why I'm here. You know that's why I'm here and you're just standing there with your one-word sentences—making me swim around in my own stupid words. You're just standing there thinking of how stupid I am.

RICHARD: I am not—

BETH: I'll do anything you want. Happily. I will give myself to you. I want to be slow and I want to be soft and I want to be with you.

RICHARD: I don't want you to change who you are, that's not what I want. I love who you are.

BETH: But you can't be with who I are!

RICHARD: I can't, but I would never want you to change for me.

BETH: What do you want? Please tell me what you want!

RICHARD: I want you to be happy.

BETH: I'm happy with you.

RICHARD: You would be for a while. Then you would start looking out again.

BETH: No, I won't. I won't look out anymore.

RICHARD: Yes, you will.

BETH: You love me, but you don't want to be with me?

RICHARD: I love you so much. I do love you.

BETH: But you don't want to be with me?

(**HE** *is quiet.*)

You don't ever want to be with me?

(**HE** *doesn't answer.* **SHE** *cries.* **THEY** *are standing at opposite ends of the room.*)

RICHARD: Look at all that passion.

(**SHE** *looks at him.*)

You're really good.

(**SHE** *runs out.*)

V-E DAY
BY FAYE SHOLITON

CHARACTERS
EVIE *(18), involved in the war effort;* **BERNIE** *(20s), her best friend's brother*

SCENE
The living room of **EVIE's** *home in Cleveland Heights*

TIME
June 1943

In this recollected meeting, **EVIE** *has been shooting pinup poses of Lil for the newsletter she sends to the troops. Lil's brother* **BERNIE**, *a young man planning to go to law school, arrives for a visit and finds that* **HE** *and* **EVIE** *are very compatible.* **HE** *has just gone to the kitchen to make himself a drink.*

(**BERNIE** *returns with his glass.*)

BERNIE: Cheers!

(**EVIE** *hands* **BERNIE** *a stack of newsletters.*)

EVIE: You stack. I'll staple. [(*To* **LIL**.) You fold.]

(**BERNIE** *and* **EVIE** *will fall into a rhythm of stacking and stapling.*)

BERNIE: (*To* **EVIE**.) So where do you gals collect all this libelous material?

EVIE: Try to get the pages a little more uniform? . . . Canteen, Mounds Club, The Statler Bar . . .

BERNIE: The Statler? How come I've never seen you there?

[**LIL:** She was in diapers.]

BERNIE: Best bourbon in town.

EVIE: Best bar.

BERNIE: Best music.

EVIE: Best dance floor.

[**LIL:** Best be going. (**LIL** *hands her papers to* **BERNIE**.) I know when to fold.

(**Lil** *exits.,* **Bernie** *and* **Evie** *work together.*)]

Evie: Lil tells me you're starting law school.

Bernie: And I walk on water. But enough about me. What about you?

Evie: Just work. Four mornings at a photography studio downtown. Afternoons and weekends in the X-ray department at Mt. Sinai for my pop. He's a radiologist. And starting this week, I drive Fridays for the Red Cross. . . . But I'm *gonna* be a photo journalist. (**Evie** *stops stapling.*)

Bernie: What.

Evie: You're not laughing.

Bernie: Did you say something funny?

(*Pause.*)

Evie: Here's a good one.

Bernie: (*Reads from newsletter.*) "Greetings from Texas, where men are men and women are men. So far, I got a desk job and do absolutely nothing. Next week, I'm getting an assistant."

Evie: Pretty easy to tell who's still stateside. (**Evie** *finds a letter.*) This one wants to know to whom he's indebted for his subscription.

Bernie: His draft board.

Evie: Mind if I use that?

Bernie: May I? (**Bernie** *looks through the mail pile and finds a letter.*) Jesus. "Air Corps Cadet Albie Lazarus." He was a fraternity brother. I didn't know he enlisted. . . . What?! He's gonna be a pilot! Hell, that clown can barely drive a car! I once saw him make a U-turn, to the right! . . . Huh. Half of these have APO addresses already.

Evie: About a third. So how come *you're* not in uniform?

Bernie: What is it with you women and uniforms?

Evie: Why. You 4-F, or something?

Bernie: Does this look like a 4-F body?

Evie: You don't need law school, pal. You already answer every question with another one.

Bernie: Do I? (**Bernie** *resumes his collating task.*)

EVIE: So what about this summer? What's doin'?

BERNIE: You tell *me*.

EVIE: I could use a sports writer. It's lousy wages, but you get all the ice tea you can drink.

BERNIE: What say we discuss it tonight? Over a burger at Mawby's.

EVIE: Can't. I'm a hostess at the Stage Door. . . .

BERNIE: Tomorrow then.

EVIE: Pop and I invited a couple sailors to dinner. You're welcome to join us.

BERNIE: What about Thursday?

EVIE: USO. . . . Tell you what. Friday. We'll grab some chow mein, then do the Statler. (**EVIE** *pulls a carnation from the vase and makes a boutonniere for* **BERNIE**.) Stay right there. (**SHE** *puts on music.*) Gotta see if you can dance.

(**EVIE** *grabs* **BERNIE** *and* **THEY** *dance, in total sync.* **THEY** *dip.*)

Not bad for a 4-F. . . .

BERNIE: I'm not a 4-F.

EVIE: I didn't think you *were*.

(**THEY** *kiss for several beats. Music starts skipping.* **SHE** *breaks away to stop the music.*)

Your ice melted.

WAITING
BY LISA SOLAND

CHARACTERS
BOB *(early 40s), married to* CLAIR *for about fifteen years, enjoys talking;* CLAIR *(late 30s), married to* BOB

SCENE
Lecture hall in the Psych building on college campus

TIME
The present

BOB *and* CLAIR *are sitting on two stools center stage in the lecture hall.* THEY *are addressing the topic of "waiting."*

BOB: (*To audience.*) We did not wait.

CLAIR: (*To audience.*) No.

BOB: We did not even come close to waiting.

CLAIR: No.

(*Pause.*)

BOB: I wanted to but... (HE *makes a head motion toward* CLAIR, *suggesting it was her fault, then whispers to audience.*) ...she's an animal.

(CLAIR *gives a small laugh and shakes her head.*)

Believe me! An animal! (*Beat.*) Never judge a camel by its hump.

CLAIR: (*To him.*) Are you comparing me to a camel?

BOB: (*To* CLAIR.) No. No. I just didn't want to use the old adage, "Never judge a book by its cover."

CLAIR: (*Agreeing with him.*) Yes, that has been overused.

BOB: (*To audience.*) So, we did not wait.

CLAIR: (*To audience, motherly.*) Though we recommend it to others.

BOB: Oh, yes. It's good to wait.

CLAIR: We just got lucky.

BOB: (*Sexually.*) I got *very* lucky.

CLAIR: He's enjoying me in my late thirties. You know...that thing they say about women...

BOB: It's true. (*Leaning in.*) All of it.

CLAIR: But we believe people *should* wait.

BOB: Yes. (*Quick beat.*) But not us.

CLAIR: No.

(**THEY** *finish each other's sentences.*)

BOB: We tried. I tried. For the first three hours...

CLAIR: ...of the first date.

BOB: ...We tried. I tried. (*Beat. To* **CLAIR.**) You weren't trying at all, were you?

CLAIR: No.

BOB: The first three hours we did fine. (*Starting to tell the story.*) I took her to Spago's on Sunset. It was still open then and she wore this...black number.

CLAIR: (*Remembering.*) Oh, yeah.

BOB: On the first date. (*To* **CLAIR.**) What were you thinking?

(**CLAIR** *smiles.*)

And she had on these pumps with little black straps. The dress was strapless but the shoes had 'em. (*Beat.*) And this bright red lipstick on her lips. (*Beat.*) I did the best I could.

CLAIR: (*Reassuring him.*) You did fine.

BOB: You ordered spaghetti and meatballs. (*To audience.*) She ordered spaghetti and meatballs. Now most women would not order spaghetti and meatballs on the first date, but she did.

CLAIR: (*Admitting it.*) I did.

BOB: Spaghetti and meatballs.

CLAIR: I like it. It's good.

BOB: I barely made it through the meal!

CLAIR: You did fine.

BOB: (*To her.*) Should I describe to them ...? (*To audience.*) I'm going to tell you how she.... (*Clears throat.*) She sat there across from me and slowly ingested one strand at a time. And the meatballs she cut into tiny, tiny little pieces....

CLAIR: (*To him.*) That's how I eat.

BOB: (**HE** *takes a deep breath.*) Yes, it is.

CLAIR: (*To audience.*) It's better for the digestion.

BOB: (*To audience.*) That's what she always says. She says that it's good for the digestion.

CLAIR: To eat slowly, yes.

BOB: (*Accusing her.*) Oh, and to take such small bites?!

CLAIR: Yes.

BOB: Well, it's good for other things too.

> (**CLAIR** *shakes her head.*)

This is the part that kills me. She orders a Coke. A Coke! I ordered a glass of, uh ... red wine, I think....

CLAIR: (*Remembering clearly.*) Yes, you did.

BOB: (*Continuing.*) ... to relax me, 'cause I was a bit nervous. You know, first date—sweaty palms, trips to the bathroom, straightening the tie....

CLAIR: You were nervous? You didn't seem nervous to me.

BOB: (*Factually, to her.*) That's because you were too busy eating! (*Continuing with story, to audience.*) She orders a Coke! (*Beat.*) Beware of women who order Cokes.

CLAIR: I like it. It tastes good.

BOB: I barely got through that meal, I'm telling you!

CLAIR: You did fine.

BOB: And of course the Coke has a straw.

CLAIR: (*To audience.*) He remembered the straw.

BOB: (*To her.*) Of course I remember the straw! (*To audience.*) What man doesn't remember the straw?!

CLAIR: Jeez.

BOB: The first time you finished...sipping...(*To audience.*)...She pulled back away from the glass and there was this...*ring of red* left around the curve of the straw and I just couldn't get that out of my head. (**BOB** *removes his glasses and wipes forehead.*) I tried to eat my pot pie...but every time she took a sip, the red line just got thicker and thicker. I thought I was going to lose my mind!

CLAIR: (*Suddenly to audience.*) So, we didn't wait.

BOB: (*Not even close.*) Oh my God, no.

CLAIR: But people should.

BOB: Yes, if they *can*, they *should*.

CLAIR: We just got lucky.

BOB: I got lucky, 'cause I'm telling you, a lot of my friends who didn't...

CLAIR: ...wait.

BOB: Yes, wait. (*To audience.*) A lot of our friends...

CLAIR: ...didn't get so lucky.

BOB: No, they didn't. *Unlucky*, I would say.

CLAIR: It's a crap shoot if you don't wait.

BOB: And we got lucky.

CLAIR: (*To audience.*) Well, we have a lot in common.

BOB: (*To* **CLAIR**) But we didn't know that then. We didn't know anything about each other!

CLAIR: No.

BOB: Next thing you know, we're totally physically addicted to each other and thought that THAT was love, so we got married. (*To* **CLAIR**, *seriously.*) And then we found out what love *really* was.

CLAIR: Yes. (*Flatly, to audience.*) It was the straw.

BOB: (*In reaction to their laughter*) You think she's joking but she's not. We keep them in the house.

CLAIR: (*Explaining the facts to the audience.*) He's dedicated an entire drawer in the kitchen, just for straws.

Bob: Not for the kids.

Clair: No, he won't let the kids go near them.

Bob: Nope.

Clair: Just me.

(*Beat.*)

Bob: That's right. (**He** *quickly turns to* **Clair**, *defensively.*) I see nothing wrong with that.

Clair: (*Shrugging, casually.*) It's fine. (*Simply.*) It's just hard to explain to your children why their daddy won't let them have one single straw, but he makes mommy use ten . . . at a time.

Bob: (*Defending.*) Hey, everyone has to give a little in the family household.

Clair: Yes, you're right, dear.

Bob: But if asked, we *would* recommend that couples wait.

Clair: (*To audience.*) But we didn't.

Bob: (*To audience.*) No.

Clair: And now I have to spend the rest of my life drinking all liquids through a plastic straw.

Bob: (**He** *quickly pulls a straw from his jacket pocket, and presents it to her.*) Thirsty?

(**Clair** *gasps in surprise.*)

WATER MUSIC
BY TINA HOWE

CHARACTERS
OPHELIA *(20s), the character from* Hamlet, *has mysteriously appeared out of the whirlpool;* **JESUS** *(early 30s) is a sexy Latino lifeguard with a passion for swimming.*

SCENE
The whirlpool at a neighborhood health club on the Upper West Side of New York City

TIME
Yesterday

(**OPHELIA** *is tossing flowers into the water.*)

OPHELIA:
"He is dead and gone, lady
He is dead and gone;
At his head a grass-green turf,
At his heels a stone."

JESUS: (*Rushing over to the whirlpool.*) Miss, Miss, it's against the rules to throw flowers in the pool. You'll jam all the filters.

(**OPHELIA** *darts up to the rim of the pool and throws in more flowers.*)

JESUS: (*Grabbing her around the waist.*) Miss, please!

(**HE** *places her back down on the floor. Feeling his arms around her,* **SHE** *guides him into a brief courtly dance.*)

OPHELIA: Lord Hamlet, thou art much changed!

JESUS: My name is Hay-zoos... Hay-zoos Avila Santo Domingo Morales. I'm the lifeguard here. I save the drowning. Whether they walk on land, swim the seas, or fly above. (*A pause, then* **HE** *bows and does a poignant bird call.*)

OPHELIA: Thou know'st the song o' the meadow lark!

(**JESUS** *sings like a tortoise.*)

The ancient tortoise!

(JESUS *sings like a lizard.*)

The lowly lizard!

(JESUS *sings like a porpoise. Ophelia claps her hands with delight.*)

And e'en the paddle-billed porpoise.

(SHE *joins him and* THEY *sing a poignant duet together.*)

JESUS: I know these songs because I was born in Costa Rica. My father was a fisherman. He caught more fish than anyone in our village. And do you know why? Because he couldn't speak like other men. He was born without a tongue. So he sharpened his ears and learned how to listen. He could hear the rain before it fell, the birds gossiping in distant jungles and the fish murmuring on the ocean floor. When he set sail in the morning, the gulls would lead him to his catch. The moment he dropped anchor, he dove into the water and swam with the very fish he was trying to lure into his nets. They told him their stories—about their ancestors who walked on land and their great cities that mysteriously sank into the sea. When I turned 12, he let me swim with him and taught me how to listen as well. Soon I was swimming great distances because the fish would guide me—showing me the safest routes and warning me of approaching storms. They'd sing to me when I got weary and spin tales about the ancient gods that once ruled the earth. Everyone thinks I swim for the glory of the miles I cover, but I do it because I long to be with the creatures of the deep. They entertain me, teach me, and finally make me a better man.

OPHELIA: (*With sudden gravity.*) Dost thou believe, my lord?

JESUS: Believe what?

OPHELIA: In a heart that's pure?

[ROZ: (*Under her breath.*) Lotsa luck!]

OPHELIA: I did possess one once, but then lost it.

JESUS: Where did you lose it?

OPHELIA: If I knew, t'would not be lost, my lord. And you?

JESUS: What about me?

OPHELIA: Where is thy heart?

JESUS: (*After a brief pause.*) In your hands.

[(*Roz mimes playing a violin.*)]

JESUS: All I've ever cared about was swimming, but now that I've met you...
I...I...

OPHELIA: (*Excited.*) Thou swim'st?

JESUS: Great distances. Next month I attempt the English Channel.

OPHELIA: The *English* Channel, my lord? In faith, I've crossed it oft!

JESUS: Thou swim'st too? I knew it! I knew it!

OPHELIA: (*Momentarily lucid.*) No, my lord, I crossed in a ship. In my youth our
family summered oft in England. We traveled by coach to Calais and thence
set sail for Dover. Verily, they were the happiest o' times.... Laertes and I
wouldst clamber to the top o' the crow's nest and there peruse the changing
horizon. At eventide, our father, good Polonius, joined us in our swaying
perch. He knew each constellation's place and wouldst point them out to us.
(*As Polonius.*) "There's Orion's Belt, mark it well...! And there, wretched
Callista, the great bear who weeps for her son she unwittingly slayed with her
own hand."

Laertes and I hung on his every word, his voice sinking and rising wi' the
swells that bore us o'er the waves. Verily, he conversed wi' the wind itself,
waving his arms as if swapping tales wi' a dear old friend. Twas he, my star-
gazing father, who unfurled the twin maps that bind the earth—the
constellations that wink above and the oceans that slumber below. Twas
those very maps that guided me 'neath the waters o' the earth 'til I popped of
a sudden into this... bubbling pool. (**SHE** *returns to the pool and gazes into its
depths.*)

JESUS: Marry me!

OPHELIA: My lord?

JESUS: You're my other half! The bride I've been waiting for.

(**HE** *gently kisses her.*)

OPHELIA: (*Moving away from him.*) My lord!

JESUS: My father told me I'd find you one day.

OPHELIA: In faith, I didst love thee once.

JESUS: Together we'll swim the waters of the earth!

OPHELIA: But then thou came'st to me in my closet, . . . "like sweet bells jangled, out of tune and harsh. . . . "

JESUS: "Sweet bells jangled?"

OPHELIA:
"That unmatcht form and feature of blown youth
Blasted with ecstacy . . . "

JESUS: Yes, ecstasy! Ecstasy!

OPHELIA: (*Pulling away.*)
"O woe is me, t'have seen what I have seen, see what I see."

JESUS: I don't care where I swim anymore—the Indian Ocean or the Dead Sea . . . I just want to be at your side. Hand in hand. Seeing together . . . listening together . . . moving through the water together. . . . (*Moving in to kiss her again.*)

WOMAN KILLER
BY CHIORI MIYAGAWA

CHARACTERS

CLAY *(mid-20s) is in debt to Joe, a drug dealer, for $16,000.* AMY *(17),* CLAY's *half-sister, loves* CLAY, *understands his predicament, but hesitates to become involved.*

SCENE

AMY's *room in her parents' house in Brooklyn*

TIME

Today

CLAY: You have to help me.

AMY: Why are you so stupid to borrow money from somebody like Joe?

CLAY: Because I have no money. I haven't been paying my credit-card bills. The collection agency is after me. I'll have to declare bankruptcy pretty soon.

AMY: If Joe doesn't get his money back, he will kill you.

CLAY: He won't. But he'll hurt me. Embarrass me.

AMY: Explain it to Mom and Dad. They'll cover it for you, I'm sure.

CLAY: You want me to tell them I owe a drug dealer sixteen thousand dollars?

AMY: You said it wasn't for drugs.

CLAY: Not all of it.

AMY: It's Rebecca, isn't it? What did you buy her? What did she ask for?

CLAY: Everything she deserves.

AMY: Clay, Rebecca is dangerous for you. She has no limits to her desire. She will devour your longing, your illusions, your sex, and your money. The empty space in her is bigger than yours. You'll disappear in her.

CLAY: That's what I want.

AMY: She's not worth giving up the chance for normal life that Timothy talks about. She's only a whore.

CLAY: Shut the hell up!

AMY: You know she is. If you don't, tell me she isn't a whore!

(**CLAY** *goes for* **AMY**. **HE** *grabs her neck.* **AMY** *gasps.* **HE** *slowly releases her, but keeps his hand on her.* **HE** *changes his energy from violent to sexual.*)

CLAY: Do you remember when we were kids, we went back every day to the school grounds after everyone had gone home, and played until the sun was dead and the air was dusky?

AMY: Some days, the sky would go orange before turning grey. Hours after that, I still had orange in my throat.

CLAY: One time there was a big hole in the ground. I think they were in the process of putting in new swings. The workers had left for the evening.

AMY: I remember.

CLAY: I hopped into the hole, made you stand still on the edge of it, and threw a stone at you.

AMY: It hit me.

CLAY: I didn't think I could really hit you. I was looking up at you from the bottom of the hole. You were a silhouette against the faint faint orange.

AMY: You hit me. I cried.

CLAY: You promised to tell Mom and Dad that you fell. When we got home, Mom flipped out seeing blood on your forehead. As soon as she asked what happened, you said—

AMY: Clay hit me with a stone.

CLAY: I hated you.

AMY: I was just a little girl then.

CLAY: You have to help me. You're my sister.

AMY: Only half. Only the half that longs for darkness, for the shadows of the unattainable.

CLAY: You know I love you.

AMY: What makes you think they'll give me the money?

CLAY: Because you're the baby of the family. And Dad is your real father.

AMY: He's your father too. We are a family.

CLAY: I've asked for money too many times already. Do this for me. Sixteen thousand dollars. Get it for me. (**CLAY** *kisses* **AMY** *on the lips tenderly.*)

WTC VIEW
BY BRIAN SLOAN

CHARACTERS
ERIC *(33), a boyish freelance photographer;* JOSIE, *(33), his friend, a stylish, Upper East Side wife*

SCENE
ERIC'S *Soho apartment overlooking Ground Zero*

TIME
The last week of September 2001

Traumatized by 9/11, ERIC *has been unable to function;* JOSIE *has dropped by to check on him.* SHE *has brought cupcakes, and then notices some of the things on the floor—the phone, about six deli cups of coffee, a full ashtray.*

JOSIE: How much sleep did you get last night?

ERIC: Mmmmmmm . . . these cupcakes are amazing.

JOSIE: Eric—when did you get up today?

ERIC: (*Indicating bag.*) Can I have yours?

JOSIE: No, and answer my goddamn question.

ERIC: I don't know . . . early.

JOSIE: And when did you go to sleep?

ERIC: I don't know . . . late.

JOSIE: You stayed up again, pulling an anxiety all-nighter. Smoking and drinking coffee and watching the news.

ERIC: I still don't get any channels.

JOSIE: God—that's even worse . . . just sitting around by yourself.

ERIC: I listened to NPR.

JOSIE: Public radio doesn't make it any better.

ERIC: It was only last night, really.

Josie: What happened last night?

Eric: I . . . I heard some sirens.

Josie: We live in Manhattan. There are always sirens.

Eric: But now—

Josie: Nothing is gonna happen, Eric. The worst is over.

Eric: We're at war, Josie.

Josie: With who? The Taliban?! They don't even have an army . . . they have *channels*. And those probably don't even work.

Eric: They don't need an army. They're here. In sleeper cells. Waiting for a signal to kill more people. Just yesterday a guy in Florida died of anthrax. Anthrax! What about that?

Josie: Anthrax?! What the hell does that have to do with anything?! It was in the fucking Everglades or something. In the middle of nowhere. What—you think there's gonna be some sort of anthrax attack here?

(*Nervous "yes" silence.*)

Okay—now you're not only being paranoid but you're missing the the point.

Eric: Let the tutorial begin. . . . "The point of terrorism is to—"

Josie: Is to inflict *terror*. The only weapon they had was surprise. And they got their one great shot to do it. What was it Dan Rather said, they lost the war the minute that second plane hit. That was it. Game over.

Eric: Thank you, professor. But when I'm in bed, trying to sleep, and I hear a bunch of sirens wailing, I tend to think the worst. It's how the whole thing began for me. Hearing all those sirens, a thousand sirens going off. It was infinite sirens to the nth degree.

Josie: But can't you tell when it's just one siren, not a thousand?

Eric: It's never one siren.

Josie: All right—there's still a difference between three sirens and three thousand sirens.

Eric: Not at three-thirty in the morning!

(**Josie** *gives up arguing this point.* **She** *turns and looks at the dresser and stuff in the room.*)

JOSIE: You know what the problem is?

ERIC: Uh—you won't let me have your cupcake?

JOSIE: You've gotta get this stuff outta here. Wasn't Will gonna take the dresser?

ERIC: Maybe. He thinks it's ugly.

JOSIE: Once you get this old stuff out and get a new roommate, I'm sure you'll feel a lot better. Instantly.

ERIC: The trick now is actually getting the new roommate.

JOSIE: There's no trick. And now that things are getting back to normal and—

ERIC: Face it, Josie. Things are not getting back to normal—they can't.

JOSIE: That's bullshit. People are going on with their lives.…

ERIC: Maybe above Fourteenth Street.

JOSIE: And don't give me your whole downtown-DMZ rant.… You act like Fourteenth Street is the friggin' Berlin Wall.

ERIC: (*Hysterical.*) Oh please—people up there have *no* idea. None!

JOSIE: Okay—you're getting hysterical again.

ERIC: Look—have you seen things getting back to normal down here? *Have* you?

JOSIE: Of course.

ERIC: Of course?! Are you kidding? Have you noticed the "missing" flyers everywhere? Or the candles in front of every fire station? Or maybe the heavily armed storm troopers on every corner? (*Challenging.*) Give me one back-to-normal example. Go!

JOSIE: Okay—let's see. Uh…yesterday. I was coming out of the Mercer Hotel when this supermodel stole my cab, right out from under me.

ERIC: What did you do?

JOSIE: I called her a fashionista cunt.

ERIC: But did she call you anything *back*?

JOSIE: Jesus!

ERIC: Aha!

SCENES FOR TWO WOMEN

AGE OF AROUSAL
BY LINDA GRIFFITHS

CHARACTERS
RHODA *(35), a teacher, a New Woman, loyal and idealistic;* **MONICA** *(29), a pretty, flirtatious former shopgirl, now seven months pregnant*

SCENE
The sitting room at Mary's school

TIME
London, 1885

RHODA *has believed that* **MONICA** *is pregnant by Everard, the man with whom* **RHODA** *was having a relationship.* **SHE** *has not spoken to him or* **MONICA** *in five months.*

(*Five months later. A dull afternoon. Mary's sitting room.* **RHODA** *and* **MONICA**. **MONICA** *is seven months pregnant.*)

MONICA: It's taken me many months to find the courage to see you.

RHODA: Five. Five months to be exact.

MONICA: I am going to die.

RHODA: Such a loss.

MONICA: When he heard what was said, how did Everard respond?

RHODA: You know that he denied it. He was above explanations. We haven't spoken since that day.

MONICA: Not a word in five months? No wonder you look so drawn and liverish.

RHODA: And you look like a wraith who's swallowed a balloon.

MONICA: It wasn't him. It wasn't Everard.

RHODA: Why should I believe anything you say?

MONICA: We did explore the amatory act on a number of pleasant occasions, but long before. The man whose child this is abandoned me. You saw him at the exhibition. He's wealthy and a shite.

RHODA: So you did lie with Everard.

MONICA: It's not Everard's. You ruined everything. You couldn't just love him, you couldn't just trust him.

RHODA: Then why didn't you speak at the time? Do you hate me that much?

MONICA: You were about to leave us all behind.

RHODA: Why are you speaking now?

MONICA: I felt it move.

RHODA: Felt it move?

MONICA: And I needed money from the real father. I've hated it all this time, and now—

RHODA: And now you love it. You felt it move.

MONICA: I feel nothing for it. But it is moving, like a fish in its watery bowl. Before I die, it deserves the truth.

RHODA: All new mothers believe they are going to die.

MONICA: My sisters are taking care of me and the man has sent money so he isn't even a complete villain. But I am so weary. I can feel the child wanting hope, sucking, searching for it, and I have none. It is as if I believed it was a lie.

RHODA: No. It isn't.

MONICA: I always felt that you had something to give me, that you could help—

RHODA: Are you shaming me? I should be ashamed. I have always been a jealous person.

MONICA: And I've been green with envy—I'll get out my whip and flay us both. Tell me about the future.

RHODA: The future? That tired old horse? Oh God, I'm weary too.

MONICA: But you believe.

RHODA: Yes. We live for the future. You must live for the future.

MONICA: I cannot. I fear I will die with this newness inside me, struggling to be born.

RHODA: This is defeat. And I won't have it. I am able to stop these thoughts with my will, can you feel my will?

MONICA: It's like a ray of cold steel.

RHODA: Then I'll warm the metal. Think. Feel. Every breath you take, you are breathing the future. The reddest blood must flow to it, the strongest muscle, your heart, must pound for the child. Hear its rhythm, feel its pulse. Let it be a drum that drowns out weakness, that dwells on life, as we must. As we must.

MONICA: As we must. Yes. We could have been friends.

RHODA: Yes.

MONICA: Good-bye, Rhoda.

RHODA: Not good-bye.

MONICA: It is a shame that sex matters are so . . . untidy.

ALL THINGS BEING EQUAL
BY FAYE SHOLITON

CHARACTERS
CARRIE *(30s), a social studies teacher, liberal, Jewish;* BERTA *(30s), a social studies teacher, liberal, African-American*

SCENE
A high-school classroom in Liberty Falls, Ohio

TIME
1976

In team-teaching the high-school social studies class, CARRIE *and* BERTA *find that their liberal views are not always in agreement.*

BERTA: Tomorrow, we're going to talk about one of those places the Constitution didn't reach: the U.S. Military. How many of you have heard of Port Chicago? . . . It's not in the textbook, children. Port Chicago was a naval installation on the Sacramento River. On July 14, 1944, something happened on the docks. The Civil Rights Act of 1964 was enacted, in some part, because of what happened that night. Look it up. This, too, is American history. (*Bell rings, scraping of chairs. Then silence.*)

CARRIE: You gonna give me a hint?

BERTA: There was an explosion.

CARRIE: With racial implications.

BERTA: Well, who do you think was doin' all the grunt work? You know, I don't think you ever told me what your daddy did during the war.

CARRIE: Is that what this is all about?

BERTA: I'm asking for a reason.

CARRIE: Fine. He was in the Army. Quartermaster Corps.

BERTA: I see. An officer?

CARRIE: Captain. Why?

BERTA: Then you know that his Negroes were nothin' more than slaves in uniform.

Carrie: No. I don't. I mean, he never…

Berta: No, I don't suppose he did. Well, my daddy was Quartermaster Corps, too. Only Navy.

Carrie: He was at Port Chicago?

Berta: He got one, maybe two days of so-called "training" before pulling ammo duty.

Carrie: How many died?

Berta: Three hundred twenty-some. Hundreds more injured. And the ones who survived? Sent right back to work, ten days later. Except some of them made a stand. Got themselves sentenced to fifteen years' hard labor.

Carrie: My God.

Berta: Oh, they were released after sixteen months. But with *dis*honorable discharges. And you know who defended them? Thurgood Marshall. … I told you there was a link.

Carrie: How come you never mentioned this when we were planning the unit?

Berta: I just get weary hearing about your mama this and your mama that. It's time we talked about your daddy.

Carrie: There's nothing to tell. He managed properties … in the city.

Berta: Properties.

Carrie: Near downtown. That's all. End of story.

Berta: But as Captain Rice…

Carrie: Actually, it was Captain Reisenfeld. And he requisitioned supplies.

Berta: And he never spoke of the men under his command?

Carrie: Hill's right. You *do* have an ax to grind.

Berta: Did he talk about his buddies? Go to any reunions?

Carrie: It's not as if he landed on Omaha Beach, for God's sake!

Berta: … Show you photographs?

(*The light dawns.*)

Carrie: … They were all black.

BERTA: Uh-huh.

CARRIE: Look. His point of reference back then was the silver screen. Negroes dug ditches. Indians carried tomahawks.

BERTA: So your sainted mama married Archie Bunker.

CARRIE: Like I said. He was a product of his time.

BERTA: So was she.

CARRIE: They divorced in nineteen sixty-two. And he's been dead for seven years, okay? Could we talk about something else?

BERTA: Carrie. Honey. When are you gonna take off those Pollyanna braids? In case you haven't noticed, we're different.

CARRIE: If you're talking about race,

BERTA: Well *some*body should.

CARRIE: That's what the whole Civil Rights Movement was for! To make sure it *didn't* matter!

BERTA: Perhaps it has to matter before it doesn't. Sooner or later, race always rears its ugly head. Somebody launches a grenade and we retreat to our bunkers. We're *wired* that way. And pretending we're not won't get us diddly squat.

CARRIE: Well, if we haven't been talking about race these last few months, what the hell have we been talking about?

BERTA: Damned if I know. But I got this feeling, keep asking myself, "What does this woman want from me?" ... Tell me, Carrie. How many black people in your address book? I'm not talking about your old housekeeper, either. I'm talking about heart-friends. Peers.

CARRIE: Well, how many white people in *yours*? Or don't you have any peers?

BERTA: What we just experienced was a moment of pure, unadulterated honesty.

CARRIE: I was merely trying to prove a point.

BERTA: Which was...

CARRIE: ...I have no idea.

BERTA: Lord, I wish you'd stop trying so hard.

(*Pause.*)

CARRIE: Have you ever had your mouth washed out with soap? When I was in tenth grade, I wrote this amazing essay about the end of civilization. How we had already proven ourselves capable of pushing the nuclear button. My teacher entered it in a citywide competition and told me it was almost certain to win.... Well, she failed to mention she'd entered another girl's essay, too. A black kid who wrote about fair housing—about the office *my mom* had co-founded!... Well, the day they announced the winner, I have to say, I got a little steamed. I had already planned where I was going to spend the prize money.... Unfortunately, my mother was passing through while I was venting to a friend.... I can still taste the soap. What's so funny?

BERTA: What that black girl was probably saying about *you.*

CARRIE: If I'm to be your heart friend, what the hell am I supposed to be doing?

BERTA: One day you will enter my world.

CARRIE: I've been waiting for an invitation.

BERTA: When you get there, I'll need you to hold it together.

(*Pause.*)

CARRIE: Does this have anything to do with why I've never met your husband?

BERTA: You've never met him, because he's been in the hospital.

CARRIE: Oh. Oh, God! You can't imagine what I thought.

BERTA: About a black man who abandoned his wife and baby. Let me guess.

CARRIE: I'm an idiot.

BERTA: He's at the V.A., Carrie.... It's where I go on Sundays.

CARRIE: ... I'll be damned.

BERTA: What?

(*Bell rings.*)

CARRIE: You know, you can be a royal pain in the ass.

BERTA: You have no idea.

AMERICAN TET
BY LYDIA STRYK

CHARACTERS
AMY KROMBACHER *(early to mid-20s)*. AMY *lives at home and is putting herself through college by working on the local military base.* ELAINE KROMBACHER *(mid-50s),* AMY'S *mother. A career military wife,* SHE *currently teaches new spouses the ins and outs of military life on base.*

SCENE
The Krombacher family's backyard

TIME
It is the spring of 2004, the one-year anniversary of the ongoing conflagration in Iraq.

AMY *is beginning to bring home stories of unhappiness on base from other military family members involved in Iraq. As this scene opens,* SHE *is reporting on co-workers affected by the war—as a way to confide her feelings to her mother,* ELAINE. ELAINE'S *thoughts are on her son, Danny, coming home soon on leave from Iraq, and on the party* SHE *is planning for him.*

AMY: Joe's wife can't stop eating. Ever since Joe deployed. She's okay 'til she starts. So she has breakfast for dinner. But it doesn't really help. 'Cause then she stays up all night. Eating. She's just exhausted all the time. My friend Wendy's started drinking. Cheap port wine, mostly. Can't get out of bed sometimes. She calls in sick. And me . . . I'm just . . .

ELAINE: You're just what . . . ?

AMY: I'm just gonna hurt someone.

ELAINE: Amy?

AMY: It's like bombs are going off. Inside of me.

ELAINE: Honey. *(A difficult pause.)* I know this war on terror isn't easy.

AMY: Who's spreading the terror?

ELAINE: Amy.

AMY: Answer.

ELAINE: Well, we're fighting for peace and security. Over there. If that's what you mean. (*Pause.*) We brought freedom. To the Iraqis. (*Pause.*) And we'll keep spreading it everywhere. Everywhere. Everywhere necessary. Until we've won. And the war on terror is over. And there's peace.

AMY: What's gonna happen when it never comes? Then we bomb again? Just keep on? Bombing. Bombing. Bomb—

ELAINE: Shh! *Stop* . . . stop. It'll be okay. We just have to trust in what our leaders say. It'll be—

AMY: Trust *who*? When all we hear is lies?

ELAINE: Oh, honey. (*A pause.*) On a brighter note, we stopped those Taliban.

AMY: The Taliban have not gone away.

ELAINE: We certainly tried.

AMY: We funded them.

ELAINE: Should we have let the Afghanis fall to communism?

AMY: If it were my choice, I'd have taken communism.

ELAINE: (*Aghast, looking around to make sure no one has heard this, in a whisper.*) *Communism?*

AMY: Yes, Mom. (*Shouting.*) COMMUNISM!!! COMMUNISM ROCKS!!!

ELAINE: (**SHE** *gets up.*) Amy, I don't think that's funny. Your father put his life on the line in Vietnam. To bring communism down. And he almost lost it. And he is not well now. And thousands died. But we won, thank God.

AMY: We were fighting the wrong enemy.

ELAINE: We'll never get it perfect, Amy. (*Pause.*) If your dad could hear you.

AMY: He doesn't listen to me, anyway. He thinks I'm crazy.

ELAINE: That's not true.

AMY: Don't lie to me.

ELAINE: Okay. He thinks you're crazy.

(*A pause.* **THEY** laugh. *The air seems to clear.*)

AMY: Communism was not the enemy is all I am trying to say. And terrorism isn't either.

ELAINE: (*Holding her chest.*) *Terrorism isn't the enemy either? Terrorism isn't—the enemy.*

(*Slowly.*) Okay. And who *is* the enemy, Amy?

AMY: The enemy's inside, Mom.

(**ELAINE** *looks toward the house, confused, dismayed.*)

Inside of us. (*Pointing her finger to her head, like a gun.*) In here. The enemy's in our heads, Mom. It's ignorance.

ELAINE: (*Exasperated now, finally turning on her.*) This is not a pretty world, missy. You have to stand for something. If they win, we lose. Is that what you want to happen? Do you want to live in their world?

(**AMY** *doesn't answer,* **SHE** *looks away.*)

Well, do you?

(**AMY** *does not respond. Elaine shouts the question.*)

Do you???

This is my world, Amy. And I'm looking around it. And it's not so bad. This is *our* world. You couldn't say those things in China. You couldn't wear those clothes in Iran. You'd be covered in a veil with slits for eyes. You couldn't even drive. You do not know, little girl, how lucky you are, how lucky. To wake up in this land, free. You'd be married off by age six. You'd be locked in a dungeon with that mouth of yours. You'd never even see the inside of a school. But freedom isn't free. Someone's got to pay. This is not a pretty world. We've got to stand for something. I am so proud of my country. I'm so proud and grateful. I pray for it every day, and I know you think that's crazy. The tired and the poor from the world over, they want to get here. No matter what they say. Everyone wants to be an American. Everyone wants what we have. This is paradise, honey. These are sacred shores. You wake up free, little girl. Do you know what that means? These terrorists—they hate us because they hate freedom. If they win, we lose. Is that what you want to happen? Do you really want to live in their world? Do you, Amy?

AMY: It's one world, Mom. And it's going up in flames.

(*A pause.* **ELAINE** *looks at* **AMY**. **SHE** *seems to be about to answer.* **SHE** *sighs.* **SHE** *looks around the yard, studying it.*)

ELAINE: We're going to need a lot of balloons. And a big old "Welcome Home" sign...

(**Amy** *looks at her mother,* **She** *shakes her head.* **She** *gets up, slowly.*)

Amy: Danny's going to die. My brother's going to die.

(**Amy** *leaves.*)

Elaine: A big old "Welcome Home, Danny" sign. Or paper cut-out letters...

AMSTEL IN TEL AVIV
BY ALLYSON CURRIN

CHARACTERS
JESSICA *(18) and* **FEN** *(18) are best girlfriends from prep school, but as they begin attending different colleges, things change rapidly.*

SCENE
A college house

TIME
The present

(As the girls remove caps and gowns, rowdy party music begins. The playing area now becomes **JESSICA's** *college house.* **FEN** *appears, dressed stylishly.)*

JESSICA: So, this is it.

FEN: It's a huge campus. I don't know how you get around.

JESSICA: I learn quickly. When I have to.

FEN: And your own little house. Daddy would have a fit if I tried to get a house all my own. I'm afraid I'm stuck in women's dorms for the rest of my natural life.

JESSICA: But you like it?

FEN: I think it's charming. So ... bohemian.

JESSICA: It's so much more than that, though. It's a relationship within a group like I've never had before. For the first time in my life, I feel like I'm actually living an adult life.

FEN: Well, don't adults usually strike up some sort of housekeeping agreement? The dishes in that sink! Honey, it looks like somebody's biology experiment in there!

JESSICA: Who gives a damn about the dishes! I am living like I've never lived before! That's the beauty of it, that's what I've been trying to tell you! I feel so much at ease here BECAUSE no one gives a damn about the dishes! God, it's so liberating.

FEN: Well ... Honey, I hate to accuse you of being outmoded, but ... well, this place looks like something out of the sixties. All you need is a couple of little naked babies running around with flowers in their hair.

JESSICA: How do you like my housemates?

FEN: REAL nice. Now, why don't we break into these Hello Dollies I made you?

JESSICA: What do you think of Sara?

FEN: I think she's a lesbian.

JESSICA: Just because a woman has a tattoo does not mean she's a lesbian.

FEN: She just makes me feel self-conscious about wearing a slip. I mean, I'm sorry I wear makeup and mousse my hair—it doesn't make me an oppressed subculture.

JESSICA: Oh, Sara is just . . . direct. And what about Juan?

FEN: He's very . . . quiet.

JESSICA: But what do you think about him?

FEN: (*Uncertainly.*) He seems real nice.

JESSICA: Oh, my God, Fen, he's so brilliant! I've never met a man like him in my entire life. He writes poetry, he studies philosophy! He speaks Coptic and there are TEETH MARKS on his books! Fen, he is so wonderful!

FEN: He certainly seems it.

JESSICA: He's in love with ideas and he plays the sax and the violin FOR PLEASURE! I mean, I've never met someone who wanted to learn so much just to know it. He's such an inspiration to me.

FEN: Speaking of inspiration . . . (*Pulls a manuscript out of her bag.*) *Underground Religion* by Jessica Abrahams. Wow.

JESSICA: You like it?

FEN: It's wonderful. I met the editor of this regional arts magazine at a career day and I showed it to him. I've got his address—if you follow up, it might amount to something.

JESSICA: Well, maybe . . . it needs some work. Anyway, Juan thinks I should try my hand at playwriting.

FEN: But I loved it.

JESSICA: He likes it, too. He just thinks I can do more.

FEN: First let's concentrate on getting this one published.

JESSICA: My writing's okay. But it's not art.

FEN: Says who?

JESSICA: You should have heard Pop's critique. Anyway, Juan doesn't think I push my boundaries enough.

FEN: What does the muse think?

JESSICA: Juan is opening my eyes to so many intriguing things. He thinks that playwriting is the ultimate form of literature because it isn't intended to be an intimate experience, but a communal experience. He equates it to writing a sermon that must appeal to atheists, Christians, Jews, Muslims, Shintos—am I boring you?

FEN: No. Shintos. Is that what you call them?

JESSICA: Do you know what he did the other day?

FEN: I would have no idea.

JESSICA: He painted a portrait of me. In the nude.

FEN: Christ Almighty.

JESSICA: Boy, what an experience. It was all about learning to trust another human being, revealing my heart and soul—

FEN: And your pussy! This is disgusting. Jesse, he's so . . . dirty.

JESSICA: Here it comes.

FEN: I mean, geniuses do occasionally come in sanitary models, don't they? Or is it a prerequisite that they go without deodorant?

JESSICA: You're acting like a snob.

FEN: If acting like a snob means requiring my boyfriends to shower once a week, fine, call me a snob! Honey, if you want to rewrite, I can help you with that. I just don't think you ought to lose your momentum with your writing.

JESSICA: I'm not going to lose any momentum—can't I just date someone without you getting your panties in a wad about my novel?

FEN: But Juan is so—

JESSICA: Adult?

FEN: Well, why can't you just date some nice Jewish boy?

JESSICA: God. I have witnessed it. It is indeed possible for a southern belle to sound like a Yenta. Fen, I'm not going to spend the rest of my life only dating nice Jewish boys any more than you have to date uptight Presbyterians. If you ever had dates, I mean. The limits are gone.

FEN: I don't see how any of this has to do with *Underground Religion*.

JESSICA: You're just pissed because I'm not doing what you expect me to do.

FEN: I've never been able to predict you.

JESSICA: Oh, but, Fen, he makes all those guys at the Academy seem like children. Now I'm actually feeling the things I've only been able to write about before. I mean, there are things that happen between people . . . things that change every perception.

FEN: I wouldn't know about that.

JESSICA: This is different.

FEN: Are you sure you're not just looking for an excuse not to write?

JESSICA: Can't you just be happy for me?

FEN: I don't know. . . .

JESSICA: For me?

FEN: I don't understand, honey.

JESSICA: I'll teach you how to lambada.

FEN: Lambada? That's like sex with your clothes on, isn't it?

JESSICA: You'll love it! You can shock Mr. Fenwick over Thanksgiving.

FEN: Well . . . I know Mama would kill me for saying so, but Juan's little ponytail is kind of cute!

JESSICA: You are wonderful! And you'll see—he really is something different! This one's for real!

DEAD MAN'S CELL PHONE
BY SARAH RUHL

CHARACTERS
JEAN *(late 20s), responsible and considerate, is trapped by circumstances;* OTHER
WOMAN *(20s–30s), a bit more worldly, is also confused by these circumstances.*

SCENE
A café

TIME
The present.

When a cell phone rings incessantly at the table next to hers, JEAN *intervenes,
only to discover the owner, Gordon, is dead. In an effort to "comfort his loved
ones,"* SHE *continues to answer his calls, and arranges to meet the* OTHER
WOMAN, *who naturally believes* JEAN *was Gordon's lover, too.*

(A café. Film noir music. The OTHER WOMAN *waiting in a blue raincoat.* JEAN
enters in a blue raincoat.)

JEAN: Hello.

OTHER WOMAN: Hello. Thank you for meeting me.

JEAN: Not at all.

OTHER WOMAN: We like the same clothes.

JEAN: Yes.

OTHER WOMAN: I suppose that's not surprising, given the circumstances.

JEAN: I don't know what you mean.

OTHER WOMAN: You don't need to pretend.

JEAN: I know.

OTHER WOMAN: Gordon has good taste. You're pretty.

JEAN: I'm not—

OTHER WOMAN: Don't be modest. I like it when a woman knows she's beautiful.
    Women nowadays—they don't know how to walk into a room. A beautiful

woman should walk into a room thinking: I am beautiful and I know how to walk in these shoes. There's so little glamour in the world these days. It makes daily life such a bore. Women are responsible for enlivening dull places like train stations. There is hardly any pleasure in waiting for a train anymore. The women just—walk in. Horrible shoes. No confidence. Bad posture.

(*The* OTHER WOMAN *looks at* JEAN'S *posture.* JEAN *sits up straighter.*)

A woman should be able to take out her compact and put lipstick on her lips with absolute confidence. No apology.

(*The* OTHER WOMAN *takes out lipstick and puts it on her lips, slowly.* JEAN *is riveted.*)

JEAN: I've always been embarrassed to put lipstick on in public.

OTHER WOMAN: That's crap. Here—you have beautiful lips. (SHE *hands* JEAN *the lipstick.*)

JEAN: No—that's—

OTHER WOMAN: I don't have a cold.

JEAN: It's not the germs. It's—

OTHER WOMAN: Put it on. Take your time. Enjoy yourself.

(JEAN *puts on some lipstick.*)

That was disappointing. Oh, well.

JEAN: I'm very sorry about Gordon. You must be—his friend?

OTHER WOMAN: Gordon didn't tell you much, did he?

JEAN: No.

OTHER WOMAN: Gordon could be quiet.

JEAN: Yes. He was quiet.

OTHER WOMAN: He must have respected you. He was quiet with women he respected. Otherwise he had a very loud laugh. Haw, haw, haw! You could hear him a mile away. (SHE *remembers Gordon.*) You must wonder why I wanted to meet with you.

JEAN: Yes.

OTHER WOMAN: You were with Gordon the day he died.

JEAN: Yes.

OTHER WOMAN: Gordon and I—we were—well—You know. (**SHE** *thinks the word—lovers.*) And so—I wanted to know…this is going to sound sentimental…I wanted to know his last words.

JEAN: That's not sentimental.

OTHER WOMAN: I hate sentiment.

JEAN: I don't think that's sentimental. Really, I don't.

OTHER WOMAN: So. His last words.

JEAN: Gordon mentioned you before he died. Well, he more than mentioned you. He said: tell her that I love her. And then he turned his face away and died.

OTHER WOMAN: He said that he loved me.

JEAN: Yes.

OTHER WOMAN: I waited for such a long time. And the words—delivered through another woman. What a shit. (*The* **OTHER WOMAN** *looks away.* **SHE** *wipes a tear away.*)

JEAN: It's not like that. Gordon said that he had loved many women in his life, but when he met you, everything changed. He said that other women seemed like clocks compared to you—other women just—measured time—broke the day up—but that you—you stopped time. He said you—stopped time—just by walking into a room.

OTHER WOMAN: He said that?

JEAN: Yes.

OTHER WOMAN: Oh, Gordon.

(*The phone rings.* **JEAN** *hesitates to answer it.*)

Aren't you going to get that?

JEAN: Yes.

(**SHE** *answers the phone.*)

Hello?

[(*On the other end: Who is this?*)]

My name is Jean.

Yes, of course.

How do I get there?

(*A pause while the mother gives directions. To the* **OTHER WOMAN**, *whispering.*)

Sorry.

(*The* **OTHER WOMAN** *shrugs her shoulders.*)

All right, I'll see you then. Good-bye.

(**JEAN** *hangs up.*)

OTHER WOMAN: Who was it?

JEAN: His mother.

OTHER WOMAN: Oh, God. Mrs. Gottlieb? Let me touch up your lipstick before you go.

(**SHE** *does.* **JEAN** *puckers.*)

DEDICATION OR THE STUFF OF DREAMS
BY TERRENCE MCNALLY

CHARACTERS
JESSIE *(40s), Lou's partner in a children's theatre;* IDA *(20s),* JESSIE's *daughter, a big-time singer*

SCENE
An empty theatre

TIME
Now

IDA *has been estranged from her mother, and wishes to make amends.* SHE *is somewhat surprised to discover* JESSIE's *affair with Arnold, their technical director.*

IDA: You two make wild love his kids can hear?

JESSIE: God, I hope not. I'm like their soccer mom.

IDA: It's cool, someone thinking your mother is sexy. How long have you two been at it?

JESSIE: Almost three years and I wish you wouldn't put it like that. I feel like such a tramp.

IDA: Ma, you couldn't be a tramp if you tried.

JESSIE: Someone was bound to find out. Better you than anyone.

IDA: Does Lou know?

JESSIE: He asked me once. I was sewing a costume for *Pinocchio* and he said, "Are you having an affair with Arnold?" and I said, "Of course not," without missing a stitch. He's never mentioned it again.

IDA: It's pretty obvious something's up.

JESSIE: It's the way I behave with Arnold, isn't it?

IDA: No, it's more the way Lou doesn't behave with you.

JESSIE: How do you mean?

IDA: He's gay, right?

JESSIE: I hate that word. Lou is a lot of things. He's good, he's fun, he's—

IDA: I'm not saying he's not all those things.

JESSIE: It's a good relationship.

IDA: But you need Arnold, too.

JESSIE: Sometimes, yes, I do. I'm not very proud of myself.

IDA: Ma, I don't blame you. If Lou's fooling around, why shouldn't you be?

JESSIE: Lou doesn't do that.

IDA: How do you know?

JESSIE: He gave me his word.

IDA: And you believe him?

JESSIE: Yes; it's called trust.

IDA: No, it's called denial. It's what men do, straight or gay. They go where their dicks take them.

JESSIE: Lou is nothing like your father.

IDA: No, I doubt I'll ever come home from school and find him screwing your best friend.

JESSIE: I'm sure you'll make another hit song out of it if you do.

IDA: What else am I supposed to write about, if not my life?

JESSIE: *Lies My Mother Taught Me.* I suppose it's a good album title if you're not the mother. You didn't even bother to change the names.

IDA: No one knows who you are.

JESSIE: I do. It's a good thing we'd moved upstate. I was mortified.

IDA: I'm sorry.

JESSIE: It's a little late for that, honey.

IDA: You'll be happy to know the new CD is about the future: life after rehab.

JESSIE: And it's called *The Curse of a Broken Heart?*

IDA: I still have a lot of issues.

JESSIE: So do I. I don't rub everyone's noses in them. I keep them to myself.

IDA: I'm a creative artist. You're just a reproductive one.

JESSIE: What the hell is that supposed to mean?

IDA: You've spent your life saying lines that were written by someone else.

JESSIE: I'm sorry, but that's what actors do, Ida. It's called the script.

IDA: I speak in my own voice.

JESSIE: That's wonderful. Just leave me out of it. And while we're at it, I don't understand your need to shock people.

IDA: I don't understand yours to please them. Wake up and smell the coffee.

JESSIE: I smell it every morning, Ida. Don't come home and tell me what's wrong with my life; I don't need my druggie daughter for that. I'm not the one on the front page of those newspapers and magazines at the checkout stand at the A&P.

(**SHE** *has begun to cry.*)

IDA: We got something all turned around. I came home to make amends to you.

JESSIE: I don't want your amends.

IDA: I have to make them. It's part of the program. I need some closure.

JESSIE: Don't make us *Oprah*, honey. Just talk to me.

IDA: I'm trying. You're not making it any easier.

JESSIE: I was way out of bounds with that druggie remark.

IDA: Thank you. Yes, you were.

JESSIE: It must have been terrible what you've been through.

IDA: It was. I should be dead.

JESSIE: Don't say that.

IDA: If you don't believe me, ask Toby. He's the reason I'm alive. You treat someone like shit and they're still there for you.

JESSIE: He loves you, Ida.

IDA: Actually, I was talking about you.

JESSIE: You're still my little girl. You always will be.

THE DIRECTOR
BY BARBARA CASSIDY

CHARACTERS
SADIE *(28) shows up at her friend* MILTON'S *apartment;* MILTON *(32) is attracted to, and possibly in love with,* SADIE. SADIE *is not uninterested.*

SCENE
MILTON'S *apartment, New York City*

TIME
3:30 AM

SADIE *has left her boyfriend, Snake, because of their difference of opinion regarding the film director* SADIE *has been talking to. This director is notorious for meeting women on the street and trying to get them in bed. Now an intoxicated* SADIE *is outside* MILTON'S *apartment.* SHE *knocks on the door and rings the bell.*

SADIE: Milton. Milton. Open up. It's me. Hey. Milton! C'mon now.

(SHE *bangs on the door some more and then after a bit sits on the floor. After a minute* SHE *bolts up, bangs on the door loudly.*)

MILTON! MILTON! OPEN THE FUCKING DOOR!

(MILTON *opens the door after a while. It appears* SHE *has been sleeping.*)

MILTON: What the fuck?

SADIE: Why didn't you answer? I've been out here.

MILTON: I think it's the middle of the night. I might be wrong.

SADIE: Oh, sorry.

MILTON: You drunk?

SADIE: A little.

MILTON: You want some coffee?

SADIE: No. Okay.

(MILTON *makes coffee.*)

What time is it?

MILTON: Three forty.

SADIE: Oh, wow.

MILTON: I gotta work.

SADIE: Sure.

MILTON: I—did something happen?

SADIE: No. No.

MILTON: What's the matter? You okay?

SADIE: Yeah. I'm okay.

MILTON: Where were you?

SADIE: Rodney's.

MILTON: With?

SADIE: I went by myself.

MILTON: Really? That's a little odd.

SADIE: Whatever.

(*Pause.*)

You ever wish you were something else? Something less messy. Like a piece of furniture. Or a triangle. A red plastic triangle. That's it. That's perfect. (**SHE** *laughs.*)

MILTON: Oh no, don't start none of that now.

SADIE: Oh, fuck. I'm so out there.

MILTON: You are.

SADIE: A lot of assholes. Out there.

MILTON: Yeah.

SADIE: I don't know if I want to spend my...

MILTON: What?

SADIE: Nothing. I ran out on him. . . .

[(*Pause. Nina enters and walks downstage and stands, gets ready for camera.*)]

Milton: When?

Sadie: Earlier...

Milton: The director thing?

Sadie: I don't know. I mean, yeah, he called and Snake was all weirded...

Milton: Uh huh.

Sadie: And sounding violent...

Milton: I don't know. You should do it.

Sadie: Do what? I got no passion. I need passion.

Milton: You don't need him.

Sadie: Who?

Milton: I meant Snake.

Sadie: I don't know what to do.

Milton: You could stay here. No, really.

Sadie: (*Putting on a street slang voice.*) I'm on to a couple a forties 'fore I hit the street.

Milton: Stop. I'm tired.

Sadie: Oh, yeah.

Milton: You smell.

Sadie: Oh, no, shut up.

Milton: Look at you. You are so fucked up.

Sadie: Okay, Buzz Kill. Can I lie on your couch?

Milton: You got more than a buzz, girlfriend....

Sadie: Don't pay attention to me. Go back to bed. I'll just stay on the couch if you don't mind. I know you have to work.

Milton: Yeah, fine.

Sadie: I'm gonna do something.

(**Milton** *exits to bedroom.* **Sadie** *stares at the apartment, at the emptiness.* **Milton** *returns after a bit.*)

Milton: I can't sleep now.

Sadie: Do you know anything about the poppy plant?

Milton: I don't know much about any plants.

Sadie: I was thinking of growing some.

Milton: You want to go to jail, eh?

Sadie: You can't go to jail for growing a plant. I'm really interested in the poppy. Poppy. I like to say that. Can I call you Poppy?

Milton: No...

Sadie: Oh. No.

Milton: Like Dorothy. Falling asleep in a field of poppies.

Sadie: Sounds nice.

Milton: The chick with the poppy garden.... Did you have sex with the director?

Sadie: I had this vision of me in my garden of poppies. It was a really nice image. And I'm not into the nature thing.

Milton: Right.

Sadie: Maybe I'll just plant the seeds from a bagel.

Milton: Great idea. It might not work.

Sadie: Of course I did. I have had sex with a lot of people. I've always wanted to smoke opium. You?

Milton: Not really. I was more interested in absinthe.

Sadie: (*Calling* **Milton** *by the name of another apparent fan of absinthe: Hemingway.*) Ernest. You're a fucking man.

Milton: Suck my dick.

Sadie: Ohhh.

Milton: Of course, I would never drink it. It's just an idea in my head.

Sadie: I really want to smoke opium. I don't know why.

Milton: You're out of your mind.

[(**Nina** *struts downstage.*)]

Sadie: Possibly, but that's irrelevant.

MILTON: Oh, that's relevant, that is very relevant. I'm sitting here with you.

(*Pause.*)

I haven't had sex with that many people.

SADIE: (*Playfully teasing.*) You're a dyke. Dykes don't have that many lovers. Do you remember your dreams?

MILTON: I don't know.

SADIE: What do you dream about? You don't remember?

MILTON: I have trouble remembering.

SADIE: I dreamt we were on vacation in, I don't know, Montana or something, and we were in this country cabin, and we suddenly realized there was a bear sleeping on the floor. And just as soon as we became aware of the bear's existence, he woke up and started attacking you, and I had to pound it with a bat I picked up. I hit it in the head, and the blood started pouring out, and it fell on the floor and was still grabbing you, and I started pounding on its head with the heel of my boot, but it wouldn't die. And more and more blood came out, but still it wouldn't die. And then I woke up.

MILTON: Wow. Some night.

SADIE: This is the kind of shit I dream about.

MILTON: You ever wonder about dreams, like what's with them?

SADIE: Yes. (*Pause.*) Like how they seem so real, even when they're so bizarre?

MILTON: Yeah, like you would never react so nonchalantly to the strangest things as often happens in dreams.

SADIE: Yeah, I think we talked about this once before. I was very into this idea. In fact, this is my idea. You remember?

MILTON: No, I don't remember.

SADIE: I hate that. You tell someone an idea you have and then six months later they come back to you with this idea they now believe is their own, and they tell it to you like you never heard it.

MILTON: It's not your idea; I thought it a long time ago. You should go to sleep. You don't have a main idea as a person. That's your problem.

SADIE: (*Rhetorically.*) I got no character, right?

DOUBT
BY JOHN PATRICK SHANLEY

CHARACTERS
SISTER JAMES *(20s), a young nun, somewhat naïve, but very enthusiastic about teaching;* SISTER ALOYSIUS *(50s–60s), the school's principal, quite authoritarian and set in her ways*

SCENE
St. Nicholas, a Catholic church and school in the Bronx, New York

TIME
1964

The two nuns are discussing Father Flynn, whom SISTER ALOYSIUS *suspects is sexually abusing a male student. He has just left the office after offering his explanation.*

SISTER JAMES: Well. What a relief! He cleared it all up.

SISTER ALOYSIUS: You believe him?

SISTER JAMES: Of course.

SISTER ALOYSIUS: Isn't it more that it's easier to believe him?

SISTER JAMES: But we can corroborate his story with Mr. McGinn!

SISTER ALOYSIUS: Yes. These types of people are clever. They're not so easily undone.

SISTER JAMES: Well, I'm convinced!

SISTER ALOYSIUS: You're not. You just want things to be resolved so you can have simplicity back.

SISTER JAMES: I want no further part of this.

SISTER ALOYSIUS: I'll bring him down. With or without your help.

SISTER JAMES: How can you be so sure he's lying?

SISTER ALOYSIUS: Experience.

SISTER JAMES: You just don't like him! You don't like it that he uses a ballpoint pen. You don't like it that he takes three lumps of sugar in his tea. You don't like it that he likes "Frosty the Snowman." And you're letting that convince you of something terrible, just terrible! Well, I like "Frosty the Snowman"! And it would be nice if this school weren't run like a prison! And I think it's a good thing that I love to teach History and that I might inspire my students to love it, too! And if you judge that to mean I'm not fit to be a teacher, then so be it!

Sister Aloysius: Sit down. (**Sister James** *does.*) In ancient Sparta, important matters were decided by who shouted loudest. Fortunately, we are not in ancient Sparta. Now. Do you honestly find the students in this school to be treated like inmates in a prison?

Sister James: (*Relenting.*) No, I don't. Actually, by and large, they seem to be fairly happy. But they're all uniformly terrified of you!

Sister Aloysius: Yes. That's how it works. Sit there.

THE ELEKTRA FUGUES
BY RUTH MARGRAFF

CHARACTERS
ELEKTRA *(20s) is the punk-rock angry rebel of the family.* CHRYSOTHEMIS *(20s) is a super proactive and healthy sisterly creature (she sprang up into a sister position in reaction to being earlier sacrificed—when she was* IPHIGENIA*—by her father to appease the gods). The scar on her throat is only seen close up, when* SHE *tells one of her many secrets.*

SCENE
Agamemnon's grave

TIME
Today

In this neoclassical-Americana sister drama of the 2000s, ELEKTRA *is the outcast of the family.* SHE*'s heartbroken, and in love with her father (Agamemnon).* SHE *will never marry now that he is gone, and* SHE *is insanely jealous of Iphigenia for getting the chance to be sacrificed. Recently* SHE *has been chained like a dog outside her royal home. (*SHE*'s mad at her mom for killing her dad.) In this scene, called "Shut up," the sisters spar for survival, sometimes almost in code.* CHRYSOTHEMIS *reveals her alliance with her mom at the very moment* ELEKTRA *is about to enlist her help in a blood vendetta.*

(Slash (/) means overlapping argument, interrupting each other.)

CHRYSOTHEMIS: I'm your sister.

ELEKTRA: I don't believe I won't be terminated—

CHRYSOTHEMIS: I'm your sister.

ELEKTRA: If I cooperate—

CHRYSOTHEMIS: Come, dear sister, I am not your foe but it's about your foe . . . your dreary wrath / and your profanity is, oh dear, it's so loud. I overheard, I said I overheard them say . . .

ELEKTRA: I don't know you or your happy-go-lucky malarkey Disney politics. . . .

CHRYSOTHEMIS: They say you better bend before the strong, you better shorten your sails, better look a little harmless . . . / if you don't shut up, well, don't blame me if you can't turn to—

ELEKTRA: My father is dead. My sister's dead. My brother might be dead.

CHRYSOTHEMIS: No, he isn't—see—and that is the terrific news. I was here this morning at the cemetery and somebody left this gleaming lock of curls on my father's grave.

ELEKTRA: They killed my sister and they killed my father. . . . This is my father's grave.

CHRYSOTHEMIS: And he was my father.

ELEKTRA: This is holy ground.

CHRYSOTHEMIS: It's been hard on all of us.

ELEKTRA: You have no right to transgress holy ground.

CHRYSOTHEMIS: Maybe I should spend more time at the cemetery.

ELEKTRA: Get off the ground.

CHRYSOTHEMIS: Maybe I should holler and bellow at the top of my lungs the way you do.

ELEKTRA: Get off.

CHRYSOTHEMIS: On the other hand I'm getting by, I carry on.

ELEKTRA: Get away from me.

CHRYSOTHEMIS: I sort of bend before the hateful.

ELEKTRA: Get lost!

CHRYSOTHEMIS: I mean I do run errands for the sake of the stepfamily. Which is probably compromising but I am entitled to my own adjustment!

ELEKTRA: Get out of here!

CHRYSOTHEMIS: You're not the only one in this family!

ELEKTRA: This is where they quenched my father, mangled him and cleft his soul, my father slew his thousands . . .

CHRYSOTHEMIS: They say there's no turning back but you could turn back now. . . . I'm telling you they're gonna kill you if you don't—I hope nobody saw me come here.

ELEKTRA: I am not doing very well.

CHRYSOTHEMIS: They told me not to tell so don't tell anybody, but I feel like I can tell you . . . as somebody I can turn to—

ELEKTRA: Where do you turn?

CHRYSOTHEMIS: Turn to me.

ELEKTRA: When you've got nowhere to go.

CHRYSOTHEMIS: (*Leaning closer, as if to tell her the secret* SHE *has been holding back,* SHE *suddenly resembles Iphigenia.*) Lying next to you for years in the shared room, our necks were parallel, our throats were quiet all those nights when they'd come bending down to kiss us both good night in the slant of light from the doorway—

ELEKTRA: When it's dark and you feel so blue.

CHRYSOTHEMIS: Daddy slipped and caught me by the neck but that was random. . . . We were so very close in age—

ELEKTRA: I wanted to ask you something but I—

CHRYSOTHEMIS: They say like sisters and we were—

ELEKTRA: I know you'll think it's . . . no, no just forget it.

CHRYSOTHEMIS: You can't change what we are, Elektra.

ELEKTRA: Oh, God! No. Shut up! No.

CHRYSOTHEMIS: You shut up, I'm entitled to my own adjustment.

ELEKTRA: Shut up! Shut up! Shut up!

CHRYSOTHEMIS: No, you shut up, you're not the only one in this family. Shut up!

ELEKTRA: Oh, God, she mocks me. Shut up!

(*Pause.* CHRYSOTHEMIS *turns away.*)

CHRYSOTHEMIS: And if they told me anything it would be just like telling Mother when it used to be the same as telling you because we told each other everything.

ELEKTRA: Oh, God, who told her that?

CHRYSOTHEMIS: Just between you and me.

ELEKTRA: Who does she believe?

CHRYSOTHEMIS: I hope nobody heard what I just said. I'll go forth upon my errand.

EYES OF THE HEART
BY CATHERINE FILLOUX

CHARACTERS
SEREY *(18), a Cambodian woman, Americanized, niece to* THIDA SAN, *strong and vulnerable;* THIDA SAN *(50), a Cambodian woman suffering from psychosomatic blindness*

SCENE
An apartment living room in Long Beach, California

TIME
Late 1980s

Eyes of the Heart *portrays a Cambodian immigrant family's pursuit of a new life in the U.S., as they struggle with the damage the Khmer Rouge inflicted upon them.* THIDA *has recently run away after revealing what happened to her daughter Oun (Pronounced Own).* SEREY, *whose single father wants to arrange a marriage for her, realizes how much* SHE *needs her aunt. Before* THIDA'S *husband, Sipha, a doctor, was taken away by the Khmer Rouge, he warned* THIDA *to take off her eyeglasses (the Khmer Rouge killed people with glasses) and saved her life.*

(**SEREY** *enters as* **THIDA** *sits by the window.*)

SEREY: You're really *pissed* at my dad. (*Explaining the word.*) Angry.

THIDA: Correct.

SEREY: He has that effect on people. When you ran away it made me think of the camp. We lived in a hole, Aunt, before we got assigned a refugee number in Thailand. It was just he and I, and a jerry can of water. He'd stay up at night, wouldn't let me stray anywhere. I found out later it was 'cause the Khmer Rouge from the next camp raped girls.

THIDA: On the day the Khmer Rouge came into Phnom Penh, a statue of the Buddha cried real tears.

SEREY: I'd ask him to show me my mother's photograph over and over. The only thing pretty. I'd ask, where was she in the photo. At home? Where would she go after the picture was taken? The color of the blouse? The little scarf? If I could just get back to where she was in the picture. He'd never say anything, just stare off. He'd put the photo back in the plastic bag, fold it in a square and pin it back to the inside of his undershirt. I miss her so much but I didn't even really know her.

(**SEREY** *is filled with grief for what* **SHE** *can't have and won't ever know.*)

THIDA: Serey? The photo as you describe it would not be taken in her house. She would be in the studio at a photographer's: a room with a red velvet drape. After the picture was taken she would accompany your father for a tea at an outdoor café with white tablecloths and silver. They would hold hands and watch the sun setting, the villas changing color. There would be a soft wind. They would have sandals, which they would slip off under the table. Their feet would touch. Her blouse is pink, I'm certain, and the scarf blue.

SEREY: I'm sorry about Oun.

THIDA: You are a stubborn one, like her. She [my daughter] was a fighter.

SEREY: Did you choose your own husband?

THIDA: No, it is my parents who chose him.

SEREY: Did you love him?

THIDA: He saved my life warning me take off my glasses [because I would have been killed for it]. Our last moment together, I understood what love was.

(**SEREY** *kisses her aunt and exits.* **THIDA** *remembers when* **SHE** *was pregnant with her daughter Oun in Cambodia.*)

THIDA: I stand in the blue-green water, feel my baby kick. Hear the sound of waves breaking, smell the salt air. At Kep I waded in the aqua water, lay on the white sand beach. Sipha would rub my shoulders. . . .

FOREIGN BODIES
BY SUSAN YANKOWITZ

CHARACTERS
SARAH *(16), white;* KATE, *a few years older, her Black girlfriend*

SCENE
KATE'S *bedroom.* KATE *sits on her bed in her underwear, talking to* SARAH, *who is in the bathroom.*

TIME
The present

Foreign Bodies *explores our profound, often unconscious, fear and hatred of "the other" in society.* SARAH *is the daughter of a lawyer who is defending Tom, the accused killer of a prostitute. As* SARAH'S *father grows increasingly obsessed with the case, the boundaries between his life and that of his client become blurred, affecting not only him, but his wife and daughter.*

KATE: What are you doing in there? Swimming the Channel?

SARAH'S VOICE: I felt dirty.

KATE: Can't be too white, huh?

SARAH'S VOICE: Hey, Kate, it's me, Sarah, remember?

KATE: How many baths do you take a day? Three? Four?

SARAH'S VOICE: Depends on the day. . . . Are you really mad because I was a little late?

KATE: We don't have much time, babe.

SARAH'S VOICE: (SHE *can be heard getting out of the tub.*) I *know*, but what could I do? The kid could have died! She was thrashing around in the deep end. Like, her chin was sticking up over the water and her face was all red. The lifeguard was making out with his girlfriend and, you know, the other kids were goofing, and nobody noticed.

KATE: She had a cramp?

SARAH'S VOICE: No. Gum.

KATE: Huh?

SARAH: (*Emerging from the bathroom, wrapped in a towel.*) Bubble gum. Like, she had it in her mouth while she was swimming and then she must've swallowed and sucked the gum into her windpipe. It, you know, choked her, she couldn't breathe or shout, nothing. So I pulled her out and gave her artificial respiration. That's what got the gum dislodged. I mean, it flew out on a big gush of water....

KATE: Gum, a killer. A wad of pink bubble gum could kill you. Nothing's safe.

SARAH: So that's why I was late. Sorry.

KATE: You saved a life. That's great. And it will look good on your resume, too!

SARAH: Hey, yes, I didn't think of that!

KATE: Hurry up. My folks are going to be home soon.

SARAH: Good. Great. Wonderful. They can quiz me about the case, too.

KATE: Give me a break, Sarah. Give yourself a break.

SARAH: How? Nobody else does! He's my dad. Not that I see him. He's hardly home anymore. Then I catch him on the tube, looking like shit. And he's getting fatter, too. You know, he really thinks he's doing something good. You should hear him talking about the criminal justice system and prejudice and scapegoats and how he's working pro bono—

KATE: Pro boner, you mean. Pro Tom's boner.

SARAH: That is gross, Kate!

KATE: He could get off the case. I mean, he chose it. He went to his closet and put on his good suit and his do-good brain and offered them free of charge to a white boy who slices up women.

SARAH: Black people aren't the only ones with problems, Kate! Like, Tom's homeless, remember? You're not. And my father believes he's innocent....

KATE: Your father's got his conscience on backwards.

SARAH: At least he's got a conscience! Oh, I don't know. I hate the whole thing— and I hate *him*!!

KATE: Well, sure you do. *Everybody* hates him.

SARAH: Thanks, Kate. That makes me feel much better.

Kate: Sorry.

Sarah: Trust me, it's no fun being in my shoes.

Kate: You're not wearing shoes. (*Tickles* **Sarah's** *feet.*) Your toes are so pink.

Sarah: Tom's an expert on toes. He worked in a shoe store.

Kate: I was talking about *your* toes.

Sarah: I know, I know! It's awful. My mind keeps jumping to Tom. Just like my dad. He's obsessed. You should hear the dinner-table conversation. Like, Tom's upset because his aunt didn't visit. Tom's prints weren't found anywhere. Tom asked for cigarettes and my dad forgot to bring them. We should pay for Tom's dental work. God, it's like he's married to the guy!

Kate: Your mom must love that.

Sarah: She can't complain. Like, she called him a corporate hack. Practically begged him to take the case.

Kate: I'm begging now. Please, honey. Don't waste our precious little time.

Sarah: (*Climbing into bed.*) Lots of nights my dad goes to sleep on the sofa....

Kate: I bet he rues the day he took this on, rues the day.

Sarah: Who knows? He's so out of it. Like yesterday my mom told me he asked to come to one of my basketball games.

Kate: Hey. Right. I used to see him in the bleachers on Saturdays. He was a big fan in the old days. So was I.

Sarah: Maybe I'll join up again....

Kate: You were hot on the court, really hot. And your jump shot wasn't bad either.

Sarah: I'm crazy about you, too. You know I am. I'm just freaked out these days. Like, I can't get my head on straight.... You think maybe I could move in with you? I mean, just a few weeks?

Kate: Here? Uh-uh. I don't think so.

Sarah: No? Why not? I've stayed over plenty of times.

Kate: Yeah but... it's different now.

Sarah: What do you mean?

KATE: (*Miserably.*) . . . It's my mom. . . . She sort of . . . she hinted maybe I shouldn't spend so much time with you.

SARAH: Your mom?! I thought she liked me.

KATE: It's because of Tom. A lot of people feel that way. They say they look at you—and they can't help it, they think of him.

SARAH: That's sick! (*Jumps out of bed and runs across the room.*)

KATE: Where are you going?

SARAH: To take a bath!

GRIEVING FOR GENEVIEVE
BY KATHLEEN WARNOCK

CHARACTERS

DELILAH PECK ANDREJEWSKI O'CONOR *soon-to-be* **FERRARO** *(early to mid-30s), the middle Peck sister, is a rock-and-roll musician, seamstress, and Girl Scout leader.* **DANNI PECK** *(around 40), the oldest sister, builds and repairs guitars.*

SCENE

The breakfast room of **DELILAH'S** *house in a working-class Baltimore neighborhood. It's also a workroom for a sewing business (***DELILAH** *makes costumes for strippers) and where* **SHE** *keeps musical equipment.*

TIME

A late-summer afternoon, mid-1990s

DELILAH *is about to get married, but her older sister,* **DANNI,** *shows up unexpectedly from New York. Genevieve, their mother, tries to get* **DANNI** *into the wedding, but* **DELILAH** *is resistant. Genevieve,* **DELILAH,** *and another sister, Angel, have just left to go to their mother's house for dinner, leaving* **DANNI** *alone.* **DELILAH** *returns;* **DANNI** *is drinking a beer.*

DANNI: You forget something?

DELILAH: I have to do some stuff first. . . . (*Pause.*) I'm kinda surprised you came.

DANNI: You're getting married. Again.

DELILAH: If at first you don't succeed . . .

DANNI: Hope springs eternal.

DELILAH: I never know what the hell you're talking about. (**DANNI** *shrugs.*) Why are you really here?

DANNI: Why couldn't I just be here for the wedding?

DELILAH: Because you disapprove of me. And when you don't like something, you stay away. Far away.

DANNI: I don't disapprove of you.

DELILAH: You think you're better than me.

Danni: By what standard?

Delilah: There you go again … never give a straight answer. Well, that's about what I'd expect from you. Well, I'm better than you at getting married.

Danni: Repeatedly.

Delilah: Without you. I mean in the wedding.

Danni: You can do whatever you want.

Delilah: You gonna hit Mom up for money again?

Danni: No.

Delilah: Because, you know, the bank is closed. You should think about paying her back what she's given you.

Danni: I think about paying her back all the time.

Delilah: So if it's not money, what is it?

Danni: I'm here to put her out of my misery.

Delilah: Oh, grow up! Your problem is you pay attention to what she says. You have to let it go in one ear and out the other. Remember, it's MOM we're talking about. You could come up and sit at the table with us, you know. It would be nice. For Mom.

Danni: No. I go up there, and with the cats and the dust, in half an hour, I'm not breathing.

Delilah: It's not that bad.

Danni: Yes, it IS! Around here, nobody ever hears me. Nobody believes me. I miss Dad. He liked me.

Delilah: Why can't you do it to make her happy?

Danni: Why is she happy when I can't breathe? You know why you never see me? Because you don't set foot out of Baltimore, except to tour, and when I come here, I go back to New York with more than a case of bronchitis. I think maybe she's right. Maybe I can't take care of myself. If I just did things her way, I might be happy.

Delilah: Please. She doesn't have that kind of control over us.

Danni: You say from the great distance of four blocks from her house. Where she is sitting right now making you dinner.

DELILAH: I don't need to run away like you did.

DANNI: What do you need?

DELILAH: Nothing from you.

DANNI: Are you sure? (**DELILAH** *leaves.*) Maybe you need me to be the fuckup. Maybe you need someone who didn't make it as a musician. Maybe you need me to be the bad daughter so you can give up that role. Hey, I'm only too happy to stop by every couple years. No need to say thanks. Just give her a beer and prop her in the corner and listen to her wheeze! (**SHE** *slams her bottle in the trashcan.*) Damn.

HOTEL SPLENDID
BY LAVONNE MUELLER

CHARACTERS
LITTLE JADE GIRL *(18)* and **CHILD OF GOD** *(17) are Korean women who have been abducted from their homes and made sex slaves for the Japanese Army.*

SCENE
Hotel Splendid, a "comfort station" in the jungles of Japan

TIME
1942

Military bugle is sounded. Lights go up slowly on LITTLE JADE GIRL.

LITTLE JADE GIRL:
>   30 uniforms
>   bud off of me today
>
>   men heave their legs
>   keening, rocking
>
>   groans above me
>   I pretend it's children calling after kites
>
>   my soul floats up
>
>   every night I wash used condoms
>   hang them on a line
>   each night
>   I empty latrine buckets
>
>   my breasts are black with fleas
>   fleas in my eyelashes
>   I shave off wounds of hair
>   glory in my bald head

(**SHE** *flings off a wig. Her head is bald.*)

>   once I made myself beautiful
>   now I only want to be plain
>
>   nothing stops life's fuel

this rapid turnover, man after man
   dividing me

   my divided

I dream about the *real* world
   now I live somewhere else

old aide-de-camp
homing in on me
squat thighs
real eye moving
his hard rounded paunch
   makes it difficult to aim

I hear the crackling step of guards

bicycle-orderly
folded bicycle on his back
his mother sewed prayers into his uniform
he shows me pictures of his wife
puts his binoculars on her thick hair
her lips of scarlet soo-yoo berries
   I hold the picture crying to it:
   take me in
   take me in

he bites my breast and pounds his chest against me

bending a coin in his teeth
preening carrier of the regimental flag
used to the harsh morning wind
skin baked hard as pavement
flies me high on the mat

skulking guard laid land mines today
he cracks his wrists like castanets
wires from his pocket scrape my thighs
he drinks butterfly brandy mixed with kerosene
smells stays on me like thrush.

[**LITTLE JADE GIRL:**
   (*To soldier.*) Will you win the war?

   (*Lights up on soldier.*)

SOLDIER:
> *Never ask that question*
> *questions are taboo.*]

LITTLE JADE GIRL:
> On the island where I was born
> I dive for shells, abalone, seaweed
>   catch crabs big as dogs
>
> in the *real* world
> I started diving at ten
>   depths of five meters
>   holding my breath two minutes
>
> with a drop-net
> I cradle newborn fish
> warm rankness of the sea
>   still rubs my skin
>
> I give the Sergeant garlic
> 12 cloves
> in a folk tale
>   when a bear asked to be human
>   god gave him garlic
>
> be human, I pray
>
> I feel him build
>   tall spreading panicle
>   this sword leaf
>
> he bends me like the white pompoms of cane
> snorting
>
> an army of one
> he ruts close to the ground
> grinding action of the sea
>
> think of the ocean
>
> water saves me
> undulating waves
> like lantern parades
> wave after wave of soft tints
> I give myself to pain

as fish give themselves
to the deepest water

one last groan
he spills
warrior quickness breaks the surface

smell of dead limes

I lie face up
held together
   by the weed structure of common water

he puts the garlic pieces on his ox tongue
slobbers them
opens my legs
forces his mouth in my vee
up
up
spits each gelatinous clove in me
   phlegm pellets
   sticking

he washes his penis in the provided rubber tube
   of salt water and permanganic acid

another careening soldier
volplaning like a glider
lands on me

ugly stretched neck
wide lappet face
yanking at my white belly
hoeing at my moist flank
scrabbling into vents
squawking
picking out my human spore.

(**LITTLE JADE GIRL** *now begins taking scraps of rags from her mat, making a rag doll. Light up on* **CHILD OF GOD**, *who is watching her.*)

CHILD OF GOD: (*To* **LITTLE JADE GIRL** *in a harsh whisper.*) Little Jade Girl, the forest out there can save you.

LITTLE JADE GIRL: Not so loud. Somebody might hear you. And don't call me Little Jade Girl. Not out in the open. Use my Japanese name, Shina.

CHILD OF GOD:

    Why aren't you sleeping?

LITTLE JADE GIRL:

    I was thinking of that first day here
    oh, nothing
    nothing is so terrible as the first day.

CHILD OF GOD:

    I wanted to throw my body in snow... bury myself in white.

LITTLE JADE GIRL:

    By the last soldier, my left side was paralyzed.

CHILD OF GOD:

    That's when I started saving stones.

LITTLE JADE GIRL:

    Why do you want to do that?

CHILD OF GOD:

    Since ancient time, stones were always used against the enemy.

LITTLE JADE GIRL:

    It won't do any good here.

CHILD OF GOD:

    In the memory of old stones... I soothe myself.

LITTLE JADE GIRL:

    Nothing soothes me.

CHILD OF GOD:

    When a man is on top of you, turn your head to the trees. That's where we'll run away and be free.

LITTLE JADE GIRL:

    When I was a girl, I hung poems on the trees. Now tree-rats hang from the branches.

CHILD OF GOD:

    We have to run away.

LITTLE JADE GIRL:

    If we escape, those left behind will be punished.

CHILD OF GOD:

    We'll *all* escape.

LITTLE JADE GIRL:

They'll catch us...bring us back here for the water torture....I know...I know about water.

CHILD OF GOD:

What are you doing?

(**LITTLE JADE GIRL** *is placing the rag doll in a crudely made sling on her back.*)

CHILD OF GOD:

Why do you put rags on your back?

LITTLE JADE GIRL:

It's my baby.

CHILD OF GOD:

Not a real one.

LITTLE JADE GIRL:

Nothing is real here.

INFINITE SPACE
BY ROB HANDEL

CHARACTERS
JESSICA *(17) wears sweat-soaked running clothes;* KIM *(40) is a celebrity interviewer (probably blonde).*

SCENE
A typical suburban teenager's bedroom, somewhere in America

TIME
The present

In the first scene of Infinite Space, *we discover a teenager,* JESSICA, *who has been a captive and seems to be living in a constantly shifting hallucination. One moment her hands are tied together with duct tape; the next moment they're not; the next she is tethered to her bed by a six-foot rope. At this moment there's a knock on her bedroom door; she conceals the six-foot rope under her desk and positions herself so that the visitor won't see her feet.*

JESSICA: Come in.

(*Enter* KIM.)

KIM: Hi.

JESSICA: Hi.

(JESSICA *gestures to the chair where* SHE *wants* KIM *to sit.* KIM *sits.*)

JESSICA: Sorry if I smell. I'm a big runner. I've been running at least three times a day.

KIM: (*Surprised, indicating window.*) Don't the camera crews—

JESSICA: I'm faster than them.

KIM: Of course.

JESSICA: I used to read *Runner's World* from the grocery store. And *Self.*

KIM: But you couldn't—You weren't able to go running when you were . . .

(*Trails off.*)

JESSICA: (*Helpfully.*) When I was in captivity? No. But I ordered athletic wear. You can really barely see it. The weight gain. I don't know what they're giving you such a hard time for.

KIM: You've been following—You've heard about that.

JESSICA: You can't see ten pounds. I mean, come on.

KIM: (*A hint of weariness.*) It's not ten pounds. (*Suddenly this conversation strikes her as absurd.*) I didn't realize you were a fan.

JESSICA: Oh, yeah. I watched you every day.

KIM: You don't have that—when people meet me sometimes—you don't seem at all starstruck.

JESSICA: I'm a celebrity, too.

KIM: Right.

JESSICA: I thought you'd want to interview me after I escaped. You understand why I had to wait a week since the press conference, right? I didn't want to tell my whole story all at once and have people get bored.

KIM: Sure. You say you ordered athletic wear?

JESSICA: I would tell him what I wanted out of the catalog, and he'd order it for me. He'd order whatever I wanted in the way of clothes. He was always asking me if I was comfortable. "Are you comfortable?" I should save this for the cameras. Or did you want to practice the interview ahead of time?

KIM: No, actually, I wanted to meet you ahead of time so we could agree on whether there's anything in particular I should ask you about. Normally my producer would be talking to your lawyer or representative about this, but I understand you always speak for yourself. So I felt I should do the same.

(JESSICA *smiles.* KIM *smiles back. Then* JESSICA *is back to business.*)

JESSICA: You can ask about anything except whether I was physically abused.

KIM: Sure.

JESSICA: That's standard in these cases.

KIM: Even a yes or no?

JESSICA: I'm willing to talk about anything else.

KIM: Sure. Of course, people, you know—it will kind of be the elephant in the room. Some people feel that other victims can feel empowered by hearing—

Jessica: I would like to talk about my faith in Jesus Christ. That's more important, right? You know, Jesus can make a raped woman a virgin again. He can do that, and he can give a nine-year-old girl the strength to wait as long as necessary and become as strong as necessary to escape from captivity. Even if it takes eight years.

Kim: That is so powerful and so interesting, Jessica. Will you say that again, just like that, in the interview?

Jessica: I don't know. About the raped woman? It might distract people if I said that on the air. I was making a point about my faith to you, as a woman to a woman.

Kim: Sure. I think what it is—is people want to know that it's possible to go through something as extraordinary as what you went through and yet be able to have a normal life.

Jessica: It's only been a week that I've had a normal life. But I believe if you have faith, if you really want to be free, you can get access to the strength you need. There are some problems adjusting. I don't know how long they'll last. There's the light thing. Bungee cords, they're a problem.

Kim: Why bungee cords?

Jessica: He used bungee cords at first. They were in his car. Then in the house he switched to duct tape. I guess he didn't think to bring duct tape with him. Do you know the duck joke? A duck walks into a store, goes up to the manager, says, (*Using a really annoying duck voice.*) EXCUSE ME! DO YOU HAVE ANY DUCK FOOD? The manager says, No, I'm sorry, we don't have any duck food. The duck looks disappointed, goes away. The next day, the duck comes into the store. Goes up to the manager. EXCUSE ME! DO YOU HAVE ANY DUCK FOOD? The manager says, No, I told you yesterday, we don't have any duck food. The duck looks sad, goes away. Next day, duck comes into the store, goes up to the manager. EXCUSE ME! DO YOU HAVE ANY DUCK FOOD? Manager says, No, and if you come in here again, I'm going to nail your little webbed feet to the floor! The duck looks heartbroken, goes away. Next day, duck comes into the store. Goes up to the manager. EXCUSE ME! DO YOU HAVE ANY NAILS? The manager says no. DO YOU HAVE ANY DUCK FOOD? (**She** *cracks up laughing.*) Saying duct tape always reminds me of that joke.

Kim: I've never heard that one before. I guess we're set. If you think of anything else, you can call my cell any time. The number's right there.

(**KIM** *leaves her card on the desk and shakes* **JESSICA'S** *hand.*)

JESSICA: Thanks, Kim.

KIM: Thank *you.* I'll see you Monday.

(**KIM** *exits and we hear her footsteps descend the stairs.* **SHE** *has left the door open.* **JESSICA** *rises and walks quickly toward the door, falls down.* **SHE** *is still tied to the desk. On the floor, she silently chastises herself.*)

THE INTELLIGENT DESIGN OF JENNY CHOW

BY ROLIN JONES

CHARACTERS

JENNIFER MARCUS *(22, Asian-American)*, ADELE HARTWICK *(late 40s–early 50s)*

SCENE

The kitchen

TIME

Now, right now

JENNIFER MARCUS *is agoraphobic, obsessive-compulsive, and a genius at creating robotic missiles. Her mother,* ADELE HARTWICK, *is a workaholic who, along with her husband, adopted Jennifer from a Chinese orphanage and has provided her with an affluent life.* SHE *does not understand* JENNIFER'S *desire to communicate with her birth mother, nor why* SHE *cannot get out of the house and behave normally.*

JENNIFER MARCUS: (SHE *picks up her* [RUBIK'S] *cube and tool kit and walks to the kitchen where* ADELE *is sitting, waiting, staring off into space, with a drink in her hand.* SHE'S *plowed.*) Oh.

ADELE HARTWICK: Hi.

JENNIFER MARCUS: How was your trip?

ADELE HARTWICK: It was what it was.

JENNIFER MARCUS: How was the acquisition?

ADELE HARTWICK: It happened. How come the garbage is still in the back, Jennifer?

JENNIFER MARCUS: I forgot.

ADELE HARTWICK: What are we going to do with you, Jennifer?

JENNIFER MARCUS: Welcome back, Mom. (JENNIFER *turns to leave.*)

ADELE HARTWICK: No. We're not finished.

JENNIFER MARCUS: I'm tired.

ADELE HARTWICK: You're tired? No, you're not. You haven't been in fourteen-hour negotiations. Your secretary didn't forget to book you a room. You weren't rerouted three times this week. You didn't have to fire a lifetime employee, someone who's been with the company for twenty-eight years and barely makes enough to support his family. And you sure as hell didn't do it the same day the company picked up a two-thousand-dollar dinner. You're not tired, Jennifer. I'm tired.

JENNIFER MARCUS: Okay. Then you should probably go to bed.

ADELE HARTWICK: No. I can't go to bed because my house is in disarray.

JENNIFER MARCUS: What are you talking about?

ADELE HARTWICK: Take out the garbage. Do some dishes. Am I asking too much?

JENNIFER MARCUS: I've been busy.

ADELE HARTWICK: Online. With your little cyberboyfriend . . .

JENNIFER MARCUS: You're drunk.

ADELE HARTWICK: . . . Hello, cyberfriend. Can you find my mommy for me?

JENNIFER MARCUS: Whatever.

ADELE HARTWICK: You think you're a princess. . . .

JENNIFER MARCUS: You're totally plowed.

ADELE HARTWICK: . . . A little Chinese princess? Isn't that what you think? Think your father and I stole you away from the queen? We're keeping you from your life as the emperor's daughter, huh?

JENNIFER MARCUS: Shut up.

ADELE HARTWICK: What happened to you, Jennifer?

JENNIFER MARCUS: You happened to me.

ADELE HARTWICK: Oh, is that right? I ruined your life? Me, who got on a plane, brought you back here. Put you in this house, put you into every accelerated program, every activity. Fed your brain.

JENNIFER MARCUS: I didn't ask for this house and I hated those classes.

ADELE HARTWICK: (*Reliving it.*) Ms. Hartwick, Mr. Marcus. Your little girl's a genius. What do you do, Jennifer?

JENNIFER MARCUS: I don't care.

ADELE HARTWICK: You can't even imagine. Of course you can't, you weren't there. You were out on the playground. They give you a handbook.

JENNIFER MARCUS: Oh, of course, the handbook . . .

ADELE HARTWICK: Page one. Never tell them they're a genius.

JENNIFER MARCUS: Never tell them you're good at anything. . . .

ADELE HARTWICK: Page two . . .

JENNIFER MARCUS: How to deprive your child of joy and wonder while preparing her for a life of infinite servitude.

ADELE HARTWICK: She abandoned you . . .

JENNIFER MARCUS: Yeah? Then how come her name is on the birth certificate? (*The following dialogue overlaps until "GO!"*)

ADELE HARTWICK: . . . left you on a doorstep . . .

JENNIFER MARCUS: How would they know that?

ADELE HARTWICK: . . . and you want to *replace* me?

JENNIFER MARCUS: This isn't about the fucking garbage cans.

ADELE HARTWICK: You don't know what we've done for you.

JENNIFER MARCUS: It's maybe I'll like her more. Isn't that it?

ADELE HARTWICK: You had so much potential. . . .

JENNIFER MARCUS: She loved me.

ADELE HARTWICK: A brilliant child. And I am . . .

JENNIFER MARCUS: And I'm going to find her.

ADELE HARTWICK: . . . totally mystified by what has happened to you.

JENNIFER MARCUS: Did you hear me? I'm getting the fuck out of here.

ADELE HARTWICK: Go. GO! (**JENNIFER** *heads for the front door.*)

JENNIFER MARCUS: I'm going to find her. I want to meet my real mother.

ADELE HARTWICK: Yeah, and how are you going to do that?

JENNIFER MARCUS: I'll fly.

ADELE HARTWICK: You got a passport?

JENNIFER MARCUS: I'll get one.

ADELE HARTWICK: You got a travel visa?

JENNIFER MARCUS: I'll contact the embassy. (**JENNIFER** *opens the front door.*)

ADELE HARTWICK: Yeah? And how are you going to get to the airport, huh? How are you going to get out the front door? (**JENNIFER** *stands in the door frame.* **SHE** *is breathing hard.*) They make names up, Jennifer. They do that, you know? They just fill in the blank. And that's the truth. There's probably a thousand birth certificates with her name on it. And that silly scarf you wear around . . . probably the nurse's. The truth? That woman abandoned you. And your father and I took two years filling out the paperwork, getting signatures and mortgaging our lives into the stratosphere so we could get on a plane, to a scary country where we knew *no one!* So we could save your life. (**JENNIFER** *keeps putting one foot out the door and then bringing it back in.*) We would never give up on you. We love you. And that is why I push you. That is why I won't let you accept this as your life. And I'll be damned if I'm going to let you throw it away, let you spend it with flunkies like Todd, people with not an *ounce* of ambition. (**JENNIFER** *is trying not to lose it in front of* **ADELE**, *who slowly walks toward her.*) Listen to me. Listen. My daughter is brilliant. My daughter is an exceptional young woman. And I am not going to let her waste away.

(**ADELE** *tries to hug* **JENNIFER** *from behind*).

JENNIFER MARCUS: (*Freaking out.*) Don't you touch me! Don't you ever fucking touch me again! (**SHE** *runs away from* **ADELE**, *back to the kitchen, shaking her hands frantically.*)

ADELE HARTWICK: I live in the real world, Jennifer. I'm real. And in the real world, women get screwed out there and if you're not prepared they will squash you. So blame me, lash out at me for your condition, but don't—

JENNIFER MARCUS: I'm going to find her. I'm going to China.

ADELE HARTWICK: Sure, go to China when you can't even take out the garbage. Keep dreaming.

JENNIFER MARCUS: I'm going there. You watch me. (**SHE** *runs to her room,* [*past Mr. Marcus*]. **ADELE** *shuts the front door.*)

[MR. MARCUS: What the hell is going on down here?]

ADELE HARTWICK: (*Loud.*) The only way you're going to get to China is if this house grows wings.

[MR. MARCUS: Adele...] (**ADELE** *exits,* [*followed by Mr. Marcus*]. **JENNIFER** *sits down at her computer, typing feverishly.*)

ADELE HARTWICK: (*Offstage, loud.*) I'm real. This house is real, Jennifer. And you can hide in your room and log on if you want to. But that's not real! That's a dream! (*We hear a door slam.*)

JENNIFER MARCUS: Dear Dr. Yakunin. It's me, Jennifer Marcus. I know you haven't heard from me in a while, but I need to talk to you immediately. You're the only person I know who'll understand. Find me, please. I need your help. (**SHE** *stops typing.*) I'm going to build a robot. (**SHE** *hits a button on her computer and we hear a loud "bling" noise.*)

INTIMATE APPAREL
BY LYNN NOTTAGE

CHARACTERS
ESTHER *(35), a plain African-American woman, looks focused and determined as* SHE *sits at a sewing machine table, trimming a camisole with lace;* MRS. DICKSON *(50) owns the boarding house where* ESTHER *lives and looks out for her interests.*

SCENE
A simple bedroom in Lower Manhattan. The only outstanding items in the room are a bright, colorful quilt and embroidered curtains.

TIME
1905

MRS. DICKSON: (*Offstage.*) Don't be fresh, Lionel. I know your mama since before the war. (MRS. DICKSON, *fifty, a handsome, impeccably groomed African-American woman, enters laughing.*) There you are. Mr. Charles was admiring the bread pudding and I told him that our Esther made it. It seems he has a sweet tooth.

ESTHER: Mr. Charles is overly generous, come, the pudding ain't nothing special.

MRS. DICKSON: And did I mention that our most available Mr. Charles was promoted to head bellman at just about the finest hotel in New York? Yes.

ESTHER: But he still fetching luggage.

MRS. DICKSON: Not just any luggage, high-class luggage.

ESTHER: And is high-class luggage easier to carry?

MRS. DICKSON: I reckon it is easier to haul silk than cotton, if you know what I'm saying. (MRS. DICKSON *laughs.*) And he sporting a right smart suit this evening.

ESTHER: Yes, it cashmere.

MRS. DICKSON: You can tell more about a man by where he shops than his practiced conversation. 'Cause any man who's had enough tonic can talk smooth, but not every man has the good sense to shop at—

ESTHER AND MRS. DICKSON: Saperstein's. (**ESTHER** *laughs.* **MRS. DICKSON** *examines the embroidery.*)

MRS. DICKSON: Lovely.

ESTHER: It's for Corinna Mae's wedding night.

MRS. DICKSON: Don't tell me you've been in here all evening? Corinna Mae is getting ready to leave with her fiancé.

ESTHER: I wish I could find my party face. It really is a lovely affair. You done a fine job.

MRS. DICKSON: Come now, it ain't over yet. Put aside your sewing and straighten yourself up. There. You'll have a dance before this evening's out.

ESTHER: Please, Mrs. Dickson, I can't, really. I'll just stand there like a wallflower.

MRS. DICKSON: Nonsense, I've danced a half a dozen times, and my feet are just about worn out.

ESTHER: If I had your good looks I'd raise a bit of dust myself. Ain't nobody down there interested in me.

MRS. DICKSON: Esther, you're being silly. You've been moping around here for days. What's the matter?

ESTHER: If you must know, I turned 35 Thursday past. (*A moment.*)

MRS. DICKSON: Oh Lord, I forgot, child. I sure did. Look at that. With Corinna Mae carrying on and all these people, it slipped my mind. Happy birthday, my sweet Esther. (**MRS. DICKSON** *gives her a big hug.*)

ESTHER: It's fine. You had all this to prepare for. And I been living in this rooming house for so long. I reckon I'm just another piece of furniture.

MRS. DICKSON: Never. You were a godsend when you come to me at 17. Yes. I remember thinking how sweet and young you was with a sack full of overripe fruit smelling like a Carolina orchard.

ESTHER: And now? Twenty-two girls later, if you count Lerleen. That's how many of these parties I have had to go to and play merry. I should be happy for them, I know, but each time I think why ain't it me. Silly Corinna Mae, ain't got no brain at all, and just as plain as flour.

MRS. DICKSON: Your time will come, child.

ESTHER: What if it don't? Listen to her laughing. God forgive me, but I hate her laughter, I hate her happiness and I feel simply awful for saying so. And I'm afraid if I go back in there, she'll see it all over my face, and it's her day.

MRS. DICKSON: There are a number of young men open to your smile. A sour face don't buy nothing but contempt. Why, our Mr. Charles has had three servings of your bread pudding.

ESTHER: And he shouldn't have had any. (**ESTHER** *laughs.*) He weighs nearly as much as your horse.

MRS. DICKSON: Nonsense, he weighs more than poor Jessup. Shhh. He is a good man, poised for success. Yes.

ESTHER: But he's been coming to these parties for near two years and if he ain't met a woman, I'd bet it ain't a woman he after. I've been warned about men in refined suits. But still, Esther would be lucky for this attention, that's what you thinking. Well, I ain't giving up so easy.

MRS. DICKSON: Good for you. But there are many a cautionary tale bred of overconfidence. When I met the late Mr. Dickson he was near sixty and I forgave his infatuation with the opiates, for he come with this rooming house, and look how many good years it's given me. Sure I cussed that damn pipe, and I cussed him for making me a widow, but sometimes we get to a point where we can't be so particular.

ESTHER: (*Snaps.*) Well, I ain't going down there to be paraded like some featherless bird. (*A moment.*) I'm sorry, would you kindly take this down to Corinna Mae?

MRS. DICKSON: I'll do no such thing. You can bring it down yourself. (**MRS. DICKSON** *starts for the door, but abruptly stops.*) It tough, Esther, for a colored woman in this city. I ain't got to tell you that. You nimble with your fingers, but all Corinna Mae got be her honey-colored skin. And you good and smart and deserve all the attention in the room, but today's her day and all I ask is that you come toast her as I know she'd toast you. Put aside your feelings and don't say nothing about Sally's piano playing, the girl's trying. For God's sake, this is a party, not a wake.

ESTHER: Let me fix my hair.

KISS AND CRY

BY TOM ROWAN

CHARACTERS
FIONA *(25), a gorgeous and charismatic actress;* LAUREN *(35), a playwright/
director, fiercely intelligent and driven*

SCENE
Their New York apartment

TIME
The late 1990s

LAUREN *and* FIONA *have lived together as domestic partners for several years,
but now that* FIONA'S *movie career is taking off,* SHE'S *been finding ways to
deceive the public regarding her personal life.* LAUREN *is packing to go to
Edinburgh to direct the play she wrote for* FIONA, *but* FIONA *is committed to a
film production and unable to go.*

LAUREN: It's not too late to change your mind and come with me. It would do
you a lot of good.

FIONA: I wish I could. I so wish that. You know how much I wish that. But this
is gonna be a dream come true for you anyway.

LAUREN: My dream of Edinburgh always included you. I wrote this play for you.

FIONA: Gina will be brilliant.

LAUREN: Not the point.

FIONA: I'd give anything to be there, but the schedule just . . .

LAUREN: I know.

FIONA: And actually, we should be glad they moved up the filming of *Vampire
Campus 2: Sophomore Year*. Now it'll be all over by the time we go into
rehearsal for our off-Broadway gig—which is our main event, right?
Edinburgh is just a one-act. This one's gonna be your masterpiece.

LAUREN: Yeah, but who knows when it's finally gonna happen? Sharon said she
might not be able to get the theatre we really want until after the holidays,
and it still depends on—

FIONA: (*Worried.*) Just make sure we're done by mid-March.

LAUREN: Excuse me? What if we're a hit? It's open-ended.

FIONA: Nothing's open-ended in the movie business.

LAUREN: I'm not *in* the movie business.

FIONA: Well, I am. And I have to keep that March–April time free. They're already talking contracts for *Vampire Campus 3: Junior Prom.*

LAUREN: I sure hope you don't think I'm gonna wait around for you to finish vampire graduate school.

FIONA: Touché.

LAUREN: Is that the kind of career you want?

FIONA: No, you know it isn't. That's why I'm trying to get Lex to delay the contract on that one. I haven't said anything because I don't want to jinx it, but . . . he thinks he can maybe get me a screen test for *Moonlight on a Ranch.*

LAUREN: A movie of the book by Seth Brown?

FIONA: Exactly. (*Grins.*) Prestige Project! It's been a *New York Times* best-seller for seven months!

LAUREN: I know, I work in a bookstore, remember? I think it took me forty-five minutes to read that novel. Counting my barf break.

FIONA: You're awful. I thought it was lovely.

LAUREN: Then you must have a secret life as a suburban housewife.

FIONA: How come you have to belittle my projects all the time? Aren't you a little bit proud of me? I could win an Oscar and you'd still be looking down your alternative culture snob nose at me, wouldn't you? I'm close to being a movie star, Lauren. And it's building. They're predicting *Vampire Campus* will end up as the biggest money-maker of the summer. And if I get *Moonlight on a Ranch*, it could be *huge.*

LAUREN: Since when is it about money? I thought we understood that *reaching people* is the most important thing.

FIONA: Exactly. So what do you have lined up in Edinburgh? Four performances in a fifty-seat theatre? *Vampire Campus* played to two and a half million *opening weekend.*

LAUREN: And I'll bet it really changed their lives.

FIONA: Well, maybe their lives didn't *want* to be changed. Ever think of that? What the fuck's wrong with *entertaining* people? You're always talking about like, *connections*, right? Movies connect! People are *talking* about *Vampire Campus* all over the country! The *world* soon. Scotland, even! Did you know that movies are one of the main topics of social conversation? Almost as big as sports, and certainly ahead of politics—only the weather has a clear advantage. I'm being discussed around water coolers and bars all across the nation! Don't tell me that's nothing. You can't do that from a converted garage in the East Village.

LAUREN: I'd rather touch twelve people's souls in a basement theatre than drown twelve million in inane, violent, sexist bullshit.

FIONA: So if it's not postlesbian radical . . . whatever!—then it's automatically garbage, right? I used to buy into that, but you know what? I don't feel like an outcast from society! I'm connecting with the world! I'm making waves! I'm rocking the boat!

THE LANGUAGE OF KISSES
BY EDMUND DE SANTIS

CHARACTERS
ZAN, *a well-kept retired college instructor, late 40s to early 50s;* MARA, *early 20s,* ZAN'S *estranged daughter*

SCENE
On a farm in Gideon, Ohio

TIME
June

MARA, *a high-strung young woman in her early twenties, has surprised her mother,* ZAN, *by suddenly returning home after a three-year-long absence and asking to stay a while.* ZAN, *a good-looking woman in her forties, is not enthusiastic about this plan as* SHE *has a relationship going with the handyman, Blue. In the beginning of the scene,* MARA *has just described how* SHE *was attacked in her apartment elevator.*

MARA: He didn't. Penetrate me. He...came on my shoe. (*Laughs, then gets teary.*) It was scary.

(ZAN *puts her hand on* MARA'S *shoulder.*)

MARA: They couldn't convict him. Not enough evidence or something!

ZAN: Your shoe?

MARA: There's never enough evidence! You notice? If I was a man there'd be enough evidence, you bet there'd be. You know, if I was a man being stalked.

ZAN: (*Takes* MARA'S *face in her hands.*) Mara. Did you stalk someone?

MARA: What?! (*Pulling away.*) No! I'm not lying! And I never stalked anybody when I was living here. That was—God, you'd believe anybody else before you'd believe me! You think I could make something like that up? This guy was everywhere I went! I felt trapped! I didn't know where else to go. So can I crash here or not? I'm not going to beg you.

(*The sound of the tractor sputters out.*)

ZAN: Yes...you can stay.

MARA: Thank you. I'll start looking for an apartment in Mallory tomorrow, I promise, and a job. I don't expect you to support me. I could find something in an office. Or waitressing. I haven't done it in a while. Just haveta get used to being treated like dirt again. This water's terrible. (*Refills her glass at the sink.* SHE *looks out the window.*) Who's that?

ZAN: Where?

MARA: On the tractor?

ZAN: The handyman.

MARA: Oh, you have a handyman.

ZAN: The guy who—He's handy. He helps out. He built the . . . gazebo thing.

MARA: I figured you had somebody to help out. He's so cute.

ZAN: He's not . . . cute. It's not high school.

MARA: Well, from here he is. What's wrong with him?

ZAN: (*A little too quickly.*) There's nothing wrong with him. He's a great help. I don't know what I'd've done without him.

MARA: Ma, you have a crush on him, don't you?

ZAN: Mara . . . no, that's not. . . . I know, I have an idea—why don't you go freshen up? I'm about to put out lunch for Blue, if you'd like I could make you a sandwich.

MARA: Blue?

ZAN: The handyman.

MARA: Blue?

ZAN: It's his name. Don't make a big deal out of it.

MARA: I won't. I'm starving. I would love a sandwich. Thank you. I'll run my bag up to my room and use the bathroom. I wanna look good for Blue.

ZAN: Oh.

MARA: You don't want me to look good for Blue?

ZAN: No, of course, I always want you to look your best but—

MARA: I'm just being playful. Don't tell me, he's gay!

ZAN: No, I meant—you'll have to sleep on the foldout couch in the addition while you're here, do you mind?

MARA: Why, do you and Helen have sewing circles up there now?

ZAN: It's Blue's room.

MARA: Blue's room? Oh, of course, how silly of me. "Blue's room." He lives here?

ZAN: (*With the slightest bit of an edge.*) What of it?

MARA: Why are you treating me so coldly? All I said was, "Does he live here?"

ZAN: Yes!

MARA: Does he pay rent?

ZAN: It's a special situation.

MARA: So he does the work and gets room and board in return and and...

ZAN: The place needs work. Constant maintenance. The land was going to waste.

MARA: But...it's...my...room.

ZAN: It was your room. It's Blue's home now, too. It's his room. I can't just take it away from him.

MARA: Then I'll sleep on the couch and use the washroom in the ADDITION! It's fine, it's more private anyhow. Though I don't see why Blue, if he's living here, isn't the one staying in the ADDITION! And P.S., the addition is the room Dad died in.

ZAN: Well, there are no ghosts here.

MARA: I'll still have to come upstairs for a shower.

ZAN: You can use the shower in the basement, I had it fixed up nice down there.

MARA: With all those spiders! I hate that! I'll clean up after myself, don't worry, okay? I promise. Does Blue shower upstairs?

ZAN: Shower wherever you like.

MARA: You're right, what'm I thinking, I'm grateful you're even letting me stay. You're only my mother. I'll shower in the basement. I'll sleep in the basement if you want me to. You don't get any of my jokes, do you? I'll stay out of your hair. You'll see.

Zan: I don't care what you think.

Mara: You're fucking him, that's it, isn't it, that's why you've been acting so weird!

Zan: Could you do me a favor and not use language like that around Blue? It upsets him.

Mara: Excuse me, you're sleeping with him, aren't you?

Zan: Go put your bag in the addition.

Mara: I'm out of line.

Zan: I don't want you to say or do...anything...to...upset...him....He's extremely sensitive and—

Mara: What'm I going to say, what'm I going to do, don't worry, I won't even talk to him, okay, would you prefer I stay completely to myself because I can crawl into a cocoon for weeks at a stretch. I got good at it.

MEASURE FOR PLEASURE: A RESTORATION ROMP

BY DAVID GRIMM

CHARACTERS

DAME STICKLE *(50s), a Puritan lady who tends to meddle in the life of her niece;* HERMIONE GOODE *(25), a beautiful country lass who may appear flighty but has a keen wit, a quick mind, and a passionate nature*

SCENE

The garden of DAME STICKLE'S *home*

TIME

1751, during the forty days known in the Christian Calendar as Lent, which end with the Spring Solstice

DAME STICKLE *is urging her niece to marry Sir Peter Lustforth (60s), a country gentleman of lower birth who has risen in the ranks through cleverness and subterfuge.*

STICKLE: By sweet King Jesu, hussy, I will not let you refuse! Before your mother died, she made me swear to her an oath that I would raise you properly and see you decently disposed. And now you have a chance to make a suitable alliance—

HERMIONE: Suitable? Egad! Let's overlook for just one moment that he's almost thrice my age; let's overlook that he's a cretin; let's overlook that he smells bad; the fact he's got a wife already should repudiate his suit! And don't you mention that annulment—! If a man may cast his wife aside whenever he should choose, what surety is left I will not meet an equal fate?

STICKLE: If more wives feared their husband's wrath, more marriages would last.

HERMIONE: A wrathful husband has one fate: to be made cuckold fast.

STICKLE:
You churl! You slut! To wish him thus and question his intent?
Has he not planned a sacred feast to mark the end of Lent?
A celebration to unite as one all sinful, errant souls,
To save you from damnation and from hell's hot burning coals;
And seeks he not your hand at that most sanctified of times—

HERMIONE: (*Aside.*) Oh here we go—I hate it when my aunt resorts to rhymes!
She'll hear no reason, brook no logic, set her mind in stone—

STICKLE:

Attempt no disputation, girl. By Jesu, cease to groan!
God's providence has chosen you a husband in good time
To lift you from your sink of vice, your swamp of moral slime,
And with all pious pity place you properly beside
An ardent, wealthy Christian man to be his blushing bride.

HERMIONE: Oh aunt, I beg you, cease this cadence. I can stand no more.

STICKLE: Then do as I instruct you, or I'll cast you from my door!

HERMIONE: He's old, he's fat, he's lecherous, he drinks, he uses snuff!

STICKLE: The choice is yours: Submit or you'll be destitute!

HERMIONE: Enough! (*Aside.*) Egad, this heptometrical prosody has rankled all my brain. (*Aloud.*) I'll do your will; I'll marry him.

STICKLE: Oh, my darling girl— Come, let me clasp thee to my breast. (*Aside.*) I wouldn't trust a word she says; this harlot's always lying. (*Aloud.*) On Easter day thou wilt be Lady Lustforth. I hope you shall conform yourself to all that will require.

HERMIONE: I will, for as in everything, obedience is king.

STICKLE: (*Aside.*) Obedience my foot! But I will fadge some method to ensure the bond is set. (*Aloud.*) Be jocund, child. This alliance will provide you comfort and security. Your dead mother would be pleased. Now I must go discuss the banns with our good Reverend Puke. I'm sure he'll have a word or two of guidance for thine ear. I shall return forthwith, dear girl. Ah, praised be Jesu. Praise the king.

MISS WITHERSPOON
BY CHRISTOPHER DURANG

CHARACTERS

VERONICA *(mid-40s to late 50s), a smart but worried woman, whose nickname is Miss Witherspoon;* **MARYAMMA** *(any age), an intelligent, graceful spirit guide in the netherworld*

SCENE

Bardo, the netherworld where dead people await their reincarnation

TIME

The present

Chronically depressed for most of her life, **VERONICA** *committed suicide and is now doomed, ironically, to reincarnation—a fate* **SHE** *refuses to accept.*

VERONICA: I'm back, I'm back, hooray, hooray!

(**MARYAMMA** *comes rushing in, angry.*)

MARYAMMA: What did you just do?

VERONICA: I'm back!

MARYAMMA: Did you just commit suicide at two weeks old???

VERONICA: It wasn't my fault. You sent me where there was a vicious dog.

MARYAMMA: Yes, but you chose. . . . Oh forget it, that was a wasted lifetime. And that poor couple are going to suffer and have guilt, and try to make it up with the next child, who's going to be spoiled and will take no responsibility for anything and then will get drunk at age sixteen and drive a car without a license and kill two people—you see what you've done?

VERONICA: I didn't do it. If that's how they behave, that how they behave, it's not my fault.

MARYAMMA: Your aura is worse than before.

VERONICA: Look, I was thinking. I don't want Saint Peter. I want to go to the Jewish heaven which is like general anesthesia. Can you arrange that please?

MARYAMMA: This isn't a spa.

VERONICA: Not only do I not like life on earth, I realize I don't like to be conscious. I don't want to be here talking to you. I would consider it a wonderful favor if you could arrange for me to be put under.

MARYAMMA: The general anesthesia afterlife is just what happens to the people who don't believe in the afterlife. And you can't just choose the Jewish heaven. Plus I sort of misspoke. It's not only Jewish people. It's also people like Jean-Paul Sartre and Camus. You know, people who don't believe in an afterlife.

VERONICA: I want blankness, I want nothing.

MARYAMMA: Between grief and nothing, I'd choose grief, William Faulkner wrote. Later Jean-Paul Belmondo took the same quote in the movie *Breathless* and said, "I'd choose nothing."

VERONICA: (*Brief pause.*) Why are you telling me this?

MARYAMMA: What you said just made me think of it, that's all. You're choosing nothing. It's a negative choice, nothing. People who go to a restaurant and order nothing, don't eat. Their bodies don't get nourishment. Nothing is as nothing does.

VERONICA: I don't remember those lines in *Breathless*.

MARYAMMA: Oh, you saw the film?

VERONICA: I didn't see the Godard version. I saw the Richard Gere remake on HBO one night.

MARYAMMA: I hate when they make remakes of classic films. It's terrible. It's like when someone says a beautiful sentence, and then some jerk later comes and says, "Let me paraphrase that for you."

VERONICA: Yes, Rex always hated remakes too. Gosh, even saying his name makes me angry. Is there a hell and can you check if he's there?

MARYAMMA: What do you have against Rex Harrison?

VERONICA: I told you, I was married to him. And he wasn't very nice.

MARYAMMA: I explained before, you were married to the soul of Rex Harrison but not when he was Rex Harrison. He had similarities, but he was a coal miner in eighteen seventy-six. In your last life you kept recognizing him when you'd see the actor Rex Harrison, but you were actually recognizing your husband from eighteen seventy-six, not the person who won the Oscar for *My Fair Lady*.

VERONICA: What are you talking about? I remember going to the Oscars with Rex Harrison.

MARYAMMA: You're blurring memories, dreams, and fantasies. It's partially that brown tweed aura of yours—thoughts get stuck in it.

VERONICA: I thought you said we could remember our past lives up here.

MARYAMMA: I did. But people are all on different levels of development, and because of your continuing negative choices, your level of development is fairly messed up.

VERONICA: You're very critical, and you're not very encouraging. I'd like you to go away now, and if I can't be under general anesthesia, then I'd just like to sit and stare and try to think nothing for a while.

(VERONICA *sits in her chair, hoping to end the conversation and to zone out for a while.*)

MARYAMMA: Well, two years have gone by since we started this converstation. . . .

VERONICA: What?

MARYAMMA: So it's time for you to reincarnate again.

VERONICA: It can't be. I just got here.

MARYAMMA: Good-bye.

(MARYAMMA *exits.*)

(*Whoosing sounds again.* VERONICA *is suddenly in that same place in her chair—air whooshing up at her hair, the light from below, sounds of rushing through the air, being sucked downward. Once again her legs are being pulled by some force, back down to earth. Lights dim or almost go black on* VERONICA.)

NIGHT TRAIN TO BOLINA
BY NILO CRUZ

CHARACTERS
TALITA (*early teens*) *is waiting in a convent for her stepmother to come and take her to America;* CLARA (*early teens*) *has run away from her village to the city.*

SCENE
A convent in Latin America

TIME
The present

Although TALITA *tries her best to distract* CLARA, *the newly arrived girl longs to be reunited with the boy she ran away with, who is in the nearby infirmary of the convent.*

TALITA: When the little stick points to seven and the big stick points to twelve, that's the time the bell rings. That's seven o'clock. That's the time we have to wake up. Sister Nora taught us how to tell time. Have you ever seen a cuckoo clock? It goes cuckoo...cuckoo...and a little bird comes out of the clock. Sister Nora has one in her classroom. Right around this time the bell rings. When the bell rings it's time to go to sleep. (*The bell rings and lights dim.*)

CLARA: (*Frightened.*) What happened to the lights?

TALITA: It's time to go to sleep. The cuckoo clock must be going cuckoo... cuckoo....Are you afraid? Nothing's going to happen to you. I used to be afraid like you. Natalia, the girl who used to sleep in your bed, was afraid, too. She was always afraid the roof would cave in at night and soldiers would come in here.

CLARA: I want to leave this place. I want to get out.

TALITA: You can't. They won't let you.

CLARA: Why not?

TALITA: Because this is where you belong. Who brought you here? Was it your father?

CLARA: No.

TALITA: Who did?

CLARA: A man from the city. He was cleaning the church steps, and I told him my friend was sick. He took us into a little room inside the church. He gave my friend medicine. Then he took us to the hospital in a car. But they didn't want us in the hospital, because there were no beds. So he brought us here, me and my friend. You know where the infirmary is?

TALITA: Yes.

CLARA: That's where they took him. He's sick.

TALITA: Was he dying? Did a soldier shoot him?

CLARA: No. His hand is infected.

TALITA: I clean the floor of the infirmary. I see people die every day. When I used to live at the Santa Rosa Mission I was sick in the infirmary and I saw a boy die next to my bed.

CLARA: He's not going to die! Don't say he's going to die!

TALITA: Shshhhhhh.... They'll hear you outside. We're supposed to be sleeping. See, I hear someone coming. Someone's coming this way, pretend that you're sleeping. [(*Sister Nora enters the room.* **SHE** *goes over to* **TALITA'S** *bed and covers her. Then proceeds to* **CLARA'S** *bed and does the same. When Sister Nora exits, both girls open their eyes. Whispering.*)] Run to the door and see if she's gone.

CLARA: You do it.

TALITA: (*Runs to the door and sees if the nun has left.*) She'll be back later. She's Sister Nora. She's nice. When I can't sleep, because I have bad dreams, she tells me bedtime stories. Except she always falls asleep, instead of me. Then she starts snoring.

One time she took us to the zoo and I saw a monkey called Nunu. He was sitting like this. (*Sits on* **CLARA'S** *bed and crosses her legs.*) Like a little man with his legs crossed. He wasn't a boy. He was a woman. Not a woman. A monkey mother. Her little monkey was sleeping and she came to me and looked into my eyes like this. (*Moves her head from side to side.*) Then she went like this with her lips. (*Makes monkey sounds, does monkey movements and spins around.*)

CLARA: (*Laughs.*) Do it again.

TALITA: Good. I made you laugh. (**CLARA** *becomes serious again.* **TALITA** *repeats motions.*) The little monkey would put her hand to her nose, like if she was going to sneeze. Like if she had a cold. Like this. (*Places hand on her nose, breathes in and out through her mouth and spins. Laughs.*) She looked like she wanted to be my mother. (*Pause. Faces forward.*) I don't have a mother. I used to have two mothers. I used to. Not anymore. One lives in America and one disappeared from home. My papi says she was kidnapped by soldiers. Do you know what kidnap means? (**CLARA** *shakes her head.*) It means that they steal you. The soldiers that come to our village, they come and do bad things. They put people in bags of rice and take them away. Then they throw them into a pit.

Were you at the Santa Rosa Mission? (**CLARA** *shakes her head.*) That's where my father took me, so my American mother can come for me. I'm going to be her daughter.

If I show you a secret, promise not to tell anybody. (**CLARA** *nods.*) Stand there and close your eyes. I don't want anybody to know where I hide my secret. Come on, close your eyes and stand there. Go on over there. (**CLARA** *closes her eyes and walks away from* **TALITA**. **TALITA** *pulls out a bundle from under her bed cushion.*) Open your eyes. And don't tell anybody I showed these to you. (**TALITA** *takes out a pair of shoes from inside a pillowcase.*) My mother in America sent them to me in a letter. In a little box. They didn't fit me when I got them. So my mother gave them to my sister, because she had bigger feet. Now they are small on me, because my feet got big. Try them on. They'll fit you. You have small feet. (**CLARA** *tries them on.*) Aren't they beautiful.

But you see my sister scratched them. She never took care of them. She was going to break them and get them dirty, so I took them away from her. She was sleeping one night and I took them from under the bed. I put them inside a sack, I dug a hole and buried them inside the ground, so she wouldn't wear them again. Wait. Let me see if someone's coming. (*Runs to the door and takes a peek.* **SHE** *runs back to* **CLARA**.) The next day everybody in my house was looking for the shoes. And I didn't tell. I didn't say anything. I used to go out at night and dig them out of the ground and wear them for a little while, even if they were big on me. Then I would polish them with my nightshirt and dab a bit of saliva to make them shine. They would shine so much you could see the bright moon reflected on them. Go see if someone's coming. (**CLARA** *goes to the door.*)

CLARA: No one's out there.

TALITA: She'll make her rounds again. Then she'll sit by the door and fall asleep. Let me wear the shoes.

CLARA: But they don't fit you.

TALITA: It doesn't matter. (*Places shoes on top of her head.*) One day I will melt them into a hat. My grandma had her gold tooth melted into a wedding band. I could do the same with my shoes. And I'll have a hat. Maybe a purse. (*Holds them by the strap, as if they were a purse.*) Maybe a pair of gloves, like the ones rich ladies wear to church.

CLARA: Keep them how they are.

TALITA: When I look at them, I remember the smell of back home. Walking on the moist grass. The moon shining on my shoes. My grandma's face.

CLARA: You miss your grandma.

TALITA: Sometimes.

CLARA: I miss Mateo. When will I see him again?

TALITA: Pretend you're sick. They'll take you to the infirmary to see a doctor, then you can see him.

RABBIT HOLE
BY DAVID LINDSAY-ABAIRE

CHARACTERS
NAT *(mid-60s), a good-hearted, outspoken woman who fiercely loves her children;* BECCA *(late 30s), her daughter, somewhat uptight and still grieving over the death of her 4-year-old son, Danny, months earlier*

SCENE
Danny's room in Larchmont, New York

TIME
The present

(NAT *and* BECCA *are sorting through Danny's things, deciding what to keep and what to throw away.*)

NAT: (*Holds up toy.*) Keep or toss?

BECCA: Toss.

NAT: (*Another.*) This too?

BECCA: Yeah.

> (NAT *puts both toys into the garbage bag.* BECCA *finds* The Runaway Bunny. *She flips through it.*)
>
> Remember this one? (*Holds up the book.*)

NAT: That was *your* book.

BECCA: I know.

(BECCA *puts it in the keep box.* NAT *pulls a Curious George doll out of the toy box.*)

NAT: (*Holds it up.*) Monkey?

BECCA: Um, keep, I guess.

(SHE *does.*)

NAT: Howie doesn't mind this?

BECCA: It was *his* idea. After that open house. Seems his grief goes out the window when it comes to maximizing profits. (*Beat.*) Sorry. I don't even know why I said that. Just being mean.

(*They go back to work.*)

Besides, it's not like we're getting rid of *everything*.

(*Something stops* NAT. SHE'S *holding a pair of Danny's sneakers. They're smaller than* SHE *remembers.* BECCA *glances over at her and realizes what's happening.*)

(*Simply.*) Don't do that. (*Takes the sneakers.*) Quick and clean, like a Band-Aid. (*Places the sneakers in a garbage bag.*) Otherwise we'll never get through it.

(BECCA *grabs a Kleenex from the bureau and passes it to* NAT *without missing a beat.* SHE *carries on as if the moment never happened.*)

Did Izzy tell you I was taking a continuing ed class? We're reading *Bleak House*. Isn't that hilarious? He handed out the syllabus and I just laughed. *Bleak House*. Of course, no one knew what I was laughing at, which was *great*. (NAT *looks up at her.*) It's in Bronxville so no one knows me. I'm normal there. That's what I like best about it. I don't get "the face" every time someone looks at me.

NAT: What face?

BECCA: You know. (*Demonstrates—solemn pity.*) "Oh, hi. How ya doin'? Hangin' in there?"

(NAT *laughs a little.*)

I hate it.

(*Together,* THEY *strip the robot sheets off the bed.*)

And you know what's nice? These ladies don't even *talk* about their kids or their husbands or any of it. I think they're just so happy to be away from all that. It's probably the *last* thing they wanna talk about. Because I'm sure most of them are bored housewives, right?

NAT: I don't know. I've never met these people.

BECCA: Well, that's who takes Westchester continuing ed classes, isn't it?

NAT: I guess.

BECCA: Sure, and they're just so happy to be talking about Dickens instead of what's for dinner. "Yay, we're reading literature." It's like they're in college again. Who'd *wanna* talk about their families? I know I don't.

(*Beat.*)

Anyway, I like it. I like that I'm just a lady taking a class. And next week we start *Madame Bovary*. That oughta get the ol' girls goin', huh?

NAT: I don't know that book.

BECCA: No, I know.

(**NAT**, *packing up more toys, accidentally flips the switch on an obnoxious yapping dog. It's loud.*)

NAT: What the hell? (*Trying to turn it off.*) How do I—? *That's* annoying.

BECCA: (*Over the noise.*) Try listening to it for hours on end! (*Switches it off.*) Izzy gave him that. Only people without children give these kinds of gifts. Or people who want to punish parents.

SCENES FROM AN UNFINISHED LIFE
BY LEIGH KENNICOTT

CHARACTERS
EFFIE *(teens), the older sister, who has suffered sexual abuse;* **FLORRIE** *(teens), the younger sister, whose whole life is a reaction to that abuse*

SCENE
EFFIE'S *bedroom in rural Colorado*

TIME
Summer (a flashback)

(**EFFIE** *is ransacking her room, opening drawers and pulling contents out of cupboards.* **SHE** *seems frantic.*)

FLORRIE: What are you doing!

EFFIE: I can't find it.

FLORRIE: What?

EFFIE: Shh.

FLORRIE: What!

EFFIE: Be quiet.

(*A pause while* **FLORRIE** *surveys her sister.*)

FLORRIE: Can I help?

EFFIE: No.

FLORRIE: (*With finality.*) You're sleepwalking.

EFFIE: I'm not.

FLORRIE: I can prove it.

EFFIE: Don't.

FLORRIE: I'm turning on the light.

EFFIE: Nooo!

(**She** *lunges for her sister, who is at the light switch.* **She** *misses, and the light goes on.*)

Florrie: There. See what you did?

(*Indicating the clothes strewn all over the floor.* **Effie** *stops and looks around.*)

Effie: I know I did it. That's not sleepwalking.

Florrie: But you do it every night.

Effie: (*Hotly.*) Did *you* ever lose something precious that you just know is somewhere close but you can't put your finger on it?

Florrie: Let it go.

Effie: I can't.

Florrie: Get to bed. I'll help you put everything back in the morning.

Effie: Nope. Tonight's the night. I feel it.

Florrie: You won't get it back this way, Effie. Please.

Effie: But I can. I will.

Florrie: Effie, it's awful what happened, but can't you just—put it away for good? Jesus will forgive you. It wasn't your fault.

Effie: Jesus! Where was he?

(**She** *sings.*)

"Jesus loves the little children,

All the children of the world. . . . "

Florrie: Maybe it's just—we're not children anymore.

Effie: I thought he would protect me.

Florrie: Come on. Don't blaspheme. Let's go to bed.

(**She** *guides* **Effie** *toward the bed.*)

Effie: It hurt so much, Florrie. It bled.

Florrie: Does it still? 'Cause if it does—

Effie: No! You can't tell anyone.

Florrie: I'm going to. And you can't stop me.

SECOND.
BY NEAL UTTERBACK

CHARACTERS
LAUREN *(30s), a successful New York surgeon;* **VICK** *(30s),* **LAUREN'S** *partner, a tough, no-nonsense reporter*

SCENE
A Manhattan apartment, snow falling

TIME
Christmas

LAUREN *and* **VICK** *have had very little time together during the last nine months, because* **LAUREN** *has been flying coast to coast to care for her dying mother. Their relationship has become somewhat distant.*

VICK: God, look at.... There's something in the air, *something*.... You're lucky your plane made it in. It's the end of the world out there.

LAUREN: Are you listening?

VICK: Hank called.

LAUREN: ... Hank who?

VICK: Your Hank.

LAUREN: My Hank?

VICK: Yes, you remember, your ex-husband, *Hank*.

LAUREN: When did he call?

VICK: I don't know. Yesterday.

LAUREN: Here?

VICK: Where else would— *Yeah*, here.

LAUREN: What did he want?

VICK: Didn't say.

LAUREN: He didn't say?

VICK: He didn't say.

LAUREN: Did you talk to him?

VICK: He left a message. I don't know.

LAUREN: Did you save it?

VICK: No.

LAUREN: Vicky.

VICK: *Lauren.*

LAUREN: Why do you do things like this?

VICK: Why don't you just call him back? Didn't you see him when you were home?

LAUREN: No. (*Pours herself more wine.*) This wine is horrible. Did you get this? What is this crap? (*Looks at the bottle.*) Australia? They don't make wine in Australia.

VICK: Clearly they do.

LAUREN: Well, not very well.

(LAUREN *takes the paper and sits on the sofa down right. Silence.* VICK *playfully slinks over to* LAUREN *and waits.*)

LAUREN: What?

VICK: What?

LAUREN: What?

VICK: *What?*

LAUREN: I'm reading.

VICK: I want to play.

LAUREN: And I want to read.

(LAUREN *sees* VICK'S *reaction.*)

VICK: I haven't seen you for eight months.

LAUREN: Nine. And it's not like I didn't come home every other week.

VICK: I was going through some old boxes.

LAUREN: Oh?

VICK: Spring cleaning.

LAUREN: It's Christmas.

VICK: And do you know what I found?

LAUREN: I couldn't possibly guess.

VICK: Try.

LAUREN: I don't want to try.

VICK: Come on, guess.

LAUREN: The Ark of the Covenant.

VICK: The first poem you ever wrote me.

LAUREN: I wrote you a poem?

VICK: When we first met.

LAUREN: Huh.

VICK:
Listen:
I wash your feet and I believe in hope
Faith in you is my sanctuary from an uncertain tomorrow
Your sweat and tears baptize me and I am reborn.

LAUREN: . . . Is that it?

VICK: Isn't it beautiful?

LAUREN: If by beautiful you mean ridiculous, then . . .

VICK: You wrote this for me when we first met.

LAUREN: Vicky, I was in medical school. I was so high on amphetamines I probably thought I was Gertrude Stein.

VICK: Where did that woman go?

LAUREN: Gertrude Stein? She's dead.

VICK: Who are you?

LAUREN: Can I read please?

(*Silence*)

VICK: 'Cause, it's just that we used to have sex all the time and this year... twice. TWICE. And the second time wasn't even really sex, it was like (**SHE** *wiggles.*) and nakedness. And I know you've had your mother and everything, but I have needs too.

LAUREN: My mother was on her deathbed. I'm off my cycle. I'm exhausted. I'm—

VICK: But in *addition* to everything else.

LAUREN: What everything else?

VICK: Not wanting to join the gym with me when you said you would.

LAUREN: *Might.*

VICK: Not wanting the dog you said we were going to get.

LAUREN: I don't want a dog.

VICK: You said.

LAUREN: When did I say this, Vicky?

VICK: When we moved in together. You said.

LAUREN: No, Victoria. I never said.

VICK: She said, she said.

LAUREN: Things change, things evolve.

VICK: Who are you? You are, like, Lauren's evil twin sent to sabotage our relationship. And you look heavy.

LAUREN: Fine, we'll have sex—I look heavy?

VICK: You've put on weight; you have, and don't placate me.

LAUREN: I'm not.

VICK: You are.

LAUREN: I want you. Oh, baby, oh, baby.

VICK: ...I could *kill* you for this, you know?

(**LAUREN** *contracts slightly. A sensation.*)

VICK: What's wrong?

LAUREN: Nothing. (*Silence. [T and JOHN, with backpack, enter.]*) I did see Hank.

VICK: You did? How often?

LAUREN: Often.

VICK: You lied to me?

LAUREN: I lied to you.

VICK: Why?

LAUREN: Because I had to.

VICK: You had no choice?

LAUREN: Because I chose to.

VICK: Are you screwing around on me?

LAUREN: Vicky.

VICK: Who are you?

STILL LIFE WITH PARROT AND MONKEY
BY PAULA CIZMAR

CHARACTERS
GLORIA *is an offbeat 20-ish housewife from The Valley.* FAITH—*40 but wishing* SHE *were 25—is an avid gossip and has a habit of dropping in on* GLORIA, *her daughter, at the worst possible times.*

SCENE
The well-used kitchen in GLORIA *and her husband, Danny's, modest stucco bungalow; it's on an undistinguished street in the San Fernando Valley, an area on the other side of the hill—and the other side of the 101 freeway—from the city of Los Angeles.*

TIME
Midafternoon

GLORIA, *who hears strange voices that somehow seem like the spirit of Frida Kahlo, has just found out through the grapevine that her neighbor has reportedly had episodes where she spontaneously bursts into flames. At her kitchen table,* GLORIA *is applying mascara. Suddenly,* SHE *stops. Shudders.* SHE *grows very still. Shudders again. Looks around, as if something or someone is in the room with her.*

GLORIA: Uh. Hello? (*No response. Another violent shudder. She looks toward the living room.*) Danny? Is that you? Danny? (GLORIA *listens. Nothing there. Then:* SHE *starts to gasp and lightly convulse.*) Danny? (GLORIA *tries to shake it off. Another shudder. Her ears perk up. Listens.*) Ohmygod. Ohmygod. (SHE *shudders, shakes. Groans. In a low voice.*) O-o-o-o-o-o . . . Glo-o-o-ria. (SHE *shakes again, more violently, then stops. In her own voice.*) Gramma? (GLORIA *shudders again. In a low voice.*) Glo-o-o-ria. (*In her own voice.*) Gram? (GLORIA *shudders again.* SHE *waits, unnerved.*) Hello? (*Nothing happens.* GLORIA *shakes herself.*) Jesus.

(GLORIA *listens again. Nothing.* SHE *relaxes, starts to apply her makeup again. From offstage, a voice.*)

FAITH: (*Offstage.*) Gloria!

(GLORIA *practically jumps out of her chair.*)

GLORIA: Stop!

(**FAITH**, **GLORIA'S** *mother, 40-ish but looking barely 20, enters the kitchen.*)

FAITH: Huh?

GLORIA: Ohmygod, ohmygod.

FAITH: What's the matter with you?

GLORIA: Ohmygod, you scared me.

FAITH: Me?

GLORIA: Oh wow. I just—I just— Never mind.

FAITH: (*After giving* **GLORIA** *the eye.*) Strange things going on all over the place. Got you spooked.

GLORIA: I guess.

FAITH: Are you okay?

GLORIA: Well, it's not every day that you hear about someone you know just bursting into flames.

FAITH: Mm-hmm. Out of the blue, she's on fire. Poor Sylvia.

GLORIA: I gotta take up a collection for her or something.

FAITH: Yeah. And bring something over. Salad. A Jell-o mold.

GLORIA: I'll make that Caesar salad thing I got from Marie. You chop up those little green onions and you soak the potatoes and the little green onions in mayonnaise and lemon juice and something overnight. Worcestershire or something. Tabasco. And then you pour the whole thing over lettuce the next day.

FAITH: I got three heads of lettuce, just waiting to go bad in my crisper. Use them before they turn brown.

GLORIA: You can't use your kind of lettuce. It's gotta be that gourmet stuff, that stiff stuff. Romaine.

FAITH: It's all gonna go bad. I was gonna make tacos, then your father went to Vegas with Uncle Ray.

GLORIA: I think I should go over there. But it's too weird. I'm gonna go sometime tomorrow when they're not home.

FAITH: You gonna call and hang up or what?

GLORIA: I'll just go when they're not there.

FAITH: How are you gonna know?

GLORIA: Ma, I don't want to be there if it happens, you know? I mean, what are you supposed to do, are you supposed to ignore it and pretend it doesn't happen, or what?

FAITH: You gotta put the fire out. Whole house could go up.

GLORIA: I don't think anything else burns. Just her.

FAITH: Huh. Nothing else. And it's actual flames.

GLORIA: That's what Sylvia said.

FAITH: So you're gonna take up a collection?

GLORIA: Yeah. And make the salad. Or what should I bring? Huh? Is the salad a good thing?

FAITH: Yeah. Salad.

GLORIA: Or bring over something they need?

FAITH: Uh-huh.

GLORIA: Like what, you know?

(**FAITH** *can't help herself. Starts to giggle. Tries to hold back—it turns to spasms.*)

GLORIA: What?

FAITH: (*Trying not to laugh.*) Buy her— Buy her—

GLORIA: Ma, will you stop it?

FAITH: (*Laughing.*) Buy her—

GLORIA: Ma, this is serious.

FAITH: (*Choking.*) Buy her a fire extinguisher.

GLORIA: Ma.

(**FAITH** *can't stop laughing.* **GLORIA** *slugs her in the arm.*)

GLORIA: Ma. (*As* **FAITH** *doesn't stop.*) Ma— Jesus, you're embarrassing.

FAITH: If she— If she— If she catches on fire—

GLORIA: Ma—

FAITH: You can ho-hose—you can hose her down!

GLORIA: Jesus, Ma.

FAITH: Let's go to Costco.

GLORIA: It's closed.

(*Another titter, then* FAITH *bursts out laughing.*)

(GLORIA *looks at her, shakes her head. Then, suddenly,* SHE *shudders. Her eyes go wide.* SHE *can feel the strange voice rising up in her throat. Struggles against it.*)

GLORIA: Gl— Glor—

FAITH: Honey?

(GLORIA *panics, rushes out.*)

GLORIA: I gotta go.

(GLORIA *is gone.* FAITH *looks after her. Utterly confused.*)

CHARACTERS

EMILY *(20), a college student home on spring break, smart, confused, and daughter of* LAURIE *(50s), a well-respected English professor, who is kind, but ambitious, and facing difficult issues: menopause; anger over the war in Iraq; her father, in a home due to Alzheimer's. In this scene,* EMILY *confronts her mother about her liberal bias, which is more biased, and destructive, than* LAURIE *would like to admit.*

SCENE
LAURIE's *living room*

TIME
Late evening

LAURIE *is in her home watching Frankie Avalon sing "Venus" on TV.* SHE *is wearing pajamas.* EMILY *walks in.*

EMILY: Mom. Are you still up?

LAURIE: (*Turns off the TV.*) Yes. I'm watching this fabulous reunion on public television of all these pop stars I liked in high school—Bobby Vinton, Frankie Avalon.

EMILY: Who?

LAURIE: Oh come on, Emily. You never heard (SHE *starts to sing.*) "Venus, if you will, please send a little girl for me to thrill." It still makes me weep.

EMILY: Did you just say "a little girl for me to thrill?"

LAURIE: It doesn't bear deconstructing.

EMILY: When I think of you and music, it's always Mahler.

LAURIE: Always Mahler could get a little overbearing.

EMILY: Okay, Mahler and Phil Ox. You know, that antiwar folk singer Daddy likes who hung himself.

LAURIE: Ochs, honey, Ochs. God, I'm old. But I must say, it's sort of fascinating culturally. Here are these truly bubble-gum pop stars—I mean people who were in beach-blanket-bikini movies—and now they have reunions on public television right after Daniel Barenboim and the Chicago Symphony.

EMILY: I guess.

LAURIE: No, seriously, as an evolution it's very interesting. It's like thirty years from now you're seeing Britney Spears on stage at the Metropolitan Opera.

EMILY: She's already been there for the MTV awards.

LAURIE: Sorry. I told you I'm old. Where have you been?

EMILY: Out.

LAURIE: Honey, spring break's only two weeks and you've been out every night. Don't you want to spend some quality time together?

EMILY: Mom, I've tried, but you're always screaming at the television.

LAURIE: I wasn't tonight.

EMILY: It's after midnight. How many times can you listen to the same Headline News every twenty minutes?

LAURIE: They can always slip in a fast one.

EMILY: You can slip in a fast one, too.

LAURIE: What do you mean by that?

EMILY: I met this guy at a bar.

LAURIE: Oh, I'm so glad you're seeing other people than Richard.

EMILY: Mother, I'm still with Richard. That doesn't mean I can't talk to someone else at a bar.

LAURIE: Sorry. Just checking.

EMILY: Anyway, this kid turns out to be a student at this college and when I asked him how he liked it, he tells me about this bitch professor who almost got him thrown out for plagiarism.

LAURIE: You met Woodson Bull?

EMILY: He likes to be called Third.

LAURIE: Oh, Christ, yes, Third. Like our president, Grandpa Bull, Daddy Bull, and Baby Bear Bull.

EMILY: Mother. He has nothing to do with the president. He's a bartender.

LAURIE: Then he must be writing a term paper on what it actually feels like to earn a living. Because he certainly doesn't need to work.

EMILY: His family has no money. His father is a small-claims lawyer in Ohio.

LAURIE: He told you that?

EMILY: Yes. You categorized him and you got him totally wrong.

LAURIE: Emily, please, not tonight. I spent the entire day with Grandpa at the clinic. He asked me twice: "Where do you live?" and "Do you have any children?" Please, just tell me what a wonderful mother I am and how much you love me.

EMILY: Mother, you almost ruined this kid's life.

LAURIE: That's a little hyperbolic, isn't it? In the big picture this kid will be fine.

EMILY: You don't know that.

LAURIE: If Frankie Avalon can land on public television, then Woodson Bull the Third will be fine.

EMILY: God, you are the most arrogant, glib, impossible woman. Daddy's right, for all your endless babbling about open perspectives, you're the most limited person I know.

LAURIE: I don't believe your father said that.

EMILY: How would you know? You never listen to him. You joke about giving him steroids. You are completely unfair to Daddy, you're completely unfair to Richard, and you were *completely* unfair to Woodson Bull.

(LAURIE *is silent.*)

You decided he plagiarized because you needed that to be true. Just like they decided there were weapons of mass destruction because they needed *that* to be true.

LAURIE: Don't compare me to this administration.

EMILY: Mother, you had an agenda. If he were a gay, Native American playwright, you wouldn't have touched him. Just like you never bother to mention that Rena, my beloved sister's partner, is cheating on Zooey, just because Rena's a published poet.

LAURIE: Your sister's partnership is none of my business.

EMILY: But my partnership with Richard is?

LAURIE: Richard is thirteen years older than you and a bank teller who plays guitar on Saturday nights in a bar in South Philadelphia. He doesn't even want to be a musician. He just wants to chill. Emily, you can do a lot more with your life than spend it with a man whose ambition is just to chill.

EMILY: You mean I could be like you are with Daddy. Just be with a man I silently resent.

LAURIE: I love your father.

EMILY: You resent my father because he's not a star and you can't go to your stupid dinner parties and brag about him. You're not a power couple. You've totally eclipsed him.

LAURIE: Emily, I'm very hot and I'm going to bed.

EMILY: Just so you know. Richard got a job in a bank near his parents in Trenton and I'm moving in with him next month. I'll wait tables until I figure out what I want to do.

LAURIE: What the hell are you talking about? Emily, do you really think life will be more equitable when you're a thirty-year-old waitress at the Rusty Scupper in Trenton?

EMILY: I want out of your world, Mother. I don't want to judge people on their schools, their influence, or the success of their latest essay in *The New York Review of Books*.

LAURIE: This is idiotic.

EMILY: This is my chance not to be you.

(**LAURIE'S** *beeper starts beeping*.)

What's that?

LAURIE: I have a beeper now so the police can beep me anytime Grandpa's missing. I have to go. Honey, we'll talk about this in the morning.

EMILY: I don't know if I'll be here in the morning.

(**LAURIE** *exits*.)

V-E DAY
BY FAYE SHOLITON

CHARACTERS
EVIE *(18) dreams of a career as a photojournalist.* **LIL** *(22) is* **EVIE'S** *best friend. The girls are working on their next newsletter for the troops.*

SCENE
EVIE'S *living room, Cleveland Heights, Ohio*

TIME
1944

LIL: Your Local Libel column in time for Valentine's Day, '44. Twelve engagements, three weddings, two disengagements, four stork arrivals.... and two expecting-to-be-expecting. Anything you care to add?

EVIE: Just put it on the pile, Mr. Winchell.

LIL: I'll have you know this represents three hours of kibitzing over at the Colony Emporium.

EVIE: Whenever did you find the time?

LIL: What's that supposed to mean? This isn't about Ralph again.

EVIE: I know. It's your life.

LIL: Exactly. And besides, I don't hear you complaining about his column, which he delivers every month like clockwork.

EVIE: My *good* writers are all in uniform.

LIL: Somebody has to stay back and *make* those uniforms. What is your beef, exactly?

EVIE: Of all our friends...he's not for you.

LIL: He's smart.

EVIE: He's dull.

LIL: And sweet. A true gentleman.

EVIE: What in God's name do you two talk about? Textile chemistry?

LIL: I guess you're the only one allowed to be in love.

EVIE: Oh please.

LIL: Don't deny you love my brother.

EVIE: He knows exactly how I feel.

LIL: Last month, on his furlough? He was the happiest I've ever seen him.

EVIE: We had a swell time. We always do.

LIL: He mentioned something about a ring. Well?

EVIE: Did *he* put you up to this?

LIL: Because you'd best not break his heart. Not now that he's over there.... It's your patriotic duty, ya know....

EVIE: To what?

LIL: *You* know. Whatever he wants!... If it weren't for you...

EVIE: What.

LIL: Nothing.

EVIE: Look, Lil. We got *things* to do here, you and me!

LIL: So we'll talk after we get the issue out.

EVIE: No, darling. Things to do *first*.

LIL: And if I settle down with Ralph, I'll be settling.

EVIE: That fella can't even *dance!*

LIL: He's steady. Secure. You said so yourself. And people will always need warm clothing!

EVIE: So you'll never want for sweaters. But marry Mister Steady and Secure and you'll never leave the house, let alone open that gallery of yours. What about your *dreams?*

LIL: War does funny things to dreams, honey.

EVIE: Yeah. Every now and then, it makes them come true. (**EVIE** *fetches a magazine.*)

LIL: What.

EVIE: The new *Life*. Look at those photographs!

LIL: They're good.

EVIE: Read the credits.

LIL: "Margaret Bourke White."

EVIE: Yeah. A woman, like you and me! From *here*! And you know what she's doing while we sit here on our duffs, spreading gossip? She's somewhere in Europe or Africa, living her dreams! She flew a B-17 raid over Tunis, Lil! She photographed Stalin, for Pete's sake! She's recording the entire war, and damn the torpedoes!

LIL: That's funny, coming from *you*, of all people. I'm sorry. I shouldn't have said that.

EVIE: When Bobby died, he died a *hero*. And if she's killed, at least there will be a record she *existed*! What will they say when *we're* gone? What kind of monument are *we* gonna leave?

LIL: Are you or are you not going to marry my brother?

EVIE: Of course I am! But we're talking about our lives here!

LIL: What about *his* life?

EVIE: He'll be fine, Lil.

LIL: I hope you're right. For *his* sake.

EVIE: What's that supposed to mean?

> (LIL *takes a photographer's black cloth and puts it over her head.*)

What are you doing with.... Put that down!

LIL: Ooooooooooooo.

EVIE: Give me that!

LIL: Ooooo. I'm the ghost of Margaret White.

EVIE: She's not dead, Lil. In fact, she's more alive than either of us will ever be. (EVIE *snatches the hood from* LIL's *head. From O.S., a pile of mail drops through the slot.*)

WRINKLES
BY REBECCA BASHAM

CHARACTERS
ELLIE *(35), a women's studies professor who has just found out that her grandmother is gay and is not handling the news well;* LOUISE *(57), her mother (the gay grandmother's daughter) and a therapist*

SCENE
The grandmother's living room in rural Kentucky

TIME
1984

LOUISE *is calling from offstage.* ELLIE *is asleep on the couch.*

LOUISE: Ellie? Ellie! Open the door. I know you're in there. (**ELLIE** *groans and pulls the blanket over her head to hide.*) Your car is in the driveway. (*Sound of keys jangling.*) Fine. I'm coming in. (**LOUISE**, *perfectly dressed and coiffed, enters and surveys the mess.*) Oh my. Ellie? Eleanor? I know you're in here, I'm just afraid to look too hard; goodness knows what might jump out and bite me. (*Pulls Lysol from purse and sprays indiscriminately.*) Your granny would have a fit if she could see this mess. (*Pause.*) Eleanor Abigail Veronica Sampson! Where in the world are you?

(**ELLIE** *raises her hand out of the blanket but continues to keep her head covered.* **LOUISE** *crosses to her and removes the blanket.*)

ELLIE: Hi, momma.

LOUISE: Hi, Ellie.

ELLIE: Why are you still using my confirmation name?

LOUISE: When you're in trouble, mothers always call your entire name.

ELLIE: I'm in trouble? Have you talked to Gran yet? I'm not the one in trouble.

LOUISE: I never really understood why you picked Veronica for your confirmation name anyway.

ELLIE: Have you talked to Granny?

LOUISE: Yes, she stopped by on her way out of town.

ELLIE: And I'm the one in trouble?

LOUISE: It appears so.

ELLIE: Hey, how did you get in here? I have your key.

LOUISE: Mom gave me hers.

ELLIE: Oh.

LOUISE: Why is your car full of boxes?

ELLIE: Granny told you I was moving.

LOUISE: No, she didn't. Where?

ELLIE: I haven't decided yet. Because it was different—unique.

LOUISE: Huh?

ELLIE: Veronica. Not Mary or Elizabeth like everybody else. Veronica had an air of individuality.

LOUISE: Conversion.

ELLIE: Huh?

LOUISE: You were six when I decided to join the Catholic Church. Obviously it was too late to instill true Catholic devotion.

ELLIE: And that's a bad thing, I take it. The Church is nothing but an oppressive force driven to control women and to . . .

LOUISE: I've got it, honey. I'm an atheist now, remember?

ELLIE: Yeah, that bothers me a little.

LOUISE: I'm sorry. Freedom of expression, however, is every person's right.

ELLIE: Oh, I don't care that you're an atheist—I am, too. I just care that it took you so long to figure that out. First we were Baptist, Pentecostal for about a minute, then Catholic—as Catholic as they come—you were the queen of Catholicism.

LOUISE: Saint would be more accurate. We all know there's nothing worse than a convert.

ELLIE: I resent the time it took you to figure it all out. Martha and Christine and I—we paid for your insecurities.

LOUISE: Interesting.

ELLIE: Don't start.

LOUISE: I didn't start anything. Watch your hormones.

ELLIE: They're fine, thank you. And if you're an atheist, then using my confirmation name means you're a hypocrite as well.

LOUISE: How long has it been since you took a bath?

ELLIE: Umm, Friday I guess.

LOUISE: And today is Tuesday; don't you think it might be time?

ELLIE: Probably.

LOUISE: Who's taking your classes?

ELLIE: It's fall break! I'm hibernating.

LOUISE: Interesting.

ELLIE: MOM!

LOUISE: At least I tried to make you girls presentable and socially acceptable. Mom never made us go to church even once. I was 19 years old before I ever entered a church. She forbade our going because "organized religion was the one true sin." My friends' parents were scandalized.

ELLIE: Our friends' parents thought you were a Holy Roller about to burst into tongues, then a martyr vying for sainthood. Talk about embarrassing.

LOUISE: They did not. I have always been looked to for direction and advice.

ELLIE: I need to take a bath. (**ELLIE** *begins to unwind herself from the blanket.*)

LOUISE: Why are we talking about all of this ancient history?

ELLIE: You started it.

LOUISE: I did not.

ELLIE: Did too.

LOUISE: I did not. Don't be so childish. Why are you attacking me for twenty-year-old crimes?

ELLIE: Some issues need to be attacked.

LOUISE: Now?

ELLIE: Better late than never.

LOUISE: Fine. Let's tidy up a little bit, and then we can have a talk and clear the air.

ELLIE: (*Overreacting.*) NO! I am not cleaning at your command. I did that too many Saturday mornings when I was a kid. We will talk amidst the evidence of my existence—a few tissues and three-day-old pizza.

LOUISE: I can't do that.

ELLIE: You can if you try—really hard, I know. Just have a seat and let's chat.

(**LOUISE** *steps gingerly through the mess on the floor and sits on the easy chair, obviously supremely uncomfortable.*)

See, not so bad.

LOUISE: (*Nervously.*) Uh-huh.

ELLIE: What do you want to chat about? Reagan's call for 24.6 million to start the Star Wars plan, or the downward economic spiral we find ourselves caught in at the moment?

LOUISE: Very funny. I want to know—I want to know—I want to know—

(**LOUISE** *jumps up and grabs the pizza box triumphantly from under* **ELLIE'S** *nose.* **SHE** *runs out into the kitchen and reappears without the box, calmly seating herself again in the easy chair. She is ultracalm and professional.*)

I want to know why you're moving.

(**ELLIE** *ignores her dash with the pizza box, blows her nose and throws the tissue on the floor.* **LOUISE** *stares at it obsessively, but doesn't move.* **SHE** *will sneak picking up the tissues throughout the rest of the scene and put them in her purse.*)

ELLIE: I'm tired of living there. Seems like the walls were closing in on me.

LOUISE: Interesting.

ELLIE: I'm not a patient, Mom. You don't have to be noncommittal. Just look at me and say, "You're a crazy freak." I can take it.

LOUISE: (*Calmly.*) My child is not a crazy freak. You're obviously going through some life crisis that you need to share in order to master these impulses.

ELLIE: Couldn't you once, just this once, talk to me like a mother talks to her daughter and not the way a therapist talks to her patients? (*Childlike.*) Pretty please with chocolate syrup, whipped cream and a cherry on top?

LOUISE: I can try, although I can't help but notice that your inner child is—

Ellie: MOM!

Louise: Sorry. So, why are you moving?

Ellie: I need a change. I don't know why that's so hard to understand. I've lived in that tiny, cluttered hole of an apartment since I was working on my dissertation. I'm ready to let go of my grad-school frugality.

Louise: Okay, completely understandable. You're mature and ready for a real life.

Ellie: I am.

Louise: But your actions are contradictory to your desires. A mature adult doesn't leave her apartment in the middle of the night and abandon half of her earthly possessions.

Ellie: Maybe I'm in the middle of a cleansing period. Isn't that what you call it?

Louise: We do. But what is it you're trying to cleanse? That type of period doesn't just occur out of nowhere. There's always a catalyst.

Ellie: Let's see. Maybe I can regress myself through hypnotherapy and figure out just what it is that's made me a little on edge lately. . . .

(**Ellie** *assumes a meditation pose and closes her eyes.* **She** *moans for a beat, and with eyes still closed, recounts.*)

. . . Wrote dissertation for three years and lived on macaroni and cheese with tuna, maybe it's a vitamin deficiency–related apartment issue. Ohmmmm. Brought up without a father because he disappeared when I was 12. Maybe it's fear of abandonment that compels me to abandon my apartment. Never hurts to leave before you're left, but then an apartment can't really leave you, so maybe that's fallacious. Ohmmmmm. Multiple forced religious experiences brought on by an overzealous need to control fate by a primary parent. Perhaps I am exorcising my demons by leaving them to wallow in an empty hovel. OOOOOHHHHMMMMMM!

Louise: ELLIE! That's uncalled for; you can't blame me for everything.

Ellie: (*Insistent.*) OHHHHMMMMM. Perhaps lack of parental responsibility. A mother who cannot, will not take—

Louise: Stop it, you little brat.

Ellie: OHHHHMMMMMM. Or maybe it's because my grandmother is gay at seventy-eight. (*EYES snapping open.*) Did you ever think of that one?

YOGA WARRIOR

BY KATHERINE BURKMAN, SUSIE GERALD,
ANN C. HALL, DEBORAH BURKMAN, AND
RICHARD ESQUINAS

CHARACTERS

JOAN *(30s) and* JUDI *(30s) are participating in a yoga retreat.*

SCENE

A country trail

TIME

Now. In fact, in the moment.

At present, they are hiking. Previously, JUDI *asked* JOAN *to have a baby and give it to her.* JOAN *agreed, but now has second thoughts.*

JOAN: Look at those birds. I just love listening to the sounds in this place.

JUDI: Slow down a little, Joan. I thought I was the one in good shape.

JOAN: Oh, sorry. I'm used to walking really fast. But you're right. If we slow down, we'll take in more of this gorgeous landscape.

JUDI: And meditate. If we stop talking, we can walk and meditate at the same time.

JOAN: I've *been* meditating, Judi. A lot. And I've come to a decision.

JUDI: A decision about what?

JOAN: I hope you'll understand, Judi. (*Pause.*) I've decided to keep the baby.

JUDI: (*Aghast.*) My baby!

JOAN: No, actually, my baby.

JUDI: But Joan, you agreed. You all but signed in blood. You made me feel that I was a new woman.

JOAN: I know, and believe me, I'm sorry, Judi. And anyway, I can't believe Jack would have agreed. And this way, he'll never know. A baby may be just what this marriage needs.

JUDI: Never know what! Joan, I'm way out of breath. Let's sit here under this tree and . . . bring you to your senses.

(THEY *sit.*)

JOAN: No, no, Judi, I was out of my mind, lost my senses and now I've found them. I do have to thank you. I feel a hundred times better than before we came here. I don't know if I can explain what happened.

JUDI: Well, you'd better begin trying. You can't just go keeping my baby without some major explanation. I'm devastated.

JOAN: If it were just me and Jack doing you a big favor, and we could be around as aunt and uncle, I might have considered it. I did consider it, didn't I? I sort of agreed. Right after Phil adjusted me?

JUDI: Sort of? I thought you did agree.

JOAN: You see, I thought that when Phil finally adjusted me, that I would have not only a new body but also a new generosity of spirit—I truly thought I could do this for you, crazy as it seems, seemed to me. But Judi, here we are on the fourth day of the retreat and something happens when he makes those adjustments in class.

JUDI: Tell me about it.

JOAN: I'm trying to, but you won't listen.

JUDI: I'm listening.

JOAN: It's hard to explain.

JUDI: Try.

JOAN: Judi, I know I will have a baby, but he's the father.

JUDI: He? Who?

JOAN: Phil.

JUDI: Oh Joan, don't be absurd. He has a girlfriend.

JOAN: I don't mean physically, Judi. I mean spiritually. The spiritual father.

JUDI: You've been telling me for years just how unspiritual you are. You always make fun of me when I talk about my inner child or my communing with nature. Now, here you are hiking like a . . . like a disciple of Carl Jung, and you plan to keep my baby because of some supposed spiritual connection you made with a man you don't know outside of a few adjustments in a dumb yoga class.

JOAN: Dumb?

JUDI: Well, ever since you started mooning over Phil, I've kinda had a chance to pull back. And he's just a guy, you know. And you, I hardly recognize you. You have no idea what it's like to lose a baby, Joan. It just makes me want to walk over to that cliff and jump right over. (*Gets up as if to do it.*)

JOAN: (*Pulling her back down.*) Now settle down, Judi. No need to get drastic here. It's just that the adjustment wasn't what I thought it would be.

JUDI: For heaven's sake, Joan, all he did was adjust your back in Child Pose. How does that make him a spiritual father of your unborn child?

JOAN: Ah, that's it. I've never been so aware of what my body can do. I've never thought about birth in this way. Judi, I can breathe. I was dead. I just didn't know it. And believe me, I'll always be grateful to you. You can be the baby's godparent. His spiritual adviser.

JUDI: Joan, my baby is a girl. Don't you remember?

JOAN: No, I don't think so, Judi. I think this is a baby boy.

JUDI: May I remind you, Joan, that you're not even pregnant yet?

JOAN: I know, Judi, but in a sense I am. I just can't tell you how... enabled I feel.

JUDI: That's because we're on a retreat in beautiful surroundings and you have no responsibilities and everything's unreal. Believe me, I've been on these retreats before. When you get back, you'll be just where you were before you came, and when you think about having this baby boy, you'll start thinking diapers, babysitters, end of freedom. Trust me.

JOAN: Then why do you come on retreats if what they give you melts away when you get home? Maybe I've been the spiritual one all these years and you've just been faking it, nibbling away at spirituality but not taking any real bites, not letting your yoga practice feed your soul.

JUDI: How dare you! I'm just fighting for my little girl here. (**SHE** *begins to cry.*)

JOAN: (*Also crying.*) And I'm fighting for my little boy.

SCENES FOR TWO MEN

APPARITION
BY ANNE WASHBURN

CHARACTERS
Two demons. C (older) wears, perhaps, a Victorian waistcoat; his horns are tipped and gilded. D (younger) is feral.

SCENE
A suburban backyard

TIME
Night. A full moon.

C: I took the bus here. Have you ever been on a bus? Probably not. They're very complicated. They're easy to get into, once they are there, but you have to know where they will appear. I have a bus schedule, obtained with great difficulty. There is a map, which shows everywhere the bus goes and, most importantly, it shows the space you must stand on to stop it. There are diagrams. There are also series of lists which tells when the bus comes, and this information must be very exactingly coordinated with a watch (**HE** *taps a pocket.*) and a calendar (**HE** *taps another pocket.*) and also, it is my contention, with some third piece of instrumentation, or an as yet undiscovered reference material because there is a variable between my calculations and the actual manifestation of the bus, which I have not been able to identify. I very, very rarely take the bus. It's tremendous.

Neighborhoods are very interesting places. It's exciting to walk right up driveways, right up driveways and into backyards. I've been walking right up driveways and into backyards. I could sort of smell where you were, but I couldn't exactly smell where you were. And all the little fences make it harder.

Wouldn't you like to eat something? I have something very good in the paper bag.

D: Ate.

C: Oh. You look like you ate. What did you eat?

D: Dog.

C: Oh. Okay.

D: Or cat. Smallish. I ate something smallish.

C: Like a dog or a cat.

D: It was this big. (*Indicates breadloaf-sized.*) And it wiggled.

C: So you don't want what I have in the paper bag?

D: What's in the paper bag?

C: Well, I don't know. Isn't that funny? I didn't pack it. They packed it for me and said: This is really good. I'll give it to you, if you're still hungry. (*Hands to* D.) There you go.

D: This isn't for hungry. This is dessert. (D *sniffs cautiously and speculatively.*)

C: That isn't its skin. That's just paper. The taste is inside. You should reach in and pull it out if you want to smell it.

(D *begins to.*)

C: (*Immediately.*) But don't shake it! They said: Don't shake it, you'll wreck it.

> (D *sniffs again.*)

> If you don't want it, or if you're only going to ruin it, then you can give it back to me.

> (D *clutches it to him, protectively.*)

> Okay. You can hold on to it instead. I don't mind. How long have you been here?

D: Tonight.

C: And where were you before that? You were just in that backyard? The one with the stand-up swimming pool?

D: No.

C: The one next to it.

D: Uh-huh.

C: Oh. Okay. How come you want to be where there's all these houses?

D: I like all the little dogs and the cats. I like a lot of little animals better than one or two big ones.

C: Oh. Huh. I guess they're . . . juicier?

D: Because of the tiny bones. I like to crunch all the tiny bones. All at once. That's what I like.

C: Oh, yes. I like that, too! Crunch crunch crunch. I was saying that and they said: Oh, you'll like what's in the bag.

(D *sniffs it suspiciously.*)

Where do you go in the daylight?

D: I go where there is a pile of leaves. I go under it.

C: Oh. A big pile of leaves. Like that pile there.

D: Yes. First I pull the big thick branches out. Then I go under.

C: Oh. Okay. Do you know that when they make a big pile of leaves like that, they let it sit there for a day, or sometimes for a few days, but then what they generally do is they pick it all up, all of it, and they throw it into a metal can or else they burn it. So. They do this in the daytime, they *move* those big piles of leaves. They would move it right off you.

D: Oh.

C: So actually, it's very very lucky, very unusual, that you went in that pile of leaves and then . . . it was left there, over you. But that's so interesting, but I guess you didn't know that.

D: Uh-uh. Or I go under the house part, where it's dark.

C: In the basement? You go into the basement?

D: No, I go into the under.

C: Into the, um, the . . . crawl space. Under the house.

D: Yes. Or into the basement.

C: Is the basement door unlocked?

D: Or I bash the glass.

C: You break the glass out.

D: Yes, if I have a big rock. Sometimes there is a little dog in the basement also.

C: Ah. Okay. You sleep in the leaves, or you bash into the basement and you eat the little dog. Okay. What if it was a little—what if, when you go into the basement, there's a . . . a basket there, and there, inside the basket, there's a little . . . do you know what a baby is?

D: (*Negative.*) Uh-uh. (*A beat. Affirmative.*) Uh-huh.

C: Okay. Good. So if you went into the basement, you go into the basement and in the basement, in a basket or in a container, some kind of a container, there is a baby there, would you eat that also?

D: Um...

C: If you bashed open the basement, with a big old rock, or, maybe a valuable lawn ornament, whatever, and inside the basement there's a baby girl, hmmm, would you eat it?

D: Um...

C: I could see how you might eat it by mistake.

D: I might! It might be very dark in there! Also, it might be dressed in fur, like a little dog. It might look like a little dog dressed in a sweater, lying on its side. Also they make the same noises, they make the same noises, they go: (*Imitates whining.*) I might eat it if it was dark. Little bones.

C: Oh. (*Beat.*) Okay. (*Beat.*) Open the bag.

D: Not hungry.

C: I am. Open it.

D: Um. But what if there was, what if there was, another baby. What if there was another baby, in a place that I could show you. Crunch. It could be very— you could be very happy to have it in your mouth. Oh, I think you would enjoy it.

C: Come on. Open the bag

D: Yes, or I could, there I could, oh, look! Here I am in the forest! Here I am in the middle of the forest and look! There is no peoples anywhere! And there is...um...trees and, well, I swoop down and I eat big animals sometimes and I reach out and I grab at night the something smaller sometimes...but like an owl! Like I have a mouth full of big owl. Feathers. *Pfew.* But a lot of crunching. Or many tiny owls all at once. That could happen, too. Yes, I have optimism. Here I am, la di la, all happy in the big forest in the dark! See how easy? Whee. Okay. Okay, here I go. You can come with me if you want but okay, lets go. Let us go to the big dark forest in the dark and in the middle of the big ol' tree. Yes, hurrah. Yes.

C: Open it. Just open it.

D: (*Whimpering.*) *Ur ur ur arrrr.*

C: That's right. It's all right. Open it. Now!

(**D** *cries out in rage and frustration.*)

AUNTIE MAYHEM
BY DAVID PUMO

CHARACTERS
FELONY MAYHEM *(30s), Latino, maybe petite, former drag queen;* **DENNIS** *(16), not white, probably black or Latino*

SCENE
FELONY'S *apartment, somewhere in Hell's Kitchen, Manhattan*

TIME
Midwinter, about 5:00 AM

(**FELONY MAYHEM**, *neat and trendy-looking, enters the apartment, flicking on the hall light, and enters the bedroom door, turning on the bedroom light.* **HE** *is wearing a winter coat or jacket.* **DENNIS** *enters after him, shyly, with his hands in his pockets.* **HE** *is wearing baggy jeans, a sweatshirt, sneakers and a down jacket.*)

FELONY: Come in, sweetie. I told you it was a mess. Don't be shy now. (**HE** *takes his coat off and drops it on the bed or chair.*) Can I check your coat?

DENNIS: I'm not shy.

FELONY: Oh, that's nice. Not shy, huh.

DENNIS: Nope.

FELONY: Ready to party?

DENNIS: Yup.

FELONY: Terrific. Check your coat?

DENNIS: Are you a cop?

FELONY: Am I a cop? Do you really still ask that? That's so cute.

DENNIS: Are you?

FELONY: (*Extending hand.*) Pepper Anderson, policewoman. Pleased to meet you. (*Waiting for a reaction*— **DENNIS** *doesn't get it.*) No, honey, I'm not a cop. Can I check your coat?

(**DENNIS** *takes his coat off.* **FELONY** *takes it and puts it on the chair near the door.*)

Dennis, right? Take your shoes off, sweetie. Get comfortable.

FELONY: You're a little young to be out so late, don't you think?

DENNIS: I'm 22.

FELONY: Oh, 22. Not just 21, but 22.

DENNIS: Yup.

FELONY: Yup. Old enough for a drink?

DENNIS: What do you got?

FELONY: Let's see. Vodka and . . . Kool-Aid, I guess.

DENNIS: Eeww.

FELONY: It is a little ghetto. Even for me. Straight up then?

(DENNIS *shakes his head no.*)

You sure? It's good for you.

(DENNIS *nods his head yes.*)

Well, I think I might have a little nightcap. Or morning cap, as the case may be. You can take your shirt off.

(FELONY *exits to the kitchen.* DENNIS *takes his shirt off and drops it on the bed.* FELONY *speaks offstage from the kitchen as* DENNIS *looks around.*)

I don't think I've seen you out before.

DENNIS: I been around.

FELONY: (*Offstage.*) Really. You have? Because I think I would have remembered you. In fact, as soon as I saw you I thought to myself, "He's the one."

(FELONY *enters and stands in the doorway with a filled martini glass, staring at* DENNIS.)

Oh yeah, you're the one, all right. I'm sure of it.

(FELONY *walks to* DENNIS. HE *runs his fingers through* DENNIS'S *hair, unbuttons the top button of his pants, and walks away.* DENNIS *undoes his pants and takes them off.*)

Lucky me I just happened to be walking out of The Cock Pit and you just happened to be walking by.

(**FELONY** *picks up* **DENNIS'S** *pants and shirt and puts them on the chair with his jacket and shoes.*)

In fact, it was looking like a pretty beat night until you showed up, looking like a little cutie with that handsome face of yours, and that sweet little body. (*Pulling back the bed sheets.*) Hop in.

(**DENNIS** *climbs into the bed and pulls the sheets around his waist.* **FELONY** *sits near him on the bed.*)

So, is this all you do? For money?

DENNIS: Yeah.

FELONY: Really? Nothing else?

DENNIS: Not right now.

FELONY: Hmm. Any plans? Any goals?

DENNIS: I don't know.

FELONY: Well, do you like doing this?

DENNIS: I don't know.

FELONY: Well, you can't do this for the rest of your life, can you?

(**DENNIS** *shrugs.*)

Is conversation extra?

(**DENNIS** *shrugs again.*)

Fine. Let's get going then. I'm gonna freshen this. You sure you don't want some?

DENNIS: No, thanks.

(**FELONY** *gets up.* **HE** *looks up and down* **DENNIS'S** *body under the sheets.* **HE** *holds his hand out.* **DENNIS** *takes his underwear off under the sheets and hands them to* **FELONY**. **FELONY** *walks to the door.*)

FELONY: Dennis, would you check that drawer? I think there are some condoms in there.

(**DENNIS** *turns left, away from* **FELONY**, *to look in the night-table drawer.* **FELONY**, *unseen, takes all the clothes off the chair and leaves the room.* **DENNIS** *finds a condom and sits, nervously playing with it.* **FELONY** *returns with a full glass and sits on the bed.*)

So, what shall we do?

DENNIS: What do you want to do?

FELONY: Oh, I don't know. What's your specialty?

DENNIS: I don't know.

FELONY: Sucking? Fucking?

DENNIS: I guess.

FELONY: Or maybe . . . we should dance! (**FELONY** *gets up on the bed and starts to dance.*)

DENNIS: Dance?

FELONY: Sure. Rhumba? Tango? Hustle?

DENNIS: What?

FELONY: Oh, come on. It'll be fun. I'll teach you. It's easy.

DENNIS: (*Realizing the chair is empty.*) Where are my clothes?

FELONY: Your clothes? I threw them out. Come on. Get up. I'll show you.

DENNIS: You what?

FELONY: I threw them out the front window. They're all over the street. Come on. I'll let you lead.

DENNIS: Where are my clothes, really?

FELONY: I told you, I threw them out the window.

(**DENNIS** *gathers the sheets around him.*)

You know what, maybe I should lead to start.

(*Wrapped in the sheet,* **DENNIS** *runs out of the bedroom to look for his clothes.*)

All right, you can lead.

DENNIS: (*Offstage.*) Are you fucking crazy?! What the fuck did you do?!

FELONY: I told you what I did.

(**DENNIS** *comes back into the bedroom.*)

DENNIS: What the fuck did you do that for?!

FELONY: Real sorry. Tell you what. I'll go get your clothes if you go get me my bag.

DENNIS: Your what?

FELONY: Oh, don't pretend.

DENNIS: What the fuck are you talking about? Give me my fucking clothes!

FELONY: (*Moving in close.*) What did you throw out? My driver's license? My gym clothes? (*Livid.*) My fucking palm pilot?

DENNIS: Throw out. . . . I didn't—

FELONY: (*Pinning him against the bed.*) Sunday night, one or two-ish, in front of Bar Baque, distressed green vintage leather, almost ripped my shoulder out of the socket. Ring a bell?!

DENNIS: It wasn't me!

FELONY: It wasn't you? That's funny, 'cause he looked just like you!

(**FELONY** *pokes* **DENNIS** *in the chest.* **DENNIS** *falls back on the bed.* **DENNIS** *jumps back up and grabs* **FELONY**.)

DENNIS: Give me my fucking clothes!

FELONY: (*Poking him hard repeatedly with both hands.*) Get your fucking hands off of me!

(**DENNIS** *swings.* **FELONY** *blocks it, gets in a few hard punches to his face and stomach, and a knee to his crotch, knocks him to the ground and sits on top of him, twisting his arms behind his back and pinning his face to the floor.*)

I had three hundred dollars worth of MAC in there. I had to cancel my Capital One!

DENNIS: Stop! I don't have it!

FELONY: Give me my bag and I'll stop!

DENNIS: (*Breathing heavily.*) I don't have it. It's gone!

FELONY: Gone? And vintage is such a bitch to replace!

DENNIS: (*Starting to hyperventilate.*) I don't have it! . . . I don't have anything! . . . My clothes! . . .

FELONY: You messed with the wrong little faggot this time, faggot!

DENNIS: (*Barely able to breathe.*) My jacket.... Please.... I don't have anything....
I don't...

FELONY: Why's he keep talking about his jacket? Do I look like I give a shit
about your jacket?!

(**DENNIS** *can barely breathe.*)

I'm talking to you, punk!

(**DENNIS** *doesn't answer.* **FELONY** *realizes something is wrong.*)

What the—

(**FELONY** *loosens his grip.* **DENNIS** *flips over.* **FELONY** *sees* **HE'S** *not breathing.*)

Oh... shit.

(**DENNIS** *pulls away from* **FELONY** *and crawls to the bed, trying to breathe.*
FELONY *falls back on the floor.*)

DENNIS: I'm... I'm... sorry... I'm—

FELONY: Okay... I... I forgive you.

DENNIS: I'm... I'm... I'm sorry.

FELONY: It's okay... oh fuck. (*Tries to be calming.*) Just breathe, okay? Calm
down. Relax.

DENNIS: I'm... I'm... I'm sorry—

FELONY: (*Frantic.*) Breathe, motherfucker! Don't you have an inhaler or
something?

DENNIS: My... my... jacket—

FELONY: (*Tries again to be calm.*) Don't talk. Just breathe... breathe.... I'm not
going to hurt you any more. Just breathe... breathe... that's it—

DENNIS: I'm... I'm...

FELONY: Ssshhhh. Don't talk, just breathe.... It's okay.... Just breathe...
breathe.... Oh, fuck.... That's it, Dennis. Just breathe... relax... nice and
deep... breathe—

(**DENNIS'S** *breathing slowly comes back.*)

That's it... just breathe.... I'm not going to touch you.... Just breathe...
nice and easy—

(*Slowly* **DENNIS** *regains his breathing.* **HE** *calms down a little and pulls the sheet around his waist.*)

Mother fuck! Are you okay? (**DENNIS** *nods yes.*) Did I hurt you? (**DENNIS** *nods yes.*) I'm sorry.

DENNIS: I'm sorry, too. I had no money is all.

FELONY: Okay.

DENNIS: I'm sorry about your MAC.

FELONY: I got more.

DENNIS: Are you gonna call the cops?

FELONY: Call the cops? Why would I call the cops?

DENNIS: (*Getting worked up again.*) Please don't call the cops. I've never been arrested. I'll do whatever...what...what—

FELONY: Dennis, look at me. (**DENNIS** *looks at* **FELONY**.) No cops. I have absolutely no use for cops. This has nothing to do with cops, okay?

DENNIS: (*Catching breath.*) Okay.

FELONY: Just relax...Jesus...mother fuck.

THE BATTLE OF LIGHT AND DARKNESS

BY STEPHEN FIFE

CHARACTERS
VINCENT VAN GOGH *(28) is just beginning his career as a painter, after having failed as a preacher.* THEO *(25) is* VINCENT's *brother.*

SCENE
A clearing in the woods near their father's parsonage in rural Holland

TIME
1881

VINCENT: What did you think of that last batch of drawings I sent you?

THEO: Well . . . to be perfectly honest . . .

VINCENT: Which is just how I want you to be . . .

THEO: The action of your figures wasn't clearly enough expressed. Not articulated fully enough.

VINCENT: Yes, exactly. You're right.

THEO: But your landscapes are getting better. I see real progress.

VINCENT: Here, look at these. I drew them all since my last letter.

(HE *hands* THEO *a sheaf of drawings.*)

Do you see how a softer edge has come into the work? And how much stronger my touch is?

THEO: They're better. It's true. I still can't be sure if they're sellable, but—

VINCENT: Oh, damn sellable! Who knows what's sellable?

THEO: That's what they pay me for.

VINCENT: They're good, I just know they are.

THEO: Yes. They're a real improvement.

VINCENT: And do you know why they're good, and why everything is possible now?

THEO: Why?

VINCENT: Because I'm in love.

THEO: What?

VINCENT: I've fallen in love, boy. Can you believe it? And I see everything differently now.

THEO: That's wonderful, Vincent. I'm happy for you. (*Pause.*) So who is she? Someone I know?

VINCENT: Yes.

THEO: She must be from the village then...

VINCENT: Well...

THEO: Caroline Roos. I always thought you two made a good match.

VINCENT: Not Caroline.

THEO: Then Clara Fitzwillem?

VINCENT: No.

THEO: Anna Eindhoven? (**VIN** *shakes his head.*) Elizabeth Stoffels? (**VIN** *shakes his head.*) Oh, I know... Helen... What's-her-name, the new teacher—

VINCENT: Not her either, Theo.

THEO: Then who? I'm completely stumped. (*Pause.*) Oh—is it one of your models? One of the women you've sketched?

VINCENT: I sketched her, that's true.

THEO: Well, you'll have to help me out then. I don't know most of their names.

VINCENT: You know this one's name.

THEO: I do?

VINCENT: Yes. (*Pause.*) It's Kay.

THEO: Who?

VINCENT: Kay Vos.

THEO: Our *cousin* Kay?

VINCENT: Yes.

THEO: You're joking?

VINCENT: Not at all.

THEO: Please, Vincent.

VINCENT: I've never seen so much beauty before, so many shades and colors. I never realized that nature, that life, could be so—

THEO: But she's our cousin! Our mother's sister's daughter.

VINCENT: I know. And I love her.

THEO: Vincent! Just think about this for a moment. (*Pause.*) Cousin Kay has a small child.

VINCENT: I know.

THEO: Her husband died a short time ago.

VINCENT: Yes. She confided her grief very freely to me.

THEO: Oh? And did you confide in her, too?

VINCENT: Yes.

THEO: So you told her your feelings?

VINCENT: That's right.

THEO: And what did she say?

VINCENT: She said no. She said she could never love me that way.

THEO: Really? Well, I think that's for the best.

VINCENT: Do you? Well, I never will, and I'm going to change her.

THEO: Show some common sense, please! We're not children anymore, are we?

VINCENT: All I know is I love her, and I will make her love me.

THEO: You can't make somebody love you. Either they do or they don't.

VINCENT: She's put a block of ice in my path, but I will melt it.

THEO: Oh Vincent.... This is very bad news.

VINCENT: I will melt down that block of ice, Theo. You'll see.

THEO: Have you discussed your feelings with Father or Mother?

VINCENT: No.

THEO: Well, did Kay say anything to them before she left?

VINCENT: No.

THEO: Then that's fine. Let's just drop it before it goes any further.

VINCENT: I can't.

THEO: Vincent!

VINCENT: She has so much life in her, Theo. So much warmth, so much love. . . . I can't let her waste it.

THEO: There's nothing more you can do.

VINCENT: I'm going to Amsterdam, and I will change her.

THEO: You'll ruin everything, Vincent. Everything we've been building up.

VINCENT: Oh Theo, if you were in love—

THEO: Well, I'm not. Thank God one of us isn't.

VINCENT: What it must be like to wake up in the morning next to someone you love! And then to come home at night, after working all day, and to look in those eyes—the eyes of someone who loves and needs you . . . that would be paradise!

THEO: And what if she never returns your love?

VINCENT: Then I will never marry. That's it. In any case, I'm telling Father tonight and leaving for Amsterdam tomorrow. (*Starts to exit.*)

THEO: What about the train to Amsterdam? You don't have money, do you?

VINCENT: (*Stops.*) No.

THEO: And where were you planning to stay when you got there? Or do you think that Uncle will be so happy to see you that he'll put you up in his house?

VINCENT: I was hoping you'd help me with money. (*Pause.*) But if you won't, I understand. I will manage.

THEO: How?

VINCENT: I've managed before.

THEO: Vincent, I'll give you the money if you promise to wait a few days and think this over. . . .

VINCENT: No.

THEO: I'm sure Cousin Kay would find you far more persuasive in a calm frame of mind—

VINCENT: Don't lecture me, Theo. Either give me the money or don't.

THEO: (*Gives* **VINCENT** *money.*) Don't make it impossible to come back here. There's nowhere else for you to go now, and—

VINCENT: (*Holds up his hand.*) We're going to be all right, don't worry. We'll have our success, whatever happens.

BETRAYED
BY GEORGE PACKER

CHARACTERS
LAITH *(20s), a Kurdish Shia from Sadr City, a suburb district of Baghdad.* HE'S *an interpreter at the U.S. Embassy, mistrusted by Americans and in danger among Iraqis. The* RSO *(20s) is the Regional Security Officer, American, responsible for diplomatic security at the U.S. Embassy in Baghdad.*

SCENE
The RSO's *office in Baghdad.* LAITH *is seated before the polygraph machine, not yet hooked up.*

TIME
2007

RSO: What are you so nervous about?

LAITH: I'm not nervous.

RSO: (*Laughing.*) Why are you hyperventilating?

LAITH: What?

RSO: Breathing hard.

LAITH: I know what happens to FSNs [Foreign Service nationals] you want to talk to about something work-related.

RSO: What happens to them?

LAITH: They disappear.

RSO: Tell me about your work. What do you do?

LAITH: I'm an interpreter in the political section.

RSO: Tell me more.

LAITH: I go with Bill Prescott to meetings. I interpret for him with Iraqi politicians. I write reports on Iraqi politics. I give information about the Arabic press.

RSO: Are you Sunni or Shia?

(**Laith** *folds his arms across his chest and doesn't answer. The* **RSO** *takes his zip cuffs off his belt and lays them on the table.*)

Laith: I'm a Feli Kurd.

RSO: A what?

Laith: Kurdish Shia.

RSO: Huh. (**He** *is momentarily stumped.*) Where do you live?

Laith: Sadr City.

RSO: Are you a Sadr guy?

Laith: I'm an Iraqi.

RSO: That's nice. I bet there's a proverb about it. So are you one of Sadr's guys?

Laith: No way.

RSO: Do you get phone calls from Sadr's guys?

Laith: I'll be lucky if I get a phone call from Sadrists. My supervisor will be very happy.

RSO: Why's that?

Laith: It's our work.

RSO: Do you know what an EFP [explosively formed projectile] is?

Laith: Like the really big IEDs [improvised explosive device] from Iran.

RSO: Do you know how many Americans may have been killed by EFPs? Do you know who's planting them?

Laith: Of course, the Shia militias, mostly Jaish al-Mahdi.

RSO: And you're talking on the phone with these guys?

Laith: My supervisor gave me instructions.

RSO: You know what? I'm really dissatisfied with this conversation. I don't feel like I'm getting any cooperation from you at all.

Laith: I don't know what you want.

RSO: No cooperation, just bullshit.

Laith: I'm telling you the truth.

RSO: You're not a Sadr guy, but last week you wrote an e-mail to the military liaison office asking about a detainee named Sami Abdel-Rahman. They forwarded it to me. (*The* **RSO** *looks triumphant.* **LAITH** *shrugs.*) Who told you that?

LAITH: I was asked by one of my contacts in Sadr City.

RSO: The same one that sent you here?

LAITH: Sent me here?

RSO: To work at the embassy.

LAITH: No one sent me here. Bill Prescott knows my background. You gave me a lie detector.

RSO: Yeah, you did better that time. Now you're not cooperating and it's starting to piss me off. So we're going to do it again.

LAITH: Why now? The annual polygraph is in September.

RSO: That's right, but you're choosing not to cooperate so I have to do a special one for you. Just sit still. (*The* **RSO** *begins to strap* **LAITH** *to the machine.*) Sit motionless. Don't close your eyes. Don't swallow. I said don't swallow. What's the name of your contact in Sadr City?

LAITH: Hazem al-Khafaji.

RSO: How do you know him?

LAITH: From school.

RSO: Did you ever conspire with him against the lives of American personnel in Iraq?

LAITH: No, never.

RSO: Why did you place seventeen calls to him between January and April?

LAITH: Bill Prescott told me to open a channel.

RSO: Did he tell you to send an e-mail to the military liaison office?

LAITH: No.

RSO: Asking about Sami Abdel-Rahman?

LAITH: No.

RSO: Do you know what Sami Abdel-Rahman is accused of?

LAITH: I think he was caught when they did the sweep in Shaab.

RSO: Planting EFPs on coalition patrol routes.

LAITH: I didn't hear that.

RSO: You're hearing it now. He has coalition blood on his hands. Did you give Sami Abdel-Rahman information about coalition patrol routes?

LAITH: No!

RSO: Are you lying to me? If I stop this test and report the results to D.C., we'll see what happens to you.

LAITH: How could I know the routes? I don't have classified access.

RSO: You're the guy who wanted the green badges, right?

LAITH: For our security.

RSO: Green would have gotten you past the outer checkpoint without a search.

LAITH: Maybe it would have saved someone's life.

RSO: That was the first red flag to me. Did you hear Prescott or anyone in the embassy talking about patrol routes?

LAITH: Never.

RSO: Why did you send the e-mail?

LAITH: Because my contact asked me to do him a favor.

RSO: You use your job here to do favors for the enemy.

LAITH: It's a kind of courtesy, to show good faith. I sent the e-mail on my state.gov account and I know you can read them. I wasn't trying to hide.

RSO: State.gov is for official business, correct?

LAITH: Yes.

RSO: Did you have official clearance to ask about the status of that detainee?

LAITH: I'm telling you, it was part of my job. I was trying to keep the channel open.

RSO: No official clearance.

LAITH: Maybe I should have asked Bill.

RSO: Did you ask about the status of any other detainees?

Laith: No. I mean, once, yes. The brother of my friend was brought in on a mistake.

RSO: No? Yes? No? This machine is going off the charts.

Laith: Yes, for my friend.

RSO: So you're using your official position to do favors for friends? Enemies, friends, doesn't matter just so long as they're Iraqi?

Laith: My friend was going to tell some people about my job.

RSO: Your friend was?

Laith: Someone I know. He began to guess where I work and he was threatening to tell the JAM [Jaysh al-Mahdi, Sadrist JAM militia] in his neighborhood. So I had to do this for him.

RSO: You know what? The simpler the answer, the happier this machine. It doesn't like complicated answers. It doesn't trust them. Complicated answers means you aren't cooperating. It means you are fucking lying to me.

Laith: Every day, every day I'm risking my life for this embassy.

RSO: You are trying to fuck with the United States.

(*Calmly,* **Laith** *removes the polygraph wires from his body, takes off his badge and phone, and places them on the table.*)

What's this?

Laith: I'm resigning my position.

RSO: You can't. You've been fired.

B'SHALOM
BY MERON LANGSNER

CHARACTERS
ISSAM *(early 20s) and* GILAD *(mid-20s) are two college students serving as day laborers on a construction site in New York the summer after 9/11.*

SCENE
A vacant lot with lots of rubble to be cleared

TIME
Summer 2002

ISSAM *is a Palestinian-American who immigrated as a child.* GILAD *is an Israeli immigrant, former IDF (Israel Defense Forces) paratrooper, and a more recent arrival. Both had been finding some common ground while piling up rubble, until events took an unexpected turn.*

(GILAD *tells* ISSAM *about a bombing in Tel-Aviv and* ISSAM *returns from checking a news broadcast, visibly shaken.*)

GILAD: The foreman. He is an asshole.

ISSAM: Yeah, well at least he isn't around much.

GILAD: He has charming views of us.

ISSAM: Whatever, man.

GILAD: You saw the news?

ISSAM: Yes.

GILAD: Fucked up.

ISSAM: Be quiet.

GILAD: Not like it was your town.

ISSAM: Close enough. (*Small pause.*) You hear anything about your people yet?

GILAD: No. If I couldn't get through in the first couple hours, I won't be able to know till afternoon at best. (*Small pause.*) Same thing happens every time. It's routine already.

Issam: I have a cousin. . . . He was studying to be an engineer. He left school.

Gilad: Sorry to hear that.

Issam: Haven't seen him for years and years. Good kid though, as I remember him. Heard from my mom we were starting college the same time. He was a little older than me. Used to beat on me a little when we were kids, but always got me ice cream.

Gilad: Glad he went to school.

Issam: He left school.

Gilad: You said you haven't heard from him in years.

Issam: I just saw him on TV. In the trailer.

Gilad: What are you talking about?

Issam: He's dead.

Gilad: They're talking about the victims on TV? (**Gilad** *starts to move toward the trailer.*)

Issam: No. (**Gilad** *stops. Stares at* **Issam**.)

Gilad: What is it then?

Issam: CNN was showing a tape from Al Jazeera [an Arab satellite news agency based in Qatar].

Gilad: What is it?

Issam: My cousin is dead. He left school, and now he's dead.

(*Silence.*)

Gilad: And he was on the news.

Issam: Yes.

(*Beat.*)

Gilad: A tape played by Al-Jezeera.

Issam: That's what I said.

(*Beat.*)

Gilad: He was dressed all in white, wasn't he?

Issam: Shut up.

(*Beat.*)

GILAD: With a flag and a gun and an explosives belt.

(*Beat.*)

ISSAM: I said shut up.

(*Beat.*)

GILAD: *Ben zonah.* [Son of a whore.]

ISSAM: Watch it.

GILAD: In Dizzingoff. You think maybe Times Square will be next? Every news agency in the Gulf would have a festival.

ISSAM: (*Quietly.*) He was a good kid. Always got me ice cream.

GILAD: A worthless fucking piece of shit terrorist coward.

ISSAM: They bulldoze houses, don't they? The families. My aunt and uncle and the rest of the cousins.

GILAD: Impressive checks are written from Saudi Arabia. What's the price on a kid today? Is it more if they kill an old woman? How is the brainwashing? I guess it's fun, lots of promises of sex in paradise, fame for the family, a great honor for everyone. What do they do with the tapes if the bombers come to their senses? You're not a little embarrassed that making kids commit suicide to kill other kids is considered heroism? Do you think the pictures of schoolchildren with bomb belts are cute? You were in the city when the towers came down, do you want to build a bigger one so it's easier to hit the next time?

(*Pause.*)

ISSAM: Gilad. Watch it.

GILAD: Making conversation. Waiting for the news from home. You know how it is. News, weather, body counts, obituaries. (*Imitates a radio newscast.*) *Kol Israel mi Yerushalyim.* [This is the beginning of a newscast, "To all of Israel from Jerusalem."] It is beautiful and sunny and thirty-two degrees Celsius, with a suicide bomber body count of only fourteen today and peace talks still suspended. The UN has declared that the IDF [Israel Defense Forces, the army] should hand out chocolates at the borders to terrorists as they enter Jerusalem. Hundreds of assholes paraded in the funeral of the *ben zonah* who may or may not have killed my—

ISSAM: *Coos emmek!* [Your mother's genitals.] SHUT UP! (*Pause. Silence.* **THEY** *stare at each other.*)

GILAD: Am I making the provocation?

ISSAM: You're a piece of shit.

GILAD: My neighborhood is blown up by your family and I am the piece of shit?

ISSAM: He was desperate.

GILAD: Tell me. What desperation allows you to do this. The men who flew planes into buildings here, were they desperate? Did your family dance in the streets when they got the news? If you were close enough to die, do you think they would dance any less?

ISSAM: Fuck you! You think it's easy? I was scared to go outside for a month. In New York. I was catching shit in school. At the fucking PC capital of the universe. You think I liked it when I heard rumors about Atlantic Avenue? You think it's not embarrassing to be identified with that shit?

GILAD: You're not part of that shit? You didn't just tell me your desperate cousin became a martyr?

ISSAM: He threw his life away after you people made it hell. I'm pissed to no end about it.

GILAD: You're pissed? Be pissed at the terrorist with the peace prize for your situation, don't scream at me.

ISSAM: I didn't do it, asshole. Don't take it out on me. I'm sick of all the shitheads over here trying to take it out on me. I don't need some other asshole making a special trip from over there doing the same.

(*Pause.*)

GILAD: Over here we can get along. Right?

ISSAM: I like to think so.

(*Pause.*)

Are you going back?

GILAD: I have to wait for news. I may have a funeral to go to. (**THEY** *get back to work.* **THEY** *do not speak.* **GILAD** *puts things down and starts to go.*)

ISSAM: You going?

GILAD: I'm getting fuck-all done here. I'm gonna go home and try to get news.

(*Pause.*)

Watch the foreman. He's an asshole. (**HE** *collects his things, starts to exit.*)

ISSAM: Gilad. I hope your people are okay.

GILAD: I hope your cousin rots in hell. (**GILAD** *deliberately knocks over a pile that they've stacked.* **HE** *exits.*)

BURNING THE OLD MAN
BY KELLY MCALLISTER

CHARACTERS
BOBBY *(late 20s), bit of a smartass;* MARTY *(early 30s),* BOBBY'S *high-strung older brother*

SCENE
The lobby of Jo's run-down motel in the middle of the Nevada desert

TIME
The night before the Burning Man Festival, summer

The brothers are traveling to the Burning Man Festival, an annual desert gathering based on radical self-expression, to bury their father's ashes, as he wished. On the way, BOBBY *smoked a joint in the backseat and set their mother's car on fire.* MARTY *has called their mother to tell her.*

BOBBY: *(Takes the box of ashes from the table, sits with it on the couch.)* I can't believe you called Mom. What are you, 12?

MARTY: You set the car on fire.

BOBBY: It was an accident. Jesus. I said I'm sorry.

MARTY: Not even noon, and you're smoking Mary Jane.

BOBBY: Wake and bake. Don't knock it 'til you try it. And did you just say Mary Jane? Geek.

MARTY: So says the loser. The completely irresponsible loser who runs to Mommy whenever things get rough.

BOBBY: Fuck you, geek. You're the one who called Mom. Just turn around and go home. You don't belong out here.

[*(JO goes to the window and looks out, pretending not to listen.)*]

MARTY: You don't belong anywhere! Jesus, what is your problem? It's bad enough we have to do this. Why do you insist on making it worse?

BOBBY: Why do you insist on being a drag? He was very specific. We're supposed to take his ashes to the Burning Man and let him go.

MARTY: I'm familiar with his instructions. I was there when he wrote them. Unlike you.

[JO: Excuse me?]

MARTY: Where were you then? Oh, that's right. You were at the movies.

[JO: Excuse me?]

MARTY: The movies. Dad's dying, and you go to the movies.

BOBBY: It was a *Godfather* marathon, and Dad told me to go.

MARTY: Of course he did. He knew you wouldn't let him have his privacy, so he pretended to feel better and sent you away. Because you couldn't accept the reality of the situation.

[JO: Do you still want me to call a cab?]

BOBBY: Why is it that everything you say sounds like it crept out of your ass, covered in cellophane?

MARTY: Why don't you take that cab to the nearest bus station, and go home? I'll take the old man.

BOBBY: Why don't you go fuck yourself! (*Grabs the box.*) I swear to fucking God, I will dump him out right here if you don't shut up and leave me alone.

MARTY: Put him down!

BOBBY: At least I didn't leave him alone in a room with a gun in it!

MARTY: You shut up about that! God, I hate you!

BOBBY: I hate you back! You should have known better!

[(*There is a very loud explosion outside.* JO *jumps back from the window.* **BOBBY** *and* **MARTY** *continue to argue, oblivious.*)]

MARTY: How was I supposed to know he'd pull a Hemingway? He asked me to get him a Bible, and I went to get it! Excuse me for trying to help him make amends with his lost God.

BOBBY: Oh, please. How could you fall for that? Did you really think our father would ever, ever seek God again?

MARTY: Put him down before you spill him.

BOBBY: I'll put him down when I get to Burning Man!

[JO: I think your car just blew up.]

MARTY: I am sick of fighting with you! What happened, happened, and there's nothing more to say about that. You need to let it go. I know we don't get along, okay? I know we're not buddies anymore. I've known that for a long time. But unfortunately, the Old Man wanted us to do this together. And that's exactly what we're going to do. We're going to get through this, as quickly and cleanly as possible, and then we can go back to pretending we don't know each other for the rest of our lives. Now, please, put him down, and be reasonable.

CAVEMAN
BY RICHARD MAXWELL

CHARACTERS
C, *the man, around 40;* A, *the other man, around 40*

SCENE
C's *home, somewhere remote*

TIME
Today

A *and* C *work together in the warehouse.* A *wants what* C *has, including his wife.* W, C's *wife, has just cleared the table and left the room, leaving* C *and* A *alone.*

C: She gets upset. She can't handle it by herself.

A: What kind of accent is that?

C: She doesn't have an accent. . . .

A: I like her voice. . . . This your place?

C: You bet.

A: All yours?

C: Yeah.

A: You don't pay rent?

C: No, I do not.

A: Well, well . . .

C: What's on your mind, Angelo?

A: Anthony.

C: Yeah.

A: Yeah. Okay. Let's get to business.

C: What's going on down on the floor?

A: Yeah.

C: ... Go.

A: People are confused.

C: About what?

A: Well, it all comes down to whose system, whose model you want to use. The one that we use now is, if you worked on their system, I mean for their system, what's to stop me from, okay, it's like—what is the goal from our side? You know what I'm saying? I could work for you and we'd be good, we could make it happen, right? And that's fine, and we'd be fine, you know? But what if you and I were to, come to see what would come of this some kind of thing and where we didn't have to show the differences. You know? What would they say?

C: Yeah ...

A: We could give a statement or whatever that shows that they're the same?

C: No.

A: Why not?

C: Because they're not the same.

A: Then we got a problem here, like I said. Because we can't agree on which system to use. On one hand you have the old way, which is more traditional and established ... which most everybody knows, but it's really for old people—and then you have the new way that I like better because the young people feel better about it—people who are new are looking at the old model and saying, "What is this?" So basically it is about the old way versus the new way. And I don't care really, but we need to decide—and I'm, like, well let's decide.

C: How long have you worked here?

A: How long ... nine months.

C: Nine months. That's it? You know how long I have worked here?

A: I don't know. I got here, and you were here.

C: I'm here for eighteen years, son. (*Smile.*)

A: Yeah. Well, like I'm saying. I have worked in it for over nine months and have been involved in pretty major projects. I saw a lot of pride from people. And different people have different ways of dealing with it.

C: Whoa, whoa, whoa. Pride? You talk about pride. That's funny to me, because you don't know what pride is. How long have you been working here? Nine months. You know? What time did you get up this morning? What time did you get home? See? That's pride, son. I have worked in these places, and I have seen this place go from the worst to a little bit better. Okay? I know about pride. Yeah, when you have worked for eighteen years, then you can talk about pride. You understand?

A: Yeah. Well, I don't know.

C: Exactly. You don't know.

A: Yeah, well, like I said. I don't know....

C: Back up, son... pride. Pride goes back. 1728. Before that, the Middle Ages. There have been transitions but it's still the same. Delivering frozen foods: taco, chicken, hot bagels, pizza... whatever. Delivering to: IFH, Robert E. Lee, Wolf... Le Fleur Foods. Dos Amigos, IGA, Solo. Texas, Georgia, Oklahoma, North Carolina, Virginia. Store-brand and controlled-brand environments. Six hundred stores. Twenty-eight thousand items—wholesale food. Tobacco, alcohol. Wide distribution. I'll tell you what.

A: Well, like I said. I don't care. I'm just like well, let's pick a system and stick with it. You know, I don't care, new, old, it doesn't matter. Let's just pick one.

C: We have a system. (*Pause.*) Let me explain to you. I worked in the warehouse and they were using the younger people's system and it was a newer system. Their way is all about speed and that's not right. Speed and you make mistakes. You know? And after that I swore I would never do it their way again. I'll tell you what.

A: But that's their system, though with the starter pieces...

C: Well, it's a cold reality, son. But it's not a big deal. Cheer up. (*Smile.*)...Great things come at a price. There's nothing you can do. It might be depressing for you. But it's a cold reality and there's nothing you can do, son.

(*Pause.*)

A: Yeah, but you know what?...I would never have worked under their system. The old way.

C: That's different from what you just said....

A: Yeah, well....

C: Yeah? Why not?

A: Because.

C: Why not?

A: No. I won't do it, actually. I'll never do it. . . . I wouldn't do it.

C: Why not?

A: Well, I have my reasons.

C: What are they?

(*Pause.*)

A: 'Cos. It gives me a headache sometimes! What about the new system? I don't see what's wrong with it. People are talking about the new system. There's a manual on it that's out now. . . . What do you think about it, buddy?

C: Well, I will make the final decision on this. Yes. I will make the final decision on this. And what I decide you will have to accept. So I'm not just thinking about you, but you, me, and everyone else here . . . so yeah. And everyone else seems to be fine with the old way. That's my experience. . . .

A: But I'm telling you what everyone else thinks and they think the old way stinks.

C: Yeah, that's not my experience.

A: Everybody who I talk to says it doesn't work.

C: Well, that's not my experience.

A: Aww! You don't know! Your experience! You don't know! You don't know the people! Why don't you try it. Just try it and see what the people think!

C: No, son!

A: Son?!

C: It won't work!

A: Come on!

C: It doesn't work!

(*Pause.*)

A: We'll see.

C: Okay. You don't tell me which system is best. I tell you. Really.

A: Okay, guy. No, I got it.

(*Long pause.*)

I'm looking at your body. You got a funny body.

C: Oh?

A: Yeah. Look at it.... Let me see something.... Okay... this is your chest, right...?

C: What about you. Look at you.

A: What.

C: You look like Neandrathal.

A: Who's that?

C: You're big. No question.

A: I know.

C: Right? You weren't always this big....

A: Yeah!

C: How did you get so big?

A: Yeah, you know what it is?

C: Yeah.

A: You know what it is?

C: Yeah.

A: Phosphogates.

C: What are they?

A: Phosphogates. Yeh. Yeah. Phosphogates. That's what it is. But you gotta eat.

C: Yeah?

A: Yeah. Phosphogates.

C: Okay, I got it.

(*Pause.*)

    I'll tell you what.

A: Yeah.

C: Those can make you crazy.

A: No no no no. Listen.

C: Be careful, son.

A: They don't make you crazy. What I'm talking about is a catalyst. It's all Catalytic Converters. What you're talking about? Those aren't steroids. Cortisol. Cortisone. Prednisone. Those aren't—they're converters—for the anabolic. Picture rings. Just picture rings. And these rings form with other rings and you get the picture. Rings. Steroids just affect the body size. You might be thinking about what are called corticosteroids. That's different. . . . I can't remember his name—English bloke?—had chickens. And one was on the hormone. And one wasn't. What happens? You know what happens? The chickens have a red hat on their head, right? For the chicken who was not on the hormone was really small. Had this LITTLE small thing—

C: A crown?

A: Yes! A crown. Little thing. Crown. And the other one?

C: Was big . . .

A: Exactly. Nice big one.

C: All right.

A: But I also work out. The chickens weren't working out, exactly. You gotta work out. So? That's all. You know. If you keep taking them, and keep taking them, then maybe you'd go crazy. But that's true with most things. That's true with everything! But you're not going to go crazy. They're not going to make you crazy. I mean they could make you crazy. But they're not going to make you crazy.

C: Yeah.

(*Pause.*)

A: All right?

C: All right. That's inneresting.

CORPS VALUES
BY BRENDON BATES

CHARACTERS
CASEY *(24), athletic build, closely cropped crew cut—dressed in long-sleeved T-shirt and thermal underwear;* WADE *(60s),* CASEY'S *Dad, a larger man, walks with a limp*

SCENE
The kitchen of WADE'S *farmhouse*

TIME
Late November 2004. After midnight.

CASEY, *a Marine, was in Iraq, but given a leave for the funeral of his mother.*

CASEY: Dad . . .

WADE: (*Reentering.*) Yeah?

CASEY: . . . I'm not going back.

WADE: Pardon?

CASEY: I'm not returning to duty.

(*Pause.* WADE *laughs.*)

WADE: You have to go back. You have six months left.

CASEY: I know.

WADE: You got an entire company counting on you.

CASEY: Half my company has been wiped out.

WADE: Well the *other half* is counting on you.

CASEY: I'm writing a letter to each member of my platoon, explaining myself, asking for their forgiveness. . . .

WADE: What?

CASEY: Encouraging them to do the same.

WADE: Encouraging them to do what?

CASEY: To walk away from the war.

WADE: Have you lost your mind?

CASEY: I'd rather rot in jail than—

WADE: (*Interrupting him.*) What are you saying?

CASEY: I'm saying I'm done with this war.

WADE: Listen. . . . Go get some much-needed rest. You've had a rough couple of months. And we just buried your mother. It's hard for you to . . . think straight.

CASEY: I'm thinking perfectly clear.

WADE: Listen. . . . War is messed up. Believe me, I know. But, right or wrong, you made a *commitment*. A commitment to those men who fight beside you. Think about your squad members. Your *brothers*. Look at me, Goddammit!!

(**CASEY** *looks at him.*)

Remember when you told me you wanted to enlist? I sat right here; you sat right there. I looked you in the eye and I told you, in full detail, the horrors I faced as a Marine, the horrors *you* would face as a Marine, what would be expected of you wearing that uniform. Remember all that?

CASEY: Yes.

WADE: And you *still* enlisted. You *still* made that commitment. So, be a man and face the consequences. (*Turns his back on* **CASEY** *and heads for the bedroom.*)

CASEY: I killed a young boy.

(**WADE** *stops.*)

A young Iraqi boy. In Fallujah. Couldn't of been 15 years old. Shot him right through the throat. He was firing at me from an elevated position. Bullet nicked my helmet. I got down, took aim. He stood up for some stupid reason. And I fired. He fell three stories.

WADE: You did what you had to do.

CASEY: I heard a woman scream as soon as he hit the ground. I couldn't tell where the scream came from, but I knew it was his mother.

WADE: Listen, we're going to get you some help. You can see a doctor.

CASEY: (*Ferociously.*) I DON'T NEED A DOCTOR!!!

(**WADE** *seems shocked.*)

I need to walk away from this war. That's what I need. And I'm prepared to face the consequences.

WADE: Are you?

CASEY: Yes.

WADE: When I was in Nam, a kid by the name Justin Shear, Private First Class Rifleman, went over the hill and disappeared. They found him a month later in a place called The Dog Patch in Da Nang. He got busted. They sent him back to our company. The C.O. made him walk *point* day after day, until... I don't need to tell you what often happens to the point man.

CASEY: I'll just tell them I refuse to fight.

WADE: (*Laughs.*) Oh...okay!

CASEY: I'll just flat out refuse.

WADE: You think they're going to grace you with mercy? This is the military. Not Little League.

CASEY: I know that.

WADE: They will work...you...over.... Do yourself a favor: Finish the six months, get out, and protest when you *get back*. No shame in that.

CASEY: Yes, there is.

WADE: Marines did it all the time during Vietnam.

CASEY: There's no way in hell I can spend another day contributing to this war.

WADE: What the hell you gonna do then? Go run, hide in the woods? Escape to Montreal? What?

CASEY: I'm going to Washington.

WADE: D.C.?

CASEY: Yeah, Katie is vice president of a grassroots organization that's connected to Charlie Waltz, the editor of the *Pittsburgh Post-Gazette*. Mr. Waltz is a board member for the organization Vietnam Veterans Against the War.

WADE: Oh, for crying out loud!

CASEY: (*Continuing.*) He's going to print my letter—(*Holds up letter.*) *this* letter— in the Sunday edition and, then, drive me down to a huge rally at the Capitol.

(**CASEY** *pulls out a purple flyer from his back pocket.* **HE** *unfolds it.* **HE** *hands it to his father, who looks at it.*)

He says I can *speak* at the rally.

WADE: Speak at the rally?

CASEY: Yeah.

WADE: What do you mean, *speak at the rally?*

CASEY: You know.... Tell my story.... Inspire others to stand against this war....

WADE: Jesus Christ. Is this Katie's idea?

CASEY: No! It's mine.

WADE: Bullshit.

CASEY: She tried to talk me out of it.

WADE: I find that hard to believe.

CASEY: (*Shrugs.*) All she's doing is introducing me to Mr. Waltz.

WADE: Pph.... So—okay, fine—you speak at this thing, get people hootin' and hollerin', and then...what?

CASEY: And then...we...*rally.*

WADE: And *after* the rally? The rally *ends*, everyone goes *home*. What happens *after* the rally?

(**CASEY** *shrugs.*)

WADE: Oh, for crying out loud! You're going back. And I'm taking ya. (*Rises.*) Get your stuff, throw it in the truck, we're leaving at dawn. (*Points at him.*) If I wake up and you're missing, I will hunt you down. You hear me?

CASEY: So be it.

(**THEY** *stare at each other.*)

DEWEY BOY AND WOOKIE
BY DWIGHT WATSON

CHARACTERS
DEWEY BOY *(30s or 40s) and* **WOOKIE** *(20s) are prison guards about to execute a condemned man by pulling the switch on "Old Smokey," a monstrous wooden-framed electric chair.*

SCENE
A room with antiseptic walls and floors, recently scrubbed, in the State Prison Center for the Penalty of Death by Electrocution. The room is bare except for the chair, the white walls, the chamber door, and a large plate-glass window.

TIME
The present

(Dressed in institutional uniforms, **DEWEY BOY** *studies the morning newspaper while* **WOOKIE**, *unshaven, gruff, and irritable, paces about.)*

WOOKIE: *(With growing frustration.)* Come on, Commissioner. Flip the light! Let's send the "Ol' Boy" home!

DEWEY BOY: Relax, Wookie.

WOOKIE: What's he waitin' for, huh? A thunderbolt?! *(In the direction of the audience.)* Hell, Commish, we got the power, so just gimme some kinda sign!

DEWEY BOY: What'sa matter with you, Wookie?

WOOKIE: Nothin'. Ain't nothin' the matter with me. I just hate wastin' the taxpayers' money. That's all. Time and money. Get this thing over with!

DEWEY BOY: Twelve sharp. Nothin's gonna happen 'til twelve sharp. Not a minute before.

WOOKIE: Why make such a damn big fuss out of this thing?!

DEWEY BOY: They gotta do it by the book, Wookie.

WOOKIE: I say we burn the book, fry his ass, and go home. *(Chanting.)* "Fry his ass and let's go home! Fry his ass and let's go home!"

DEWEY BOY: Shut up, Wookie. This ain't no baseball game. We're 'bout to make history here.

Wookie: History? I ain't makin' no history! It's a job, Dewey.

Dewey Boy: Well, show a little respect.

Wookie: Respect?! You tryin' to make me feel bad? Is that it, Dewey Boy? You want me to feel sorry for Ol' Tom Dooley there? Is that it? Well I don't! I don't feel sorry for him, Dewey Boy, and I ain't gonna sit here and listen to you get all sentimental about Ol' Tom Dooley there. I say, let him hang!

Dewey Boy: (*Reading the paper.*) James.

Wookie: What?

Dewey Boy: His name is James.

Wookie: Don't give me his name!

Dewey Boy: James Duncan.

Wookie: Fried Chicken.

Dewey Boy: James P. Duncan.

Wookie: Crispy Fried Chicken! I'm gonna eat me some fried chicken. Finger lickin', lip smackin', crunchy, spicy chicken!

Dewey Boy: (*Reading the paper.*) Says here that "James P. Duncan has an IQ of sixty-two."

Wookie: Sixty-two, huh? That makes him near genius, don't it?

Dewey Boy: He's retarded, Wookie, retarded.

Wookie: Retarded?! An IQ of sixty-two in your high school, Dewey Boy, would make him the graduation speaker.

Dewey Boy: Read this.

Wookie: I ain't interested.

Dewey Boy: (*Pushing the newspaper into* **Wookie's** *hands.*) Go ahead, read it.

Wookie: (*Reading.*) "It's only a little critter, but it might be worth a million dollars."

Dewey Boy: Not that. Here.

Wookie: (*Reading.*) "James P. Duncan's lawyer believes it's un . . . cons . . . tit. . . . un . . . con . . . sti . . ."

Dewey Boy: Unconstitutional.

WOOKIE: Don't tell me it's unconstitutional! I know it's unconstitutional! I was just breathin'.

DEWEY BOY: (*Reaching for the newspaper.*) You want me to read it?

WOOKIE: (*Slapping the paper into* **DEWEY'S** *hands.*) No, I don't! I don't want you to read anything to me. I don't want you to talk to me. I don't want you to look at me. I just want you to leave me alone.

DEWEY BOY: (*Reading.*) "It's unconstitutional to give the death penalty…"

WOOKIE: I told you, Dewey Boy, I told you, I ain't interested.

DEWEY BOY: "…unconstitutional to give the death penalty to people with limited mental abilities."

WOOKIE: (*Shocked.*) What?! His lawyer says you can't kill stupid people?

DEWEY BOY: (*Reading.*) Ah…those with "limited mental abilities."

WOOKIE: Yeah, well, that excuses about everyone, doesn't it? Except what's-his-name? Einstein.

DEWEY BOY: Albert.

WOOKIE: I know his name's Albert.

DEWEY BOY: (*Reading.*) He says, "It's doubtful that James P. Duncan knows the difference between right and wrong."

WOOKIE: It don't matter! There's a special look in a mean, mad dog's eye…you just know he's bad!

DEWEY BOY: You just know?

WOOKIE: Yeah, his eyes bulge…his head comes unglued…ears spin in different directions…and his tongue…his tongue is like something sticky he's trying to cough up. And anybody who has ever seen a mad dog…knows you better shoot first. Bam! Or else he just might bite you and make *you* mad. And then *your* head comes unglued…and *your* ears spin…and *your* tongue begins to look like some strange-lookin' gravy dinner you left for months in the 'frigerator. And then, there you are, crazy, hangin' out with this crazy dog, standin' in the middle of the damn road…just waitin' for a chance to bite someone else on the butt so you can make *him* crazy. Once you see a mad dog's eyes, you know, Dewey Boy, you know. You better shoot, then and there. Bam!

DEWEY BOY: Bam?

WOOKIE: (*Demonstrating.*) Bam! Yes, bam! And then cut off his head and send it to the state capital.

DEWEY BOY: The capital?

WOOKIE: Don't you know nothin'! Put it in a box, wrapped in brown paper, and ship it to the capital.

DEWEY BOY: Why would anyone ship a dog's head to the capital?

WOOKIE: Because, Dewey Boy, it's the job of the government to keep track of all the mad dogs in the country. They gotta make sure they don't spread rabies.

DEWEY BOY: I see. Have you sent heads to the capital?

WOOKIE: Sure. A time or two. Book rate. It's our duty, Dewey Boy.

DEWEY BOY: Did the government reply? I mean, did you get a report?

WOOKIE: Why, sure. Once I got a real friendly letter from the FBI thankin' me for the head, and askin' me to fill out their questionnaire.

DEWEY BOY: Just suppose, Wookie, that the dog ain't mad. Maybe he just ate some garbage... maybe... just maybe... he's chucking down a big ol' piece of fat he found... and he's just havin' a hard time swallowin' it. What then?

WOOKIE: Look! I just told you, Dewey Boy, you just know! You can see it in his *eyes*! That's why they got Ol' James P. Dooley there blindfolded.

DEWEY BOY: It's *Duncan*, Wookie, and the blindfold is supposed to keep the eyes from popping out of their sockets. It's not 'cause he's crazy.

WOOKIE: You really care about that Old Boy, don' ya? I mean, you don't want him to die, do ya? No. You want the devil to live so he can kill again, don't ya?

DEWEY BOY: No, that ain't...

WOOKIE: (*Stalking* **DEWEY**.) Maybe set him free to kill your mother, Dewey Boy?

DEWEY BOY: Now, wait just...

WOOKIE: How'ya like that, huh? Maybe kill your sister, or your baby brother, or how 'bout your ol' bird dog, huh? Yeah, uh-huh, let's set him free to steal that spit-polished, stripped-down, prized Camaro you drive....

DEWEY BOY: Whoa... now....

WOOKIE: . . . kill and rape your wife, if 'n you was ever lucky enough to git one.

DEWEY BOY: (*Topping* **WOOKIE**.) Take it easy, Wookie! You just made me an orphan without a dog and wheels all in one breath! It's just that this IQ thing got me to thinkin', that's all.

WOOKIE: Thinkin? Shit . . . feelin's more like it. And once we start feelin' for his kind . . . ain't nobody safe.

(*Slight pause.*)

DEWEY BOY: Yeah. Maybe you're right.

WOOKIE: Bet on it. (*Sticking out his tongue; looking for gum.*) Got any gum?

DEWEY BOY: Nope.

WOOKIE: (*Sticking out his tongue again.*) You see anything on my tongue?

DEWEY BOY: You mean, like a sore?

WOOKIE: Yeah, anything.

DEWEY BOY: Nope. Looks a bit like a wet cucumber, bumpy and a tad green.

WOOKIE: It just don't feel right. Probably just hunger. What time is it?

DEWEY BOY: Eleven fifty-seven.

WOOKIE: Jesus! What difference does a minute or two make?!

DEWEY BOY: Duncan's lawyer asked for a stay of execution, and so who knows, the governor might call at eleven fifty-nine.

WOOKIE: Yeah. Well, while we're waiting, I say we put the lawyer's ass in the chair to test the current.

DEWEY BOY: Wookie, if it's unconstitutional to execute a guy with a limited IQ, the governor will call.

WOOKIE: Don't that just beat all. I mean . . . we fry a guy with average intelligence or a guy who's even smart, but if the guy's got a little bit of stupid in him . . . we let him go. Well . . . I guess I'll never get the chair, 'cause I sure as hell can't figure that one out.

DEWEY BOY: They gotta play it by the book.

WOOKIE: (*Absorbed in his disgust.*) Well, this is a living hell! Waiting around like this! Seems like nobody can make up his mind in this country. I'm fed up! Do you hear me?! Fed up!

(*A warning light lights up near the switches.*)

DEWEY BOY: Wookie?

WOOKIE: (*Unaware of* **DEWEY BOY**.) I had another job offer. I did! I could've worked the assembly line puttin' together auto parts for them Japanese imports.

DEWEY BOY: Wookie! It's time. The switch.

WOOKIE: (*Ranting.*) But I said, "Hell no! I'm gonna do somethin' to help America!"

DEWEY BOY: It's time, Wookie! Almost time to throw the switch!

WOOKIE: (*Startled,* **HE** *then moves to the switch.*) The switch? The switch! Well, all right, now! Git rid of that newspaper, Dewey Boy, and let's go to work! Yes sir, America is back at work again.

END ZONE
BY BOB SHUMAN

CHARACTERS
ARTHUR TRAINER *(late 30s) is a freelance composer and percussionist;* **NORM TRAINER** *(late 40s) is a sporting goods salesman and former football player. Their father, Lucian (late 70s), a retired football coach, is asleep in the adjoining room.*

SCENE
A motel. It's about a mile down the road from a prep school in the Northeast.

TIME
A while back, in November. Before dinner.

(**NORM** *helps* **ARTHUR** *fix his pants.*)

ARTHUR: Jesus Christ.

NORM: Get out of the way so I can look.

ARTHUR: I can't get it to catch.

NORM: Will you stop moving so I can see?

ARTHUR: I knew this would happen.

NORM: What the hell did you do to it?

ARTHUR: I told you I didn't want to wear it.

NORM: This is a Mauritzio suit.

ARTHUR: Haven't even seen the guy in—

NORM: Got the whole fly coming apart.

ARTHUR: You're the one who wanted to arm wrestle.

NORM: Eight years! It's been eight years since you've seen him.

(**ARTHUR** *furiously tries to fix the fly again.*)

ARTHUR: Where is this mother?!

NORM: So you gotta act right this weekend.

Arthur: Get this clasp . . .

Norm: Your father spent forty years at this school.

Arthur: . . . so I can zip . . . up . . .

Norm: Somebody better recognize him.

Arthur: . . . my . . . pants . . .

Norm: MY pants.

Arthur: . . . get these runners . . .

Norm: Just get him over to the campus in the morning.

Arthur: . . . like THAT.

(*Pause. The fly is fixed.* **Norm** *looks at* **Arthur**, *unbelieving.*)

Norm: You're kidding.

Arthur: (*About the pants.*) You can take them back to the thrift shop when you get home.

Norm: You actually got that to work?

Arthur: Got all this baggage.

Norm: You need to go through it.

Arthur: I could beat you if we arm wrestled.

Norm: Can't even talk to him.

(*Pause.* **Norm** *takes the CD* **Arthur** *has been wrapping.*)

Arthur: What do you think you're doing?

Norm: I need it for Clayt [the prep-school headmaster].

Arthur: That's not for him.

Norm: He saw you playing the industrial piping in New Hope.

Arthur: I want it back.

Norm: Quite the musical aficionado, this headmaster.

Arthur: It's for Dad.

Norm: I don't want to hear about you being an artist, we've all seen how far you've come with that.

[LUCIAN: (*From his bed, in his sleep.*) Who you talking to?]

ARTHUR: Coach.

NORM: (*Suddenly.*) He's up.

[LUCIAN: Who's that?]

NORM: You woke him.

ARTHUR: (*Calling.*) You all right, Coach?

NORM: Be quiet, will ya!

ARTHUR: Should we get him?

NORM: Shut. Up!

ARTHUR: (*Quietly.*) Is that you, Coach?

(*Silence.* NORM *checks on* LUCIAN.)

NORM: He'll sleep a little longer....

(NORM *drinks.*)

ARTHUR: I'd like to help but...

NORM: I really don't think...

ARTHUR: I don't have any money....

NORM: ...it's worth talking about

ARTHUR: You keep bringing it up.

NORM: Pull up your pants!

ARTHUR: I'm out of work.

    (*Pause.*)

    I could beat you!

NORM: Yeah, right.

ARTHUR: I don't want to beat an old man.

NORM: I'll kill you!

ARTHUR: Start! (*They don't arm wrestle.*)

NORM: Send him a different CD.

ARTHUR: Last one's for Coach!

NORM: That's mine!

(**NORM** *and* **ARTHUR** *begin arm wrestling, grunting and groaning through their dialogue.*)

NORM: My wife can't take it—

ARTHUR: You said you'd take care of him—

NORM: We need you to help us—

ARTHUR: He can't come to New York—

NORM: Then move back to Georgia.

ARTHUR: You know what it would be like?

NORM: I can't pay taxes.

ARTHUR: You can't expect me—

NORM: I haven't paid my taxes in two years.

ARTHUR: Bullshit.

NORM: You're dead!

(**NORM** *slams down* **ARTHUR'S** *hand on the table and wins.*)

ARTHUR: That's not fair.

NORM: Beat ya!

(*Pause.*)

ARTHUR: You lied!

NORM: His bawling and moaning and his emphysema, flushing his medication down the toilet.

ARTHUR: You pay your taxes. . . .

NORM: Don't believe me. Everything I'm telling you is true.

"FLOATING HOME" from AN INTIMATE HISTORY OF EXILE
BY ADRIÁN RODRÍGUEZ

CHARACTERS
ABEL *(30s) considers himself a Cuban exile, although he has lived in this country for twenty years.* **FATHER ALFREDO** *(60s) is a parish priest.*

SCENE
Union City, New Jersey

TIME
2000

(**FATHER ALFREDO**, *wearing glasses, is lighting candles.* **HE** *looks around to ensure that* **HE** *is alone and then lights a cigarette with one of the candles.* **ABEL**, *now in his thirties, wearing winter clothes, enters stage right and startles* **FATHER ALFREDO**.)

ABEL: I don't believe in God. . . . I haven't believed in God for a long time.

FATHER ALFREDO: You did believe at one time, yes?

ABEL: Yes, Padre, I did . . . I think I did.

FATHER ALFREDO: And?

ABEL: Now I don't. Not for a long time.

FATHER ALFREDO: Yes, you said that already.

ABEL: I'm sorry. I repeat things a lot these days.

FATHER ALFREDO: So as not to forget?

ABEL: No. I never forget anything.

FATHER ALFREDO: Never?

ABEL: I never forget anything. I can remember how your ring felt on the back of my head when you lowered me into the water . . . here, right at the base where it folds into the neck. . . . It was cold, smooth.

FATHER ALFREDO: You didn't cry.

ABEL: You don't forget anything, either.

FATHER ALFREDO: No. I forget many things, most things.

ABEL: You married me here in this church almost ten years ago. You baptized my son here six years ago.

FATHER ALFREDO: I marry so many people every year that they start to melt away. And baptisms, forget it, thousands of clean-smelling babies who smile at me before they cry out.

ABEL: Abel. My name is Abel.

FATHER ALFREDO: Of course. Abel. Rosa's son.

ABEL: Yes.

FATHER ALFREDO: She was...

ABEL: Yes, she was.

FATHER ALFREDO: ...always smiling.

ABEL: (*Pause.*) Not always.

FATHER ALFREDO: No?

ABEL: I repeat things because...

FATHER ALFREDO: It's just a saying, you know. Nobody smiles all the time.

ABEL: No, I suppose not.

FATHER ALFREDO: Go on. You were talking about...

ABEL: Repeating things. I repeat things because I like to be sure that I'm understood. That *I* understand.

FATHER ALFREDO: Do you?

ABEL: What?

FATHER ALFREDO: Understand?

(*Long pause.*)

ABEL: I haven't believed in God for a long time.

FATHER ALFREDO: Why are you here today, Abel?

ABEL: What makes holy water holy?

FATHER ALFREDO: Holy water?

ABEL: Yes. What makes holy water holy?

FATHER ALFREDO: It's been blessed.

ABEL: That's it?

FATHER ALFREDO: That's it.

ABEL: So it's just regular tap water? It's not imported from the Holy Land or anything like that?

FATHER ALFREDO: It's no longer regular after it's been blessed.

ABEL: Right. Like the wine.

FATHER ALFREDO: Not exactly. (*Takes out a cigarette.*) Do you mind?

ABEL: No. Please, go ahead.

(**FATHER ALFREDO** *lights cigarette and takes two drags.*)

FATHER ALFREDO: Is there anything else I can do for you?

ABEL: The Virgin, Padre.

FATHER ALFREDO: Immaculate Conception? That's a very complicated theological concept. I'm not sure I can explain it correctly. I don't think I have the time to—

ABEL: No, no, no. I mean la Virgen de la Caridad.

FATHER ALFREDO: What about her?

ABEL: It's dark. There's a storm, a huge storm. These three men, fishermen I think, are floating aimlessly. They're disoriented. Yet they're certain of one thing—they're going to die.

FATHER ALFREDO: I'm not sure what they were feeling, what they were certain about.

ABEL: Then the Virgin appears and they are saved. Saved by a hallucination.

FATHER ALFREDO: Not a hallucination, a divine apparition.

ABEL: Okay, apparition. It's dark. There's a huge storm. These three fishermen are floating aimlessly, disoriented. Yet they're certain that they're going to die.

FATHER ALFREDO: You did it again.

ABEL: What?

FATHER ALFREDO: Repeat yourself.

ABEL: I know. I'm trying to understand.

FATHER ALFREDO: *What* are you trying to understand?

ABEL: Were they men of faith?

FATHER ALFREDO: Who?

ABEL: *Los tres Juanes.* Were they believers? Did they pray to the Virgin, did they summon her to rescue them?

FATHER ALFREDO: Why does that matter?

ABEL: *Or,* did the Virgin selflessly appear to save these desperate Godless men without being summoned? Was she looking after them regardless of the fact that they did not believe in God, or the Savior, or the Immaculate Conception, or...

FATHER ALFREDO: Why does that matter?

ABEL: (*Stands up, almost to himself.*) Is it the sea? Is there something so uniquely dangerous about the sea that the mother of God would look after even those who would deny her existence? These ordinary fishermen...

FATHER ALFREDO: Abel.

ABEL: ...who were probably not very virtuous, maybe even criminals—

FATHER ALFREDO: Abel!

ABEL: Yes...Padre?

FATHER ALFREDO: The answer is yes. She looks after all of us. *All* of us.

(*Long pause.*)

ABEL: Can I buy some holy water?

FATHER ALFREDO: (*Laughing.*) Why do you want holy water?

ABEL: It's not important. (*Takes out money from his pocket.*) Could I just buy some?

FATHER ALFREDO: (*Waving the money away.*) Take as much as you'd like. Over there. Take as much you'd like.

ABEL: Thank you.

(**FATHER ALFREDO** *puts his hand behind* **ABEL'S** *head and looks into his eyes.*)

FATHER ALFREDO: Can you really remember how my ring felt?

ABEL: I remember everything. It was cold, smooth. Just like now.

FATHER ALFREDO: Good-bye, Abel.

ABEL: Good-bye . . . Padre.

(**ABEL** *fills two plastic jugs with holy water.*)

ABEL: Better safe than sorry.

A FREE COUNTRY
BY STEPHEN MOST

CHARACTERS
Mac *(late 40s–early 50s), an Irishman down on his luck, lives alone in a shantytown shack;* Leon *(30s), African-American, is on the lookout for a place to escape the rain and cold.*

SCENE
A Seattle shantytown

TIME
1930

Mac *sits on the bed inside his shack in one of many squatters' settlements across the country that became known as Hoovervilles, with ironic reference to President Hoover, who had no remedy for the Great Depression except the hope that "prosperity is just around the corner." His shack is sparsely furnished. In addition to the bed, there is a stove, whose dull glow indicates a fire within, a tinderbox, and a stand or table holding a kerosene lamp. On this rainy winter night in 1930,* Mac *lights the lamp. Then* Mac *raises a bottle of whiskey and unscrews the cap.* He *is about to drink when someone knocks at the door.* Mac *hides the bottle.*

Leon: Anyone there?

(*Silence.* Leon *knocks again.*)

Hey, is anyone in there?

Mac: Hold your horses. I'm comin'.

(Leon *stands in the doorway. Though tall and wearing a hat and coat,* He *seems beaten down by the weather.* Mac *looks carefully at* Leon. *Outside in a driving wind, rain continues to fall.*)

Leon: Mind if I come in outa the rain? Tryin' to make it to my shack, but it's hard to see out there. Headed for your light.

(Mac *says nothing.*)

The way sure is slippery. Almost fell over.

Mac: With them boards on the mud, it's a regular skid road.

Leon: I can make it. Just wet, that's all.

Mac: A goddamn tide flat.

(**Leon** *steps close to the light.*)

What happened to you?

Leon: Nothin'. I'm okay.

Mac: You been in a fight.

Leon: Got out of a fight.

Mac: Lookin' for trouble?

Leon: Can't help it if trouble finds me. Guy tried to cut me. Didn' let 'im.

Mac: Looks like you can defend yourself.

Leon: When I have to.

Mac: And fend for yourself.

Leon: We all doin' that.

Mac: It's an ill wind that blew ya here. Blew us all here.

(*For a moment* **Leon** *watches* **Mac** *sink into the privacy of his despair.*)

Leon: I better be goin'. So long, brother man.

Mac: Hold on.

Leon: You don't mind?

Mac: Mac's the name.

Leon: Leon.

Mac: Ain't seen you before.

Leon: Only been here couple weeks.

Mac: Big sprawl o' shacks. Too many men to keep track of.

Leon: Growin' every day. President says prosperity's 'round the corner. All I see 'round the corner is more shacks like this one.

(**Mac** *laughs bitterly.*)

Mac: Take your hat off.

LEON: Mighty kind.

MAC: Play cards?

LEON: Not any more.

MAC: You quit?

LEON: Play a game, 'fore you know, you playin' for keeps.

MAC: Wasn't gonna bet. Got nothin' to bet.

LEON: I don't play.

MAC: You religious?

LEON: Bible never said nothin' bout bid whist and blackjack. Closest it gets is, "Time and chance happen to all."

MAC: Time and chance. That's what happened to me. Time and chance—and a stacked deck.

LEON: A stacked deck. Yes, indeed.

MAC: And there's no beatin' the odds.

LEON: Is cards how you pass the time?

MAC: Never went in for solitaire.

LEON: Didn't mean you playin' by yourself. You a hermit?

MAC: Oh, no.

LEON: Never met a hermit.

MAC: When someone comes by, we usually talk.

LEON: Guess you wouldn't.

MAC: What?

LEON: Meet a hermit. Not in a city.

MAC: You could.

LEON: Prob'ly wouldn't.

MAC: Not likely.

LEON: What do you talk about?

MAC: With a hermit?

LEON: When somebody comes by.

MAC: Depends. If it's someone I knew in the old days, we talk about old times: people we knew, things we did. You know. If not, well, politics and women.

LEON: That's it?

MAC: What about you?

LEON: What about me?

MAC: Is that what you talk about?

LEON: Politics and women?

MAC: More interestin' than weather. Nothin' you can do about the damn weather.

LEON: Nothin' I can do about politics. And women— If I had lovin' on my mind, I sure wouldn't go through your door.

MAC: What door would you go through?

LEON: I ain't tellin' you.

MAC: Days go by, don't even see a woman's face. Single men. That's all there is 'round here. Men with no work. And no place to go.

LEON: This is just a stop on my road. Unless Lady Luck does me in.

MAC: For me, it's all come down to this.

LEON: This ain't so bad. Roof ain't leakin'. Got a stove. Firm walls. This is nice cardboard. Nice and thick. Where'd you get this?

MAC: Know where the glass company's at? They give out that cardboard they put between panes.

LEON: That's good stuff. Say, do you cook on this stove?

MAC: Coffee now and then.

LEON: No food, eh?

MAC: Rats would get it. Walls ain't that thick.

LEON: So you get soup tickets, go to the Salvation Army.

MAC: *Starv*ation Army's more like it. Stand in line for a bowl o' oatmeal or stew. And then they sing at ya. Depresses the hell outa me.

LEON: Gotta eat somehow. Some folks say we in a Depression. Like a big hole people can't get out of. Or it's the way we're s'posed to feel.

Mac: You depressed?

Leon: Not me. There's no Depression for us colored folks.

Mac: You're here, ain't ya? These times are hard for everybody.

Leon: Times are no tougher now than they been, for us. Only difference is the white folks got it rough. And that makes things better, way I see it.

Mac: Oh, does it now?

Leon: It does. 'Cause we all on the same level. You got nothin', we got nothin'. All of a sudden, we no lower than you. In fact, we got somethin' you ain't got.

Mac: Yeah?

Leon: We know how to make it through tough times.

Mac: I survived plenty o' tough times. Don't think I was livin' high off the hog when the Crash came. Far from it. Far from it.

GOD'S EAR
BY JENNY SCHWARTZ

CHARACTER
TED *(30s), husband and father of a recently deceased 10-year-old son;* GUY
(30s), much like TED. THEY *are drinking beer and watching a game.*

SCENE
A bar

TIME
Now

GUY:

Is your wife a wife-wife?

Or is she one of those take-charge, split-your-lip, bust-your-balls, pull-your-chain, cook-your-goose, get-your-goat, rip-you-to-shreds, kick-you-when-you're-down types of gals?

TED:

Somethin' like that.

GUY:

Best a both, huh?

Lucky guy.

Lucky guy.

Lucky guy.

TED:

You want her?

Take her.

She's yours.

GUY:

Free of charge?

TED:

Small fee.

GUY:

Thanks.

Thanks, man.

Generous offer.

You got a generous spirit.

And that's a rare thing to come by in this day and age.

Trust me on that.

Take it from me.

Trust me on that.

Take it from me.

But I got my own little lady back home to contend with, if you know what I mean.

You know what I mean.

How much we talkin'?

TED:

Zero down.

GUY:

Money-back guarantee?

TED:

No questions asked.

GUY:

You got a recent photo or what?

(**TED** *hands* **GUY** *a photo.*)

TED:

Her name's Mel.

Short for Melanoma.

But you can change it.

GUY:

Say, not bad.

Those your kids?

TED:

Those?

No.

No.

Those are...

No.

I should warn you, though, because you can't really tell in the picture:

Her vagina is green and her urine is blue.

GUY:

Green, huh?

What, you mean, like, fertile ground?

Or, like, green with envy?

Or, like, cold . . . hard . . . cash?

TED:

Somethin' like that.

GUY:

And is it a green-green or, like, more like a pastel?

TED:

Actually, it's—

Well, I don't want to say lime, but—

GUY:

And is this a permanent situation or—

TED:

Let me put it this way:

If she's wearing, say, a green camisole or a green bustier or a green negligé or what have you, it might bring out the green in her vagina.

Or it might not.

Vaginas are . . .

What's the word?

GUY:

Mercurial.

TED:

Mercurial.

But it's really only a slight hue.

I just thought I should mention it because of . . .

GUY:

Company policy.

TED:

Company policy.

So what do you think?

Take her out for a test drive?

Little spin around the block?

One-time offer.

Won't last.
Vaginas sell themselves.

Guy:

Does she need a lot of light?

Ted:

A little.

Guy:

Water?

Ted:

The usual.

Guy:

Wish I could.
Wish I could.
Wish I could.
But like I said, I got my own little lady back home to contend with, if you
know what I mean.
You know what I mean.
How 'bout we do a trade?
My little lady for your little lady?

Ted:

For keeps?

Guy:

Trial basis.
And if we're not completely satisfied, then no big deal, no harm done, no
big whoop, no sweat.
I think I got a recent photo here someplace.

(**Guy** *hands* **Ted** *a photo.*)

Her name's Meg.
Short for Smegma.
But you can change it.

Ted: (*Looking at the photo.*)
That your daughter?

Guy:

Sure is.

TED:

> That your son?

GUY:

> Sure was.

TED:

> Huh...
> I thought you said your little lady was a little lady.

GUY:

> Did I?
> No kidding.

TED:

> Don't kid a kidder.

GUY:

> Did I?
> No shit.

TED:

> Don't shit a shitter.

GUY:

> Now, don't get me wrong.
> I love her to death and all.
> She's the mother of my kid and crap.
> But between you, me, and the lamppost, my little lady is not the little lady
>   I married.
> How 'bout Melanoma?

TED:

> Can I have my recent photo back?

GUY:

> Is she the little lady *you* married?

TED:

> Gimme my recent photo back.

GUY:

> Gimme gimme never gets.
> Crybaby.

TED:

> Who you calling crybaby?

GUY:

Wuss.

TED:

Who you calling wimp?

GUY:

Creep.

TED:

Who you calling loser?

GUY:

Moron.

TED:

Who you calling reject?

GUY:

Lamebrain.

TED:

Who you calling jerk-off?

GUY:

Jackass.

TED:

Who you calling candy ass?

GUY:

Limp dick.

TED:

Who you calling pecker head?

GUY:

Pansy.

TED:

GIMME MY FREAKIN' PHOTO!

GUY:

TAKE YOUR FREAKIN' PHOTO!

TED:

YOUR WIFE DOESN'T KNOW DICK ABOUT DICK!

(**Guy** *gives* **Ted** *back his photo.* **They** *calm down.*)

What's your favorite part of your job?

Guy:

I'm a people person.

Ted:

I like numbers.

Guy:

It's not that I *don't* like numbers....

Ted: (*Telling a joke.*)

What's the difference between your wife and your job?

Guy:

What?

Ted:

After twenty years, your job still sucks.

Guy:

Beauty is in the eye of the beer holder.

Ted:

Good one.

Guy:

Beauty is in the eye of the beer holder.

Ted:

Good one.

Guy:

Beauty is in the eye of the beer holder.

Ted:

Good one.

(**They** *laugh.*)

Guy: (*Seriously.*)

I feel for you.

Is all I'm sayin'.

I feel for you.

Ted:

I don't know you from a hole in the wall.

GUY:

I don't know you from Adam.

TED:

I don't know you from Adam's house cat.

GUY:

Beat it.

TED:

Can it.

GUY:

Shove it.

TED:

Save it.

GUY: (*Giving him the finger.*)

Save this!
I don't know you from a hole in the ground.
But I feel for you.
Man.

TED:

Hey, man, don't call me "man."

GUY:

Sorry, man.

TED: (*Giving him the finger.*)

Feel this!

HOUSE, DIVIDED
BY LARRY LOEBELL

CHARACTERS
YOUNG LOU *(21), a college senior, is having an argument with his brother,*
YOUNG DOUG *(19), a Vietnam War resister.*

SCENE
The brothers' living room in Philadelphia

TIME
August 1971

YOUNG LOU: You're going to what?

YOUNG DOUG: Break into the Camden draft board.

YOUNG LOU: Are you nuts?

YOUNG DOUG: That's the action.

YOUNG LOU: I've been asking you for weeks. Why tell me now?

YOUNG DOUG: Some people felt they had to tell their families. We reached a consensus.

YOUNG LOU: How democratic of you.

YOUNG DOUG: We decided if anyone wanted to tell we all should. Even this Justice Department isn't stupid enough to indict everyone's spouses, siblings, and parents as co-conspirators.

YOUNG LOU: Right.

YOUNG DOUG: The people in this group, Lou, they're pretty amazing. They look out for each other. Some of them are religious. Quakers and Catholics. There's a couple of priests.

YOUNG LOU: They know you're Jewish?

YOUNG DOUG: Oh, man, I forgot to tell them. It was on the back page of the activist application but I skipped over it because it's complicated. I didn't know if they meant by birth or practice. I was going to come back to it but—

YOUNG LOU: Come on.

YOUNG DOUG: No, really. I worried that once they knew my foreskin was gone, they'd want to kick me out of the whole antiwar movement.

YOUNG LOU: Very funny.

YOUNG DOUG: All they want to know is that I can hump a ladder fifty yards.

YOUNG LOU: You're sure they don't want to have someone to blame if it gets screwed up.

YOUNG DOUG: You know, I'm sure that's their motivation. Ending the war, keeping some kids from being drafted, that's just a cover. Fucking up some Jewish college kid, that's their real purpose. (*A beat.*) Look, I know you're big into your religion all of a sudden, going to services and all, but this action has nothing to do with who practices what particular—

YOUNG LOU: You should come some time.

YOUNG DOUG: To synagogue? I've got better things—

YOUNG LOU: Like what?

YOUNG DOUG: Like trying to save my life. Trying to save my country.

YOUNG LOU: By what? Pouring pig's blood on draft records?

YOUNG DOUG: We're going to do more than that. We're going to try to actually keep them from putting a few thousand local kids in uniform.

YOUNG LOU: Yeah? How?

YOUNG DOUG: By stealing their Selective Service records and destroying them.

YOUNG LOU: You want to give him a heart attack?

YOUNG DOUG: Who?

YOUNG LOU: Dad. You want to kill him? You're talking about committing a felony.

YOUNG DOUG: This has nothing to do with him.

YOUNG LOU: The hell it doesn't. He didn't testify at your draft hearing so now you have something to prove.

YOUNG DOUG: He could have made my case a hell of a lot easier.

YOUNG LOU: So now you're pissed at him. You're pissed because he supports the war. You're pissed because of Mom. You're pissed because he likes Nixon. You're pissed at him for everything. It's all one thing to you. You want to pay him back. You want to punish him.

YOUNG DOUG: You like Nixon. You think I'm paying you back?

YOUNG LOU: I like him because of Israel.

YOUNG DOUG: Yeah, well, Dad likes him because of Vietnam. He thinks what we're doing there is just dandy.

YOUNG LOU: He believes "my country right or wrong."

YOUNG DOUG: Because that worked so well for all those patriotic German Jews.

YOUNG LOU: I don't want to fight with you.

YOUNG DOUG: So how come he *didn't* come to my draft hearing, if that's what you think this is about?

YOUNG LOU: We're not having that conversation right now.

YOUNG DOUG: No, let's have it since you brought it up. I spend three months getting ready and all he has to do is show up and say that even though he disagrees with me he understands the depth of my conviction. He didn't even have to utter the words conscientious objector. But does he do it?

YOUNG LOU: You want to know why he didn't come to your goddamn draft hearing, Doug? He didn't want to. He has convictions, too. You had a perfectly good student deferment you were throwing away. You think he should ignore what he believes because you say he should?

YOUNG DOUG: You know what? Maybe I do. Maybe I think that's what fathers do. Support their kids. He's gotten inert. So have you. Do something.

YOUNG LOU: I do lots of things. But you don't mean do something. You mean do what you think I should do.

YOUNG DOUG: Why are you so *gung ho* to defend him?

YOUNG LOU: That's a stupid question. He's in shock. He just lost his wife. He's trying to figure things out.

YOUNG DOUG: Yeah, well, in case you've forgotten, you just lost your mother, and so did I. What's that an excuse for? There are other things going on in the world.

YOUNG LOU: He just wants us to be the way we were. Before mom died.

YOUNG DOUG: Yeah, well, you can forget about that ever happening.

I JUST WANNA GET TO PHOENIX

BY JOHN LANE

CHARACTERS

FRANK (mid-30s), very macho (or at least he thinks he is), dressed in an overcoat and business suit; RICHARD, in age and dress somewhat similar to Frank, but more subdued in his behavior

SCENE

A hotel room in Salt Lake City

TIME

The present

En route to a business meeting in midwinter, FRANK and RICHARD are forced to stay overnight in a cheap motel room with one double bed when their flight is grounded. FRANK is clearly agitated about having to share a bed with another man.

FRANK: (*Looks at the bed again.*) Tell you what. Why don't I just take some of the bed covers and bunk out here on the floor.

RICHARD: Frank, there's not enough covers, and that floor is *cold*. This room is cold. Let's get real. When was the last time either one of us actually slept on a floor?

FRANK: I suppose you're right. But Jeez, this bed is—small.

(RICHARD *takes off his trousers and socks.* HE *has on only a T-shirt and shorts. He gets under the covers on one side of the bed and sits up.* FRANK *awkwardly lies down atop the covers on the other side of the bed with his socks and trousers still on.*)

RICHARD: Are you going to sleep like that?

FRANK: Actually, I'm not quite ready to go to sleep.

RICHARD: We're up eighteen hours straight, crammed on a flight, waiting in airports for hours, and you're not ready to go to sleep?

FRANK: Give me a minute or two. (*Looks around the room.*) Is it just me, or do you get the impression that these rooms normally rent by the hour?

RICHARD: Come on, Frank. This is Salt Lake City. Does the word Mormon mean anything to you? They don't even drink coffee, for Christ's sake. Do you think they're gonna allow hookers on the street?

FRANK: You gotta admit, this *is* the kind of hotel where guys go to get a little action on the side. Hell, most of us get a little on the side now and then. Don't you, Richard?

RICHARD: Not while I was married. And when I got divorced, I was single again. And when you're single, you don't have to get it on the side.

FRANK: I'm not saying I did it a lot—but there were a few times—when Christine and I weren't getting along. Sales is a high-pressure job. A man's gotta have some outlet. And on the road there's no shortage of opportunities. (*Pause.*) By the way, Richard, I wouldn't want any of this to get back to the company. This *is* strictly between you and me. Right?

RICHARD: Sure thing. Just two guys talking. It stays in this room.

FRANK: What about you, Richard? You're single now. You're a good-looking guy. You must have to fight 'em off with lead pipes.

RICHARD: Like you said, there's lots of opportunities.

FRANK: That's for sure. This is the new millennium.

RICHARD: But it's not the seventies. You do have to worry about stuff like AIDS.

FRANK: Aw, that's just something fags gotta worry about.

RICHARD: Frank, I think *gays* is a better word. *Fags* is sort of—offensive.

FRANK: Well, if it really bothers you. Not that I see the difference. (*Pause.*) Speaking of this, uh—gay—thing. To be truthful, that's why this goddam bed has got me spooked.

RICHARD: Come on, Frank. We're just gonna sleep here. We gotta make the best of a bad situation.

FRANK: Don't get me wrong. It's not like you're gonna do anything to me, or I'm gonna do anything to you. It's just that—

RICHARD: You just haven't slept in a bed with a man before.

FRANK: Well, not in a long time. When I was a kid, of course, and I think—one time back in college. We went to a basketball tournament in Boston. There were five of us in this hotel room overnight.

RICHARD: (*Playfully.*) So did anything happen?

FRANK: Hell, no. I mean, who knows? We were all drunk. The only thing I remember is that I woke up with a monster hangover.

RICHARD: (*Pause.*) Frank, I don't wanna spook you any further, but I'm curious. Have you ever been—attracted to a man?

FRANK: (*Very uncomfortable.*) Jesus Christ. Don't bring that up now! That's not the thing we should talk about here.

RICHARD: I'm just curious, Frank. Have you ever been attracted by a man at all?

FRANK: Attracted? Well, in a way. But not sexually. Definitely not sexually.

RICHARD: And who was this guy?

FRANK: There's no *one* person. I mean, every so often you see a really good-looking guy, an athletic guy or something, and you can—appreciate him. You can see why he would attract a woman.

RICHARD: But would these guys—attract you, too?

FRANK: Attract me? As I said, I can appreciate them. I suppose you could say they attract me—in an intellectual way.

RICHARD: Didn't you say good-looking, athletic guys? Doesn't sound like you're attracted to their—intellects.

FRANK: Come on, Richard. What are you doing here? Playing shrink? (*Pause.*) Hey, I'm really feeling tired now.

RICHARD: Sorry, Frank, I guess I'm just giving you a bad time. Pushing you a little. See, it's my theory that we're attracted to both sexes in various ways. Sexually and otherwise. You're attracted to women—primarily—but men could attract you, too. Nothing wrong with admitting it. That's all I'm saying, Frank? (*Pause.*) Frank?

FRANK: (*Sleepily.*) Yeah. I'm still here.

RICHARD: Did you hear what I said?

FRANK: Yeah. Look, Richard. Let me lay it on the table. I'm tired, really tired. And yes, pardon me, but I *am* uptight about sleeping in a bed with another guy. It's nothing personal. It's not like I think you're actually—gay—or anything.

RICHARD: But what if I were? What if I were gay?

FRANK: (*Bolts up in bed.*) Jesus! You're not, are you? Are you playing mind games with me?

RICHARD: Yes.

FRANK: Yes? What does that mean? Yes, you're gay? Or yes, you're playing mind games?

RICHARD: Yes, to both.

FRANK: Jeez! You? You're gay? But you were married. How could you—?

RICHARD: As I was just saying, I think all of us are attracted to both sexes in some ways. I was young back then, and marriage was the thing to do, and I liked Tracy, and we decided to get married, and—that's how it happened. Later on, I discovered a lot of things about myself.

FRANK: Oh, Christ, now I'll never get to sleep.

RICHARD: Why? You're nervous. You're afraid I might—

FRANK: No, of course not. (*Second thoughts.*) You *wouldn't* do anything, would you?

RICHARD: No, that's not my style—and besides—oh, forget it.

FRANK: No—besides what?

RICHARD: You're really not—my type, Frank. You can relax. You're really quite safe.

FRANK: (*Somewhat calmer.*) Well, anyway I'll just sleep this way—on top. It's more comfortable.

(**FRANK** *gets up to get his overcoat.* **HE** *again lies down on top of the bed and uses the overcoat as a cover.*)

FRANK: (*Rethinking the situation.*) Uh, Richard, you said I'm not your type? You mean—I don't attract you at all?

RICHARD: Well—not really.

FRANK: I mean, I look okay, don't I? I'm not ugly. I'm masculine. I try to keep in shape.

RICHARD: It's nothing personal, Frank. You're just not my type. (*Pause.*) You sound disappointed.

FRANK: No, it's just that— Hell, let's just get some sleep. I just wanna get to Phoenix.

RICHARD: Yeah, let's get some sleep. Good night, Frank.

(*Both men turn on their sides-back to back.* **RICHARD** *reaches over to turn off the lamp on the nightstand. The lights fade quickly.*)

INDIAN BLOOD
BY A. R. GURNEY

CHARACTERS
EDDIE *(16), a student who has been suspended from school for drawing one of several puerile pictures of Injun Joe from* Tom Sawyer *in a sexual situation with Glinda the Good Witch from* The Wizard of Oz; LAMBERT *(16),* EDDIE'S *cousin and foe*

SCENE
EDDIE'S *grandmother's large music room with no Christmas tree—due to her "heart." All imaginary: a fireplace with a gas jet and log that's not burning; a piano in the corner and an old cello.*

TIME
Christmas Night, 1946

LAMBERT: You could at least be polite and say hello, Eddie.

EDDIE: Oh right. (*Giving* LAMBERT *the Indian sign.*) How.

LAMBERT: How what?

EDDIE: "How" happens to be a greeting between Indians, Lambert. As you damn well know.

LAMBERT: I was still thinking about Dickens.

EDDIE: Oh really? (*To audience.*) See what a twerp he is? (*To* LAMBERT.) Maybe you should do some thinking about how you tried to mess me up with my own grandmother.

LAMBERT: By doing what?

EDDIE: Telling her what happened at school, that's what. Thanks a bunch, pal.

LAMBERT: I just said—

EDDIE: I know what you just said. But it didn't work. I'm back in her good graces.

LAMBERT: For now, at least.

(*Sounds of party, muted, offstage.*)

EDDIE: What do you mean by that, Lambert?

LAMBERT: Come into the lavatory. I'll show you something.

EDDIE: What've you got?

LAMBERT: That's for me to know, and you to find out.

(**HE** *moves to a light area downstage.* **EDDIE** *follows.*)

EDDIE: So?

LAMBERT: (*As if locking the door.*) Hold your water. Just hold your water. (*Reaches into a pocket, produces a folded piece of paper.*) How about this? (**HE** *unfolds it.*) Take a gander.

EDDIE: Oh, Jeez! (*To audience.*) It's that same damn lousy drawing I did over at the Garvers'.... (*To* **LAMBERT**.) Ted said he'd put that in the incinerator!

LAMBERT: He forgot to light it.

EDDIE: Which means you stole it. Which means once again that the Tuscaroras are a bunch of thieving rascals and scamps.

LAMBERT: Knock it off!

EDDIE: (*Making a grab for it.*) Then give it back.

LAMBERT: (*Holding it away from him.*) No...

EDDIE: May I have my own personal property back, please, Lambert.

LAMBERT: No.

EDDIE: I'll give you five dollars for it. (*Takes it out of his pocket, displays it.*) Five whole dollars. Which I'll bet you can use, too, because you don't have much money. (*To audience.*) And which is a lot of money to spend on a minor work of art.

LAMBERT: This is a valuable masterpiece, Eddie. I'll take twenty.

EDDIE: Twenty *dollars*?

LAMBERT: Two-zero.

EDDIE: You bastard! You know I don't have that much.

(**EDDIE** *makes a grab for the drawing.* **HE** *and* **LAMBERT** *get into another fight.* [*Harvey comes in.*])

HARVEY: Boys? (*Looks around, then knocks on the lavatory door.*) Boys! What's going on in there?

LAMBERT: (*Now in* **EDDIE'S** *hammerlock.*) Eddie spilled something on his pants and I'm helping him to clean up.

EDDIE: (*To audience.*) See what a natural liar he is!

HARVEY: Well, make it snappy, you two, because we're about to go in to dinner. (**HE** *goes off.*)]

EDDIE: Okay, Lambert. If you show that around to anyone, I'll just say I didn't draw it. Sometimes you have to lie just to keep the ball rolling.

LAMBERT: (*Looking at the drawing.*) Yeah, well, I notice your name on this, Eddie! I see your own personal signature.

EDDIE: Oh, shit! (*To audience.*) This is what I get for being too conceited and putting my name on a crummy work of art. . . . (*To* **LAMBERT**.) Lambert, my friend, let me tell you something, man to man. If you don't watch out, you'll grow up to be the black sheep of this entire family.

LAMBERT: You think so, Eddie?

EDDIE: I know so, pal.

LAMBERT: Yes, well, I'm going to hold on to this drawing, Eddie. So you better be nice to me tonight. And nice to me at school, too. I want to go with the gang more. When you all go to New Skateland or Crystal Beach, I want you to ask me along. And I want you to invite me to dinner so I can talk to your dad about Yale. Otherwise, I'll show this around. And I don't mean just at school, either. I'll make copies of it down at the blueprint place. And I'll mail one to your parents. And another to Peggy Nussbaumer. And I'll even mail one to your grandmother.

EDDIE: That would kill her, you prick! She's got a bad heart.

LAMBERT: Then change your attitude, Eddie!

EDDIE: You know what you're doing, Lambert. You're doing blackmail! Men have died for doing that. And women, too.

[**HARVEY**: (*Coming on.*) Come on, boys! Immediately! (**HE** *goes.*)]

LAMBERT: (*Quickly pocketing the drawing.*) Just remember the party isn't over yet, Injun Joe.

(**THEY** *come out of the lavatory.*)

IS THAT A GUN IN YOUR POCKET

BY CAROL MULLEN

CHARACTERS

JAMES *(30s) is a collection agent of sorts;* ADAM *(30s) is a down-on-his-luck inventor with a $150,000 debt he cannot afford to pay.*

SCENE

The living room of ADAM'S *apartment*

TIME

10:00 PM

(ADAM *is sitting at a desk writing a letter. On the desk are three sealed, stamped envelopes. Several crumpled pieces of paper are in and near a wastebasket next to the desk. Adam is dressed well, as if going out for a special occasion.* HE *is anxious and checks his watch repeatedly as he writes.*)

ADAM: (*Reading aloud from the page.*) Dear Mom. By the time you read this, I will be dead and, quite possibly, rotting in my apartment. (*Crumples up letter in frustration, tosses it on the floor.*) Way to soften the blow, Adam. She'll be reaching for the nitro tablets before she even gets to the second sentence. (*Reaches for a second sheet of paper, begins writing furiously.*) Okay. Let's try this again. More compassion. Less Joan Crawford. (*Reads aloud again.*) Dearest Mother. I hope you're doing well and that the sciatica hasn't been bothering you too much. I'm writing to tell you that I won't be home for Thanksgiving this year. Or ever again. (*Looks up, seems more satisfied.*) Now we're getting somewhere. (*Begins writing again, reading aloud as* HE *works.*) I've made some bad financial decisions and I'm afraid that the consequences will be dire. (*Scans the paper. Disgusted.*) Dire. Who says dire? People in Merchant Ivory films. (*Scratches out word, writes another one.*) Significant. The consequences will be significant. That sounds like I'm being audited. (*Scratches out words, writes another one.*) Fatal.

(*A knock at the door startles* ADAM *out of his reverie.*)

(*Sets down paper and pen, stands up slowly, straightens his clothes, and walks to the door.*) H . . . hello.

JAMES: (*Through the closed door.*) Adam Walker?

ADAM: Yes.

JAMES: I work for Mr. Hampton. I believe you're expecting me.

ADAM: You're early.

JAMES: It's ten o'clock.

ADAM: It's nine fifty-eight.

JAMES: Arriving two minutes early for a scheduled appointment is certainly within the standards of socially acceptable behavior.

ADAM: If I were a fruit fly, two minutes would be a big chunk of my childhood. Maybe even cut into my early adolescence.

JAMES: Are you?

ADAM: Am I what?

JAMES: A fruit fly.

ADAM: No, but—

JAMES: Then I would strongly suggest that you open the door.

ADAM: But—

JAMES: Adam, I realize this is a difficult situation. But I would urge you not to make it any worse than it already is. I would hate for things to get unnecessarily... messy.

(**ADAM** *considers, then opens door reluctantly. Enter* **JAMES**, *who is well dressed, wears thin leather gloves, and carries a small case the size of a laptop computer. The two men check each other out with appreciation.*)

JAMES: (*Points to his watch.*) Ten on the dot.

ADAM: Do you want a punctuality prize?

JAMES: Let's get down to business.

ADAM: How about a cup of coffee? Or maybe a drink. I know I could use one. If you're hungry, I can whip up some gazpacho.

JAMES: (*Sets his case on the desk.*) You know why I'm here.

ADAM: You're here for the hundred and fifty thousand dollars I owe Mr. Hampton.

JAMES: That's correct.

ADAM: I . . . I don't have it.

JAMES: You don't have all of it?

ADAM: I don't have any of it.

JAMES: I see.

ADAM: Look, I know you're going to kill me. Mr. Hampton was clear that this extension was my last one. So just . . . you know. Go ahead and do it.

JAMES: (*Shrugs, begins opening the case.*) All right.

ADAM: (*Incredulous.*) That's it?

JAMES: (*Stops what he's doing.*) Excuse me?

ADAM: You're going to take my word for it? Isn't there some kind of paperwork to sign? Don't you need to call in and double check with someone? I mean, what if Mr. Hampton has decided to let things slide?

JAMES: (*Continues opening the case.*) He's not the governor. There are no reprieves.

ADAM: What . . . what's in that case?

JAMES: (*Removes a gun from the case, begins attaching a silencer.*) This is my colleague.

ADAM: You're going to shoot me with that? What are you, a Size Queen? You could kill a charging bull with that thing! Don't you have something . . . smaller?

JAMES: This is a one-size-fits-all type of tool.

ADAM: (*Sinks into the couch, stricken.*) There won't be anything left to identify. Thank God the dry cleaner writes my name on the inside of my collars.

JAMES: (*Turns to* **ADAM**, *gun in hand.*) Should we do this here, or would you prefer another room?

ADAM: I can't believe it. I'm going to die. I'm really going to die. And all because of fucking Paula Abdul.

JAMES: What are you talking about?

ADAM: I lost a twenty-five-thousand-dollar bet on *American Idol*.

JAMES: You bet on *American Idol*?

ADAM: I was desperate. I hoped I could pull together some of the money I owed Mr. Hampton, so maybe he'd break my legs and we'd call it even.

JAMES: (*Amused.*) Don't tell me. You thought that Mariah Carey wannabe was going all the way.

ADAM: She should have won! I can't believe she was eliminated so early. That bitch Paula. She'll cut you. I wouldn't have figured you for an (*Meaningful pause.*) *American Idol* fan.

JAMES: (*Ruefully.*) I've been addicted since day one. I wouldn't have figured you for a gambler.

ADAM: Oh, I'm not. Clearly.

JAMES: But I thought...

ADAM: I'm an inventor. I borrowed the money to build prototypes. I thought that once I sold my patents, I'd pay Mr. Hampton back. Unfortunately, the market isn't ready for my waterproof cell phone.

JAMES: A waterproof cell phone?

ADAM: Cell phones are completely portable, right? You can take them anywhere. Except in the water. You're showering or taking a dip in the pool and you hear the phone. You know you're missing a call, but you can't do anything about it. My Wet Chat 1000 would have changed that forever.

JAMES: Why didn't it sell?

ADAM: There was a small glitch, an electric shock kind of thing, but I was working through it. Another few weeks, a little tinkering, and I would have been a millionaire.

JAMES: You said prototypes. Plural.

ADAM: I've also got a great line of glow-in-the-dark items. Toothpaste. Chewing gum. Margarita salt. But as it turns out, there are low-grade traces—and I'm talking miniscule, barely measurable amounts—of highly toxic chemicals involved in the phospho-luminescence process.

JAMES: You're still...tinkering with those, too?

ADAM: I am. Or...I was.

MEASURE FOR PLEASURE:
A RESTORATION ROMP
BY DAVID GRIMM

CHARACTERS
SIR PETER LUSTFORTH *(about 60), a country gentleman of lower birth whose cleverness has helped him rise in rank;* CAPTAIN DICK DASHWOOD *(about 30), a handsome man with a passion for wine, women, and grandeur*

SCENE
The Lustforth home

TIME
1751, during the forty days known in the Christian Calendar as Lent, which ends with the Spring Solstice

LUSTFORTH: But Dashwood come, uncork thyself. Pour forth the vintage of your tale. My ears do thirst to taste its curious draught.

DASHWOOD: My story is a bitter grape, yet I will crush it thus: It doth involve a woman.

LUSTFORTH: Aye, as all good vintners can attest: 'Tis woman drives a man to wine.

DASHWOOD: 'Tis no mere whining this, Sir Peter, for I am in love.

LUSTFORTH: In love? Again? Pish, Dashwood, but you've drained the contents of that bottle many times. How can there be a drop left in't?

DASHWOOD: So did I think myself; yet by my troth, she fills me up anew.

LUSTFORTH: And so you long to fill her up.

DASHWOOD: No, friend, this love is true! No more for me th'inconstant life of a buzzing bee which passeth every changing hour by supping from a diff'rent flower. Her blossom yields all dreams and hopes.

LUSTFORTH: Then Dashwood, wherefore play the corpse? A lady hath no usage for a man who's dead, lest she be married to him.

DASHWOOD: Ah, if it were not for my ill-fame of having loved too often and too well, I would have had her even now. Yet that dear creature holds my heart to ransom for my past and will not give, even for begging, that which I have had most freely up 'til now.

LUSTFORTH: Ah, women are such prudes! What boots it that a man must bed a sea of wenches, whores, and slatterns? Is't your fault you had to wade knee-deep in cunt before you found her? Man must do what man must do to find the island of his bliss.

DASHWOOD: And now I have! Rich promises I gave her, and cajolements— Oaths that I had changed my ways—But she would none of it. And so, to teach her not to take Dick Dashwood's yearning love for granted, I thought it best to kill him off. Rumors through gossip-mills had me quite dead within the week. The word began as pox, but somehow metamorphosized to losing at a duel—I've died a dozen deaths, my friend, yet in each one, her name was the last word to cross my lips. 'T'was handsomely portrayed, I'm told.

LUSTFORTH: But if Dick Dashwood's dead, how will he win her?

DASHWOOD: By new-minting! I will adopt some wily and ingenious guise and woo my love anew. I'll say I've come to town to seek my fortune. Or to see St Paul's and pray. Nay; a man of God would only be suspected for a lecher. Tosh, I'll fadge it well anon. What's most important is I act with haste, for I've a rival to her warm affections.

LUSTFORTH: What? A rival? How?

DASHWOOD: Alas, I've never seen the man. But I have heard he's three score old and of a face and form repellent. Egad, Sir Peter, but I'd shoot him dead if e'er he touched my sweet and pure Hermione.

LUSTFORTH: (*Aside.*) Hermione? Nay, could it be—? (*Aloud.*) What sort of woman is this—this—?

DASHWOOD: Hermione Goode. She is niece and ward to one Dame Stickle, a Puritan residing hard by Bishopsgate.

LUSTFORTH: (*Aside.*) By hell's own breath, what fickle fate!

DASHWOOD: You say—?

LUSTFORTH: She is, I'll wager, your most perfect mate.

DASHWOOD: If such a one draws breath, 'tis she. But this same Stickle keeps an eagle eye on her, repelling all advances, which goes hard. Which brings me to the crux: I need your help.

LUSTFORTH: (*Aside.*) Aye, to an honest grave, thou poxy dog—"In face and form repellent—"? I'll repel thee from thy life!

DASHWOOD: Without some cunning pretext of propriety, I'll never get within her reach and all my hopes for love are lost. Sir Peter, what am I to do?

LUSTFORTH: (*Aside.*) But slit your throat and there's a start, y'canting cankered coxcomb!

[LADY VANITY: (*Offstage.*) Husband! Coo-eee! Where hast thou gone, my stallion? (*At the sound of her voice,* **LUSTFORTH** *freezes in his tracks. Pause.* **HE** *gets an idea.*)]

LUSTFORTH: (*Aside.*) Ha, ha! See now how I will use him for my sport. (*Aloud.*) Dick—you must live here with me.

DASHWOOD: Here, Sir Peter?

LUSTFORTH: Here. And I'll equip thee with thy newfound life and form thee as a tailor does the latest fashion. What say you to a music teacher? Yes, a genius of the arts. Henceforth wilt thou be known as Don Fidelio—A man of sterling reputation for whom love is as a foreign land: oft dreamt of, never visited. I'll put it out you are a distant cousin to my wife who has come hither for to master her in finer learning. (*Aside.*) And thereby master thee, thou knave!

DASHWOOD: Oh, 'tis an excellent device, good Lustforth. But your wife, will she not mind?

LUSTFORTH: Mind, my dear Fidelio? She hasn't got one! Wives have minds the like their husbands give them; mindful husbands give them none. But see your manner be not shy with her. She has a deep abhorrence of timidity. Fear not, as you instruct her, to make exorbitant demands. Be rough and ready in your nature, friend; be hard and it will please her well.

DASHWOOD: (*Aside.*) "Rough and ready"? "Make demands"? "Be hard and please her well"? What sort of husband's this?

LUSTFORTH: My home is yours, Fidelio! My comforts and my wife are here at your disposal. Use them as you would your house and dog.

DASHWOOD: (*Aside.*) I smell a rat. (*Aloud.*) You are too kind, Sir Peter.

LUSTFORTH: (*Aside.*) Aye, two kinds of face, the better to outface your plan.

DASHWOOD: (*Aside.*) Why does he mumble so and snicker 'hind his hand?

LUSTFORTH: (*Aside.*) I will be rid of you 'ere long, you cad, and tift the field.

DASHWOOD: (*Aside.*) I'll play along his game to see what fortunes yield.

(*The two men smile at each other obsequiously and laugh.*)

LUSTFORTH: Fond Fidelio, come, let us go to her.

DASHWOOD: Loving Lustforth, lead the way.

OPUS
BY MICHAEL HOLLINGER

CHARACTERS
DORIAN *(late 30s), a brilliant, but unstable, musician who cannot stay on his meds;* **ELLIOT** *(late 30s), also a musician, more controlling than creative, and* **DORIAN**'s *ex-lover. Both are members of a string quartet and their recent breakup is causing tension for the group.* **DORIAN** *has resorted to drastic measures in order to get* **ELLIOT**'s *attention.*

SCENE
DORIAN's *new apartment*

TIME
The present

(In darkness, "God Only Knows" by the Beach Boys begins to play. After a few moments, a loud buzzer is heard; the music continues. Again, the buzzer, more insistent; the music continues. Finally, the buzzer sounds over and over. Lights up on **DORIAN**'s *apartment. A few packing boxes are on the floor, a boom box (now seen to be the source of the music) sits atop a chair.* **ELLIOT**'s *open violin case rests nearby.* **ELLIOT** *has just entered;* **DORIAN** *holds a short plunger.)*

A slash (/) indicates overlapping dialogue.

DORIAN: Nelly! Perfect timing!

ELLIOT: Where is it?

DORIAN: I was just about to unclog my toilet....

ELLIOT: Knock it off.

DORIAN: *(Indicating the boom box.)* And listen-they're playing our s—

  *(**ELLIOT** pushes him hard, knocking him backward into the room. **DORIAN** recovers his balance.)*

  Well, that's the most physical we've gotten in months.

ELLIOT: You've crossed a line.

DORIAN: I take it you got my note.

ELLIOT: I almost called the police, you know that?

DORIAN: What would you tell them? "My lover—oops, co-worker-kidnapped my violin"? Sounds a little squishy.

(*A brief standoff. Then* **ELLIOT** *walks past* **DORIAN** *and exits into an offstage room.*)

Sorry for the mess in the bedroom. I haven't had a chance to unpack everything. Anything, really. Oh, I got some of your clothes by mistake. Good thing you sewed name tags in them.

(**ELLIOT** *re-enters and crosses to another interior exit. Before* **HE** *disappears.*)

It's not in the kitchen.

(*Sounds of pans clattering, cabinets shutting.* **DORIAN** *starts flipping the plunger, catching it by the handle.*)

You haven't told me what you think of the new place. Not as nice as ours, of course. BUT, older buildings have their charms: clawfoot tubs, cast iron radiators . . . nice wide window ledges for those too timid to face a bare bodkin.

(**ELLIOT** *re-enters.*)

I told you it wasn't in the kitchen.

ELLIOT: You think this is some kind of joke?

DORIAN: I wanted to see you.

ELLIOT: You see me every day.

DORIAN: Outside of rehearsal.

ELLIOT: Well, here I am. Happy?

DORIAN: God, no.

ELLIOT: I step out for a bite. I come home to practice the Brahms and find a ransom note (**HE** *pulls a note out of his shirt pocket, printed words taped to it like a ransom note.*) taped to my music stand.

DORIAN: I thought you'd appreciate the fact that I cut the words out of *Chamber Music Monthly.*

ELLIOT: You've crossed a line. I don't know who you are.

DORIAN: The feeling's mutual. (*Beat.*) You treat me like an employee, won't even make eye contact anymore. Bad enough that our playing suffers....

ELLIOT: Have you been taking your meds?

DORIAN: Ah, here we go....

ELLIOT: I'm just asking.

DORIAN: Blame it on the crazy one....

ELLIOT: I never said—

DORIAN: I flushed them down the toilet. All of them. (*Beat.*)

ELLIOT: You shouldn't have done that.

DORIAN: So I discovered.

(HE *holds up the plunger.*)

At the very least, I should have taken them out of the bottles. I was about to pour Drano down, but I thought it might react with the lithium.

(ELLIOT *shakes his head and walks away. Pause.*)

They flatten me out, make me feel dead. Make it so I can't hear the music / anymore.

ELLIOT: I don't care, just tell me where it is!

(*Pause. Sensing* ELLIOT'S *intransigence,* DORIAN *jams the plunger onto the seat of the chair, making it stick, then exits into the bedroom.* ELLIOT *removes the plunger and places the open case upon the chair.* DORIAN *re-enters carrying the violin.* ELLIOT *takes it quickly and looks it over. As* HE *places it in its case.*)

DORIAN: It was under my pillow. You know how I hate to sleep alone.

(ELLIOT *closes the case.*)

ELLIOT: The others are going to hear about this.

(HE *heads toward the exit.*)

DORIAN: You don't have to go so soon, you know.

(ELLIOT *wheels around.*)

ELLIOT: What did you expect me to do?

DORIAN: When?

ELLIOT: Tonight!

DORIAN: I don't know. I thought you might like to play duets. It's been a while.

(**ELLIOT** *looks away.*)

I don't mind your being testy. Even furious. At least it's something. What I can't take is cold. Icy, cold, objective ...

ELLIOT: Yes, well. Someone's got to maintain a grip on reality.

(**DORIAN** *lowers his head.* **ELLIOT** *studies him for a moment.*)

Give me the key.

DORIAN: Key?

ELLIOT: To my apartment.

DORIAN: Our ap / art—

ELLIOT: There is no "our" apartment; not anymore. (**DORIAN** *reluctantly produces a key, which* **ELLIOT** *pockets.* **HE** *starts out, then turns back.*) Stay away from the ledges.

(**HE** *exits. Lights fade.*)

ORSON'S SHADOW
BY AUSTIN PENDLETON

CHARACTERS
ORSON WELLES *(45), the mythic creator of* **Citizen Kane** *and* **The War of the Worlds**, *now struggling to revive a fading career with* **The Chimes at Midnight***;* **KENNETH TYNAN** *(37), the brilliant theatre critic of* **The New Yorker** *who would like to be involved in Sir Laurence Olivier's formation of the National Theatre of Great Britain.*

SCENE
The stage of the Gaiety Theatre in Dublin

TIME
1950

TYNAN *has urged a reluctant* **WELLES** *to direct Olivier in a production of Ionesco's* **Rhinoceros.**

ORSON: Good God, it's just what people say about me, I bring things on myself!—I'll do the play.

KEN: You'll what?

ORSON: I'll direct Olivier in the play.

KEN: Well, thank Christ—

ORSON: What is the play, by the way?

KEN: What?

ORSON: You've never told me what the play is.

KEN: Well, yes, I have, actually—

ORSON: My God, it's *Rhinoceros*.

KEN: Yes.

ORSON: That thing by Ionesco. That thing I saw in Paris.

KEN: Yes.

ORSON: You hate that play.

KEN: To see you flourish once again, there is no whoredom I would not undertake.

ORSON: You think this is a good idea for Larry?

KEN: What do you mean?

ORSON: It's modern, that's what I mean. It takes place this side of the fourteenth century.

KEN: That is not fair!

ORSON: Don't tell me what's not fair!

KEN: He played a modern play last year!

ORSON: He did?

KEN: Yes.

ORSON: Had he read it?

KEN: Yes!

ORSON: What was it called?

KEN: *The Entertainer*, and he had a triumph in it.

ORSON: Of course he had a triumph. He always has a triumph. It is his strategy for absolutely everything. Who directed it?

KEN: What?

ORSON: *The Entertainer.* Who—?

KEN: Tony Richardson.

ORSON: Tony Richardson.

KEN: I can't say I care for Tony Richardson.

ORSON: Thank you, Ken. And Larry had a triumph, well, what might happen if he had a strong director, he'd either have a bigger triumph or a nervous breakdown and either way we'd have a hit! Oh, Ken! What's this play about? What's the plot?

KEN: What play?

ORSON: *Rhinoceros*!

KEN: I thought you saw it

ORSON: I didn't pay attention. What's the plot?

KEN: It's about a town in which everybody turns into rhinoceroses.

ORSON: And this is—what?—my God, this is a metaphor. What are you trying to do to me, Ken? A metaphor for what?

KEN: Fascism.

ORSON: Aha. So Larry's going to play a Fascist, this has possibilities.

KEN: No, he's to play the little man, who—

ORSON: WHAT?

KEN: The hero, who stands up against the rest—

ORSON: Larry's going to play the little man? This is a plot, you're trying to make me look ridiculous.

KEN: If you think it's a plot, why don't I just leave—?

ORSON: STAY HERE! Ken, wait—let's—let's—Whose idea was this, that Larry play—

KEN: Miss Plowright.

ORSON: Plowright? Joan?

KEN: Yes.

ORSON: I directed Joan Plowright! In *Moby Dick*. You hated her.

KEN: She's grown.

ORSON: Now that she's out of my clutches? Now that Larry's rescued her?

KEN: Are they all as neurotic as you, Orson? I really must know.

ORSON: Worse than me. I at least am talented. Why would Larry let Plowright talk him into this?

KEN: She's had success with other plays by Ionesco.

ORSON: Oh.

KEN: Yes.

ORSON: She's got him by the balls, then. He's weakened.

KEN: I would not count on it.

ORSON: He's out of his depth. I'm a modernist, you know. No one is aware of that, but I'm a modernist, it's my secret weapon, wait till you see what I've done for Universal. I think I'm the man for this, Ken.

KEN: Well, then, set up a meeting, propose yourself.

ORSON: What do you mean, propose myself?

KEN: Well, who else?

ORSON: You.

KEN: I—?

ORSON: It was your idea!

KEN: You expect me to speak to—?

ORSON: Oh, Ken.

KEN: I'll stammer like a fool!

ORSON: You know, you have this habit of revering people. You've got to get over that.

KEN: I revere no one!

ORSON: Talk to him, it'll be the best thing for you.

KEN: Is this some grotesque form of speech therapy?

ORSON: I don't understand. You never stammer around me. Should I resent this? I've always been proud you never stammered around me, I've always thought it was my one undeniable accomplishment—

KEN: Oh, stop that! Stop it!

ORSON: What?

KEN: Stop this relentless, whimsical, revolting self-abnegation when you are our hope! (*Pause.*)

ORSON: I'm sorry.

KEN: So am I. I'll talk to Olivier, I mean of course I'll talk to him.

ORSON: Just talk the way you write, you terrify everybody when you—oh no.

KEN: What?

ORSON: Oh, Ken.

KEN: What?

ORSON: You can't talk to him.

KEN: Why not?

ORSON: What you wrote about Vivien—

KEN: That was ten years ago!

ORSON: You've blown it, Ken. I think we're going to have to forget the whole thing.

KEN: You want to have your work in London again, don't you.

ORSON: I want to have *Chimes at Midnight* in London, not *Rhinoceros* with Larry Olivier—

KEN: *Chimes at Midnight* has played to empty houses here, and everybody knows it.

ORSON: Empty houses?!

KEN: Orson—

ORSON: You see that? These are rumors!

KEN: Are you seriously saying that it's a rumor that—

ORSON: When and where did you hear the rumor that I've been playing to empty houses?

KEN: I heard it tonight, from the other member of the audience!

ORSON: And I'm sending you as my emissary?

KEN: (*To us.*) But I am his emissary. I have been his emissary since that afternoon when I was sixteen, since I saw *Citizen Kane* at a cinema in Birmingham one afternoon—

ORSON: Please don't tell them about *Citizen Kane*. Am I to be remembered for one movie, which I directed from my high chair?

KEN: (*Lights dimming.*) But I must tell them—(*To us.*)—how I saw it every afternoon for the remainder of that week, how I took a different girl each day, how the fifth time I saw it I put on a blindfold, to revel in Orson's use of sound—

ORSON: Don't talk to them anymore, Ken.

KEN: How I wrote that if I had my way Orson would be responsible for the entire American film industry from that moment on—

ORSON: Ken. I can't stand it. (*Pause.*)

KEN: I'm sorry. I'll talk to Olivier.

ORSON: Please Ken. For me.

OUR LADY OF 121st STREET
BY STEPHEN ADLY GUIRGIS

CHARACTERS
FLIP (37), an African-American lawyer, has returned to his roots in Harlem for a funeral and wishes to keep his homosexuality a secret; GAIL (37), his white lover, is none too pleased to keep their relationship in the closet.

SCENE
In and around the Ortiz Funeral Home, Harlem

TIME
The present

FLIP: Do not act like a faggot!

GAIL: Excuse you?

FLIP: Put your collar down!

GAIL: My collar?

FLIP: Where'd that scarf come from?! You were not wearing that scarf when we left the hotel, Gail!

GAIL: You said we were coming here as a couple, Robert!

FLIP: And I changed my mind! And you know that I changed my mind because I been tellin' you all fuckin' morning, Gail, that I changed my fuckin' mind—so just lose the scarf, do not act like a faggot, and stop calling me fuckin' "Robert"!

GAIL: What should I call you? Penelope?

FLIP: Flip, Goddamnit! For the fifty-eighth time, they call me Flip!

GAIL: Flip what? Flip a pancake? Flip a flappy Flip Flop?

FLIP: Gail—

GAIL: Maybe I should have a special name too, like . . . "Rocky."

FLIP: Stop it—

GAIL: I could be "Hercules," grow a beard.

Flip: Look! You're an "actor," right? So juss act like you're not a faggot for a few fuckin' hours if that's not fuckin' beneath you, okay?!

Gail: (*Improvise cursing.*)

Flip: I will not have this today, Gail! Do you hear me? Will not have it!

Gail: Will not have what, Robert? A relationship? A partner? The respect of the man who lies beside you at night?

Flip: You know who I am, and you know how I feel about you!

Gail: Do I?

Flip: Don't do this today, Gail.

Gail: My friends embraced you, Robert! My parents took you in!

Flip: Your friends are all gay, Gail, and your parents trumpet my race and sexuality with unconcealed glee 'cuz it makes them feel like better liberals!

Gail: I'm going to tell them you said that!

Flip: Good. Why don't you hop on the next plane and tell them in person.

Gail: Do you really mean that? Do you?

Flip: You know what? I ain't even tryin' ta have this conversation!

Gail: "Ain't even tryin'"?!

Flip: Dass what I said?

Gail: Right, "Assimilation." Going back ta the "'hood," can't be you, gotta be someone you never were.

Flip: Careful now—

Gail: No, Robert, you're the one who should be careful! Didn't you ever see *The Death of Sunny* with Shelley Winters?

Flip: Gail—

Gail: Sunny Waldman denied her Jewishness before a Nazi tribunal to avoid the death camps—and what happened to Sunny? She became a morphine-addicted harlot who ended up wandering into the forests of Bavaria to be consumed by wolves and jackals—that's what! Denial's like a pair of Prada silk pajamas, Robert—the price is just too high!

Flip: Look, Drama Empress. Just turn it down a few notches and be here for me. Quiet and dignified. Can you do that, yes or no?!

GAIL: "Turn it down a few notches"?

FLIP: Yes or no, Gail!

GAIL: I am not a drama empress!

FLIP: I am begging you, okay? Begging.

GAIL: On my worst day, I'm more masculine than you.

FLIP: Gail—

GAIL: I'm like a young Al Pacino: intense, soulful—

FLIP: Oh, you aren't a "young" anything, Gail! And you certainly, *certainly*, ain't no Al Pacino!

THE OVERWHELMING
BY J. T. ROGERS

CHARACTERS
GEOFFREY *(17), a typical white American teenager;* GÉRARD *(20s), a Rwandan house-servant*

SCENE
Kigali, Rwanda

TIME
Early 1994

GEOFFREY'S *father has brought his wife and son to Rwanda while he writes a book about a Tutsi doctor.* GEOFFREY *has befriended* GÉRARD, *the servant, who has offered to show* GEOFFREY *his country. They are in a car;* GEOFFREY *is driving. Playwright's Note: The use of a slash at the beginning or in the middle of a line of dialogue indicates that the next line of dialogue begins at that moment—creating verbal overlap.*

GÉRARD: Slowly! Slowly! / These dirt roads, you will crack the chassis! You should not go driving when you are angry, Geoffrey.

GEOFFREY: Sorry. Forgot. Sorry. Look, I'll be more careful!

GÉRARD: A woman should not speak to you like that.

GEOFFREY: Don't worry about it.

GÉRARD: Stand in your way, try to block you from going out. Jumping about like some chicken.

GEOFFREY: I said it's cool!

GÉRARD: Cool?

GEOFFREY: Yeah.

GÉRARD: Cool...?

GEOFFREY: Means good.

GÉRARD: Like hot?

GEOFFREY: Exactly.

Gérard: Cool is good *and* hot is good?

Geoffrey: Yes.

Gérard: *Fantastique!* When I go to America, I will say (*Pointing.*), "This is cool," and "That is hot," and I will sex all the women. (*Off* **Geoffrey's** *laugh.*) Why not?

Geoffrey: All of them?

Gérard: Yes!

Geoffrey: Dude, we got a lot of women!

Gérard: You watch me, Geoffrey! I will sex the black woman, the white woman, the thin woman, the fat woman—mmmm! The fat American woman! (*Off* **Geoffrey's** *laughter.*) Ah, ah, ah! This is your problem.

Geoffrey: What? / What are you talking about?

Gérard: You are embarrassed. Look at you: You are a pink man now. I see you. I watch you. You talk about a woman like you talk about a man. Treat a woman like a man. Like there is no difference. Did God not make us different? You give away your power, Geoffrey.

Geoffrey: Dude, I'm not / giving away anything.

Gérard: Then why did you let the black wife speak to you like that?

Geoffrey: Look, she's my / dad's wife.

Gérard: You should not let the black wife—

Geoffrey: Linda. Her name's Linda. And don't—she's not black. She's African-American.

Gérard: . . . I do not understand.

Geoffrey: We don't say black anymore. We say African-American.

Gérard: She is from Africa?

Geoffrey: No. Her people—you know, at one time her ancestors were—It's just what we say, to be respectful.

Gérard: Of who?

Geoffrey: Of . . . the people . . . who . . . I don't know.

Gérard: But she is American.

Geoffrey: Yes.

Gérard: She is not African, she is American. You are American, I am African. How can one be African and American? If you are American, you are American. Who does not know this?

Geoffrey: Yeah, but she's an American *and* she's— Okay. In America, okay, the white people, you know, like me, we have power. We control . . . pretty much everything. So—

Gérard: Ah! You are Tutsi! The white man is the Tutsi! (*Joking.*) I am in the car with a Tutsi!

Geoffrey: No, man! That's not what I'm—

Gérard: (*Putting his head out the window, pretending to cry for help.*) Aaaaaah! Tutsi! Aaaaaah! (*Back to* **Geoffrey**.) You are like the man hiding in your house.

(**Geoffrey** *stares straight ahead.*)

Geoffrey: What are you talking about?

Gérard: The Tutsi your father is hiding. Who is he hiding from? Why would he need to be hiding?

Geoffrey: How did you know he's—

Gérard: I am frightened, Geoffrey, to be in your house with this man. I am too frightened to sleep in your house. Here, no one is sleeping in their houses. In our village, my wife is taking our children to the church.

Geoffrey: You have a . . . what? Why aren't they— / I don't . . .

Gérard: Home is not safe. Everyone is waiting.

Geoffrey: For what?

Gérard: I pray to know. But God does not tell me. You are my friend.

Geoffrey: I know.

Gérard: I am your friend.

Geoffrey: Yeah. Totally. (*Looks at him.*) Yes! Of course.

Gérard: Then I am asking you.

Geoffrey: What do you mean?

GÉRARD: To go. To leave with you. I will get my family, and we will—

GEOFFREY: Gérard, I'm not—we're not going anywhere. / We just got here. My dad's book isn't even ...

GÉRARD: You will leave soon, Geoffrey. Do you think this is a place for you to stay? Something is coming! Closer, closer. I do not wish to be here to see it. I will do what I must. But to go, I would only need—

GEOFFREY: You want me to, to take you to—

GÉRARD: Please.

GEOFFREY: I'm just.... What can I do? I'm just a ... I mean.... What can I do?

(**THEY** *drive in silence as they stare straight ahead.*)

GÉRARD: I understand.

THE PARIS LETTER
BY JON ROBIN BAITZ

CHARACTERS
SANDY *(21), Princeton graduate, newly arrived in New York;* ANTON *(late 20s), a somewhat sophisticated New York restaurateur.*

SCENE .
ANTON's *Greenwich Village apartment*

TIME
November 1962

In this forty-year flashback, SANDY *and* ANTON *have just returned from the movie* Freud. *Although* SANDY *has visited* ANTON's *restaurant regularly for several weeks, this is the first evening they have spent together alone.* SANDY *has been talking nervously about his family, his love of the snow, his experience in college.*

SANDY: I keep talking about my family. I really have to stop.

ANTON: No, actually, you can talk about anything you like.

SANDY: The thing is this: We're in a series of wars, my father and I, Anton, you see, I want to join the Peace Corps. He didn't even vote for Kennedy, he's so assimilated, so country club. . . . I heard Kennedy's speech about the Peace Corps, and I thought, "I want to serve, I want to help."

ANTON: And you're being dissuaded?

SANDY: To put it mildly. I am expected to go into the family business. I am the only son, it's money, the business, they fiddle with money, clean it up, polish it, make more of it, magic tricks and sleight of hand and late-night phone calls.

ANTON: Sounds like medicine.

SANDY: It is. Emergencies, flights to Europe, somber joyless meetings. And dull people.

ANTON: So what? I left home and never looked back. You're 21, Sandy, and you should do what you want, my friend. It's not worth it, trying to please. It is a fucking fool's errand.

SANDY: Right.

(*There is a moment.* ANTON *is very close to* SANDY, *who finally darts away.*)

Anyway, in Princeton, the last time it snowed I went for a walk and I thought, "Where will I be when it snows again?" I cried, because I'd had such a good four years. I was just—I wandered around the campus for hours, I had this cashmere overcoat on, and it was totally soaked.

ANTON: And here you are. Eight months later.

(ANTON *touches* SANDY'S *cheek.* SANDY *nervously moves away.*)

SANDY: I love staying up all night. I do, it's my favorite thing, I don't like to sleep. I have never been able to sleep.

ANTON: New York was not intended for sleep. If you want to sleep, move to Baltimore.

SANDY: No, I never wanted to live anywhere else. I never will, I'm a New Yorker.... (*Looking around.*) I like your place. It's very Bohemian. Very hectic.

ANTON Hectic. God, I've never heard that before. Is that bad?

SANDY: No, it's unrestrained. Your friends, the people I've been meeting—so much energy unfettered, so little kept inside, you do whatever you like— Well, you should see my parents' house, I mean, you know, it's all Duncan Phyfe stuff, you can't really ever quite relax. You can't... what's that? What's *Flair*...? (SANDY *points to the* Flair *magazine art.*)

ANTON: A magazine, which was published for a very short time, twelve issues only, I worked there, I made myself over there, after Bendel's.... I worked there when I was kicked out of the army.

SANDY: I remember seeing them when I was a kid.

ANTON: It was fun, it folded, too expensive, rather ahead of its time. The cover always had a hole in it, revealing some bit of art underneath. Something hidden peeking out. One day I'll show them to you. But right now, I'm sorry to say, I really, really only want to kiss you.

SANDY: (*Not looking at* ANTON.) I know.

ANTON: May I, do you think?

(SANDY *shakes his head "no."*)

SANDY: I mean, I don't know.

ANTON: You've never done this, have you? You waited until you graduated, right? You couldn't bear to confuse yourself any more while you were at school, so you waited until...

SANDY: Right. I mean, tenth grade, this boy and I jacked off together and I...he never wanted to talk about it, and then, nor did I.

ANTON: Sandy, I am, by nature, a deferential man, so I shan't pursue this.

SANDY: (*Disappointed.*) Oh. Really?

ANTON: (*Laughing.*) Too much. Don't look so disappointed. I mean, you're gorgeous and tortured and Jewish, and terribly unsure of yourself in a cocksure sort of way, which I adore, but I'm not going to take you. I'm not built for that.

SANDY: (*Bellicose.*) I'm not—what does me being Jewish have to do with anything? And I don't think I'm cocksure, at all, whatever that means, at all, I just...

ANTON: (*Smiling.*) You what? You've been coming into my restaurant, kitty cat, staring at me for a week. Sitting alone at a table reading fucking Genet? And Proust, no less, sitting around, lounging with a martini and a pack of Gauloises, making notes in the margins, with a big fucking fountain pen, which incidentally stained my nice linen tablecloth, batting your eyes at me like we're at the Princeton library.

SANDY: Yeah, well. You looked happy. Like someone having fun. It's sort of contagious. I thought I might catch it.

ANTON: Well, God knows, one wouldn't want that. I mean, you might die.

(**SANDY** *kisses* **ANTON.** *His hands explore* **ANTON'S** *body.*)

SANDY: I'm really sorry about the tablecloth.

ANTON: Right. I don't think I can forgive you, they're very expensive and— Are you all right, I don't want to—

SANDY: No, I'm not, I'm... (*Kissing him, shuts* **ANTON** *up.*) I'm on the verge of detonating. I've wanted to do that for years—and in October during the missile crisis, when the whole world was about to explode, I thought, I am going to die without ever—

ANTON: Look. Wait. This is my hand. I want you to hold it. Feel it. Okay? Take your time. My hand. You want to know me? Look at me. Look.

(**HE** *kisses* **SANDY** *again, and removes his jacket, unbuttons his shirt.*)

It's good to know who you're touching, and what it feels like. Last time it snowed you were one person, now you're another, okay?

SANDY: What's going to happen to me?

ANTON: Nobody knows the answer to that question. It's pointless. Look at me. It's pointless.

(**SANDY** *kisses* **ANTON** *hungrily, voraciously. The lights fade down, with both men undressing in the near dark, lit mostly by the snow, which is illuminated by the streetlight outside the window.*)

THE PRIVATE LIVES OF ESKIMOS
BY KEN URBAN

CHARACTERS
Marvin *(20s), a disaffected urban dweller in mourning for his sister;* **Tom,**
Marvin's *co-worker (late 20s)*

SCENE
An office cubicle

TIME
A few years in the future, or right now

Because of his sadness, **Marvin** *has stayed home to grieve, thus missing two weeks of work, while his office amigo,* **Tom,** *has covered for him.*

Tom: Hey. You okay, bud?

Marvin: My phone. I must have lost my phone. It's not here.

Tom: No worries. You just left it at home. No worries.

Marvin: No, I had it, I had it when I walked out, I had it in my—

Tom: Hey. Take it easy, Marv. You'll find it. You'll find it, bud. Okay? And if you don't, you can still get all your messages and numbers and stuff and it's all saved online and Marv?

Marvin: Can we talk, Tom? Tom, can we? She. If you don't mind. Talk? You and me.

Tom: Uh. No, if that's okay. I don't really want to hear the details. I mean, it's not like I can help or anything. I mean, you and me. Office amigos. It's not really that kind of thing. Not the kind of thing where you, y'know, tell each other things. Not really that sort of thing. Me and you.

Marvin: Sorry, I didn't mean—

Tom: I'm just not comfortable with—

Marvin: Sure, fine, it's okay, Tom. It's. It's fine.

(Pause.)

Tom: You watch any TV last night? Digital cable or satellite?

Marvin: I don't really watch TV.

Tom: Don't watch TV. You're fucking funny, Marv. Don't watch TV. Who doesn't watch TV?

Marvin: I don't know, I like to, um, read, books.

Tom: Jesus, Marv, you're totally crazy. I love it, I love it. You remind me of this bro of mine at school. He would say the craziest shit, especially if he was toasted and dude, he was always toasted.

Marvin: Is, uh, the server still down?

Tom: Yup. Sure as shit. Down.

Marvin: Do you think they'd let me go home? I'm feeling—I need to find my phone. I'm sure it's home.

Tom: Just go, man, just go. I'll cover for you. No worries. Supervisor comes here, I'll cover. No worries. I mean, isn't shit to do here except—

Marvin: Jerk off?

Tom: You know it, Marv.

REASONS TO BE PRETTY

BY NEIL LaBUTE

CHARACTERS
GREG *(mid-20s), after a huge fight with his girlfriend;* KENT *(late 20s), his friend and co-worker.*

SCENE
A workplace

TIME
Now

(At work. GREG *and* KENT *sitting around the break room of their workplace. In jumpsuits. Just finishing up their lunch-it's after midnight and they're both tired. Third-shifters.)*

(A slash (/) indicates overlapping dialogue.)

KENT: . . . and then what?

GREG: She left. Drove off. / Took *my* car. . . .

KENT: Wow. / Bitch.

GREG: Yeah. To her parents' house or some crap like that, you know?

KENT: Right.

GREG: Making a statement.

KENT: Exactly.

GREG: Threw an ashtray at me, actually, and one of those pots, you know, with the handle on it. . . .

KENT: No, what?

GREG: You know, where you make, like, pancakes and shit. . . . You *know*. . . .

KENT: That's a pan. Frying pan. / Or *skillet*, if you wanna get fancy.

GREG: Oh. / Yeah, well, one of those . . .

KENT: Whoa. *(Beat.)* I thought you said a pot.

GREG: Whatever. It went whizzing by my head—I didn't exactly take stock, I ducked. Stuck my head in the kitchen and bam!

KENT: Fuck. (*Beat.*) Just so you know, though...it's a pan.

GREG: Fine! God...

KENT: Dude, I used to work over at *Denny's*, so...I should know. 'S a pan.

GREG: OK, well, that's what she threw....

KENT: And?

GREG: And nothing. Haven't heard a word since. *Two* days.

KENT: No?

GREG: No call, no text, nothing. I rang up their place but I'm only getting the answering machine. (*Beat.*) Her mom's eating this up, I'm sure. She hates me....

KENT: Figures.

GREG: Yeah. Left a message, anyway. (*Beat.*) I'm just, like, totally *baffled* by this....

(**KENT** *nods and yawns—checks his watch.* **HE** *slaps* **GREG** *on the back.* **GREG** *flinches as* **HE** *opens up an energy snack.*)

KENT: What's that?

GREG: Power Bar.

KENT: Why're you having that?

GREG: What do you mean?

KENT: You just had lunch—now you're having one of those, too?

GREG: Uh-huh. 'S the only way I'll make it to break....

KENT: That doesn't make sense....

GREG: They're good, though. Supposed to give ya a little jolt of energy.

KENT: Yeah, but they're for, you know, like, as a supplement. If you don't have a meal or instead of—not after you already ate.

GREG: Oh.

KENT: They're not *dessert*. Even with all the chocolate on it...

Greg: Huh. (*Beat.*) I think it's carob.

Kent: Whatever! That's like having two meals.

Greg: So? That's okay. . . .

Kent: I guess. If you wanna get fat it is. . . .

Greg: I'm not gonna get fat because I had one of these things—it's all natural stuff in it. Nuts and . . . I dunno. *Seeds.*

Kent: You'd be surprised.

Greg: Yeah, but . . . I mean, athletes eat 'em all the time. Olympians and whoever.

Kent: Are you out running? Or swimming? Hmmm? I don't see you doing cardio work or, like, lifting. Nothing. *Athletes* get away with that shit because they're always active, chipping away at their bodies. Not you. (*Beat.*) Shoving anything you find on the counter over there into your stomach . . .

Greg: Kent, it's a fucking *snack*! Take it easy.

Kent: Just pointing it out—got a group of guys counting on ya is all. . . .

Greg: Fine.

Kent: And getting all chubby is not the way to win her back. / Or your face breaking out.

Greg: Nice! / Thank you. (*Beat.*) Shit . . .

Kent: Well . . . need you strong and fast for the team, man. Can't have any dead weight.

Greg: That's really sensitive, thanks.

Kent: Dude, it's for *you*—I'm throwing a little love your way, don't be a hater.

Greg: Just shut up, OK? (*Beat.*) You got me out in *right* field. How good do I gotta be?

Kent: Good enough to get us that motherfucking trophy! Huh? / (*Pumps his fist.*) Oh, yeah!

(**Kent** *stands, points to a dusty shelf above the cabinets where several other trophies stand. Nothing very new.*)

Greg: I guess . . . / Yep. (*Mock yell.*) Woooaa!

KENT: Dude, come on! Be serious now. . . . (*Beat.*) They haven't brought one a those home since I started working here—last one was in, like, *eighty-six* or something. That's pathetic! (**He** *slaps the table and sits.*) *This* is the year! Without question.

(**GREG** *nods and checks a wall clock against his watch. Yawns.*)

KENT: Third sucks.

GREG: Yep. Pretty much.

KENT: Even with the overtime . . .

GREG: Agreed. (*Yawns.*) I'm *so* beat, man. . . .

KENT: 'Cept for that new girl. *Damn*, she's good-looking! / *What?* / I'm just saying. She's a fox. . . . (*Beat.*) I gotta take a dump.

GREG: Ha! / You never change. . . . / Go for it.

KENT: Can't. I'm waiting for Carly—she's out on *rounds*. (*Grins.*) How gay is that?

GREG: Very. (*Beat.*) She pisses me off.

KENT: Hey man, don't blame her for this.

GREG: I don't.

KENT: Good, because you're the one who said it.

GREG: I *know*. Shit! (*Beat.*) 'Course, she didn't need to jump on the phone and repeat it before I even got home, though, did she?

KENT: Fuck, dude, she's a girl!—they've got, like, *sonar*. It was a done deal, second it came outta your mouth.

GREG: Yeah, well, she screwed me over but good. Steph is acting like . . . Crazy Horse. . . .

KENT: Exactly. Taking scalps . . .

GREG: Yep.

KENT: Noble savages my ass, right? (*Beat.*) They took people's *hair*! Fuckers . . .

GREG: Uh-huh. (*Checks his watch.*) . . . Anyway, I'm just, you know, I'm saying that I'd never do something shitty like that to her. All *behind* her back and everything.

KENT: Right. (*Beat.*) Fuck it, I'm gonna go.

GREG: I'll wait for ya.

KENT: Cool. (*Looks around.*) If she shows before I get back tell her I'm in the can. . . .

GREG: I'll probably flower it up a bit, but okay. Fine.

(**KENT** *nods and gathers up his trash, heading for the door.* **HE** *dumps it—half goes onto the floor.* **HE** *doesn't stop.* **GREG** *watches and shakes his head. Walks over with his own and tosses it; reaches down and collects the last of his buddy's mess, throws it out.*)

REDEMPTION
BY MURRAY SCHISGAL

CHARACTERS
GEORGE BARNABY *(60s) is founder and president of the Warwick House publishing company.* HE *is dressed stylishly: French cuffs; white-collared royal blue shirt; compatible dimpled tie; garish suspenders.* CHARLES "CHUCK" PFEIFFER *(30s), an associate editor with the publisher, has had a few sleepless nights.* HE *wears baggy khaki trousers with no jacket, and his short-sleeved shirt hangs over his trousers; no tie; shirt unbuttoned at neck.*

SCENE
GEORGE BARNABY'S *office: a cluttered desk; two chairs—one an upholstered chair behind the desk, and the other, straight-backed, in front of it. On a bentwood coat stand, we see* BARNABY'S *felt hat and his suit jacket on a hanger.*

TIME
Morning

Office and traffic noises. Knock on offstage door. CHUCK *enters.*

CHUCK: Did you want to see me, Mr. Barnaby?

BARNABY: Sit down.

CHUCK: (*Seated; crosses leg; bounces leg up and down.*) I hope this doesn't take too long. I'm reading an unsolicited manuscript that's genuinely exciting. It's about a woman who discovers that she's slowly turning into a penis.

BARNABY: That isn't why—

CHUCK: I'm also two-thirds through another unsolicited manuscript. It's about a man who marries a tomato. I personally prefer the book about the woman who discovers that she's slowly turning into a penis, but the book about a man who marries a tomato is probably more commercial.

BARNABY: Chuck, I don't want to upset you, but books of similar content were already published. As an assistant associate editor, you should have known that.

CHUCK: I did know it, sir. I was merely making chitchat.

BARNABY: Will you stop bouncing your leg up and down.

CHUCK: Consider it done. (**CHUCK** *stops bouncing his leg, folds his arms across his chest, and yawns widely.*)

BARNABY: Must you yawn? I find it most impolite.

CHUCK: (*Unfolds legs and arms.*) My apologies. Since I broke off with your niece... (*Yawns widely, covering open mouth.*) I...I haven't been able to sleep this past week. I'm fine, though. I'm fine. It won't happen again.

BARNABY: (*Rises; pacing.*) Tell me this. In the half-dozen years you've been with me, how many manuscripts that you recommended for publication have I actually published?

CHUCK: Oh, I would say.... I have no idea.

BARNABY: The fact is I haven't published a single manuscript you recommended since you've been at Warwick House. (**HE** *moves to stand near* **CHUCK,** *puts his hand on* **CHUCK'S** *shoulder.*) It won't do, Chuck. It simply won't do.

CHUCK: (*Staring up at him.*) What won't do, sir? I don't understand.

BARNABY: I cannot justify your position at Warwick House.

CHUCK: Why's that? Have I done something to displease you?

BARNABY: To my knowledge you haven't done a damn thing.

CHUCK: Then I don't understand why you're displeased.

BARNABY: Now I don't want you to get upset and start crying.

CHUCK: It's the furthest thing from my mind. Why should I start crying? You've been like a father to me. (*Impulsively,* **CHUCK** *wraps his arms around* **BARNABY'S** *waist.*)

BARNABY: (*Strokes* **CHUCK'S** *head.*) I have been like a father to you. That's what makes this so painful.

CHUCK: Are you going to discharge me?

BARNABY: I'm afraid I have to. (*Moving away from him.*) If there was anything I could do...

CHUCK: What could you do? What could anybody do? I'm a total mess. I don't know who I am, what I am. I can't eat, I can't sleep. I have angst, I have ennui, I have diarrhea. I don't know what I'm doing on this planet!

BARNABY: All right, all right, don't upset yourself.

Chuck: I'm not upset. (*Screams.*) I'm hysterical!

Barnaby: As well you should be, after what you've endured this past week: your analyst passing away before you finished your analysis; my niece asking you to leave her apartment so my nephew could move in with her; and as of today you're out of a job.

Chuck: It's unbelievable, isn't it?

Barnaby: It certainly is. Good-bye, Chuck.

Chuck: (*Rises; shakes his hand.*) Good-bye, Mr. Barnaby.

Barnaby: Keep in touch.

Chuck: (*Urgently.*) How frequently?

Barnaby: (*Embraces him.*) I can't let you go. I can't!

Chuck: And I don't want to go. I don't!

Barnaby: I never had a son of my own.

Chuck: Neither did I.

Barnaby: (*Steps away from him.*) If only you were man enough.

Chuck: I am man enough. I am. I'd do anything to keep this job. I'd sell my soul to the devil to keep this job.

Barnaby: Would you?

Chuck: Would I what?

Barnaby: Would you sell your soul to the devil to keep this job?

Chuck: Could I ask for a substantial raise?

Barnaby: You won't have to ask. I'm putting on the table the job of senior editor, a salary of one hundred thousand per annum, a private editorial assistant, and your own personal fax machine.

Chuck: Do you have something specific in mind or are we merely making chitchat?

(**Barnaby** *takes* **Chuck** *under the arm and leads him to sit in the upholstered chair behind the desk.*)

Barnaby: We'll see if you're man enough. (**He** *moves to sit in the other chair; leans over the desk; whispers, conspiratorially.*) In the last issue of *Gigolo* magazine there appeared a chapter from a novel-in-progress called *The Glass Cage* by John Naughton, an inmate at the Leone Correctional Facility in Plattsburg, New York. He's been serving a twenty-year-to-life sentence for manslaughter, bank robbery, kidnapping, and sodomy.

CHUCK: (*Whispers, conspiratorially.*) Manslaughter, bank robbery, kidnapping, and sodomy.

BARNABY: Chuck, never in my—

CHUCK: Did he do them all at once or on four separate occasions?

BARNABY: To my knowledge they were done all at once. During his lunch hour.

CHUCK: I better write this information down. (*Writes on desk pad.*)

BARNABY: In my thirty-three years of publishing, I haven't witnessed such a furious, avaricious attempt to gain the rights to a single piece of fiction.

CHUCK: (*As* HE *writes.*) John Naughton, manslaughter, bank robbery, kidnapping, and sodomy. All done during his lunch hour.

BARNABY: It appears an inmate he shared a cell with mailed the chapter from his novel-in-progress to *Gigolo* magazine. I'm told Naughton went absolutely berserk and broke the inmate's arms and legs. It appears that he has no interest in getting his work published.

CHUCK: (*As* HE *writes.*) Naughton has no interest in getting his work published. He breaks arms and legs.

BARNABY: Every piece of mail he receives, he returns unopened. He refuses to meet with any publisher or agent. (*Leans closer to* CHUCK.) It occurred to me that if we could arrange for you to be in that prison to negotiate a contract with him . . . (CHUCK *stops writing, stares at* BARNABY, *dumbfounded.*) Don't you get it? The success of the people who own the rights to that book will be astronomical.

CHUCK: Mr. Barnaby . . .

BARNABY: I'm not going to hold anything back from you, son. Warwick House has had it. At the rate we're going, we can't last the year. We're broke, bankrupt, penniless. It'll only be a matter of time before we're locked up and shut down for nonpayment of our bills.

CHUCK: But I don't understand.

BARNABY: What don't you understand?

CHUCK: (*Hysterically.*) Why do I have to go to prison to get a personal fax machine!

BARNABY: (*Rises.*) You don't have to go to prison. You can walk out that door and go on your merry way with your dead-end life, moving from job to job, from failure to failure, rejected by your fiancée, deserted by your analyst, a nobody, a nonentity, a piece of feces floating on a vast, empty ocean.

CHUCK: With all due respect, I'd rather be a piece of feces floating on a vast, empty ocean than be in prison with a convict who breaks your arms and legs for just trying to get his novel published!

BARNABY: And I thought you loved Natalia.

CHUCK: I do love Natalia. The only reason I'm still alive is because I love Natalia. Without her I would have given up on this miserable, godforsaken planet a long time ago.

BARNABY: Am I to presume that you don't love Natalia enough to spend a few insignificant weeks in prison for her? Is that how deep your love is for the only woman you claim to be in love with?

CHUCK: But she loves your nephew!

BARNABY: Nonsense! Poppycock! I know my niece as intimately as I know myself. She doesn't love my nephew. And he doesn't love her. They belong to the look-how-kinky-we-can-be-that-you-can't-be generation. Take my word for it, Natalia loves you. And yet... she's a woman, a woman who needs what every woman needs, reassurance, support, prospects for a stable and secure future. She'll give you her love in abundance as soon as you become the man she can depend on to fulfill those needs. And who is that man? He's an ambitious man, a financially prosperous man, a man who is esteemed and admired by his colleagues. I guarantee you, once you're a senior editor, once you're earning a salary of one hundred thousand per annum and have a private editorial assistant and a personal fax machine, she'll drop Ted and come running back to you so fast you won't know what hit you.

CHUCK: Are you sure I'll be in prison for only for a few insignificant weeks?

BARNABY: Absolutely. You're a first offender. There'll be no cash in the cash box. My lawyer will cut a plea bargain with the prosecuting attorney.

CHUCK: And I become a senior editor at a salary of...

BARNABY: Everything I said.

CHUCK: And Natalia?

BARNABY: She'll be waiting for you, wide-eyed, open-armed and with trembling, ruby-red lips.

CHUCK: When do I go to prison?

BARNABY: Today. Now. We don't want another publisher contacting Naughton before we do. I spoke to my lawyer. To get into prison all you have to do is commit a felony.

CHUCK: That shouldn't be a problem. May I ask what the felony is?

BARNABY: Robbery and assault. Chuck, guess who the victim is.

CHUCK: Ahhh . . . a public school teacher?

BARNABY: No. The victim of the robbery and assault is me.

CHUCK: You, Mr. Barnaby? I couldn't assault you.

(BARNABY *takes presidential or horror mask from desk drawer and gives it to* CHUCK *as a disguise.*)

BARNABY: My lawyer scrupulously planned everything. Don't louse it up. Now put on the mask. When the police pick you up it can be used as evidence against you.

CHUCK: I can see that some excellent planning has gone into this. (*Puts on mask.*) Exactly what is the plan?

(BARNABY *overturns chairs; opens desk drawers.*)

BARNABY: The plan is for you to wreck the office while searching for the cash box in my desk drawer. You find the cash box. When you hear me walking in, you hide behind the desk. I go to the hanger to put on my jacket. You jump up from behind the desk and hit me on the head with this baseball bat, hard enough so that I fall down on the floor. (HE *hands* CHUCK *a baseball bat.*)

CHUCK: That shouldn't be a problem. (HE *bangs the bat on the desk, then takes a few practice swings at* BARNABY'S *imaginary head.*)

BARNABY: You take this cash box . . . (*Removes metal box from desk drawer; puts it on desk.*) . . . leave the office, use the back stairway to get to the lobby and go directly to your room at the Hotel Istanbul. When I get back on my feet, I'll call the police and tell them that, in spite of your wearing a mask, I recognized your voice and I'm convinced you stole the cash box.

(He *tears off* Chuck's *entire shirt in one quick swipe, exposing* Chuck's *naked torso.* Chuck *stares down at his nipples, nonplussed.*)

As further evidence I'll give them your shirt, which I tore off your back during the robbery. My lawyer suggests you hide the cash box and mask under your mattress. That will further implicate you when the police search your room.

Chuck: Consider it done.

Barnaby: I'll leave the office now and re-enter. Don't forget, you hit me on the head with the baseball bat, hard enough so I fall down on the floor.

Chuck: That shouldn't be a problem. (Chuck *swings the bat several times at an imaginary* Barnaby's *head.*)

Barnaby: Incidentally, my lawyer is acquainted with the warden at Leone, Warden William E. Crawford. He's writing his memoir. It's titled *Redemption*. I suggest you touch base with him. It might earn you some brownie points.

(Barnaby *exits office.* Chuck *crouches behind desk.* Barnaby *re-enters, play-acting the role of innocent victim;* He *moves to put on jacket at bentwood coat stand.*)

Barnaby: Ah, what a day, what a lovely day it is. Unfortunately I have an enormous amount of work to do.

(*Once his jacket is on,* He *turns to face desk, his knees buckle, his fists are clenched at sides, his eyes are shut in fearful anticipation of an assault. When* Chuck *doesn't respond,* He *repeats himself, miming the same motions* He *performed previously.*)

Ah, what a day, what a lovely day it is. Unfortunately I have an enormous amount of work to do.

(He *turns to face desk, his knees buckle, his fists are clenched at sides, his eyes are shut.*)

Chuck?

Chuck: (*Rises behind desk, bat in hand, mask on face.*) Yes, Mr. Barnaby?

Barnaby: (*Without moving; eyes shut.*) Why the delay?

Chuck: You have to turn around. I always have trouble hitting a man on the head with a baseball bat when he's facing me.

BARNABY: Very well, I'll turn around. (HE *turns around, his knees buckle, his fists are clenched at sides, his eyes are shut.*) Go ahead. Get it over with, quickly!

(*But* CHUCK *doesn't budge;* BARNABY *turns to face* CHUCK; *eyes open.*)

Chuck, will you get on with it?

(CHUCK *takes off mask and puts it and baseball bat on the desk.* HE *moves to exit.*)

CHUCK: It's no use, Mr. Barnaby. I can't do it. I'm going home.

BARNABY: Go home. Quit. I knew you weren't man enough. I knew— (*On second thought.*) All right, go home. Wear the mask when you leave by the back staircase and take the cash box with you. Don't forget to hide the mask and the cash box under your mattress. I'll manage without you.

CHUCK: (*Slipping on mask.*) You're not . . . ?

(BARNABY *puts cash box under* CHUCK's *arm.*)

BARNABY: I have no choice in the matter. You may well ask what compels me to take such drastic action to save Warwick House. Perhaps I can enlighten you. Have you ever wondered why I've worked for thirty-three years, six days a week and until 2:00PM on Sundays? Why I've lived my entire adult life as a bachelor, cooking my own meals, sleeping alone in a king-size bed and washing my own underwear?

CHUCK: Natalia and I talked about it, frequently. We couldn't understand why you did it.

BARNABY: Obviously, you haven't my resolve. You haven't sacrificed every scintilla of respite and leisure in the pursuit of a single, obsessive goal: to be on top, to be with the big boys, to stand like a colossus at the pinnacle of our profession, rich, prosperous, free of the humiliation of anonymity.

CHUCK: Mr. Barnaby, I couldn't hit you. I couldn't . . .

(BARNABY *leads him out.*)

BARNABY: Go. Go straight to your hotel room and wait for the police. I'll take care of everything.

(CHUCK *exits.* BARNABY *lifts his felt hat from the coat stand and puts it on;* HE *picks up bat from desk, judges the weight of it in his hand, perhaps takes a swing or two.* HE *gets down on his knees; puts bat beside him; clasps hands; looks upward.*)

BARNABY: Our father who art in heaven, hallowed be thy name. Thy kingdom come, thy will be done, on earth as it is in heaven. Amen.

(**HE** *takes the baseball bat in both his hands, wags it over his head. After a few feeble taps on his head, squealing with fright,* **HE** *screws up his courage and smashes the bat down on his head, crumbling to the floor. Sound: we hear the crack of the bat hitting his head. Blackout.*)

TAKE ME OUT
BY RICHARD GREENBERG

CHARACTERS
DARREN *(late 20s), the best player on the championship baseball team, the New York Empires;* **KIPPY** *(20s or 30s), his teammate*

SCENE
The New York Empires' locker room

TIME
The present

DARREN *has recently come out as a gay man to the media, but his arrogance (and perhaps his deep insecurity) trumps his ability to see how this announcement changes things for himself and his teammates;* **KIPPY**, *his best friend on the team, tries to help* **DARREN** *cope with the fallout from his decision.*

DARREN:
   I am so freakin' *sick* of this *welcome* I'm getting.

KIPPY:
   Welcome?

DARREN:
   Ever since fuckin' Mungitt went on TV.
   Alluva sudden I'm a *victim*.
   Fuck that!
   I want slurs—brickbats—epithets.
   Do you know what I'm *getting*?

KIPPY:
   What?

DARREN:
   Offers!

KIPPY:
   Like . . . ?

DARREN:
   Endorsements for, like, cheap furniture.

KIPPY:

Those can be very moving.

DARREN:

Fuck this shit, Kippy.
Do you know what I'm *getting*?

KIPPY:

... Offers?

DARREN:

Compassion.
I need compassion?

KIPPY:

Nah.

DARREN:

Don't you have compassion for me. You *envy* me!
This is how it is with me, this is how it's always been,
take your fuckin' compassion an' stick it up your ass,
'cause you're not gettin' *me* there!

KIPPY: (*Hugs him with compassion.*)
I know how it is, man, and I *feel* for you.

DARREN: (*Throwing him off.*)
You fuckin' faggot.

(KIPPY *laughs,* DARREN *quiets down, gets somber.*)

Ya know what it is, Kippy.
They think they've figured me out.
They think my secret's out.
And what's gonna follow is this cavalcade of revelation.
IS THAT WHAT EVERYBODY THINKS?
You think you're gonna get this *torrent* of *me* comin' at ya?
You think you *know* me? You think you know my *secret*?
Shit, that wasn't a secret—that was an omission. I've *got* a secret—but that's
    not it.

KIPPY:

What is?

DARREN:

... Wha-?

KIPPY:

What is your secret? You said you have a secret.

DARREN:

. . . I don't *have* a secret, Kippy.
I *am* a secret.

KIPPY:

Even from me?

(*Beat. The question slides away.*)

DARREN:

I'm sick of baseball.
I want out.

KIPPY:

Oh, bullshit.

DARREN:

I mean it—I might walk right out of all this—

KIPPY:

Nobody playing the way you're playing "walks right out" of it— Nobody
    making your salary "walks right out" of it—

DARREN:

How do you know? What makes you sure'a that?

KIPPY:

The world's old, there've been a lot of people; I extrapolate.

DARREN:

Maybe I'm somethin' that's never been seen before.
Maybe I'm somethin' brand-new. Maybe—

KIPPY:

I *play* with you.
I play on your team (which is not to say that I play on your team, but)
    I . . . play on your team.
I know you.
I know you when you're playing.

DARREN:

. . . Things are . . . changing.
I'm changing.

KIPPY:

I like you better now.

DARREN:

Bullshit.

KIPPY:

No, I liked you before—*loved* you in a manly sort of way. But now you're . . . more human.

DARREN:

What was I before?

KIPPY:

Sort of . . . godly.

DARREN:

And now I'm human?

KIPPY:

Yeah.

DARREN:

Kippy?

KIPPY:

Yeah, Dar?

DARREN:

Isn't that a *demotion*?

TAKE ME OUT
BY RICHARD GREENBERG

CHARACTERS
DARREN *(late 20s), one of the best baseball players in the major league, who just recently outed himself;* **MASON** *(early 30s), his shy gay accountant*

SCENE
The New York Empires' locker room

TIME
The present

MASON'S *burgeoning friendship with* **DARREN** *has changed his life and made him a complete baseball fanatic.* **DARREN,** *who has become more human over the past few weeks, realizes his own vulnerabilities and both the benefits and the consequences of coming out.*

MASON: (*Singing.*)
   "Oh my man, I love him so, he'll never know...."

(**HE** *giggles.*)

DARREN:
   Are you drunk?

MASON:
   I *had* a beer.

DARREN:
   You had a keg.

MASON:
   No. Just one.
   The great advantage of an extremely narrow life is the slightest deviation produces *stag*gering results.

   (**HE** *giggles.*)

   Oh, I'm sorry if I'm silly.

DARREN:
   No, it's kinda cute. Kinda endearing....

MASON:

Oh . . . well . . . yes, it is. . . .

DARREN:

. . . So, Mason, I was wonderin'. . . .

MASON:

Yes?

DARREN:

If I retire now, will I—

MASON:

Oh no no no no no *no*—not the night you won the World *Series*! My God, man, have you no sense of oc*ca*sion?

DARREN:

I just need to be alone for a while.

I just need to get real quiet.

I'm not who I was when the season started.

MASON:

Neither am I—isn't it *great*?

DARREN:

But ya see, unlike you, I *liked* who I . . .

But I guess I really wasn't that then, either.

MASON:

. . . Darren, I truly, deeply feel I should be responding to your *crise* right now, but all I keep thinking is, when do you get the *ring*?

DARREN:

The—

MASON:

The championship—

DARREN:

Oh, next year.

MASON:

Well, then you *have* to come back, you don't have a choice—

DARREN: (*Flashing rings.*)

I already have two others.

MASON:

Oh! Is *that* what those are?

DARREN:

What didja think?

MASON:

I didn't know. I just thought you had terrible taste! Wow! Look at them.

DARREN:

Yeah—

MASON:

Well, all you have to do is look at them, and you'll know.

DARREN:

Know what?

MASON:

Who you are. Your ontological quandary will be dispelled.

DARREN:

They just mean I was on a winning team, that's all.

MASON:

That's a better start than most of us get. Don't diminish it, it would be too ungrateful.

DARREN:

(*Still sad.*): I s'pose. (*Beat.*)
I guess I have to go to this *party*. (*Beat.*)
Do you wanna come?

MASON:

Huh?

DARREN:

Wanna be my date?

MASON:

Don't you have a date?

DARREN:

No.

MASON:

How can you not have a date?

DARREN:

I told you—I don't know people.

MASON:

But you didn't mean that.

DARREN:

But I did. (*Beat.*) Come on. We'll get photographed together, splashed over alla tabloids.

Everybody'll think you're my long-awaited *boy*friend. Those two gay guys down the hall will drop dead. (*A hitch as he hears this, brief, then.*)

Then I won't hafta kiss you in the elevator like we've both been dreading.

MASON:

. . . Okay. Um. Yes! But do I look . . . all right?

DARREN:

You look okay. . . .

You could maybe use an accessory—

MASON:

I don't—have—

DARREN: (*Pulling off one of his rings.*)

Hey—wear this.

MASON:

What?

DARREN:

Yeah—it'll be a goof—come on. (**HE** *slips the ring on* **MASON'S** *finger.*)

That feels weird, doesn't it?

MASON:

Wow.

(**MASON** *spreads his fingers in front of him to inspect the ring.*)

DARREN:

Hey, Mars—it's gonna be a roomful of *jocks.*

(**HE** *folds his fingers into a fist, demonstrates looking at the ring that way.*)

MASON:

Oh . . . oh.

DARREN:

So—whaddya say?

MASON:

Sure. (HE *starts to leave with* DARREN, *pauses.*)

Um—would it be all right if I met you there? If I stayed here just a little bit longer?

DARREN:

You know where the place is?

MASON:

I do, in fact.

DARREN:

Sure. Enjoy yourself.

MASON:

Thank you.

DARREN:

Hey—Mars?

(MASON *turns to* DARREN. DARREN *tosses him the ball.* MASON *catches it, gasps.*)

DARREN:

What a fuck of a season, huh?

MASON:

Yes. It was. A fuck of a season. It was . . . tragic.

(DARREN *exits. To himself, realizing it.*)

It *was*—tragic.

(*A moment.*)

(*His glance falls on the ring. Then moves to the ball. Then* HE *closes his eyes and takes a deep breath, and opens his eyes, and takes in the whole stadium.*)

What will we do till spring?

(*Fade out.*)

TIME OUT
BY ERIK SHERMAN

CHARACTERS
DAVIE *(20s), a prisoner afraid to accept his fate;* **PETER** *(20s), his older brother, more cynical and realistic, but ultimately just as vulnerable*

SCENE
A large prison cell

TIME
Early morning

(*Both characters are standing, looking at the door.*)

DAVIE: I wonder what time it is?

PETER: Ten minutes to.

DAVIE: To what?

PETER: You have to ask?

(*Pause.*)

DAVIE: How do you know?

PETER: The clock.

DAVIE: What clock?

PETER: You never noticed it?

    (**DAVIE** *shakes head.*)

    Go all the way right and look left.

    (**DAVIE** *moves chair under window, stands on it, and looks out.*)

DAVIE: I don't see it.

PETER: Not the chair. (**PETER** *pulls the table over, replacing the chair with it.*)

DAVIE: Why not the chair?

PETER: It's not tall enough.

DAVIE: Oh. And all this time I thought that you wanted to do things the hard way. (**DAVIE** *climbs on table and looks out.*) I still don't see it.

PETER: You've got to push out as far as you can, then look up so you can almost see around that corner.

DAVIE: Oh, I see. (*Walks away from door.*) You're right.

PETER: Thank you.

DAVIE: No need for sarcasm at this point. I just didn't realize that it was so late.

PETER: *Tempus fugit.*

DAVIE: I only thought...

PETER: That maybe it would be something else?

DAVIE: No, not exactly.

PETER: That maybe I had made a mistake?

DAVIE: Maybe.

PETER: Or something else?

DAVIE: Maybe.

PETER: What?

DAVIE: Nothing. (*Gets off the table.*)

PETER: Nothing. (*Looks at him.*) That would be lovely, wouldn't it. (*No response.*) Oh, yes, I'd like that too, nothing, but that just isn't going to happen. No nothing today.

DAVIE: Sometimes things happen. Or don't happen.

PETER: Things? Things? What kinds of things?

DAVIE: Good things. Hopeful things.

PETER: Ah, I see. Miraculous things, huh? (**HE** *hits home.*) Waiting for a miracle. Didn't you have enough of that? (*Laughs.*) Father will be down with the holy water any minute now.

DAVIE: You didn't have to say that.

PETER: Yup—holy water for the young heathen. Anoint me.

DAVIE: Stop it.

PETER: Baptize me.

DAVIE: Stop it.

(*Both are getting worked up.*)

PETER: Yes, my brother, bring down that liquid spirit! Wash away those original sins in the essence of truth!

DAVIE: Peter, I'm beggin' you, please stop.

PETER: Anoint me, Big Daddy, and shrive me. (*Stands very close and looms over* DAVIE, *who is cowering.*) Here it comes. . . . Lay back and have a little grace. . . .

DAVIE: (*Pushes his way back up.*) SHUT UP!

(*Pause. Both are breathing hard.*)

PETER: Touchy.

DAVIE: Like you aren't?

PETER: It doesn't matter. It just doesn't effing matter any more.

DAVIE: (*Starts to laugh.*) It's down to ten. . . .

PETER: Six, now.

DAVIE: . . . Six minutes and you're still censoring yourself? (*Laughs.*) Afraid Big Daddy is going to get mad? Wash your mouth out?

(*Pause, and then together.*)

DAVIE AND PETER: Do I have to clean that filthy cesspool? (*Pause.*)

PETER: Some things never change.

DAVIE: (HE *looks at window.*) And some things do.

PETER: (HE *looks at window.*) Too bad it's never for the better.

DAVIE: You always did refuse to hope. You always wanted to believe the worst.

PETER: Not true.

DAVIE: Oh? And when did you ever have hope.

PETER: Years ago. Before you would remember.

DAVIE: And what did you hope for?

PETER: Death.

DAVIE: Good things come for those who wait. (*Pause.*) No hopes now?

PETER: No. It just doesn't matter any more.

DAVIE: The king of despair.

PETER: The prince of resignation. And, pray tell, where has your hope gotten you? (*Looks around.*) All roads lead to Rome.

DAVIE: (*Looks around.*) Maybe that's true on the outside, but inside I could think of other things. Inside I was free. Inside . . .

PETER: (*Cutting him off.*) Inside you were ready to be just like me.

DAVIE: No.

PETER: Yes.

DAVIE: No.

PETER: It all wound up the same, anyway.

DAVIE: But in the meantime . . . in the meantime, you sat in a dank cellar and I was able to breathe.

PETER: And now?

DAVIE: I can still breathe. (*Looks around.*) At least a little.

PETER: Emphasis on the little.

DAVIE: What should I have done? Be like you?

PETER: Don't you get it yet? You are like me. (*Bitter smile.*) Ask anyone. From the start, everyone was ready to write us both off. They didn't know, didn't care, and wanted to be done with it. So they were. So even if there was a little difference—and I don't think there really was, I think it's only you wishing that there was—it doesn't matter, because we don't get the last word.

(*Pause.*)

DAVIE: What if we talked to them?

PETER: Huh?

DAVIE: Yes . . . what if we talked to them?

PETER: Talked to them?

DAVIE: (*Getting excited.*) Yes, talked to them. We're human. They're human.

(PETER *snorts.*)

They're human. Did we ever try that?

PETER: We never even had the chance. No one wanted to hear.

DAVIE: But if we tried . . .

PETER: It wouldn't matter. Do you remember what happened? Why we're here?

DAVIE: Of course I do.

PETER: (*To himself.*) Of course he does. (*To* DAVIE.) Do you?

DAVIE: Yes. (DAVIE *gets increasingly agitated during Peter's next speech.*)

PETER: But what? Our situation? Or everything that had happened? That last instant, with the grooves of your fingerprints melting into the grain of the wood? The gut-swimming waves of fear? That heart-pounding rush as the sound revved up, climbing your throat until it could pry your jaws apart and turn into . . .

(DAVIE *crosses to* PETER, *grabbing his throat, pushing him, panting. Then* HE *realizes what* HE'S *doing, stops, and looks at his hands, still grasping, but now by themselves, in the air.*)

PETER: Yeah, I guess you remember. A little better.

(DAVIE *walks away to the other side of the room, slumps to floor, burying his head in his arms. Starts weeping.*)

PETER: Hey. (*Nothing.*) Hey. (*Still no reaction.* PETER *crosses to* DAVIE *and sits down next to him.*)

PETER: Look, I'm sorry. Okay? (*No reaction.*) I was out of line—I apologize.

DAVIE: (*Sniffles.*) 'S okay.

PETER: It's not your fault.

DAVIE: (*Head still down.*) Sure it was. I was there.

PETER: You did the best you could. I didn't listen—it's my fault.

DAVIE: No, it's not.

PETER: Yes, it is.

DAVIE: No, it's not. (*Lifts head up.*) You didn't think anything—didn't do anything—that I hadn't thought of. Except you had the balls to do it. (*Looks around.*) Pax Romana.

(*Turns to window.*) How much time left, do you think?

PETER: Maybe a minute, maybe two.

DAVIE: It's a funny thing about time. Sometimes it takes forever to go by. Like when you're ready to go someplace, but you're tired and you sit, resting, eyes closed, waiting to get up and walk out. You look at your watch and it's ten minutes to go. So you let your mind wander and feel the tiredness like something you breathed in. You sit there for, oh, a half hour, an hour, and then you open your eyes and look, and only a few minutes have gone by. (*Starts to cry.*) You still have a whole lifetime to live in that last five minutes. (*Looks at* **PETER**.) I'm so scared.

PETER: (*Takes* **DAVIE's** *hand.*) I know. (*Looks over at the door.*) I'm scared, too.

DAVIE: What were we supposed to do?

PETER: I don't know. I really don't know.

DAVIE: Just live with it? Take it? Let it go on?

PETER: You and me, we were put in the wrong place at the wrong time. We got ourselves born bad. And we did the only thing we could.

DAVIE: And?

PETER: And they did the only thing they could.

DAVIE: So they're behind the door as much as we are?

PETER: (*Thinks for a moment.*) Maybe they are.

(*Pause.*)

DAVIE: Tell me a story. Like you used to.

PETER: (*Pause.*) Once upon a time, there were two heroes. They had to go through a lot of trials, fight a lot of monsters. But they did what they had to do, and when they got tired, or scared, or lonely—especially in the middle of the night when they were lonely—they knew that one day it would be better, and they wouldn't have to fight anymore.

DAVIE: We'll be able to stop fighting soon, won't we?

PETER: Yes, just a little while longer. One day is finally here.

THE WOMEN OF LOCKERBIE
BY DEBORAH BREVOORT

CHARACTERS
GEORGE JONES *(40s), an American government representative;* BILL LIVINGSTON *(50s), father of Adam, who died in the Lockerbie crash seven years ago*

SCENE
Nighttime. The hills of Lockerbie, Scotland, where Pan Am Flight 103 crashed.

TIME
December 21, 1995, the seven-year anniversary of the crash, and the night of the winter solstice

GEORGE, *in charge of the warehouse storing the belongings of victims of the Pan Am 103 crash, is hiding from the women of Lockerbie, who want to wash the clothing of the crash victims and return it to the victims' family members.* HE *runs into* BILL, *but does not realize who he is.*

GEORGE:

These women are driving me crazy!

Look.

Let me give you a piece of advice about the women of Lockerbie.

Don't be fooled by the lace on their collars.

Or the flowers on their teacups.

They're not the sweet little old ladies they appear to be.

They're tigers.

And they're ferocious.

You know what they just did?

They called in the television crews!

The *networks*.

The *American* networks.

They're all down at the warehouse

with their reporters

waiting for a statement from me!

And that's not all.

There are two hundred women with them!

Two hundred women!

With *candles*.

They're trying to create an international incident, these people.

BILL:

But I thought Lockerbie was already an international incident.

GEORGE:

Lockerbie? Hardly!

The world has forgotten all about Lockerbie.

They forgot about it two weeks after the crash.

But if those women get it back in the news...!

Well, then it will be. And then I'll *never* get out of here!

BILL:

You don't like it here?

GEORGE:

What's to like?

Lockerbie is the Siberia of the State Department!

But.

You have to do your time in places like this

before you get the better assignments.

Me, I'd rather be someplace else.

You know, places like...

Kuwait...

Tel Aviv...

The hot spots.

And if I handle this right, I just might get there.

BILL:

Then why are you doing it, if I might ask?

GEORGE:

You mean this business with the clothes?

BILL:

Yes.

GEORGE:

I have orders from Washington.

They want things wrapped up here.

Quickly.

So that's what I'm doing.

Look. This whole affair has gone on long enough.

These people should just get over it.

It's been seven years.

I mean... *move on*, for God's sake!

Get a life!
I've tried telling them that,
but of course, they won't listen.
They sent the mayor to see me.
They sent the *bishop*, for God's sake.
Next, they'll probably send in a *mother!*
The mothers are the worst.
They come clutching the baby pictures.
Johnny blowing out the candles on his birthday cake.
Little Timmy smiling with his mouth full of braces.
The mothers will drive you crazy.
There is always a mother who makes it impossible to do your job.

BILL:

What about the fathers?

GEORGE:

Oh, I have to deal with them too.
But men...
Men are different.
Thank God.
You can always reason with a man.
At least they don't shove those pictures in my face.

(**BILL** *pulls out his wallet and opens it.*)

What do you have there?

BILL:

My son's school picture from the sixth grade.
Smiling. With his mouth full of braces.
Look.

(**BILL** *shoves the picture in* **GEORGE**'s *face.*)

GEORGE: (*Pause.*)

Was your son...uh...on board?

BILL:

Yes.

GEORGE:

Oh. (*Pause.*) I didn't know....

BILL:

His body was never found.
He's still out here somewhere.

GEORGE:

(*Pause.*) I'm . . . sorry.
(*Pause.*) Um. What was his name?

BILL:

Adam. Adam Alexander Livingston.

GEORGE:

Oh, yes. Yes. I, uh, seem to recall it. . . .

BILL:

And here is a picture when he hit a home run.
In the Little League.
The game was tied and the bases were loaded.

GEORGE:

Yeah?

BILL:

Yeah! He brought them all home.
And here . . .
Here is the ticket stub
from the Yankee game I took him to on his last birthday.
I just found this a few minutes ago, in the pocket of my coat.
Funny.
I haven't worn this coat in years.

GEORGE:

Well, hey.
Hey, hey, hey.
That's great.
So your son was a Yankees fan?

(**BILL** *nods.*)

Helluva team, the Yanks.
Helluva owner.
I like George Steinbrenner.
Always have. Always will.
Man knows how to run a team.

BILL:

Yes. Yes he does.

(*Pause.*)

Mr. Jones.
Do you have children?

GEORGE:

No. No, I don't.
Don't have a wife.
Well, I had one.
Had two, actually.
But we never got around to having kids.
You know.

BILL:

Then it might be hard for you to understand
the loss that a parent feels....

GEORGE:

They say there's nothing worse.

BILL:

They're right. There isn't.
(*Pause.*) See that hill?

GEORGE:

Yeah.

BILL:

My wife is on the other side of it.

GEORGE:

Right now?

BILL:

Yes.

GEORGE:

Doing what?

BILL:

Looking for my son's remains.

GEORGE:

You're kidding.

BILL:

> No.

(**GEORGE** *rolls his eyes and whistles.*)

GEORGE:

> Women. You know?

BILL:

> They're not the only ones who feel loss.
> Men do too.

GEORGE:

> Not like that.

BILL:

> No, not like that.
> That's the difference, I guess....
> The women show it and the men don't.
> And they show it more because we don't.
> It's not fair, really, now that I think about it.
> The women have to do their own crying
> and also, the crying for the men....

> (*Pause.* **HE** *reflects for a moment on this realization.*)

> When Adam died...
> I cut off the pain.
> I had to.
> I couldn't take it.
> But then...
> I didn't feel anything else either.
> Just now
> when I was walking these hills
> and found this ticket stub from the Yankees,
> I felt something.
> For the first time in years.

GEORGE:

> You did, huh.

BILL:

> Yes.

> (*Slight pause.*)

Look at this thing.

(**He** *holds up the ticket stub and looks at it with astonishment.*)

It's a piece of paper
A *little* piece of paper.
Who would have thought
that a
little
piece of paper
like this
could have that kind of power?

(*Pause.*)

George . . . those clothes aren't just clothes.
They're not *things*.
They have *life*.
Just like this piece of paper.
Please.
Reconsider your decision.
Release the clothes to the women.

GEORGE:
Look . . . I wish I could, *really*, but—

[**WOMAN** 1 (Off. *Calls.*)—Mr. Livingston?

WOMAN 2 (Off. *Calls.*)—Mr. Livingston?]

BILL:
Over here!

GEORGE:
Who's that?

BILL:
The women.

GEORGE:
The *women?!*
Oh shit!
Look, I've got to go, I'll see you later—

(**GEORGE** *starts to run off.*)

THE WRITING ON THE WALL
BY ED NAPIER

CHARACTERS
SEBASTIAN ST. JOHN *(30s) is a slender, handsome British writer. Though he speaks with an affected East End accent,* SEBASTIAN *is, in reality, a viscount.* NELSON *(40) is a New York playwright who has temporarily moved to Hollywood to write for* Crime Time, *a television series.*

SCENE
A studio in Culver City, California, where Crime Time, *a hit TV procedural, is produced (it's written, shot—except for locations—and edited here).* SEBASTIAN'S *office is a box of glass and plasterboard.* HE *has a hot-looking couch that* HE *filched from the prop department*

TIME
The present

SEBASTIAN *is hanging a publicity poster for an episode of a crime show he wrote for BBC2—something like* Prime Suspect. *The poster can definitely be abstract—but Glenda Jackson's name is definitely on it.*

NELSON *has given his "writer's draft" of a television show to his old friend, Sid, the star of the show. (They have an almost big brother little brother relationship). However, doing this is completely forbidden in the industry.*

SEBASTIAN: Do you think if I hang this poster above the sofa it would look all right?

NELSON: Sure.

SEBASTIAN: First script for the BBC. It was fucking great. Glenda Jackson was in it.

NELSON: Cool.

(**SEBASTIAN** *stands on his sofa and, above it, pounds a nail into the wall.*)

SEBASTIAN: Small part. But she was great. Cameo role really. Dude, you don't look well. Are you all right?

NELSON: I'm fine. How about you? How are you?

SEBASTIAN: Me? I'm great. Livin' the dream, baby. Livin' the dream. This poster hung up straight?

NELSON: Looks straight.

SEBASTIAN: Yeah. But it must be really difficult for you with your wife and your kid in New York.

NELSON: Yeah. It's difficult,

SEBASTIAN: Yeah, man, seriously. Must be fucking hard. So do you ever like, you know, go to hookers?

NELSON: No.

SEBASTIAN: Didn't think so. Part 'o your problem is: You're not getting laid.

NELSON: Yeah. But that's always been my problem. I've never been with a woman who likes to fuck as much as I do.

SEBASTIAN: You. (*Points at him. Laughs.*) You're funny.

NELSON: (*English accent.*) Funny? Me?

SEBASTIAN: Yes, mate, you. Maybe you should be in Hollywood?

NELSON: Me?

SEBASTIAN: Wait. Wait a minute, mate. Wait! Seriously. (*Surveys him.*) You are in fucking Hollywood!

NELSON: (*Screams.*) AH! Pinch me. Fucking pinch me!

SEBASTIAN: I'll pinch ya. I'll twist your fucking nipples off. (**HE** *does.*)

NELSON: Ah. Sebastian, stop. God damn. It hurts.

SEBASTIAN: Now, this, mate. This is you.

NELSON: How you mean?

SEBASTIAN: The old you has reemerged. (*Smiles. Beat.*) Because lately, dude, honestly, and this is no lie, you seem different. You really do.

NELSON: How so?

SEBASTIAN: I dunno. Just totally different. Can't really put my finger on it, actually, but between this week and last, something has happened. You know what I mean?

NELSON: No.

SEBASTIAN: You seem—nervous.

NELSON: I don't feel especially nervous.

SEBASTIAN: Look at me. Look in my eyes and answer this question.

NELSON: Okay.

SEBASTIAN: Did you give Sid Rosen your writer's draft?

NELSON: What?

SEBASTIAN: I said, did you give Sid Rosen your writer's draft? (*Beat.*) And I'm going to repeat the question one more time: Did you give (NELSON *overlaps.*) Sid Rosen your writer's draft?

NELSON: (*Overlap.*) Yes, I did. I gave it to him.

SEBASTIAN: What the fuck were you thinking?

NELSON: I don't understand why it's such a big deal.

SEBASTIAN: What? What did you say? You don't understand why it's such a big deal? Did I just hear you say that? Big deal! Dude, you have no FUCKING IDEA! We're talking about a show that is now worth about two hundred million dollars, and two hundred million dollars is a BIG FUCKING DEAL TO ANYONE WITH HALF A FUCKING BRAIN! Of course, if Neil found out you gave Sid your writer's draft, he would fire you like that. (*Snaps his fingers.*) Not to worry though. All your secrets are safe with me.

(NELSON *starts to go.*)

Nelson, where are you going?

NELSON: I'm going down to the set to talk to Sid.

SEBASTIAN: No, you're not.

NELSON: I know I am.

SEBASTIAN: No, you aren't. You are going to sit down, and you are going to fucking listen to everything I have to say.

NELSON: No, I'm not.

SEBASTIAN: Don't make me force you. Because I can. And I will.

NELSON: You're insane.

SEBASTIAN: All right. Fucking go. Go on then. Do the fuck what you want. See if I care. Go! You don't fucking understand that I'm just trying to protect you. You don't get that. You go fuckin' around with a system that is specific. A system that is tried and true. Actors can not get involved in the writing of scripts in television. This is not the theatre. There isn't fucking time.

NELSON: What are you talking about?

SEBASTIAN: How much is Sid helping you with your second draft?

NELSON: What?

SEBASTIAN: I said, how much is Sid helping you with your second draft?

NELSON: He's doing the shit he always does. Making slight line adjustments to his speeches. That kind of shit. Regular.

SEBASTIAN: Because he told me he's given you like over half the script.

NELSON: Well, that's untrue.

SEBASTIAN: That's what he said. Well, what about the trumpet?

NELSON: Oh yeah. Sid suggested that the schizophrenic patient play the trumpet instead of the piano, because Sid plays the trumpet, and that way they could play a duet at the holiday party in the psych ward at the end of the show.

SEBASTIAN: Well, that's a pretty good idea, actually.

NELSON: I thought so.

SEBASTIAN: I want to tell you something, But it is paramount that you keep your mouth shut—keep my secret. So I need to know before I tell you: Can I trust you?

NELSON: I think so.

SEBASTIAN: No, you have to know so. Because if you betray me, I will hunt you down wherever you are, and I will take this fucking hammer, and I will beat your fucking head in.

NELSON: Sebastian, I won't tell anybody. God damn.

SEBASTIAN: Remember, my hammer. (*Smiles.*) Sid told me that next year he wants me to run the show.

NELSON: What?

SEBASTIAN: That's it, mate. It's as good as done. You're looking at your new show runner.

NELSON: But what about Neil?

SEBASTIAN: What about him?

NELSON: I thought he was your best friend?

SEBASTIAN: There is an old Hollywood saying, mate, that you best remember and remember well: Welcome to Hollywood. The only place in the world where your friends will stab you—in the FACE! (*Laughs.*) No, dude, seriously, if Fate is such that I end up running this show, then I will run this show. I have learned to never swim against the tide—not ever. And at the end of the day, if Neil can't learn to get along with the star of this show, then he doesn't deserve to be the show runner. You know what I mean? Because, mate, listen, you know that I am very good friends with Russell Crowe.

NELSON: No, I didn't know.

SEBASTIAN: One 'o my best mates. And fifteen fucking Oscars—Russell Crowe says that Sid is the only fuckin' actor worth watchin' on our show, because the rest of them are crap. They're boring. Fucking boring. That's what Russell Crowe says. And at the end of the day, it's really about me and my family. You know what I mean? And I am going to do whatever I have to do to ensure that my wife, my kids, and me maintain the manner of living to which we have all quickly become accustomed. And I'm not having this show tank because the star and the show runner happen to hate each other's guts, because the bottom line is: Without Sid, there is no show—so it looks like Neil will have to go, and I will have to rise! And that is the fucking bare bodkin! Which is good news for you, by the way.

NELSON: How so?

SEBASTIAN: Because, mate, as long as I'm here, you're here.

CHARACTERS
ELIJAH *(26), a Black American, sincere;* INMATE H-31887 *(30s), a Black American, manipulative*

SCENE
The reading room of a state prison in the Midwest

TIME
Present day

ELIJAH *sits in a chair, facing the audience.* HE *reads a book. Moments pass.*

INMATE H-31887 *enters, carrying a book.* HE *sits next to* ELIJAH. *Sitting with his back to the audience,* INMATE H-31887 *reads. Moments pass.*

INMATE H-31887: You can sorta lose track. (*Beat.*) It's easy for me to . . . lose my place when I'm reading. I have to follow the words with my finger. It's the only way I can hold on to the words. My mind wanders. A lot. That ever happen to you? (*Beat.*) Seems to me there are places in between these words. In between the lines. I always end up trying to read the story behind the story. That ever happen to you? You ever find yourself fightin' to figure out more? (*Beat.*) It helps when I guide my eyes with my finger. It helps. I don't read any faster, but it helps me focus. How long you been readin' that book?

(ELIJAH'S *unsure if he should answer, but he also likes to brag about the number of books he has read.*)

ELIJAH: . . . Six weeks.

INMATE H-31887: (*Calculates.*) . . . Forty-two days. How long's the book?

ELIJAH: Two hundred and fifty pages.

INMATE H-31887: What page are you on?

ELIJAH: . . . Ninety-eight.

INMATE H-31887: That's pretty good. (*About the book he's reading.*) One hundred and ten pages. Been coming to the reading room for three months. I'm only up to page thirty-five, 'cuz my mind wanders, you know? (*Beat.*) I guess it doesn't help that they only let us in here twice a week. (*Beat.*) They seem to let you in more often. (*Beat.*) They must like you. Does somebody like you ... around here?

ELIJAH: I don't know. ... I just keep to myself.

INMATE H-31887: Oh. I'll have to try that some time.

(INMATE H-31887 *stands up, positions his chair so that it's perpendicular to* ELIJAH. HE *sits. Silence. Both of them appear as if they're reading but neither of them are. They are waiting to see what each is going to do. Suddenly.*)

ELIJAH: Do I know you?

INMATE H-31887: No ...

ELIJAH: 'Cuz dudes in prison don't come up to other dudes in prison unless somebody is gonna be somebody's bitch. This is a bitch proposition.

INMATE H-31887: This?

ELIJAH: This.

INMATE H-31887: You think it happens like this? In the reading room?

ELIJAH: I think it happens when a dude in prison comes up to another dude in prison and just starts talking about books and shit.

INMATE H-31887: You like books, don't you?

ELIJAH: Yeah.

INMATE H-31887: I thought you might wanna just talk ... about books.

ELIJAH: I said I like readin 'em. Not talking about 'em.

INMATE H-31887: Have other guys been talking to you?

ELIJAH: No. No. I've been keeping to myself.

INMATE H-31887: That doesn't happen in here.

ELIJAH: I keep to myself.

INMATE H-31887: They don't let you keep to yourself in here.

ELIJAH: I make it happen.

INMATE H-31887: You're new, right?

ELIJAH: Transfer.

INMATE H-31887: How long you been in the system?

ELIJAH: Ten years. Did some time as a juvenile.

INMATE H-31887: So you know how to keep to yourself? Been managing that for ten years?

ELIJAH: Yes.

INMATE H-31887: I'm the first dude to talk to you in here?

ELIJAH: No.

INMATE H-31887: I'm the first dude you talk back to?

ELIJAH: Yeah.

(*Beat.*)

INMATE H-31887: I'm not looking for a bitch. Just makin' conversation. My mind wanders.

(**INMATE H-31887** *goes back to his book.* **He** *glides his finger along the page to guide his eyes.* **ELIJAH** *goes back to his book.* **INMATE H-31887** *reads.* **ELIJAH** *looks up from his book and watches* **INMATE H-31887** *read.*)

ELIJAH: What do you see in between the words?

INMATE H-31887: Nothing too complicated. A lot of times I end up dreaming about the stuff I cain't get in here. I can be reading a book about somebody drivin' a car and I start thinkin': "Holy hell, it's been a long time since I drove a car." Then I start remembering how long it's been. Then I start thinking 'bout where I'd go if I could drive. Simple shit like that.

ELIJAH: It's the simple shit that gets you going.

INMATE H-31887: Yes, yes.

ELIJAH: Gets everything stirred up.

INMATE H-31887: Brings everything back.

ELIJAH: You know how we had green beans for dinner last night...?

INMATE H-31887: Yeah....

ELIJAH: I take a bite of one...and I start thinking about how my sister makes these green beans. Outta this world. Good shit. Just the best stuff in the world, man. I start thinkin about that, then I start thinking about the crazy shit me and my sister used to get into....

INMATE H-31887: Don't take much.

ELIJAH: Not much.

INMATE H-31887: The five senses are a bitch, man.

ELIJAH: Makes you remember stuff.

INMATE H-31887: When I smell a certain something...

ELIJAH: Taste a certain something...

INMATE H-31887: Hear a certain...

ELIJAH: It's like pow. (*Punches his palm with his fist.*) Memories come back to me. Dreams come back to me.

INMATE H-31887: And it just swells up.

ELIJAH: Gets bigger.

INMATE H-31887: Spreads all over my skin.

ELIJAH: On my uniform.

INMATE H-31887: In my hair.

ELIJAH: Gets tangled up. Knotted up.

INMATE H-31887: And it's all "remember when such and such happened...."

ELIJAH: "Remember how it used to be...."

INMATE H-31887: And I just fall into it. Fall into those days. And I can see colors....

ELIJAH: Smell those sweet smells. Hear music.

INMATE H-31887: I reach out for it.

ELIJAH: Reach out for it.

INMATE H-31887: And then bam. (*Punches his palm with his fist.*) Smack my hand against concrete.

ELIJAH: Against those fuckin' bars.

INMATE H-31887: And I'm back in this fuckin' uniform.

ELIJAH: Bells ringing in the yard.

INMATE H-31887: Surrounded by a bunch of dickheads. Assholes. Pricks. Fuckfaces.

ELIJAH: Getting shoved around. Pushed around.

INMATE H-31887: Being told when to do it. How to do it.

ELIJAH: Sleep with one eye open.

INMATE H-31887: Breathe through your mouth.

ELIJAH: Shuffle along.

INMATE H-31887: Pay the consequence.

ELIJAH: Count the days.

INMATE H-31887: Counting the days.

(Beat.)

ELIJAH: I'm never getting out.

INMATE H-31887: Me neither.

(Beat.)

ELIJAH: I read this book last year. It was a long-ass book, but I liked it. There's this one part I can't get outta my head. It's been with me ever since I read it.

INMATE H-31887: What is it?

ELIJAH: This lady, this rich white lady is getting dressed for this party. And it's like I'm standing in the corner of her room, watching her get ready. The book breaks it down to the smallest detail, yo. It's like I'm watching her spray perfume here and there. Watching her put on her panties. Hook her bra. Lipstick here. Blush there. Slip on a silk this. Slide on a lace that. Then she's going to the party. She's riding in the back of this horse-drawn thing. And she's all nervous 'cuz some dude she's into is supposed to be at the party. He's waiting to see her. She's waiting to see him. She gets to the party. It's packed. Folks are dancing, talking, laughing, drinking. She walks around, saying hi to everybody, but the whole time she's keeping an eye out for this dude. Then she sees him. And he sees her. He's all fucked up by how great she looks. He goes over to her. And he says she looks like a angel. He tells her that her dress looks like it was made in heaven. He says it doesn't take much to make her perfect. But keep in mind, I know how hard this rich white woman worked to look good. I know about the perfume, the bra, the drawers, all that makeup. I know about the tugging, slipping, zipping, you know? But all she says to this dude is: thank you. He takes her out on the dance floor. And the book says, "They dance as if they're in the eye of the storm."

INMATE H-31887: Eye of the storm?

ELIJAH: Eye of the storm! How deep is that shit, man!?

INMATE H-31887: I don't get it.

ELIJAH: You don't get it?!

INMATE H-31887: Naw, no, I don't get it.

ELIJAH: There's this feeling . . . the book describes a feeling they share. In the middle of all this energy there is a straight-up sense of calm between them. And they just let the moment fall over them. It's like, "Yo, this shit is mad crazy and exciting, but here's my peaceful spot right here. I can watch all this energy bounce around, but I'm here with you." It's that kind of vibe. Have you ever felt anything like that?

INMATE H-31887: Maybe. Once. When I was high. . . .

ELIJAH: Sober, man. I'm talkin' when you're sober.

INMATE H-31887: If I think about it, yeah. Yeah, I think so.

ELIJAH: I haven't. And my chances of feeling a feeling like that while I'm in here are fucked.

INMATE H-31887: Definitely fucked.

ELIJAH: I can't stop thinking about it. To know what it feels like to stand in the middle of beauty, chaos, colors, sweet smells, music. . . . If only I could get the fuck outta here, you know? Find a feeling like. . . .

(Beat.)

INMATE H-31887: What, what if I could make that happen for you?

ELIJAH: What?

INMATE H-31887: What if I could get you outta here?

ELIJAH: You talking 'bout busting me out?

INMATE H-31887: I'm talking 'bout you feeling that feelin'.

ELIJAH: And how can you do that?

INMATE H-31887: The how ain't nothing to worry about right now.

ELIJAH: It's something to worry about if I get my ass shoved in maximum for six weeks. You don't get to read books in the hole, man.

INMATE H-31887: Look here, man—what your name?

ELIJAH: Elijah.

INMATE H-31887: Look here, Elijah, I can make it happen. And it can go down without you getting caught.

ELIJAH: You got the hook-up like that in here?

INMATE H-31887: I got the hook-up like that in here. Out there. All around.

ONE-ACTS FOR TWO

INTERREGNUM
BY WILLIAM M. HOFFMAN

CHARACTERS
MAN *(mid-40s);* WOMAN *(late 30s–early 40s)*

SCENE
A romantic restaurant in Williamsburg, Brooklyn. The table is set with two chairs, two wine glasses, and an open bottle of wine.

TIME
2002

MAN *is seated alone.* HE *pours some wine and drinks it. It's good stuff.* HE *checks his watch.* HE *looks at his cell phone. Did* HE *accidentally turn it off?* HE *gulps down the rest of his drink and then refills his glass.* HE *checks his watch again.* HE *is punching in a number on his cell phone as a somewhat younger* WOMAN *enters, looks around, and approaches the table.* HE *turns off the cell phone.*

MAN: Wonder Woman?

WOMAN: (SHE *smiles, nods.*) And you must be Superman! Sorry I'm late. Brrr. It's cold out there.

(HE *smiles shyly. They don't know whether to hug or shake hands. Finally,* SHE *offers her hand, and then indicates the empty chair.*)

May I?

MAN: Huh? Oh, you mean sit. For God's sake, of course. (HE *takes her coat and sits her down.*) Did you have trouble finding this place?

WOMAN: Not at all.

MAN: I mean, some people still think they need a passport to go to Brooklyn.

WOMAN: I *live* in Brooklyn.

MAN: Right, of course you do. How could I forget? You can see the Jehovah's Witnesses sign from your bathroom window, and you used to have a view of the Trade Center from your bedroom window.

WOMAN: I'm impressed you remember.

Man: I hope you don't mind, I took the liberty of ordering some wine for us.

(**She** *doesn't have to read the label to know what it is.*)

Woman: Shiraz Barossa Valley. Sensational.

Man: Bella's Garden 2004.

Woman: I'm even more impressed.

Man: You mentioned it, and I was curious, so I . . .

Woman: (*Hand to heart.*) You pay attention.

Man: Actually, I made a copy of all our chats.

Woman: And you reviewed them before meeting me?

Man: Hey, if George Bush can read our e-mail, why can't I make copies?

> (**He** *nods, smiles shyly.* **She** *toasts.* **They** *sip.*)
>
> I glanced at them. . . .
>
> (**She** *smiles.*)
>
> . . . once or twice.

Woman: I guess I assumed our words would end up in some sort of cyberlimbo.

Man: We will be convicted of cybersodomy and sentenced to Guantanamo.

Woman: I mean, we said a lot of . . .

Man: I know I said a lot of things. . . .

Woman: That you didn't mean?

Man: No, I meant every word.

Woman: *Every?* Every single word?

Man: Every *the* and *and*.

Woman: How about those hinky little *buts*, Superman?

Man: I meant everything I said online. (*Beat.*)

Woman: You know I'm not wearing any . . . (**She** *smiles at him.*)

Man: *Me neither.* Fuck. I've never done anything like . . . (*Beat.*)

Woman: And you're straight and you're HIV negative?

MAN: Yes, and I'm more than a little bit nervous. You know, this is the first time since my divorce.

WOMAN: I thought we wouldn't talk about our baggage.

MAN: Baggage. Right... it's just that you've done this before and this is my first time and...

WOMAN: We'll have our wine, just like we said. No obligations. No—

MAN: I needed to hear that. (*Beat.*) Some more of Australia's finest, Wonder Woman?

WOMAN: No. I'm okay.

MAN: I will—if you don't mind. I'm usually not much of a drinker, but this being a special occasion, what the— (**HE** *overflows the glass.*) Shit. Damn! Waiter! (**HE** *mops up the excess with his napkin.*)

WOMAN: Let me...

(**SHE** *helps him mop it up with her napkin. Their hands touch.* **HE** *tries to take her hand.* **SHE** *pulls back.*)

MAN: Lousy service in this restaurant.... Look—

WOMAN: If you'd like to meet another time, that's all right with me. Maybe I'm not your... or maybe it's too soon after your... (*Beat.*)

MAN: No! I'm fine. I...I...I don't know what to say. (**SHE** *checks her watch.*) Do you have to be somewhere?

WOMAN: (*Setting up an excuse to leave.*) As I told you, I have an appointment later.

MAN: Do you want to call it an evening?

WOMAN: We have a few minutes.

MAN: Would you like to order dinner?

WOMAN: It's all right. (*Beat.*)

MAN: (*Clearing his throat.*) Would you mind if I went to the bathroom and shot myself?

WOMAN: Just leave me money for your half of the check.

MAN: Fuck! I'm new at this. I've been real gentle with myself ever since the— Sorry. Can we start all over again? Let's pretend the last few minutes never happened. You get up.... Come on, you get up... (**SHE** *gets up.*) You approach the table.... (**SHE** *nonchalantly approaches the table.*) I'm drinking my wine, wondering when the hell you're going to show up. "Is she going to stand me up like all the others?" I'm thinking.

WOMAN: Is that you, Superman?

MAN: Wonder Woman?

(**THEY** *embrace.*)

You look exactly like your jpeg.

WOMAN: So do you. I mean from what I can see of you with your clothes on.

MAN: Well, maybe I should... (**HE** *stands up, looks around, and starts to open his fly.*) Aren't you going to stop me?

WOMAN: Hell, no.

MAN: It's a restaurant, for God's sake.

WOMAN: I know you've got a wild mind, Superman. Do it. Just a little.

MAN: I was just trying to lighten things up. I could never—

WOMAN: Not to worry.

MAN: It's no good.

WOMAN: Oh, please.

MAN: I mean I'm so nervous all of a sudden, even though we've been chatting for months, and suddenly here we are. Do you really want me to—?

WOMAN: Chill already....

MAN: Sorry.

(*Three beats as the Woman drums her fingers on the table. Either She will get up and leave or She will try to rescue the drowning man. Which will it be? She decides to plunge on in.*)

WOMAN: And so here we are suddenly in the fleshshshsh... and I know your deepest darkest secretssss.

MAN: Well, yes, you do.

WOMAN: And you know mine.

MAN: Yes. (*Relaxing a little.*) Yes, I do.

WOMAN: Like what *really* turns me on. (**SHE** *shivers.*)

MAN: God, it's so weird.

WOMAN: That's why we're here, isn't it?

MAN: Man, I have to say, you turn me on.

WOMAN: To explore our mutual *interests.*

MAN: Do you know how turned on I am? . . . Do you? . . . If you could only read my mind . . .

WOMAN: I can.

MAN (*Losing his nerve, deflating.*) Shit!

WOMAN: What now?

MAN: I can't do it! It's so difficult to chat in person.

WOMAN: Maybe we should have brought our keyboards and videocams?

MAN: It feels like we really know each other *deeply,* or this morning it felt that way, but right now, in person . . .

WOMAN: It's always awkward to make the transition to in person. To really get to know each other. Not the image of each other.

MAN: Yes, that's it exactly. (**HE** *doesn't know what to say all of a sudden.*) I'm not any good at this. Maybe it wasn't a good idea. I'm sorry. (*Raising his arm for the waiter.*) I'll get the check and— Yo, waiter!

WOMAN: So you like to make dramatic gestures, do you?

MAN: Gestures?

WOMAN: "I'll get the check."

MAN: That wasn't a gesture.

WOMAN: A moment ago you made believe you were going to flash me, but you didn't have the balls to go through with that, and now you want to skip out on me.

MAN: I was just trying to lighten things up.

WOMAN: You're just a lot of talk.

MAN: Waiter!

WOMAN: You like to shock people, and you count on them to stop you from going over the edge.

MAN: I was just nervous at meeting you. I don't make it a practice of dropping my pants in public.

WOMAN: It was bold. As opposed to—

MAN: As opposed to what? Dull? Yes, I'm a dull dullard.

WOMAN: Go over the edge. I want you to.

MAN: You want me to expose myself now? Is that what you really want?

WOMAN: You seem to want to show it off in public. Online you talked about it. You're very proud of the thing between your legs. Why not? Remember the night we sat half naked in front of our cameras and chatted for three hours? You "accidentally" flashed me that night.

MAN: I was just trying to—

WOMAN: I know exactly what you like. You explained it to me in very precise detail. Over and over for three months. I thought we'd never meet.

MAN: And I know what you like. I like what—I *love* what you like.

WOMAN: I like a man with passion, with feelings—

MAN: Is that me, or what?

WOMAN: —who wants a woman with feelings.

MAN: Yes, definitely. A woman should have feelings. I believe that a woman ... I believe that a woman should have ... I believe ...

WOMAN: Go on, damn it!

MAN: Shit!

WOMAN: What?

MAN: I thought it would be okay to meet, but I'm not that kind of—I'm just a—I just got my own place— It was just six months ago and my shrink thought ... I thought ... when I met you online, I—

WOMAN: "Recently divorced reality-based 30ish green-eyed Clark Kent dying to meet his Diana Prince. Seeking unusual and wild adventures, not the marriage noose. Only kinkish non-Republicans need contact me. I am super in all dimensions."

MAN: You memorized my profile.

WOMAN: You *do* hate George Bush, don't you?

MAN: George Bush? What the hell does this have to do with anything?

WOMAN: Well, you haven't been exactly honest with me so far. You *said* you're 30ish, but in reality, you're 45 if you're a day; you *said* you have green eyes, but in reality, they're kind of a nondescript muddy color; you *said* you're looking for an unusual, bold, adventurous kind of woman, when in reality, you're scared shitless and probably desperately miss the woman you just dumped, hoping to meet someone just like me; and as far as your dick goes, I can't say. You wouldn't show it me either on camera or here in person.

MAN: Waiter! Waiter!

WOMAN: You dragged me down here on a freezing day wearing no underwear in some kind of pathetic bait-and-switch game. So I would assume, going by your track record so far, that you voted for George Bush.

MAN: That's so low. Oh, man. I'm outta here. (**HE** *empties his wallet of all his cash, and gets up to go.*)

WOMAN: Go on, admit it.

MAN: Are you serious?

WOMAN: You voted for George Bush.

(*The* **MAN** *can barely speak* **HE'S** *so angry.*)

MAN: Hell no! No way!

WOMAN: Like I believe that.

MAN: If it was up to me I would hang the motherfucker by his balls.

WOMAN: You're all talk.

MAN: I would send him back to basic training.

WOMAN: You love his tax cuts for the rich.

MAN: I would have the pricks who hanged Saddam Hussein deal with him.

WOMAN: You love invading foreign countries.

(*Simultaneously.*)

WOMAN: Nuke Iraq! Nuke Iran! Nuke 'em all! **MAN:** Muktada Muktada, Georgie boy!

Man: Or I would send him to Iraq with his secret Christian prayer cabal and set them in the middle of a mosque in Mosul and—

Woman: Yes!

Man: I sent money to have him impeached! Fuck, I paraded in Texas with that crazy bitch Cindy Sheehan!

Woman: All right!

Man: I think he's a monster!

Woman: Go for it!

Man: His daughters are so sleazy, I bet they end up crack whores—

Woman: It's Superman!

Man: —pimped out by Uncle Bubba Jeb.

Woman: (*With admiration.*) Uncle Bubba Jeb. I love it.

Man: What?

Woman: More!

Man: Are you making fun of me?

Woman: Tell me what else you would do with George Bush.

Man: You're goofing on me?

Woman: I like a man to be obsessive. George Bush is your obsession, which is totally cool. I told you I'm attracted to passionate men.

Man: I guess you are saying you're too chicken to say you voted for Bush, in which case, there is nothing much for us to say, is there?

Woman: I didn't vote in the last election.

Man: DON'T YOU CARE ABOUT THIS COUNTRY?

Woman: Your eyes are sparkling. You're so handsome when you're angry.

Man: You really don't hate George Bush?

Woman: I'm not very political. But I admire people who are. I'm perfectly willing to go along with your fetish. (*Proclaiming.*) George Bush is a mass murderer! Dick Cheney is a Nazi! Donald Rumsfeld—

Man: So it would be all right with you if I were a Republican? (**She** *shrugs*) That's obscene. Would you sleep with a serial killer, too?

WOMAN: Actually, I don't think much about Bush.

MAN: How can a thinking person not hate him?

WOMAN: I love the way your eyes light up when you say what you'll do to the man.

MAN: You do have a mind, don't you?

WOMAN: You're alive. (*To a neighboring table, as in the Frankenstein movie.*) He's alive!

MAN: And otherwise I'm dead?

WOMAN: I wouldn't say dead. Let's say obsession puts color in your cheeks.

MAN: Let me get this straight: You don't hate the son of a bitch? That's sick.

WOMAN: And you're Mr. Mental Health? "If it was up to me I would hang the motherfucker by his balls"?

MAN: Man, you're a sick puppy.

WOMAN: I'm politically agnostic.

MAN: Anyone who doesn't hate George Bush is sick.

WOMAN: You are so hot.

MAN: I'm not sure I could possibly be involved with a person who doesn't hate George Bush.

WOMAN: Well, how 'bout we forget the involved part?

MAN: He's going to be our president for two more years!

WOMAN: Could you fuck a woman who doesn't hate George Bush? Or does she have to be certified ideologically *glatt kosher* before you poke her?

MAN: I'm passionate about the fate of this country.

WOMAN: What you're passionate about is not being intimate with me. (**SHE** *gulps down her wine and pours herself another glass.*)

MAN: Me poking you is your idea of intimacy?

WOMAN: Yup. That's why I came here. To get intimate, flesh on flesh. Isn't that why you came here? Or were you really looking for a "relationship"? Did you want to rub feelings as well as privates? If that's what you were looking for, why didn't you just say so?

MAN: And what would you have said?

WOMAN: I would have said, "No, thank you, sir, I just wanna fuck."

MAN: And I thought I was burned out. Your marriage must have been a doozie. Did he beat you? Did he hang you up by your tits and burn you with a blowtorch? Or maybe you would have liked that? You're probably so cynical you can't feel anything any other way.

WOMAN: Have you come yet?

MAN: Where the fuck is the waiter? Waiter!

WOMAN: All because you miss your wife—

MAN: She's not my wife anymore, thank God.

WOMAN: —and because I don't hate George Bush.

MAN: Hating George Bush is a core value of mine. I don't compromise on core values. Some things are bigger than our petty little egos. Not that that would make any sense to you. I gather all you value is what tickles your clit. Look, you go on. I'll take care of the check. Jesus, where is our fucking waiter?... (*Beat.*)

WOMAN: When I was married we used to watch old movies and make lovely gentle love in our bedroom. We could see the Twin Towers from our windows. They were an eyesore during the day, but they really were something to look at after the sun went down. Steve and I watched them being bombed the first time. I was alone the second time. He had just started to work in Windows on the World. I could see everything up close with my Bausch and Lombs. People jumping, et cetera. No, I didn't see Steve up there that day.

Now, obviously, there's going to be a third time and so forth in New York or L.A. or D.C. or London or Paris, and there will be a Holocaust Two in Israel, less messy this time, because all the Jews will be ash in seconds. It could happen now as we sit here. You see that guy over there? He could be wearing a vest, or one day I'm walking down the street and the sky explodes, and I rush home to save my cat and my building isn't there, or my legs aren't there, or Brooklyn is gone.

So go on and hate that poor dumb shmuck in the White House if it makes you feel any better. He doesn't have a clue. He can't protect us, nor can Hillary—who will be the first *female* president—hoorah!—nor that nice little Obama with the round brown eyes, who will be the first *black* president—hooray!—nor the terrified, constipated ranters on the Left and Right. And being nice to *them*—the enemy whose name we dare not speak—hey, I'm getting old enough to look good in a veil—being nice won't stop them. They'll kill us by bombs, by rat poison, or by machete, if they have to. And since we're unwilling to go after *them* and nuke *them* first and kill millions of *them* before they kill millions of *us*, we're fucked.

So hate George Bush. Impeach him. Assassinate him. It won't change things. Not at all. And you want to know something? I don't really care. Me, I smoke a little dope and pick up lonely kinky guys on the Internet. How much do I owe?

(*Beat.* **HE** *takes her hand.*)

Don't! (**SHE** *tries to pull away.*) Leave me alone!

(**SHE** *is crying.* **HE** *won't let go of her hand.*)

Please!

(*Beat.*)

MAN: (*Very gently.*) My name is Jim. What is your name? Would you tell me your name?

WOMAN: (*Finally.*) Cathy.

THE OTHER WOMAN
BY DAVID IVES

CHARACTERS
THOMAS *(40s), a novelist;* EMMA *(late 30s), his wife*

SCENE
THOMAS'S *study. A desk with books, papers, a small lamp. A chair in front of the desk. Books.*

TIME
The present

Middle of the night: a clock chimes three times. THOMAS *sits in the glow of the desk lamp, writing at a laptop. Darkness around* THOMAS. EMMA *enters out of the dark from right, barefoot, in a nightgown.* THOMAS *doesn't notice and keeps working a moment.*

EMMA: It's too dark.

THOMAS: Jesus, you spooked me. What are you doing up? Time is it...? Three...? I was just going to wrap up and come to bed. Three hours, three paragraphs. I shouldn't have drunk so much at that party.... (EMMA *says nothing, looking at him steadily.*) What's the matter? Emma? (*No response.*) Emma...?

EMMA: I'm so afraid. (SHE *sits on the edge of the chair.*) I'm so afraid.

THOMAS: Emma...you're sleeping, honey. You're asleep. Don't you want to go back to bed? Come back to bed, honey. Come on.

EMMA: (*Who seems to us in no way somnambulistic.*) I'm so afraid.

THOMAS: What are you afraid of? What is it? Emma, what's the matter?

EMMA: Not here.

THOMAS: What?

EMMA: Not here.

THOMAS: What's not here?

EMMA: Is it still night?

THOMAS: Yes.

EMMA: How night?

THOMAS: Very night. It's late. Come on.

EMMA: *Don't you patronize me. I'm afraid.* (*That stops* THOMAS.) I'm so afraid.

THOMAS: Okay. Okay...

EMMA: Where are you going?

THOMAS: (*Who has not moved.*) Nowhere. I'm right here.

EMMA: Will it be morning soon?

THOMAS: Come back to bed. Everything's going to be all right.

EMMA: Nothing bad can happen in the daylight.

THOMAS: What...?

EMMA: Nothing bad can happen in the daylight.

THOMAS: I know.

EMMA: Will you tell her that?

THOMAS: Tell who?

EMMA: Tell her that.

THOMAS: I will. I'll tell her tomorrow. Now everything is fine. Go back to bed.

EMMA: (*Sighs heavily; reluctant, resigned.*) All right. All right....

THOMAS: Everything is fine. Everything is good.

EMMA: Not you. Not you. (EMMA *exits.*)

THOMAS: It's so unreal, it's so wild, for a second I can hardly believe it happened. Everything's the way it was before. I'm alone. The room is empty. The laptop is on the desk. I write it all down, of course—as much as I can remember— just so I won't forget it. This visitation. And when I go upstairs a while later, Emma is in bed, fast asleep. Peaceably asleep. The way she always sleeps. The way she lives. With a kind of preternatural calm, a serenity that I admire but never seem able to attain myself. Unruffled, and unrufflable. That's Emma. And afraid—? Never. Not Emma.

(*Lights change to morning.* EMMA *enters in a robe.*)

EMMA: Good morning.

THOMAS: Good morning. (*Kiss.*)

EMMA: You're up early.

THOMAS: Yeah. Sort of a restless night.

EMMA: Too excited. The new book.

THOMAS: Must be. How did *you* sleep?

EMMA: Wonderfully. Gone with the light. (*Sits in the chair.*) What a fun party.

THOMAS: Yeah. Very fun.

EMMA: A lot of people I didn't know. Interesting people. The Nielsens always have such good parties. You know Terry's going around the world in June. I should call her. So you did good work?

THOMAS: Yeah. I think I might've cracked it.

EMMA: Good. (*Off his look.*) What's the matter?

THOMAS: Nothing. Nothing.

EMMA: Full day today. Meeting about the power plant.

THOMAS: The power plant...

(*A small pause.*)

EMMA: The leakage. The river, the chemicals? You remember?

THOMAS: Yes, I remember.

EMMA: The way you were looking at me...

THOMAS: Darling, I hear every word you say.

EMMA: ... like I was crazy. How about you? What's on the docket?

THOMAS: Emma, you don't have something on your mind, do you?

EMMA: Something on my mind...?

THOMAS: I mean, you're not worried about anything. Anxious, or afraid...?

EMMA: No, why? Afraid? That's a strong word. Why do you ask?

THOMAS: I don't know, you just seem... anxious, lately. A bit on edge.

EMMA: I'm sorry. When?

THOMAS: No particular time. Just . . .

EMMA: No. I feel good. I feel *very* good. That power plant certainly troubles me.

THOMAS: Maybe something about me?

EMMA: What is all this? Did I miss a chapter?

THOMAS: No, I'm just . . . you were talking in your sleep last night.

EMMA: I was? God, did I say anything embarrassing?

THOMAS: No. Well, I didn't know you were sleeping with that car mechanic.

EMMA: No, come on. What did I say?

THOMAS: I don't know. I couldn't quite make it out. You seemed pretty worked up, pretty tense about something. Afraid.

EMMA: I didn't know I talk in my sleep.

THOMAS: You never have. I mean, not to my knowledge.

EMMA: Huh. Funny. So she's going mad at last, huh. Just tell them the chemicals from the power plant did it. Then sue those bastards for everything they've got.

THOMAS: Well, it's daylight now. Nothing bad can happen in the daylight.

(*Pause.*)

EMMA: *What?*

THOMAS: I just mean—I wouldn't worry about it.

EMMA: I'm not worried. Talking in my sleep. How *odd* I'm not talking in my sleep right now, am I? I mean, how would I know?

THOMAS: But you would tell me if there was something. I mean something more personal than the power plant—?

EMMA: Darling, I tell you everything. And you hear every word I say.

THOMAS: Right.

EMMA: It's a nice arrangement. (*Kisses him.*) Dinner out tonight? What do you say?

THOMAS: Sure.

EMMA: Anton's? For the amazing appetizers?

Thomas: Sounds good to me.

Emma: (*Stretches; sighs happily.*) All right. All right. I'm going to clean up.

(**He's** *still staring at her.* **She** *snaps her fingers in front of his face.*)

Wake up!

(**Emma** *exits.* **Thomas** *watches her go.*)

Thomas: The day is uneventful, the amazing appetizers are eaten, night falls, and Emma slips peaceably off to bed. (*Lights change back to night. Music comes back up.*) Needless to say, I get no work done. No real work. Because after Emma goes to bed I spend the night waiting, listening for something. A sound. A footstep in the hall. A strange woman wandering the house.

(*Clock strikes three, offstage.*)

Three o'clock chimes.

(**Emma** *enters, barefoot, in her nightgown.*)

Emma: Don't let me be in there.

Thomas: Be where?

Emma: It's too dark.

(**Thomas** *turns off the music.*)

So will I be hanging off the ceiling upside-down? Otherwise? (**She** *waits urgently for an answer.*) So? *Otherwise?*

Thomas: Otherwise . . . I think you're fine.

Emma: If brain matter was equal to landscape, Portugal would extend from the cerebral cortex all the way to mistake.

Thomas: I never thought of it that way.

Emma: What are you going to do about it?

Thomas: What do you want me to do?

Emma: Will you help? Or is the grey jacket?

Thomas: I'll help you. I just need to know how.

Emma: Useless. Pathetic. Men men men. (*Deep sigh.*) Is it still night?

Thomas: Honey . . .

EMMA: Fake. Fraud.

THOMAS: Honey, wake up.

EMMA: The orange isn't *on* the orange, the orange *is* the orange. In the basket on the cat. If I could only...

THOMAS: What. What do you want. What are you afraid of?

EMMA: If I could only.

THOMAS: Only what.

EMMA: I forgot to take my perfume.

THOMAS: What perfume?

EMMA: My *perfume*. My necessary *perfume*. By prescription.

THOMAS: Nothing bad can happen in the daylight. (*That catches her attention.*)

EMMA: Nothing bad...

THOMAS: ...can happen in the daylight. Do you know who I am? What's my name?

EMMA: Book.

THOMAS: Who are you? What's your name?

EMMA: You know my name.

THOMAS: What name?

EMMA: Secret prescription.

THOMAS: Where do you come from?

EMMA: From sleep.

THOMAS: Do you know where you are? Do you recognize this place?

EMMA: No...

THOMAS: Do you know Thomas and Emma? Emma and Thomas?

EMMA: That would be fine. Amazing appetizers if all the world was a restaurant.

THOMAS: So you remember the appetizers at Anton's—

EMMA: *No. Help. At. All.*

THOMAS: I'll help you. What can I do? What do you want? Tell me.

EMMA: (*Runs a hand along his cheek.*) So sweet. (*Kisses him.*) Love me.

THOMAS: I do.

EMMA: Love me. (*Throws her arms around his neck and kisses him again.*) Love me.

THOMAS: It's like kissing another woman who also happens to be my wife.

EMMA: Love me. (**SHE** *exits.*)

THOMAS: We make love right there on the floor, and she's warm and deep and delicious. It's like I'm in the back room at some crazy drunken party—out of my mind and making love to a total stranger who wraps herself around me like a vine. Our first time but not our first time. Emma but not Emma. Emma but anonymous. It's not even Emma's body—not quite. The same body, but with different eyes looking at me. Familiar but unknown. All the while we're making love I'm terrified that she'll wake up. Yet somehow the danger of it all excites me. Nothing in my life tells me I could ever do such a thing, or that it would excite me. But I can and I do and it does, and the woman in my arms is amazing. When she leaves the room, trailing her nightgown behind her, I feel bereft. Bereft the way you feel when you've said good-bye to a lover. Ashamed the way you feel when you've betrayed her. Which I have done. I lie awake until dawn in a universe that feels light years wider, and infinitely more fragile.

(*Morning.* **EMMA** *enters, dressed for the day.*)

EMMA: I missed you.

THOMAS: I'm sorry?

EMMA: You didn't come to bed last night.

THOMAS: No, I fell asleep on the couch.

EMMA: Working till dawn now, huh.

THOMAS: Yeah. Type type type. That couch isn't meant for sleeping, I'll tell you that. I'm sort of out of it. How are you? Besides smart and strong and incredibly alluring.

EMMA: Do you know I woke up naked this morning?

THOMAS: Naked. Really.

EMMA: Naked in bed, with my nightgown at the bottom of the stairs.

THOMAS: Huh. You don't remember taking it off?

EMMA: Just sort of dropped there. I don't even remember *being* on the staircase.

THOMAS: Funny.

EMMA: Which means I would have had to be downstairs sometime during the night. But I don't remember that either.

THOMAS: Huh.

EMMA: You don't remember hearing me or anything? Moving around the house?

THOMAS: No.

EMMA: I don't walk in my sleep, do I? You said I was talking in my sleep the other night.

THOMAS: Maybe you're trying to tell yourself to sleep in the nude.

EMMA: It's just so creepy. To have done something and be totally unaware of it. To be somewhere, or have been somewhere, walking around—and have no memory of it all.

THOMAS: You slept all right otherwise? Apart from waking up naked?

EMMA: It's like I just got home from Saks and found I'd dropped a perfume bottle in my purse. A secret klepto.

THOMAS: Who knows what we do that we're not aware of. We could have whole other lives. We've done plenty of things in the past that we don't remember. It's like a whole life that we've lived and what percentage of it do we remember? A billionth of one percent? It's like we've never lived it at all. Or only the few nanoseconds left scattered in our memory.

EMMA: Tom, you're not hiding something from me?

THOMAS: No.

EMMA: *Do* I walk in my sleep?

THOMAS: No. I mean . . .

EMMA: Not to your knowledge. I guess I could've been walking around at three AM for years.

THOMAS: Three AM?

EMMA: What?

THOMAS: Nothing. Three AM. That's very specific.

EMMA: Wait a minute. Wait a minute.... (**SHE** *looks around the room.*)

THOMAS: What...

EMMA: Nothing. Part of a dream, I guess. A flash on something. Gone.... Maybe I am going off my rocker.

THOMAS: Great material if you do.

EMMA: Don't you dare. Pinned and wriggling to the page of a book?

THOMAS: Could be a big best-seller.

EMMA: No, thank you.

THOMAS: I'll cut you in for twenty percent. And buy you a new rocker. A house in Aruba.

EMMA: (*Reading from the papers on the desk.*) "...we make love right there on the floor, and she's warm and deep and delicious...."

THOMAS: (*Trying to move her away from the papers.*) No peeking.

EMMA: "I'm in the back room at some crazy drunken party—out of my mind and making love to a total stranger who wraps herself around me like a vine...."

THOMAS: No peeking.

EMMA: Looks like the book's taken a turn to the sexy.

THOMAS: Yeah.

EMMA: So. An erotic novel.

THOMAS: No. I don't know.

EMMA: That's a change.

THOMAS: Erotic elements. I'm still sort of fumbling around.

EMMA: Does it turn you on?

THOMAS: What.

EMMA: Writing sexy scenes, late at night.

THOMAS: Well—sure.

EMMA: So wake me up sometime and do something about it.

THOMAS: All right. It's a deal. Sleeping Beauty. (**HE** *kisses her.*)

EMMA: What was that?

THOMAS: What . . .

EMMA: What was that all about?

THOMAS: (*Moving back in.*) You just said . . .

EMMA: (**SHE** *pushes him away and looks at him a moment.*) I don't get it.

THOMAS: Get it? Get what?

EMMA: That kiss was so funny.

THOMAS: Just a kiss.

EMMA: It didn't even feel like you. It didn't feel like you at all.

THOMAS: How'd you like it?

EMMA: I didn't, really. I don't want a stranger on a floor in a back room. I want you.

THOMAS: You've got me already.

EMMA: You're supposed to say you don't want a stranger either.

THOMAS: I don't want a stranger either. I want you.

EMMA: Thank you.

THOMAS: (*Unbuttoning her blouse.*) So are we saving the spotted owl today?

EMMA: We're supposed to be.

THOMAS: Maybe we could save the spotted owl for another time and save ourselves instead.

EMMA: Save ourselves?

THOMAS: From the ravages of unrequited desire. Nice bra.

EMMA: Tom, do you hate my name?

THOMAS: *What*? Do I *what*?

EMMA: I'm just asking. Do you hate my name?

THOMAS: What put that into your head?

EMMA: I don't know. *Do* you?

THOMAS: No. Am I supposed to?

EMMA: I was just wondering if you did.

THOMAS: You just happened to be wondering?

EMMA: Say my name.

(*Thomas says nothing.*)

Go on. Say my name.

THOMAS: Emma.

EMMA: Say it again.

THOMAS: Emma. Emma. Emma.

EMMA: I feel like crying today. I feel like weeping and I don't know why. I felt like it when I woke up. A feeling of loss. Absence. I don't know.... (*Pause.*) I'm sorry.

THOMAS: No. Don't be.

EMMA: (*Rebuttoning.*) Maybe later?

THOMAS: Absolutely. Say hello to the spotted owl for me.

EMMA: Actually it's a kind of dove.

THOMAS: Dove.

EMMA: (*Putting a hand to his cheek.*) So sweet. Later?

THOMAS: Yes.

EMMA: 'Bye.

THOMAS: 'Bye.

(*Kiss.* **EMMA** *exits. Lights change to night.*)

THOMAS: We do make love later that evening. Not very happily. In the midst of it, Emma begins to cry. To weep, I should say. Great horrible sobs that shake her. And me. All her unruffledness, all that serenity is gone, and nothing I say can calm her. She says over and over again that it's her, but she doesn't know why it's her. She keeps apologizing for weeping. After midnight sometime she drifts off to sleep and I slip downstairs to wait...shuffle some sentences around. Stare at the screen. (*Clock chimes three.*) Three o'clock. Nobody. I still wait. At four-thirty I turn out all the lights and find my way through the house and up the stairs with my arms out in the dark in front of me—like a child imitating a ghost. I wait the next night, and the next night. Writing almost nothing. The next night. A month passes. The clock chimes. I wait.

(**Emma** *enters, barefoot, in her nightgown.*)

Emma: It's too dark up there. I'm so afraid. (*Sits on the edge of the chair.*) I'm so afraid. . . .

Thomas: I've missed you.

Emma: I couldn't be up there anymore. Hanging off the ceiling in the dark. . . . (**Thomas** *says nothing.*) Well? Mr. Book? (**He** *goes to her and tries to embrace her.* **She** *pulls away.*) What are you doing? (**He** *tries again and she pulls away.*) Thomas. What are you doing?

Thomas: Sorry. . .

Emma: So who is she?

Thomas: Who is who?

Emma: Who is she? Isn't there somebody? The woman in your book.

Thomas: Emma—that was . . . there is nobody.

Emma: The Nielsens' party?

Thomas: What?

Emma: The warm and deep and delicious stranger in the back room at a party?

Thomas: Emma, it's *fiction.*

Emma: I was looking for you at one point during that party and I couldn't find you.

Thomas: The Nielsens' party doesn't have anything to do with anything.

Emma: So which party?

Thomas: *No* party. *No* woman. No*where*. There's nobody but you.

Emma: And I stupidly thought it could never happen to us. Not here. Not in this house. Not you.

Thomas: I kissed *you* in the bedroom at the Nielsens' party, just before we left. Do you remember? The mix-up with the coats?

Emma: Do you love her, or is it just fucking?

THOMAS: There is nobody but you.

EMMA: Can I read this book?

THOMAS: I destroyed it. What there was of it.

EMMA: The whole book?

THOMAS: The whole book.

EMMA: Why?

THOMAS: I don't know. The direction it was taking. Honey, if I've hurt you or confused you or made you worry—I'm sorry. But look, everything's going to be all right. Everything's fine.

EMMA: Don't you patronize me. *I'm afraid.*

THOMAS: I'm sorry.

EMMA: Is it still night?

THOMAS: What...?

EMMA: Is it still night?

THOMAS: Yeah...

EMMA: How night?

THOMAS: Very night. It's three o'clock in the morning....

EMMA: Will you tell her that?

THOMAS: Sure, I'll tell her in the morning.

EMMA: Something tells the belltower to scream at England every hour. Depending on circumstances.

THOMAS: Emma...

EMMA: And what about the circumference of all that noise? Where does that go?

THOMAS: Emma, it's time to go to bed. Come on, honey.

EMMA: I told you, I'm afraid. I'm afraid. I'm so afraid.

THOMAS: Emma...

EMMA: Love me.

(*Simultaneously.*)

EMMA:

Love me. Love me. Love me. Love me. Please love me. Please. Please. Love me. Love me. Love me.

THOMAS:

Emma. Emma. Emma. Wake up! Wake up, Emma! Wake up! Wake up!

THOMAS: *Emma—WAKE UP!*

EMMA: (*Running a hand along his cheek.*) So sweet...

PLAY SOURCES AND ACKNOWLEDGMENTS

Anderson, Christina, © 2007. *You Are Here.* For performance and publication rights, and all other inquiries, please contact the Author's representation: Bruce Ostler, Bret Adams, Ltd., 448 W. 44th St., New York, NY 10036, 212-765-5630.

Baitz, Jon Robin, © 2006. *The Paris Letter.* Reprinted by permission of the author. Contact Jon Robin Baitz, c/o Creative Artists Agency, 162 Fifth Ave., 6th Fl., New York, NY 10010.

Barnett, Claudia, © 2007. *Henry.* Reprinted by permission of the author. *Henry* was workshopped at the 28th Mid-America Theatre Conference Playwright's Symposium and presented as a staged reading on March 2, 2007, in Minneapolis: Nancy Jones (director), Jon Herbert (HIM), Annaliisa Ahlman (HER). Please direct queries to Claudia Barnett, English Department, Middle Tennessee State University, Murfreesboro, TN 37132; cbarnett@mtsu.edu.

Basham, Rebecca, © 2005. *Wrinkles.* Reprinted by permission of the author. Contact the author at rbasham@rider.edu.

Bates, Brendon, © 2005. *Corps Values.* Reprinted by permission of the author. Inquiries should be addressed to the author, Brendon William Bates, c/o The New York Theatre Experience, Inc., P.O. Box 1606, Murray Hill Station, New York, NY 10156.

Brevoort, Deborah, © 2005. *The Women of Lockerbie.* Reprinted by permission of the author. Inquiries regarding stage performance rights should be directed to Dramatists Play Service, 440 Park Ave. South, New York, NY 10016; www.dramatists.com, tel: 212-683-8960, fax: 212-213-1539.

Burkman, Deborah, © 2007. *Yoga Warrior.* Reprinted by permission of the authors. Queries may be directed to Rosa Theatrical Management, the group's manager, Mary Lou Chlipola, 1427 Natalie Lane, #108, Ann Arbor, MI 48105; rosamanagement@gmail.com.

Burkman, Katherine, © 2007. *Yoga Warrior.* Reprinted by permission of the authors. Queries may be directed to Rosa Theatrical Management, the group's manager, Mary Lou Chlipola, 1427 Natalie Lane, #108, Ann Arbor, MI 48105; rosamanagement@gmail.com.

Wasserstein, Wendy, © 2008, Trustees of the GST-Exempt Descendents' Trust U/W/O Wendy Wasserstein. *Third.* For performance rights, please contact Dramatists Play Service, 440 Park Avenue South, New York, NY 10016. For all other inquiries, contact Phyllis Wender, The Gersh Agency, 41 Madison Avenue, 33rd Floor, New York, NY 10010.

Watson, Dwight, © 1998. *Dewey Boy and Wookie.* Reprinted by permission of the author. Additional queries should be directed to the author, Wabash College, Crawfordsville, IN 47933, or watsond@wabash.edu.

Yankowitz, Susan, © 2007. *Foreign Bodies.* All rights reserved. Reprinted by permission of the author. For inquiries, contact the author at: syankowitz@aol.com, www.susan yankowitz.com, or at 205 West 89th Street, #8F, New York, NY 10024.

Zwerling, Philip, © 2007. *The Last Freak Show.* Reprinted by permission of the author. Contact the author at the Department of English, University of Texas Pan American, Edinburg, TX 78539, or pzwerling@rgv.rr.com.

Additionally, the editors would like to thank the extraordinary writers who so graciously allowed their work to be used in this volume, as well as Applause Books, Susan Barclay, Nicole Bergstrom, Beth Blickers, Justin Cavin, Clare Cerullo, June Clark, Margie Connor, Creative Artists Agency, Marie Darden, Rochelle and Martin Denton, Elaine Devlin, The Drama Book Shop, Dramatists Play Service, Scott D. Edwards, Faber and Faber, Kenneth Ferrone, Peter Filichia, Carol Flannery, Victoria Fox, Peter Franklin, The Gersh Agency, Pam Green, Grove Atlantic Press, Peter Hagan, Heidi Handelsman, Harden-Curtis Agency, Joshua Harmon, Ken Hatch, Corinne Hayoun, Gary Heidt, Patrick Herold, Tina Howe, Dara Hyde, InterAct Theatre Company, Morgan Jenness, Linda Konner, Melissa Krupa, Jonathan Lomma, Matthew Love, Katie LeCours, Eric Lupfer, Bernadette Malavarca, Carol Mann Agency, Stuart Marshall, Lysna Marzani, Vivian Matalon, Michael Messina, Nancy Nelson and Randy Lanchner, New York Theatre Experience, Mark Orsini, Paradigm, Kathleen Peirce, Michael Petraseb, Jonathan Rand, Ross Theatrical Management, Peter Rubie, Will Scherlin, Karen Schimmel, Zachary Schisgal, Marit Shuman, the Shuman and Nolan families, Rita Battat Silverman and Steve Silverman, Keith Strunk, Ursinus College, Verso Books, Kathleen Warnock, Anne Washburn, Stephanie Weir, Phyllis Wender, Peregrine Whittlesey, Gary Winter, and Susan Yankowitz.

THE EDITORS

Joyce E. Henry is professor emerita of Theatre and Communication Studies at Ursinus College. She is the editor of *The Wisdom of Shakespeare* and author of *Beat the Bard*. She lives in Collegeville, Pennsylvania.

Rebecca Dunn Jaroff is assistant professor of English at Ursinus College, where she teaches American literature, drama, and journalism. She is the author of several essays on nineteenth-century American women authors. She lives in Conshohocken, Pennsylvania.

Bob Shuman is the owner of Marit Literary Agency in New York. He is an editor, playwright, college professor, author, and composer. A Fellow of the Lark Theatre Company, he received Hunter College's Irv Zarkower Award for excellence in playwriting. He lives in New York City. Visit his blog at http://stagevoices.typepad.com.